Merchant
Adventurer ~

William Russell Grace, mayor of New York (1880s). *Courtesy W. R. Grace & Co.*

Merchant Adventurer ~ The Story of W. R. Grace

By Marquis James

With an Introduction
by Lawrence A. Clayton

SR BOOKS

A Scholarly Resources Inc. Imprint
Wilmington, Delaware

The paper used in this publication meets the minimum requirements of the American
National Standard for permanence of paper for printed library materials, Z39.48, 1984.

Scholarly Resources Inc.
104 Greenhill Avenue
Wilmington, DE 19805-1897

Library of Congress Cataloging-in-Publication Data
James, Marquis, 1891–1955.
    Merchant adventurer : the story of W. R. Grace / by Marquis James;
with an introduction by Lawrence A. Clayton.
        p.   cm. — (Latin American silhouettes)
    Includes bibliographical references (p.) and index.
    ISBN 0-8420-2444-1 (alk. paper)
    1. Grace, William Russell 1832–1904.   2. Businessmen—United States—Biography.
3. Merchants—United States—Biography.   4. Mayors—New York (N.Y.)—Biography.
5. Judges—New York (N.Y.)—Biography.   6. United States—Relations—Latin America.
7. Latin America—Relations—United States.   I. Title.   II. Series.
CT275.G628J36   1993
380.1'45'00092—dc20
[B]
                                                                93-7475
                                                                CIP

~ Contents

~ Introduction

~ I first saw "Merchant Adventurer" one day in June 1978. I found it boxed in a warehouse on Broome Street in lower Manhattan while I was researching material for a book that I would later write on W. R. Grace & Co.'s early presence and development in Latin America. I had been researching that topic for nearly two years, having begun rather informally while visiting my father and mother in Central, South Carolina, over Christmas break in 1976.

I owe my first thanks to Dr. William H. Hunter, one of the finest physicians and gentleman scholars in South Carolina. Bill Hunter, who practices in Clemson, is an old friend of my family's, and he suggested that my father's career in South America with W. R. Grace & Co. merited some attention. Dr. Hunter is a persuasive man, as is his lovely wife Jane, whose intuitive sensibilities urged me on as well.

"There's a grand story there, Larry," they both told me. So that Christmas season I plugged in an old tape recorder and sat my Dad down to ask him what it was like to be a young gringo engineer in the nitrate fields of Chile in the 1920s. One thing led to another and, finally, to the shock and pleasure of uncovering "Merchant Adventurer," a manuscript that turned out to be the unpublished work of a two-time Pulitzer Prize-winning biographer.

In addition, I wish to thank Ramona ("Missy") Felts-Wonders, who received her master's degree in Latin American studies from the University of Alabama in 1990 while I directed that academic program; she earned my gratitude for being such a great research assistant. She, too, shared with me the thrill of uncovering layer after layer of Marquis James's life as we probed into the history of "Merchant Adventurer." Dr. Lawrence Kohl, a colleague of mine in the Department of History, University of Alabama, and a Jacksonian specialist, brought me in touch with some of the modern historiographical trends related to the periods of history about which James wrote.

Richard L. Moore, of W. R. Grace & Co., assisted me in sorting out the story of "Merchant Adventurer" within the company's history from the 1950s through the 1980s. Frederick E. Bona, also of W. R. Grace & Co., helped make this edition possible by running "Merchant Adventurer" through the final gamut of company lawyers and counselors. J. Peter Grace, the grandson of the subject of "Merchant Adventurer," graciously gave me the benefit of his recollection of events from the 1940s.

At the Library of Congress the Manuscript Division provided me with its usual superb professional assistance as I worked in the Marquis James papers several times during the summer of 1992.

And finally I would like to thank with great affection my wife, Louise, who may not have been taken as much by James and "Merchant Adventurer" as I was but who learned patiently to indulge my obsession for many months.

~ W. R. GRACE

~ ℐn January 1881, New York City inaugurated its first Irish-born mayor after a campaign that pitted reformers against the most notorious symbol of corrupt politics in America, Tammany Hall. That same year, Chile's armies sacked the Peruvian capital of Lima in the climax to the War of the Pacific, fought along the west coast of South America. While Peru, the principal heir to the once-great Spanish Empire in South America, was pummeled into humiliation, defeat, and debt by the victorious Chileans, in the United States the age of industrial capitalism was in the ascendant, rapidly transforming the country into one of the world's leading powers.

William Russell Grace, a forty-nine-year-old transplanted Irishman, celebrated perhaps his most famous achievement in public life when he took the mayor's oath of office. However, it was a bittersweet triumph, for 1881 also marked one of the most trying times for his business, W. R. Grace & Co., which he had founded in 1854 in Peru and whose commercial success was closely tied to the fortunes of that country. As Grace was sworn in, his brother Michael was working to protect the company's interests in Peru and to keep its territorial integrity from being dismembered by the Chileans.

Despite Grace's achievements, he was a relatively unknown figure in U.S. business and political history. Although a biography of him was written in the 1940s by two-time Pulitzer Prize-winner Marquis James, that book, *Merchant Adventurer: The Story of W. R. Grace*, disappeared into the archives of the family and company that had commissioned the work. Instead of being released in 1948 by Viking Press, it lay dormant and unknown to all but a few James and Grace family members and friends. Now, almost one-half century later, *Merchant Adventurer* is being released to the public in a cooperative effort by W. R. Grace & Co. and Scholarly Resources.

Allan Nevins, one of the best-known historians of U.S. enterprise, wrote in his foreword to *Merchant Adventurer* that "in this warm, nostalgic story . . . James combines his gift for biography and his close acquaintance with business history to investigate a characteristic phenomenon of American life," the personal success story. As Nevins hinted, the reader will discover a true-to-life Horatio Alger tale in the pages that follow. Grace, a young immigrant, crosses the Atlantic to the Americas and, with hard work, thrift, intelligence, good fortune, and boundless opportunities, makes good. He establishes business institutions that help shape America's history, wins two terms as mayor of the greatest city in the country, counsels presidents, and even becomes a millionaire.

That, of course, was the American success story, and Marquis James excelled in telling it. However, he told the story he wished to tell, not the one that the Grace family originally proposed to him in the fall of 1943, a "biography" of the W. R. Grace & Co. business. As James and his wife, Bessie Rowland, pored through the scores of carefully preserved letterbooks that William Grace, his brothers, cousins, and associates had accumulated for over one-half century, the outline of an extraordinary career became clear.

James was adamant in focusing his sponsors—principally Joseph P. Grace, William's son, who wished to honor his father—on a "straight biography."[1] "Why," James told Grace, "men have had books written about them with no more to justify that attention than your father exhibited in his two terms as mayor."[2] He was clearly taken by the versatility of the elder Grace's career, which had spanned from the guano islands of Peru to the highest councils of power in the United States. William Grace clearly deserved a full biography, not a story thinned down or diffused by a lack of vision. "To be of any account," the writer James instructed the patron Joseph Grace, "a book must have unity—a dominant theme which the writer must stick to and to which he must subordinate everything else. Your life-and-times and life-and-works biography rarely does this. Such books tend to be diffuse, focus on nothing and leave scattered impressions."[3]

The biography that James produced focuses on and captures the extraordinary experience of William Grace's life with a storyteller's magic. The result is, as Robert Utley observed in the introduction to another of James's classics, a book that "has lasted because it is literature as well as history."[4] Utley was writing of James's prize-winning biography of Sam Houston, *The Raven*, but his analysis applies equally to *Merchant Adventurer*: "James's strength lies in getting inside his subject and presenting him in an engrossing style that holds lay reader and scholar alike." His sensibility as a novelist and his passion for the original documentation impart credibility to his subjects.

The story of William Grace that James spins is both simple and complex. As a young man, Grace embarked for the Americas in the midnineteenth century looking for opportunities, escaping a homeland laid waste by famine. He ended up on the coast of Peru, where he found an exotic land and people. Here he began to sell naval stores to the hundreds of ships from the United States and Europe that came annually to take guano off the Chincha Islands.

Success in trade eventually drew Grace to New York in the 1860s where he established the main branch office of what evolved into W. R. Grace & Co. He left his younger brother in charge of the business in Peru. Together, the brothers, plus scores of younger relatives and talented apprentices, developed a thriving business that included, by the turn of the century, the first steamship line between New York and the west coast of South America; ventures in sugar, rubber, and railroads; and dozens of other commercial and industrial activities in many parts of Latin America.

W. R. Grace & Co. was well known as the principal shipping and trading company between the Americas. It was, indeed, the first multinational company in Latin America. Its activities predated more celebrated and notorious enterprises such as United Fruit and Standard Oil, which developed wide presences in modern Latin America. While enlarging his reputation as a businessman, Grace also found time for his successful run for mayor of New York, and for an unsuccessful attempt to sponsor a transisthmian canal across Nicaragua. For the reader interested in Grace, Latin America, urban U.S. politics, and the making of the Panama Canal—in sum, in the vast variety of endeavors in which William Grace became involved—James's biography will prove not only compelling as literature but also informative as history.

~ MARQUIS JAMES

~ Within its own domain the story of Marquis James is no less fascinating than the one he told of William Grace. There is no biography of James, one of the leading "popular" historians of midcentury America, but he surely deserves one. James himself would have argued that he was not a historian but a biographer, making that distinction in his notes to best-sellers in which he described in detail how the craftsman and artist dealt with his subjects. But a historian he was, as well as a journalist and writer of great versatility and talent, whose name was easily recognizable to readers in the 1930s and 1940s as a man who could tell a tale. When Grace family members were searching for a suitable biographer of the founder of their clan, they contracted with one of the premier biographers of the era.

James's first book, *The Raven,* was about Sam Houston. Published in 1929, it won him a Pulitzer Prize for biography. Fascinated by the man and the period, James was inevitably attracted to another giant of the time, Andrew Jackson. That biography, *Andrew Jackson: The Border Captain,* appeared in 1933. In 1937, James completed the second volume to his study, *Andrew Jackson: Portrait of a President,* and the combined effort won him a second Pulitzer in biography.

Winning a Pulitzer Prize may not necessarily bring long-term recognition. However, today, as in 1929 and 1937, it confirms near-instant fame for an author, and James was no exception. In 1937 he shared the limelight with Odell Shepard, who also won a Pulitzer in biography for *Pedlar's Progress: The Life of Bronson Alcott.*

Subsequently, James enlarged his canvas to include not only giants in political and military history but also those who built the commercial and industrial empires that were synonymous with the American success story. *Alfred I. DuPont: The Family Rebel* was the first book in this new genre for James and appeared in 1941 to critical acclaim. It was followed in 1948 by *Merchant Adventurer: The Story of W. R. Grace.* Arguably, if published, *Merchant Adventurer* could have brought James his third Pulitzer Prize.

In many ways the lives of Marquis James and William Grace intertwined. Each man enjoyed fantastic successes and some equally spectacular

disappointments. Each inherited a good name, a good family, and boundless ambition in a world where opportunities were rapidly opening. James,
born in 1891 in Springfield, Missouri, was reared in the Cherokee Strip of
the Oklahoma Territory, before it became a state in 1907. He was a late
child, for two older sisters were married when he was still a young boy. In
his autobiography, he writes fondly of his older, somewhat doting parents.[5]

His father, Houstin James, was a Civil War veteran who had migrated
from Ohio to Missouri to Oklahoma. Although he practiced law, financial
security eluded him. He dabbled in oil, but his wells never produced. When
he was almost fifty, he made a dash into the Cherokee Strip to stake a claim
against hundreds of younger men with faster horses. He fared rather well,
but farming the claim did not work out, so he tried an icehouse scheme,
with little luck. What held his family together, especially after they moved
from the claim into Enid in 1901, was his law practice. Marquis's mother
was the one who provided the more solid foundation. She cultivated the
small parcels of real estate in Enid that gave them some stability and
parlayed the windfalls that his father occasionally secured into sound
investments. From her family in Virginia came the old French Huguenot
name of Marquis.

However, in James's autobiography, written in 1945, one senses the
financial insecurity that probably drove the younger James in his life as a
writer. He was endowed with prodigious energy—and with a supportive
wife who helped him organize and produce the massive amounts of
research that gave substance to his books. In fact, by the 1940s and into
the early 1950s, he was producing books on a biennial basis. But he also
was driven to accumulate where his father had failed, to secure the financial substance that translated into security in the American dream.

James was a mediocre student throughout high school, and before he
left Enid for the wider world of journalism, he tried one year of college.
Further education was not a compelling desire; he found his higher education in books—especially in history—and this passion served him as an
entry into the fields of literature and history. His father and his father's
friends, well educated by the standards of the time, encouraged him with
suggestions and loans of books.

Drawn to the world of journalism and to the craft of printing, young
"Markee" wanted more than anything else to be a printer. He became fascinated by the transformation of thought to type to the printed word. His
early bosses, however, thought that he had a more promising gift, and he
settled on being a reporter in the front office. He never lost his fascination

with and knowledge of the printer's craft. His later meticulous attention to detail may have been cultivated by those master printers with whom he first apprenticed.

As a reporter, James typically concentrated on perfection in pnrose: "I devoted myself to a study of newspaper style, Mr. Hearst's New York *American* and Mr. Pulitzer's St. Louis *Post-Dispatch* being the models most valued. I strove to illuminate my copy with marks of erudition and taste. A cow was a bovine quadruped. Ladies had finely chiseled chins and shell-like ears."[6] Furthermore, "I labored to extract the gold of the unusual from the ore of the commonplace."

James also learned that facts were not necessarily intrinsically interesting:

> Mr. Drummond [his boss on the Enid newspaper] did not print feature stories unless verifiable. . . . A farmer might come to town and tell about the cat which had fallen into the threshing machine and come out with only part of an ear snipped off, thus lending credence to the legendary indestructibility of cats. . . . In the hands of a good feature writer that incident could be elaborated a little. Give the cat a name, such as Carry Nation. Tell of some of its other experiences: as a kitten they'd tried to drown it but it clawed out of the sack; after which Carry had been struck by lightning, tossed on the horns of a bull, sucked up by a twister and deposited on a haystack in the next township, et cetera.

For him, "Mr. Drummond missed the whole point. A journalist adaptation of the tall tale, this type of feature story wasn't supposed to be true."[7] As Utley later noted, James "was not burdened by a Ph.D. and bound by the rather dry and sterile prose of the academician. He was, in fact, taught to write for the American public that bought newspapers to read and entertain them, and the style he learned from his editors in Kansas City, Chicago, St. Louis, New Orleans, and New York served him well throughout his career."[8]

This career was interrupted by the First World War, during which he served as an army officer in France. After the war, he became the director of publicity for the American Legion and later edited the *American Legion Monthly* until 1932. James was blessed by being at the right place at the right time. Before becoming editor of the *Monthly* himself, he worked for its first editor, Harold Ross, a midwesterner with a penchant for viewing the world in the same terms as James. As he recalled, Ross had decided to "start a little local magazine of his own in New York . . . and tried to get me interested in this but I couldn't see any financial future in the thing. I went to work for him though, in spare time, and wrote under three or four different names in the early issues of his publication."

Ross called his magazine *The New Yorker* and offered to pay James in stock, but James thanked his friend and said that cash would do. Reminiscing, he thought that "possibly that was just as well, for if I had done so I might have had a good many worries that as things turned out I have never been bothered with—I mean money worries."[9] He continued to write for Ross and became a regular contributor to *The New Yorker* for the next thirty years.

James had been writing profiles for *The New Yorker* when a friend connected with a publishing house suggested that he should try something more substantial, a biography. James was flattered, but about whom should he write? Sam Houston's name came to mind. "My publishing friend thought nothing of Houston, whose name he pronounced 'Howston' as they do in New York. This offended my southwestern sensibilities."

Why Sam Houston? As a boy growing up in the Oklahoma Territory, young Markee remembered Temple Houston, a son of Sam's, who had come to live in Oklahoma because he had killed a man in Texas. "Texans thought [going to Oklahoma] was punishment enough." Temple practiced criminal law in the old Cherokee Strip along with James's father, and from him the boy learned about Temple's father. Sam Houston became a hero to him, and James later remembered him when first toying with the idea of writing a biography. A "number of bright Americans were endeavoring to write biographies in emulation of Lytton Strachey's *Queen Victoria*," and James did not preclude himself from membership in that estimable literary group.

While mulling over this idea, James was asked by Ross to go to Dayton, Tennessee, to cover the Scopes Monkey Trial for *The New Yorker* in 1925. In Dayton, according to Utley, he was transformed by a catharsis of sorts:

> There, [James] recalled, "I picked up a copy of Houston's virtual autobiography, *Sam Houston and His Republic*, which I had previously read. I used it now to put myself to sleep in the noisy little hotel. By some impulse still unexplained, when I returned home I dropped all my work . . . and informed my friends that I would come out of my shell a year from date with a red hot life of Sam Houston." He did not, but rather burned the results of the first year's labor and set forth to do serious research.[10]

James's more colorful account mentions nothing about burning his first year's efforts, but he did begin four years of intensive research. "Up to that time I may have come across the word 'research' a time or two but I am sure I didn't know what it meant."[11]

James soon discovered that most of Houston's "private papers, and a good many of the official papers relating to the Texas republic, were in the hands of one of his grandsons [Franklin Williams] who up to that time had refused to let any writer see them." Nor was Williams about to turn them over to the University of Texas Library or to the Texas State Archives in Austin: "He had a good reason for this, for at that time and for thirty years preceding, the history department of the University of Texas had for dynasty reasons been under the spell of the Austin legend in Texas." Although Houston and Stephen F. Austin did not get along personally, James said that the hatchet would have long ago been buried "had it not been for the fact that the descendants of Austin were able to carry it into the history department of the University of Texas and subtly prejudice against Houston a great deal of writing that came out of that institution."

When James showed up on his doorstep in Houston, Williams received him cordially and invited him to set up his headquarters in Williams's office while working on the biography. Neither party spoke of the papers: "I used to drop in there every day and always had a good time and I never mentioned the papers, nor did he." Until then, James had limited himself to manuscripts held in the public library and at Rice Institute (now Rice University).

Then one day Williams invited the biographer to tea. When James arrived, he found himself surrounded by about twenty people, "the Houston clan, no less. Well, I tried to make myself as acceptable as possible. I figured that Williams had got them all there to look me over. I didn't know how well I had managed to do until the next day when I dropped in the office and he opened a big black safe he had there and hauled out a box of papers the size of an army locker trunk. And there was the material in my hands."

"This is the sort of thing," he later wrote, "that one runs into in research which has proved so attractive that I have spent a good deal of my life at it since." In effect, he was also learning that the truest and straightest way to the essence of any historical subject is through original documentation. By this the historian means the letters, journals, diaries, and ledgers created by the person who is the subject of the biographer. James did not disdain those accounts written later by other historians and biographers, but he unerringly hit the mark on his first biography, that of Sam Houston. Thereafter, he continued with the consummate passion of the researcher.

~ MERCHANT ADVENTURER

~ *Merchant Adventurer* was composed during a fertile period of historical debate and research in the United States that spanned the 1930s and 1940s. James certainly must have been a party to these discussions that "revolved around several related issues: popular versus scholarly history, history as a literary craft, and the problem of historical truth," as the historian Louis P. Masur pointed out in an essay written in 1990.[12]

Masur noted the various actors in this debate, and they included some of the great historians of the era—Carl Becker, Charles Beard, Arthur Schlesinger, Bernard De Voto, and Allan Nevins among them. Nevins, especially, touted James's works as possessing the twin virtues of readability and historical credibility. In fact, he was among the foremost advocates of what has been rather loosely—and often incorrectly—styled "popular" history, and certainly James was among its foremost practitioners. Nevins promoted this idea in a 1939 article entitled "What's the Matter with History?"

> [Nevins] lamented "the comparatively barren patches in our historical writing." He blamed the drought on "the pedantic school of historians," those "dryasdust monographers" who gathered facts, accumulated footnotes, and stalked the universities where they had professionalized themselves into obscurity. The touch of the pedant, Nevins warned, was "death. . . . [H]e is responsible for the fact that today a host of intelligent and highly literate Americans will open a book of history only with reluctant dread." Although Nevins also viewed the amateur popularizer as a threat to history, he heralded the best work as "a fusion of facts, ideas, and literary grace in a single work," and he proposed the establishment of a nonprofessional historical magazine for those who believe in history as literature.[13]

(This proposal was realized later by the founding of *American Heritage*.) If literary style and historical accuracy were two of the principal bases that Nevins and others considered good history, then the ability to render sound and appropriate judgments was the third leg of the tripod. Without the interpretative dimension, all history would be mere chronicle. De Voto argued passionately for this creative reasoning on the part of the historian. Although he agreed with Nevins in the main, his solutions were somewhat different. De Voto admitted the need for "dryasdust" monographs—and presumably the dissertations on which most were drawn—as necessary for the synthesizer. It was the synthesizer, the generalist, who then could see the grand and complex sweep of history and render appropriate judgments, something both professionals and amateurs seemed unwilling to do. Like Nevins and others, De Voto also bewailed the pedantic writing style of many professional historians and claimed that a good journalistic background, which he shared with Nevins and James, was invaluable training. The division between scholar and writer should be bridged by the good historian, and James's career—at least as a biographer—fell squarely into this paradigm.

When James was first contacted by Joseph P. Grace, the son of W. R. Grace, in late October 1943, it was on the basis of James's well-known reputation for producing highly readable biographies. Grace admired James's work on Andrew Jackson and Alfred I. DuPont and told him so: "It is for this reason that I hoped some time to have an opportunity of talking with you about a biography of my father William R. Grace."[14] Prior commitments and illness postponed their first face-to-face meeting until December, when they discussed the project over lunch in New York City.

This was not the first try by the Grace family to have an appropriate biography written of their founder. Some time in the late 1930s they had contracted with Katherine Burton, who produced a manuscript entitled "Anchor in Two Continents," which reached the galley proof stage but was never published. Another history was available, albeit a shorter and less-polished one. A young Princeton student, Robert Lee Boughton, had made the Grace company the subject of his senior thesis in 1942.

Both the Boughton thesis and the Burton manuscript were made available to James and his wife at the meeting in December 1943. In early January 1944 the Jameses were introduced to D. Stewart Iglehart, Joseph Grace's longtime friend, confidant, and fellow steward of W. R. Grace & Co.'s fortunes for almost fifty years. They met at lunch at India House, the company's elegant old headquarters on Hanover Square in downtown New York. Although James and Bessie were most interested in the Grace project, they could not move on it because they were tied down by a contract signed in 1942 to write a history of the Metropolitan Life Insurance Company. This was the second project in the new genre that James had embarked on in the late 1930s: writing company histories for lucrative fees.

The first was a history of the Insurance Company of North America, which was published in 1942.[15] In November of that same year, James signed a contract with Metropolitan Life in which both parties agreed to "exchange ideas on the contents." However, "in the event there are any differences of opinion as to any parts, which you do not care to change, then the Company may re-edit the manuscript . . . and use any and all parts of it in such manner as may seem to it to be the most appropriate. In this event the Company may publish the book under any name it elects other than yours."[16] In other words, James was a paid agent; the copyright—or the property itself—belonged to the company. In this regard, he was moving away from the liberty he possessed as an independent biographer and historian, but he was well compensated—$25,000 per year, "with the understanding that it will be finished within three years . . . to begin June 1, 1943."[17] And he could count on the income, rather than taking his chances as a free-lancer.[18]

James was betting that any publication without his name on it would not give a company the cachet associated with his growing fame as a biographer and corporate historian. He probably thought that a manuscript would never be subjected to the ultimate veto. Still, he and Bessie were drawn to the possibilities of a biography of William R. Grace. "As a matter of our own personal choice, we think that a life of Mr. Grace would be more pleasant to write and more pleasant to read than any of these other things that have come to our notice," James wrote Joseph in early May 1944, perhaps seeing in the life of William a reflection of his own success story.[19] Despite James's interest, he needed to keep the bacon on the table. And at the moment, Metropolitan was providing the bacon, although that project was dragging. Therefore, James told Grace that, "as greatly as we are attracted to the subject, we would not feel right if you were to neglect an opportunity to put this matter in other hands which could go to work on it now." If, however, the Grace family could wait two years "for us to get under way [then] we have something we would like very much to talk over with you."[20]

Joseph Grace, then in his seventy-first year, was terribly disappointed and frankly told James that "Mr. Iglehart and I are both so old that to think of putting off having my father's life started two years hence would be almost impossible."[21] The Jameses relented: "Bessie and I are working on it. . . . We have been trying to turn over in our minds some possible scheme whereby we might be able to undertake the book about your father when this Metropolitan job gets out of the way."[22] With Bessie, James came into the city for a long meeting with Grace in June and later that month laid out his plan. He was not interested in producing a "company history" of W. R. Grace & Co. The man William Russell Grace was too interesting to be buried in a "life-and-times" approach. If he did that, "you won't have a biography of William R. Grace, which I understood from our first conversation to be your main object."[23]

James's proposal to Grace in his letter of June 26, 1944, is a remarkable testament to the biographer's vision. In it, James outlined precisely what he proposed to do and then, over the course of the next three years, did it. His preference was clear: a straight biography, "with a swift and compact concluding chapter summarizing the projection of W. R. Grace's life beyond the grave in the form of the Grace companies as they exist today." Joseph Grace and Iglehart wanted to bring the reader up to the present with a lengthy section—perhaps 100 or more pages—tagged on after the death of William Grace in 1904. James proposed a more elegant and literary solution, based on his long experience:

> With the rock of Grace's life to stand it on you wouldn't have to write a hundred pages to get across what you want to get across *and be sure people will read it.* If I wanted to tell people about the Grace company from the date of Mr. Grace's death on I'd rather write two pages [it worked out to about six pages in the final manuscript] that I could be pretty sure would be read than 200 I was pretty sure wouldn't.[24]

James argued that few companies had a "founder whose personality and life-experience" carried on in the business that he had "conceived and set in motion. It is still really a part of him," and to tell William's story was, in effect, to portray the company itself. James was clarifying and focusing the project for Joseph Grace and Iglehart, both seasoned businessmen but novices to the workings of the literary world. He also knew that while both men wished to honor the founder, they wanted to advertise the company as it then stood: "I do not see how it could be done better [advertising the company and its principles] than by laying before the public the story of its founder."

Other basic themes that eventually ran though *Merchant Adventurer* were also touched upon by James in the same letter. None was more important than the following interpretation of William Grace's life and the nature of the company he founded, which James subsequently wove into *Merchant Adventurer* with persuasiveness and coherence:

The primary mission would be to show how W. R. Grace founded, nurtured, guided and built a great business—a business which survives him and in which his personality and wisdom still live; a business which serves a purpose in this world far more useful than that of making money for those engaged in it. Mr. Grace formed our pioneering commercial tie with the Latin Americans. It differed from the run of such ties in that Mr. Grace was not an exploiter. He made the Latin Americans, in effect, his partners. His gain was theirs, and so on, paving the way to a hemisphere relationship which presently may be regarded as something of a model in the effort to refashion world relationships so as to render future wars less likely.

James was, in a fashion, a child of the Good Neighbor policy cultivated by the Roosevelt administration in the 1930s. One can clearly discern the glow of ebullience and optimism that was to characterize the immediate post-World War II relations between the United States and Latin America in his characterization of the Graces and their company.

More than anything else, however, James was interested in "[William] Grace, the man, not Grace the business man." With this biography, James was returning to the form that had brought him so much success in the 1930s. Although the companies—Metropolitan Life, W. R. Grace, Bank of America, Texaco—paid for his living through the 1940s and 1950s until his death in 1955, his old love was for the men who made history, richly told. Knowing that Joseph Grace and Iglehart wanted the nature and philosophy of their company also featured in the biography of their founder, James made his pitch with conviction and from much experience: "In such an account the company would not suffer, but the reverse. It was the major concern of his life and the major achievement of his life. So it would stand in the book . . . one would see the company through him and not him through the company."

Furthermore, there was a public dimension to William Grace's life that had attracted the Jameses from the beginning. Grace twice became mayor of New York in the 1880s, and he was a major actor in Democratic politics at the end of the nineteenth century. In *Merchant Adventurer,* the writers could not ignore one of the more prominent parts of his life. A straight company history would have relegated Grace's public role to secondary status, whereas in a biography "his public life, to mention one thing, could be gone into with the fullness it deserves, and with no dispersion of focus because we would be *talking* about *Grace* all the while. In such a book it would be structurally the natural thing to follow him through the lively and important events of his chief magistracy of the world's second city."[25] Joseph Grace was persuaded. From his summer home in Maine, he wrote James on the Fourth of July weekend: "When . . . you state your preference and give your reasons for them it is hard not to agree with you. I agree with you." And, Grace added, "I think Mr. Iglehart will too."[26]

James thought that he may have overpowered his new patrons, who were both elderly and had dealt with him in a kindly and cordial fashion. "It was not my intention to overpersuade either of you," James wrote, but "I really think the decision made on the premises is the right one."[27] By October 1944 he and Bessie had a contract with W. R. Grace & Co. for a biography of William Russell Grace.[28] Signed on October 11, 1944, it provided for a fee of $62,500, plus $12,500 in expenses, plus travel to South America to carry out some of the research. Similar contracts signed with Metropolitan Life in 1942 and the Bank of America in 1947 stipulated that the ownership of the manuscript reside with the company. The same general conditions were expressed in the contract between the Jameses and W. R. Grace & Co.[29]

One reviewer of the book that the Jameses later produced on the Bank of America called them "subsidized historians," and one could argue that they were by extension "bought" historians.[30] But they were given free and unrestricted access to the company's records, the principal ones for *Merchant Adventurer* being the letterbooks of William Russell Grace— and there was constant collaboration between the Jameses and Joseph Grace and Iglehart on the contents of the book. However, as far as this writer can ascertain, the Jameses did not kowtow to a version imposed on them by Joseph Grace or Iglehart. They wrote the story as they saw it, and both came to like and admire William Russell Grace immensely on his own merit.

The research and writing itself took about three and one-half years. Like most professional writers, James was involved heavily in parallel activities: writing scripts for radio plays, free-lancing articles, finishing major projects—in this case, the history of Metropolitan Life—and initiating others. Therefore, the task of researching and organizing the Grace papers fell to his wife. In early 1945, Bessie and C. W. Hopkins, a Grace employee, plunged into the papers kept at the company's old headquarters on Hanover Square. They were the principal cataloguers and initial organizers, and their notes summarizing the contents of scores of letterbooks, telegram books, scrapbooks, contracts, and other documents were used as the basis for organizing the biography. Jonathan Grossman, a young historian at the College of the City of New York, was hired to work on the public career of William Grace. The company provided other researchers as the project continued throughout 1945 and 1946. Grace executives, all mentioned in the acknowledgments at the end of the book, pitched in whenever needed.

James himself did not begin to concentrate on the project until almost one and one-half years after it was initiated. By May 1946, when he settled down to commit himself fully to *Merchant Adventurer*, a considerable amount of research already had been completed by Bessie and Hopkins. Scores of letters and documents had been transcribed into typescript and carefully filed into three large cabinets under subjects such as "Politics, 1881" and "Theodore Roosevelt."[31]

No sooner had James begun to write than the Graces wanted to see some results. Perhaps their concern was natural. Iglehart had died; and Joseph Grace had suffered a stroke in 1945, from which he never fully recovered.[32] He felt the weight of time on him and was anxious to see the project through to the end. But James resisted any pressure, explaining that "so help me I am not going to make the mistake that I did with the agreeable people of Metropolitan. They were anxious to see a few chapters, and against my better judgement, I tried to write them before I was really sufficiently prepared. . . . An old-stager like me shouldn't have made such a mistake, and I promise I won't make that same one with you."[33]

In the late fall of 1946 the Jameses began to supply Joseph Grace with some of their early draft chapters. James also asked for an additional $12,500 on December 20 to cover the growing costs of research assistance, and Grace approved.[34] With this substantial increase in their expense allowance, early in 1947 he and Bessie sailed to Peru and Chile aboard a Grace Line steamship to conduct research in South America for almost three months. There, they characteristically sought out the best researchers and historians available. In Peru, for example, they obtained the services of Dr. Jorge Basadre, the country's leading historian and director of the National Library.

Basadre's notes on the Grace-Aranibar contract, which evolved into Chapter 15 of *Merchant Adventurer*, clarified and focused the Jameses on an issue of great complexity and controversy in Peruvian history. Basadre was paid fifty dollars for his services. One can feel some sense of awe at the Jameses' ability to work with the best and pay the least.[35] Basadre also read all the chapters dealing with Peru, as noted in the acknowledgments to

Merchant Adventurer, and imparted to the manuscript the credibility that only a scholar of Basadre's rank could bring.

Few stones were left unturned. Manuel Ulloa, a talented and ambitious young employee of Casa Grace in Lima, conducted research for the Jameses in the records of the Ministry of Foreign Relations in preparation for several parts of *Merchant Adventurer* that dealt with complex diplomatic maneuvers. Ulloa later became minister of foreign relations under the second presidency of Fernando Belaunde Terry (1980–1985). In Callao, James and Bessie found letterbooks and other documents from the earliest period—the 1850 and 1860s—whose contents shed light on William Grace's early life in Peru.

By September 1947 the manuscript was nearing completion. Joseph Grace had finished reading Chapters 8, 9, and 15, and "the whole story as you put it is fine."[36] By now, he and the Jameses had settled into a pattern. Grace and one of the company's senior officers, Harold Roig, would read the chapters as they arrived from the Jameses, and then the four of them would get together at the Grace estate on Long Island to iron out any differences—and there were some differences—and move on to the next set of chapters.

Earlier that year, Grace had been disturbed by the portrayal of one of his ancestors as a "poor stick" or "poor provider." James had been referring to the father of the Eyre children, all of whom had joined W. R. Grace & Co. in the nineteenth century; one of them, Edward Eyre, rose to become one of the principal managers of the company in the twentieth century. The Eyres were the children of William Russell Grace's sister Alice. James argued that Alice's husband indeed had been a poor provider, and "it renders plausible the fact that your father undertook the support and the shaping of the careers of his children." Then he explained to old Joseph that "there are many unpleasant features of my profession. One is that I have no control over the facts." "Actually," James continued, "Eyre was a thoroughly bad egg. But he is such a momentary character in this book that all we need to say is he failed to provide for his family."

The working relationship between the Jameses and Grace and Roig continued to be cordial and mutually helpful through 1947 and 1948. W. R. Grace & Co., for example, had distinctly favored Peru during the War of the Pacific, and Joseph Grace thought that James's "presentation of the details of the supplying of torpedo boats and other implements of war to stop the war which Chili [*sic*] declared upon Peru is very graphic."[37] In fact, this support of Peru set the tone for the early business presence of

W. R. Grace & Co. in Chile in the 1880s. Known as a Peruvian house, Grace was received coolly in Chilean business circles, as noted by James and confirmed by Joseph Grace: "Mr. [Charles] Flint's reception in Santiago reveals a condition which lasted for some time as we were distinctly *outsiders* in Chili."[38]

About this time, James also was negotiating for his next big writing project, a history of the California-based Bank of America founded by Amadeo Peter Giannini. Walter Bruns, vice president of the bank, wrote Joseph Grace for a recommendation on the reputation and character of the Jameses. Grace responded with warmth and enthusiasm, helping them to secure a lucrative contract to write *Biography of a Bank: The Story of Bank of America, N.T. & S.A.*, published in 1954.

How was this book—as well as the one on Metropolitan Life published in 1947[39]—received? Let us recall that James was producing a book on the average of one every two years during this prolific period in his life. The Bank of America history was quite different from *Merchant Adventurer*, for the Jameses avoided writing a biography of the founder, since Julian Dana's *A. P. Giannini: Giant of the West* had been published in 1947. Writing in 1954, John E. Baur of the Huntington Library thought that the Bank of America's vision—largely that of its founder and his son Mario—was closely tied to California's vision, "an expanding economic giant with industry now balancing agriculture and independent of eastern banks, as Giannini fought to make it."[40] Although Baur labeled the Jameses "subsidized historians," he nonetheless said that they wrote a good book, capturing the essence of Giannini's dream of what a bank should be and what a bank should do, and that much of what California was—for good or bad—reflected this vision.

Arthur Cole's review of *Metropolitan Life* was equally positive. The Harvard historian quibbled a bit with the less-than-scholarly appearance of the volume, but he noted that the most common defect of this type of corporate history—the unconscious, perhaps unavoidable, bias of the authors—was "not a major defect in this particular study." Cole described the book as a "welcome addition to our library on business history; . . . the reader will gain much from this interesting volume." He concluded that "it does not answer all the questions that scholars might well wish to have had answered, but Mr. James emphasizes the fact . . . that institutional histories *can* be good reading."[41]

Have these books by James been supplanted by later works? Newer ones have appeared: for example, Gerald D. Nash's *A. P. Giannini and the Bank of America* (1992) and Moira Johnston's *Roller Coaster: The Bank of America and the Future of American Banking* (1990). They probably have not entirely superseded James's works, although they undoubtedly have updated his findings and put the story of the Bank of America within the mainstream of modern business history.

However, James's study of the Insurance Company of North America, *Biography of a Business, 1792–1942,* published in 1942, went aground in an unsigned review in the *American Neptune,* the premier journal of U.S. maritime history. Apparently, he either missed or chose to ignore thousands of vessels' biographies in this maritime insurance company's archives that told the story, individually and collectively, of the "hopes and fears of the politician, the statesman, and the business man" over the years of the republic's existence through the rise and fall of insurance rates. As a result, James was skewered for bias and for what he did not write:

> It is to be regretted that Mr. James does little more than bend a knee before a group of local saints. However piously he makes his genuflections he has completely overlooked the significance of the records of the Insurance Company of North America. It is apparent that little knowledge of insurance and even less of ships and shipping were brought to the book. What induced the Pulitzer Prize biographer of Andrew Jackson to venture into something for which he is obviously unfitted is not known, but the book marks a missed opportunity to give the students of both economic and maritime history a work of prime importance.[42]

Most writers have been impaled at one time or another by such reviews, merited or unmerited. Whether the charges about *Biography of a Business* were true or not, James did not approach W. R. Grace & Co.'s collection with the same cavalier attitude. By the time he and Bessie had completed *Merchant Adventurer* in the spring of 1948, little in the records of William Russell Grace and his contemporaries had been left unread or without comment. In April, Roig, then vice chairman of W. R. Grace & Co., wrote James: "Our most sincere thanks and appreciation for the fine work you have done on this book. Your extended research, sound analysis, fine writing and realistic understanding of your subject have produced an outstanding biography. The book is a definite contribution to American history and letters."[43]

On September 14, 1948, C. W. Hopkins logged in the "letter books, etc. used by Mr. and Mrs. James in connection with [their] biography of

W. R. Grace [which were] returned to [the] basement files."[44] One week earlier, W. R. Grace & Co. had paid Viking Press $10,000 "in accordance with modifications of [a] contract dated March 10, 1948," as a subvention for *Merchant Adventurer.*[45] The book, now in galleys, was scheduled for release in October 1948. The galleys needed only to be proofread once more and then page proofs would be printed. After one final reading, *Merchant Adventurer* was ready to be bound, jacketed, and sent to bookstores around the country. The price was set at five dollars per book.

Then something happened that surely no one had anticipated. W. R. Grace & Co., the owner of the book, decided not to publish it. James could do nothing. He was the author but not the owner. From inside the company came dissenting voices that apparently overrode Joseph Grace and Roig. Someone had read *Merchant Adventurer* and thought that it contained remarks and commentary prejudicial to the company's current operations in Peru and Chile. It could have been any number of officers, including William Grace Holloway, the chairman; Adolf Garni, vice chairman; or two vice presidents with long Latin American experience, John T. Kirby and Andrew B. Shea. They have all since died. The only other chief officer at the time was Joseph Grace's son, Joseph Peter Grace, Jr., who was elected president in 1945.

Peter Grace—as he has always liked to be called to distinguish him from his father—only recalls that some of the officers with long experience in Peru, perhaps Shea or Kirby, objected to James's portrayal of certain Peruvians in the nineteenth century whose descendants were still powerful in the late 1940s.[46] Unflattering comments or portrayals could be misinterpreted, and these men could hurt the company. Others have speculated that the company's operations in Chile could be harmed by the revelations in James's book of the clear and unequivocal support that the Graces had lent to Peru during and after the War of the Pacific. Although the company's presence in Peru was much heavier than in Chile, Grace had a sizable investment in Peru's southern neighbor.

In addition, in October 1948 the constitutional government of President José Bustamante was overthrown and replaced with a military dictatorship. Overall, the year 1948 was one of political instability in Peru as the old oligarchy wrestled with new forces aspiring for power. A rising middle class, a vocal laboring class, and radical socialists wanted to make the country responsive to the needs of the many rather than subservient to the wants of the few. The Grace executives who froze the James project were sensitive to the political mood in Peru. Perhaps it *was* prudent in the fall of

1948 not to sponsor *Merchant Adventurer*, which portrayed the Graces as major actors on the Peruvian scene in the late nineteenth century.

This writer has not been able to identify the specific passages or areas that offended some of W. R. Grace & Co.'s officers and halted *Merchant Adventurer*'s march to the bookstores just before the 1948 Christmas season. Perhaps the following passage too graphically demonstrated Grace's avid partisanship toward Peru:

> Other powerful interests clearly did not wish Peru to revive; they wanted that country to remain an economic, and perhaps eventually a political, dependency of Chile. The tenacity and skill with which the Graces opposed these forces, refusing to give up when Peru's cause seemed almost hopeless, form a bright and singular chapter in the history of American commercial penetration in South America. (p. 215)

Perhaps presidents bearing such distinguished Peruvian family names as Pardo and Prado were portrayed too roughly. Or perhaps James's casual mention of "the Peruvian people, whose habitual idleness" (p. 76) caused old-timers to wince and veto the entire work as too dangerous to business.

In any event, scores of galley proofs of *Merchant Adventurer* were carefully stored in the basement at the company's headquarters on Hanover Square, and the book also sank to the basement of the company's collective consciousness. But W. R. Grace & Co. is not without a strong identity with its past. In the 1960s, Richard L. Moore of the company's public relations department almost reached an understanding with Little, Brown & Company to publish the manuscript before senior Grace managers once again intervened.[47] Presumably the same type of rationale was invoked.

By the 1970s, however, W. R. Grace & Co. had divested itself of almost all of its Latin American holdings, including its vast empire in Peru. The reason for suppressing *Merchant Adventurer* no longer existed. Indeed, no one could even remember precisely why it had been suppressed back in the fall of 1948. Now, forty-five years after Bessie and Marquis James completed *Merchant Adventurer*, it is finally available for all to read.

What happened to James after *Merchant Adventurer* was thrown into a literary and historical deep freeze? Not a man to be cast down for long, his ongoing history of the Bank of America (published in 1954) kept Bessie and him busy through 1953. This project was paralleled by another book, *The Texaco Story: The First Fifty Years, 1902–1952*, published in 1953. Seemingly, James could have continued writing corporate histories as long as he wished. But something was lacking in those accounts, and by the mid-1950s he had returned to the type of writing he loved most, biographies. In the works was a biography of Booker T. Washington, a black American who must have appealed immensely to the biographer of Sam Houston, Andrew Jackson, and William Grace.[48]

James's personal life had been profoundly rearranged in the early 1950s. In 1952 or 1953 he and Bessie, his wife of almost forty years, divorced, and, in January 1954, James remarried. His new wife, Jacqueline Mary Parsons, had been educated at Swarthmore College and was employed in New York at *Life* and *Collier's* before marrying James. Henry Steele Commager, the distinguished U.S. historian at Columbia University, was James's best man. Less than two years later, on the Saturday before Thanksgiving Day, 1955, James died at the age of sixty-four. His funeral service was held at the Friends Meeting House of the Quaker Society in Rye, New York. Patrick Murphy Malin, executive director of the American Civil Liberties Union, presided and read from the Bible; Commager delivered a short eulogy.

In its obituary the *New York Times* noted that James was preparing a biography of Booker T. Washington: he "will be missed, and so will the book he did not live to write."[49] Another work, *Merchant Adventurer*, did survive his death. Although one is accustomed to long gaps between the composition of a book and its publication, especially in the academic world, *Merchant Adventurer* must hold one of the longest such records. Nonetheless, I invoke the old adage "better late than never" and trust that James would take pleasure in finally seeing this story come to life.

The book that follows is a faithful copy of the 1948 manuscript. Small errors and misspellings have been corrected, as James or his copy editors certainly would have done before going to press, but little else has been done to edit or "modernize" the narrative, other than updating capitalization and hyphenation. One might ask: Is *Merchant Adventurer* dated and biased? Yes; it was a product of its time. Is it a good scholarly work? Yes; the research is accurate and trustworthy, based on documentary evidence of the best sort, with the story fleshed out by secondary sources and by the Jameses' reconstruction of events. Is it a good literary work? Yes; James, a master of the telling detail and the revealing anecdote, combined failure, personal tragedy, and success into a narrative that makes good reading. Is it controversial? Again, yes; the author was not afraid of taking the body of evidence and imposing his view and interpretation on events as he saw them.

The basic message of *Merchant Adventurer* has not changed. It is a compelling story of a man and his time and place in North and South American history. It is also set firmly in that optimistic period in U.S. history just after the Second World War. The relations between the United States and Latin America generally were warm, still bathed by the glow of Franklin D. Roosevelt's fading, but not forgotten, Good Neighbor policy. The Cold War was only just beginning, remote from Americans busy getting on with their lives after the war. The population boom in Latin America had not yet exploded, Fidel Castro was still an angry young student at the University of Havana, and the Cuban Revolution would not erupt until 1958.

Beneath the surface, Latin America's society and economy were being transformed. However, to James, Latin America was Casa Grace in Peru; a well-run Grace Line steamship plying the ports of the Pacific; and a cosmopolitan city such as Lima, the clean and modern capital of a quaint country, whose life-style for the upper classes was elegant and fun loving. Even the term "Third World" had not yet emerged in 1948 to describe the world apart from the developed, industrial, modern worlds of North America and Europe. In *Merchant Adventurer*, William Russell Grace spans these two worlds as they come into closer contact in the second half of the nineteenth century.

~ *AFTERWORD*
~ $\top$oday, W. R. Grace & Co. would be almost unrecognizable to the company veterans of the 1940s.[50] The headquarters no longer is in New York City, the main offices having moved in 1991 to Boca Raton, Florida. The stock, now traded on the New York Stock Exchange, no longer is only in family hands. And there is no Grace Line, no PANAGRA (sold to Braniff in 1968), no Latin American "commercial house"—not since Casa Grace was pushed out of Peru by a socialist-inclined revolution in the late 1960s and early 1970s.

The company, now a major producer of specialty chemicals, manufacturing everything from water sealants to plastic wrap for foodstuffs, also has significant investments in health-care services. However, forty-five years after Marquis James was commissioned to write *Merchant Adventurer*, there is one constant of W. R. Grace & Co. that old-timers would recognize: a member of the family is still chairman of the firm. While J. P. Bolduc, president and chief executive officer, is the first nonfamily person to head the company, J. Peter Grace, Jr., continues to serve as chairman of the board after forty-seven years as CEO (1945–1992).

Lawrence A. Clayton
University of Alabama

~ *NOTES*

1. Marquis James to Joseph P. Grace, Rye, New York, June 26, 1944, Marquis James Papers, Manuscript Division, Library of Congress (hereafter MJP/LC).
2. Ibid.
3. Ibid.
4. Marquis James, *The Raven: A Biography of Sam Houston,* introduction by Robert M. Utley (New York: Book-of-the-Month Club, 1990), p. xiv. Originally published by Bobbs-Merrill in 1929.
5. Most of the biographical detail in this section is from James's autobiography, *The Cherokee Strip: A Tale of an Oklahoma Boyhood* (New York: Viking, 1945).
6. Ibid., p. 219.
7. Ibid., pp. 245–46.
8. James, *The Raven,* p. xiv.
9. From undated, seven-page, double-spaced typewritten letter by James to "Dear Don," Box 26, MJP/LC. The remaining quotes above are also from this letter until otherwise indicated.
10. James, *The Raven,* pp. xiii, xiv.
11. From letter to "Dear Don," Box 26, MJP/LC. The remaining quotes above are also from this letter until otherwise indicated.
12. Louis P. Masur, "Bernard DeVoto and the Making of *The Year of Decision: 1846,*" *Reviews in American History* 18, no. 3 (September 1990): 436–51.
13. Ibid., p. 438.
14. Grace to James, October 22, 1943, New York, MJP/LC.
15. Marquis James, *Biography of a Business, 1792–1942: Insurance Company of North America* (Indianapolis: Bobbs-Merrill, 1942).
16. Leroy A. Lincoln, president, Metropolitan Life Insurance Company, New York, to James, November 10, 1942, MJP/LC.
17. Ibid.
18. In fact, James left his old publisher, Bobbs-Merrill, for Viking to publish an autobiography of his early life, *The Cherokee Strip.* This move led to some hard feelings between James and Bobbs-Merrill, but James believed that he would fare better with Viking. Sentimentality was apparently not one of James's weaknesses when it came to business decisions. He explained in a let-

ter to the president of Bobbs-Merrill, Lawrence Chambers, that either he would try to change Bobbs-Merrill more to suit his tastes, or he would change publishers. Since James did not see much chance of changing the nature of Bobbs-Merrill, he opted to switch publishers.

19. James to Grace, May 4, 1944, Pleasantville, New York, MJP/LC.
20. Ibid.
21. Grace to James, May 22, 1944, Tullaroan, Great Neck, Long Island, MJP/LC.
22. James to Grace, June 12, 1942, Rye, New York, MJP/LC.
23. James to Grace, June 26, 1944, Rye, New York, MJP/LC.
24. Ibid. All the following quotes are from this letter until otherwise indicated (emphasis in original).
25. Ibid. (emphasis in original).
26. Grace to James, July 3, 1944, Stony Point, North East Harbor, Maine, MJP/LC.
27. James to Grace, July 10, 1944, Rye, New York, MJP/LC.
28. The original contract was signed on October 11, 1944. Although I have not seen the original contract, the above information was contained in a revision of the original dated December 18, 1946, now the property of W. R. Grace & Co., Boca Raton, Florida. Subsequent references to this small collection of papers are cited as Grace Papers, Boca Raton (GP/BR).
29. The agreement between James and the Bank of America read, in part: "We understand further that your manuscript when completed, or any portion of the manuscript if it is not completed, together with all literary and auxiliary rights to the same, shall become the property of Bank of America N.T. & S.A. and that such manuscript shall be published under your name as author except that if we shall see fit to make changes in the manuscript which will not be approved by you after reasonable and thorough discussion, then the manuscript shall not bear your name." Walter E. Bruns, vice president, Bank of America, San Francisco, to James, October 17, 1947, MJP/LC. The contract with Metropolitan Life read, in part: "Upon completion of the manuscript of the history, appropriate opportunities are to be given us to review it thoroughly and to exchange ideas on the contents thereof. In the event there are any differences of opinion as to any parts, which you do not care to change, then the Company may re-edit the manuscript, if it so decides, and use any and all parts of it in such manner as may seem to it to be the most appropriate. In this event the Company may publish the book under any name it elects other than yours." Lincoln to James, November 10, 1942, MJP/LC.
30. John E. Baur, Huntington Library, review of Marquis James and Bessie Rowland James, *Biography of a Bank: The Story of Bank of America, N.T. & S.A.* (New York: Harper and Brothers, 1954), in *Pacific Historical Review* (1954): 404–5.

31. This writer first saw the same materials in 1978 in the warehouse on Broome Street. Everything had been reboxed and repackaged in 1948 by C. W. Hopkins, but the basic organization given to the papers by Hopkins and Bessie James was preserved. Upon the recommendation of this writer, the entire collection was donated to Columbia University in 1980 and is now housed in its Rare Book and Manuscript Library. Joseph Grace was an alumnus of Columbia and had long and close ties with his alma mater.

32. J. Peter Grace, Jr., to L. A. Clayton, October 28, 1992, Boca Raton, Florida.

33. James to Grace, June 3, 1946, MJP/LC.

34. James to Grace, December 20, 1946. Penciled note on bottom of letter indicates that JPG, Sr., approved. GP/BR.

35. In all fairness there was only one reference to a fifty-dollar fee paid by the Jameses to Basadre in the records that this writer cursorily reviewed in 1978. Perhaps this payment was one of several, or perhaps fifty dollars was all Basadre requested. Records of this and other transactions are with W. R. Grace & Co., GP/BR.

36. Grace to James, September 10, 1947, MJP/LC.

37. Ibid.

38. Ibid. (emphasis in original).

39. Marquis James, *The Metropolitan Life: A Study in Business Growth* (New York: Viking, 1947).

40. Review of *Biography of a Bank,* in *Pacific Historical Review* 23, no. 4 (1954): 404–5.

41. Review of *Metropolitan Life* by Arthur H. Cole, in *New York History* 28, no. 3 (July 1947): 358–61 (emphasis in original).

42. Review of *Biography of a Business, 1792–1942,* in *American Neptune* 4, no. 2 (April 1944): 76–77.

43. Harold Roig to James, April 5, 1948, MJP/LC.

44. One-page typed memorandum by C. W. Hopkins, originally seen by this writer in the Broome Street warehouse.

45. Receipt in GP/BR.

46. "I believe that Mr. Iglehart persuaded my father that there were too many insulting comments in the book about the fathers and grandfathers of then prominent Peruvians which, if published and publicized, could only hurt the Grace Company—among these, very prominent Peruvians who could damage the Company if they were angry enough." J. Peter Grace to L. A. Clayton, October 28, 1992, Boca Raton, Florida.

47. Richard L. Moore to L. A. Clayton, April 11, 1992.

48. There is also in the Marquis James Papers/Library of Congress at least four or five boxes with manuscript typescripts of a biography that James collaborated on with Bernard Baruch. Much correspondence between the two is also included with these typescripts.

49. Obituary, *New York Times,* November 21, 1955.
50. Readers curious about the modern historiography of William Russell Grace and the company he founded are referred to Lawrence A. Clayton, *W. R. Grace & Co.: The Formative Years, 1850–1930* (Ottawa, IL: Jameson Books, 1985).

~ AN ANNOTATED BIBLIOGRAPHY

~ Manuscript Collections

Marquis James Papers. Manuscript Division. Library of Congress. Washington, DC.

Grace Papers. Rare Book and Manuscript Library. Columbia University, New York City, New York.

Grace Papers. W. R. Grace & Co. Boca Raton, Florida.

~ Books by Marquis James

1923. *A History of the American Legion.* New York: W. Green. James's first book, written while he was editing the American Legion magazine.

1929. *The Raven: A Biography of Sam Houston.* Indianapolis: Bobbs-Merrill. James's first major biography and the winner of the 1929 Pulitzer Prize in biography. It marks the first in a long line of books that he published with Bobbs-Merrill. A modern edition was published in 1990 by the Book-of-the-Month Club, New York. Introduction by Robert M. Utley.

1933. *Andrew Jackson: The Border Captain.* Indianapolis: Bobbs-Merrill.

1934. *They Had Their Hour.* Indianapolis: Bobbs-Merrill. Dramatic episodes in American history written for popular consumption.

1937. *Andrew Jackson: Portrait of a President.* Indianapolis: Bobbs-Merrill.

1938. *The Life of Andrew Jackson.* Indianapolis: Bobbs-Merrill. Combines *The Border Captain* (1933) and *Portrait of a President* (1937) into one volume, which won James his second Pulitzer Prize for biography.

1939. *Mister Garner of Texas.* Indianapolis: Bobbs-Merrill. A biography of John Nance Garner, who served as vice president of the United States during Franklin Roosevelt's first two terms.

1941. *Alfred I. DuPont: The Family Rebel.* Indianapolis: Bobbs-Merrill. Commissioned by the DuPont family, this was the first of James's many books in the genre of business history. All of his subsequent works, with the exception of his autobiography, were commissioned or contracted.

1942. *Biography of a Business, 1792–1942: Insurance Company of North America.* Indianapolis: Bobbs-Merrill.

1945. *The Cherokee Strip: A Tale of an Oklahoma Boyhood.* New York: Viking. James's recollections of his youth. This was his first book with Viking, breaking with his old publisher, Bobbs-Merrill.

1947. *The Metropolitan Life: A Study in Business Growth.* New York: Viking.

1953. *The Texaco Story: The First Fifty Years, 1902–1952.* New York: Texaco.

1954. (With Bessie Rowland James.) *Biography of a Bank: The Story of Bank of America, N.T. & S.A.* New York: Harper and Brothers. James's last book and the only one in which his first wife Bessie was formally listed as coauthor.

Merchant
Adventurer ~

~ Foreword

~ Marquis James's penchant for the sturdy individual-
ists of our history, which has twice led him to a Pulitzer Prize, finds a sympathetic new subject in W. R. Grace, the Irish immigrant boy who not
only opened new fields to American commerce but also became an outstanding mayor of New York and a powerful amateur in national politics.
In this warm, nostalgic story, made possible by his access to the files of
W. R. Grace & Co., James combines his gift for biography and his close
acquaintance with business history to investigate a characteristic phenomenon of American life.

Grace's success story is a symbol of his age. In reading it we are
made aware again of the kind of personal character that went into the
shaping of the nation. The story of the opening of the west coast of South
America, Dollar Diplomacy, the ramifications of the Grace business—in
Peru, in Chile, in Central America, and on both coasts of the United
States—form as fascinating a pattern as that of an earlier kind of empire;
and a study of the heart and brains that shaped it, in the person of W. R.
Grace, is a contribution to our knowledge of the forces that make history.

Equally interesting, and of special significance in an election year, is
the story of how such a man, from his modest beginnings, won political
mastery of New York through sheer honesty and goodwill, and influenced
the destinies of Grover Cleveland and other national figures. New York in
the second half of the last century has never been more vividly brought to
life; for this story takes us along its teeming waterfront, into the heart of
the mercantile world when Wall Street was coming to power, behind the
scenes of its politics, and into its quiet homes and comfortable suburbs. As
with Sam Houston before, James has again found in local history a man for
us to regard as a national figure.

Allan Nevins
1948

3

~ Preface

~ This book is about William R. Grace, an Irish boy of distinguished family who ran off to sea in 1846, shortly before his fourteenth birthday. At nineteen he was in business in Peru. In the course of the next fifty years that business made the name of Grace what it remains to this day: the best-known commercial name on the west coast of South America, from Panama to Cape Horn. Those were stimulating times on the West Coast. The means by which W. R. Grace got where he did, make, I think, a good story. Grace did not stop with the creation of a great international business, which is still in the hands of his descendants. No citizen of the United States of his time did more to promote understanding between the peoples of the two continents of this hemisphere.

If that were the whole of W. R. Grace's career it might not be surprising that today he should be almost wholly unknown to the American public. But that is not all.

Grace married a Maine sea captain's daughter whom he had met at sea, those being the days when Yankee master mariners often carried their families with them about the world. When his business became large enough, Mr. Grace moved to New York and ran it from there. He entered politics on the reform side and became one of the three or four great mayors of New York City's history. (La Guardia and O'Dwyer are the kind of mayors his record brings to my mind.) Grace's influence in behalf of good government and his courage in public places went far beyond the confines of the city he governed so well. He was an important factor in Grover Cleveland's three races for the presidency, two of which were successful. Had Mr. Cleveland paid more attention to Grace and less to Tammany and similar political machines the Cleveland reputation would be bigger than it is.

That historians should so generally have lost sight of this phase of Grace's career does seem surprising.

Another thing. A shelf of books, including some very good ones, has been written on the golden age of the American merchant marine in the days of the down-easters and the clippers. Almost nothing has been written on the decline of that exhilarating era, which was a swift process beginning with the Civil War. It was during this decline, when the sailing ship, and nearly all ships bearing the American flag, were being swept from the seas, that Grace built up the last of the great sailing fleets. He did not buy a steamer until 1893.

Such is the career this book endeavors to portray. No biography with which I have been concerned has been drawn so largely from sources that have not previously seen the light of day. The principal source is Mr. Grace's correspondence, preserved over a period of fifty years. This remarkable collection, comprising more than fifty thousand letters, was offered by the Grace family and company, with no strings attached. A considerable proportion of the early letters are in Spanish, which Mr. Grace used as easily as he did English. Mrs. James spent a year and a half with these papers before I came on the scene at all. We found additional manuscript material in South America and in the United States. Thus, through favoring circumstances rather than any special talents of ours, this book should give a fresh aspect to a number of things that have been dimly perceived heretofore.

M.J.
Rye, New York
1948

1 ~ An Eventful Boyhood

~ In the spring of the year 1832 a young Irish country gentleman named James Grace took his family for a sojourn in the village of Riverstown, where the air carried the briny smell of the Cove of Cork, a mile and a half away. The house they got to live in could not have been an expensive establishment. Though comfortable enough, Mr. Grace's material circumstances were below the average of his class; and they were reduced, indeed, from what some of his forebears had been able to enjoy for hundreds of years. His wife—born Eleanor Mary Russell, and always called Ellen—also was of genteel Irish stock, with an admixture of Scotch. Her maternal grandmother was a Calvinist.[1]

The Graces had been married three years and they had two baby daughters. On May 10, 1832, at Riverstown, a third child was born—this time a boy. He was christened William Russell. Fourteen years later when Billy Grace's venturesome career was to carry him, on his own, across the ocean, Ellen saw in the fact that this child had been born almost within sight of saltwater the operation of cause and effect.[2]

Billy's first journey, however, was by land—to the Grace home in the hamlet of Ballylinan, Queen's County (now Leix). That was a trip of ninety-six Irish miles, equaling one hundred and eighteen English miles. It was a jolty ride, too, Irish roads being what they were. The mail coach's schedule from Cork to Athy was fourteen hours. At Athy a conveyance from the Grace farm doubtless met the family and carried it four miles to Ballylinan, a place of four hundred and fifty inhabitants and one hundred and one houses.[3]

The best of these houses—a rambling one-story, slate-roofed affair built of stone—was the residence of James Grace. It stood a short distance outside the village, and probably the stone came from the ancestral quarry which James Grace still operated. Mr. Grace's landed property consisted of three farms, aggregating one hundred and fifty-four Irish acres. This is the same as two hundred and fifty-two English acres—Irish acres, like Irish miles and Irish imaginations, being larger than their English counterparts. Two of these farms had come to James Grace by successive inheritances from his great-great-grandfather, yet no Grace had ever owned them. They were held under lease, and an Irish farm lease might run for nine hundred and ninety-nine years. Property thus held could be passed from father to son, as if owned in fee simple. The third and smallest of the farms—sixty-five English acres—James Grace apparently owned outright. This farm he leased to Patrick Bolger. The others, including the quarry and a limekiln, were worked under his own supervision.[4]

Queen's was one of the most productive of Irish agricultural counties, and this was moderately good Queen's land, indicating that James Grace and his recent forebears had not abused the soil, as was so common in Ireland. From these properties, James Grace appears to have made a fair living, but little more. For one thing, he does not seem to have possessed the energy of his grandfather, who had done handsomely with the same holdings, and, in addition, had profitably operated a cotton mill at Ballylinan. The mill had gone the way of the Irish cotton industry generally, due to adverse duties and to the introduction of new machinery that fostered the rise of the English industry in Lancashire. Moreover, James Grace found his stone quarry almost useless, because of the opening of similar quarries near Carlow, handier to the canal for transportation to Dublin. In James Grace's father's time, had a rich relative and neighbor—Richard Grace, M. P.—succeeded in his design to run the canal through Ballylinan, the money-making possibilities of the Grace quarry would have been a different story.[5]

Still, James Grace rubbed along. Though he might shy a boot at his serving man, he treated his working people well, really, and retained their loyalty. This was a help in providing for an increasing family. Two more boys—John and Morgan—followed William. Then there was a girl, Sarah, and finally another boy, Michael Paul. With Billy's older sisters, Alice and Ellen Mary, that made seven children.

They led a robust outdoor life, with no want of companionship. There was a flock of youthful cousins from two small neighboring farms, and, of course, the children of villages and of the farm folk in the Grace employ. All the young Graces learned to ride well—even John, whose legs were crippled by an illness in infancy so that he used crutches. James Grace bred and raised good horses, an occupation traditional in the Grace family.

In fact his manner of running his place showed considerable evidence of the sporting and improvident traits inherited from well-heeled ancestors. As a grown man, James Grace's eldest son remembered his boyhood home as provided with "more horses than cows, more guns than spades, more dogs than pigs."[6]

Billy was not tall for his age, but he was well set up and strong. He had blue eyes, tawny hair, and an excellent temperament for a first son, being a daredevil and a natural leader. He was hotheaded and a fighter. He taught John to fight, so that the crippled boy could hold his own against most boys of his size who had sound legs.

Billy liked to excel and was displeased with himself and with the world at large when he did not excel. The boys of the neighborhood played a game of "follow the leader" on horseback. Though most of the mounts were a nondescript assortment of ponies and donkeys, William rode a superannuated hunter—a gift from his father. The old thoroughbred was over at the knees and touched in the wind, but still game and able. Billy did all the foolhardy things he could think of, and the others made attempts, at least, to follow. So Billy led his crowd to a stone wall which edged the steep bank of a small stream. The far bank was ten feet below the near one. "Who dares follow me now?" shouted Billy, and put his old horse at the wall. No one followed, and some thoroughly scared boys crept up to the wall and looked down. There was Billy, safe on the other bank and pleased as Punch. In a moment, Irish perception was equal to the occasion. It turned out that one boy had seen a guardian angel riding by Billy's side. Another had heard a banshee's cry stifled in the banshee's throat. (As was well known in Ireland, a banshee's wail foreboded death.)[7]

Billy Grace and his gang reconnoitered and doubtless invaded the woods of the neighboring estates and of the important gentry. Nearest to hand was Raheen, the seat of Sir Anthony Weldon, whose family owned the farms James Grace and his Ballylinan cousins held under inherited lease. There was also Boley, homestead of the late Richard Grace, M. P., and now in the hands of one of his sons. Just beyond Boley, not more than two English miles from Ballylinan, was the most notable estate in the district—Gracefield, which a contemporary gazetteer of Ireland described as "the seat of the ancient family of Grace." When Billy was growing up, the widowed Mrs. Kavanagh, born a Grace, was mistress of Gracefield. She had taken down the great mansion and replaced it with a smaller "lodge" which was still a showplace of the region.[8]

It may be that boyish trespasses were the only occasions on which James Grace's sons and their Ballylinan cousins got a close look at the splendid abodes of their remote kinsmen. Certainly no intimacy existed among the manor-house Graces and Kavanaghs of Boley and Gracefield and the minor-gentry Graces of Ballylinan. James Grace's great-grandfather had been born in the old mansion at Gracefield; but being the second son he had not inherited the property. And James Grace's grandfather, the cotton mill owner, was a favorite at the hunting parties at Gracefield, and at Mantua House, another elegant Grace estate in Roscommon County. The passing of this enterprising man seems to have ended ordinary social intercourse this side of the grave between the great and the small Graces. In death, however, they came together again—in the family burying ground at Arless, five miles from Ballylinan, where Graces mighty and humble had been laid to rest for generations.[9]

~ In his Ballylinan home, Billy Grace was exposed to a social and political atmosphere probably more enlightened than he would have found at Boley or at Gracefield. The world "Gracefield" is English "Ballylinan," Irish: and therein lay the nub of the matter. In Ballylinan James Grace and his family were closer to the Irish people and to their peculiar and tragic problems than they would have been in almost any manor house.

The name Grace came neither from the Anglo-Saxon nor the Celtic but from the Norman French. It had once been Le Gros, then Gras, then Grace. A Le Gros came to Ireland in the thirteenth century during the first stages of the Anglo-Norman conquest of that island. A forebear of this Le Gros, a count by title, had been with William at Hastings in 1066. For the first three or four hundred years of their stay in Ireland the Grace family was immensely powerful, as was essential for the success of an alien invader. Various heads of the house lived in fortified castles, and hardly dared stick their noses out of them unattended. The invaders' policy was to keep their alien blood pure, and to exterminate or enslave the Celts. At first the law against intermarriage worked fairly well in the great families, but among their rank-and-file followers it scarcely worked at all. Then in the big families also a breakdown began, especially among younger sons who hadn't too much to hope for anyway.[10]

But the main thing that parted the one-time alien invaders from their brethren across the Channel was religion. The Catholic Church was well established in Ireland before the Anglo-Normans came storming in. That much invaders and invaded had in common. When the pope refused Henry VIII a divorce and Henry outlawed the Roman Church in his realm, neither he nor his successors got anywhere with that idea in Ireland, Ulster excepted. Almost invariably Irish families, great and small, remained true to the old faith and bore with the harsh political and economic disabilities that in time were imposed upon Catholics. Yet in other matters the big Irish houses upheld the English monarchs, and fought under their colors in wars without number. They helped to put down the recurring Irish uprisings instigated by native "patriots," or "rebels," according to the point of view. The most recent of these had been in 1798, the year James Grace was born. Scars of that brief struggle could still be seen within a few hours' ride of Ballylinan. In that affair all the Graces of whom there is any record had sided with the king.

When James Grace's children were beginning to become aware of their surroundings, Graces were still wearing the king's coat; and James's third son, Morgan, one day was to wear it as an army surgeon. All the same, this little Grace clan, Catholic in religion and preponderantly Celtic by blood, was pretty much Celtic in thought. William Grace grew to manhood with no love for the English, politically speaking. He never forgot the sufferings of the Irish poor, or rid himself of the distrust of authority as exercised in Ireland. A proud boyhood recollection dealt with the time he had helped to frustrate that authority. William was working in a field with a number of his father's laborers when a member of the constabulary turned up to arrest one of them. The man had escaped without his coat. Immediately all the other workers removed their coats to make identification of the fugitive more difficult.[11]

Young William Grace could speak a little Gaelic, the common tongue of the older farm laborers. Indeed, Billy's English was salted with a rich Irish brogue. When he got out in the world he rid himself of all but a trace of the accent, but he could put it on full force when he chose. In the later years of his life someone asked Mr. Grace the first book he had studied in school as a boy.

"Radamaydaisy," replied Mr. Grace.

"How is that?" the questioner asked.

"Reading Made Easy," said Mr. Grace.[12]

Another item of William Grace's early reading was a paper to which his father apparently subscribed—*The Nation,* organ of the Young Ireland movement. William remembered hearing his elders tell of the struggle to get the paper started. Once launched, in 1842, *The Nation* was

an instantaneous success. Driven out of the public reading rooms, it flour-
ished nevertheless. It was read in the forges, in taverns and cottages, and
wherever Irish working people gathered. The five pence a copy it cost
was the better part of a day's wages for a farm laborer. Yet a hat would be
passed and the sum raised. On Saturday a boy would go to the nearest
town and bring back a copy. Half the people in Ireland were unable to
read, but they could listen while others read aloud the speeches of Daniel
O'Connell, discussions of the plight of Irish agriculture and trade, native
ballads, poetry, news. In later life, William Grace remembered particularly
the contributions of Sir Charles Gavan Duffy and Thomas Osborne Davis,
the early *Nation*'s most brilliant writers. Davis was a Protestant.[13]

The fact that *The Nation* was cherished in his household seems to
throw light on James Grace's political leanings. He may even have been a
personal acquaintance of Daniel O'Connell. At any rate, William told of
having, as a youth, met and spoken with that Irish idol. The greatest Irishman of his generation, O'Connell was no firebrand. He discouraged violence and professed loyalty to the Crown. By peaceful and reasonable
means he accomplished much. "His earnest, devoted & intelligent patriotism has ever been held in reverence by me," William Grace wrote forty
years later, enclosing a contribution toward a monument to O'Connell.[14]

O'Connell's greatest achievement was the emancipation of Irish
Catholics. Time was, and that as recently as James Grace's grandfather's day,
when a Catholic was barred from certain trades and professions; when he
could not hold office or vote or serve on a jury; when he could not marry a
Protestant or appoint a Catholic guardian for his Catholic children; when he
could not purchase land, or inherit it, except from another Catholic. The
right of primogeniture was denied to Catholics unless the eldest son changed
his faith. Otherwise, landed property was divided among all the sons. This
served to break up Catholic holdings. Yet Catholics, even the poorest, were
obliged to contribute to the support of the Anglican Church.[15]

Some of the worst of these restrictions had been abolished when
O'Connell went to work. He did away with the rest.

A vicious land system remained. The preponderance of all cultivators
of the Irish soil held their land by lease. Long leases, which might run for
generations as in the case of James Grace, were not so bad. There was
incentive to make and preserve improvements, and to take care of the soil.
But there existed a system of subletting which sometimes brought five middlemen between the owner and the tiller of the soil. Each got his profit,
leaving the cultivator little for himself. Often this cultivator was a tenant-at-

will, who could be dispossessed any time. He had little reason to keep up fences and buildings or to protect the soil. Most of the horse manure from the streets of Dublin not shipped to Scotland was dumped into the River Liffey.

This way of doing enslaved the rural poor to a greater extent than the Anglo-Norman conquerors had done. Small farmers with ten acres worked nine acres to pay what they owed and lived on the produce of one. They ate practically nothing but potatoes. They lived in one-room hovels, which the family shared at night with a pig or a cow, if fortunate enough to own one. This was the condition of half of Ireland's eight millions.

In such an agricultural economy even a partial failure of the potato crop could bring hunger and death. This happened in 1845.

~ *S*uffering was widespread and the *Times* of London wrote: "There would be something highly ludicrous in the impertinence with which Irish legislators claim *English* assistance if the circumstances were not of the most pitiable kind." Fortunately the British government took a more humane view, and acted promptly and effectively. But when the potato crop failed again in 1846, and for the third time in a row in '47, relief measures were in no way adequate—though gifts of supplies poured in from many parts of the world. It was Europe's worst famine in time of peace.[16]

"Groups of families [were seen] sitting or wandering on the highroad, with faltering steps and dim, patient eyes," wrote John Mitchell in *The Nation*. "Sometimes I could see, in front of the cottages, little children leaning against a fence when the sun shone out—for they could not stand—their limbs fleshless, their bodies half-naked, their faces bloated—children that would never, it was plain, grow up to be men and women."[17]

As a relief measure a program of public works was begun. The road past James Grace's house was improved by men fighting off starvation. To take care of his own workmen, James Grace drained ten acres of bog on one of his farms. The workmen themselves wondered where the "ould Gintleman" got the money to pay them. One of James Grace's small-landowning cousins in Ballylinan went into debt, and eventually was obliged to sell his leasehold to Sir Anthony Weldon. At length James Grace had to give up the struggle, put the farms in charge of an overseer, and move his family to Dublin, where he took a post in the tax administration as supervisor of excises. William entered Dr. Cahill's College in Dublin, a Jesuit institution of high scholastic standing.[18]

Conditions in Ireland grew worse. Uncoffined dead were buried in trenches. In the three desperate years, half a million died of hunger or of sickness caused by it. An equal number fled the country, mainly to the United States. Many perished of illness at sea. On the ship *Larch,* bound for Canada, there were one hundred and eight deaths among four hundred and forty passengers; on the *Virginius* two hundred and sixty-seven deaths among four hundred and seventy-six.[19]

In the spring of 1846, before his fourteenth birthday, Billy Grace decided that stricken Ireland was no place for him. He ran off to sea. Little is known of his doings in the two years that elapsed before he came back. Possibly he made only the round voyage from Dublin to New York, working his passage, though the seamanlike appearance the boy presented on his return almost dissipates that assumption. One is struck also by the partiality that W. R. Grace showed, to the end of his days, for seafaring men—particularly old-timers "in sail." At all events, the boy spent considerable time in New York City. While in New York, William had several jobs. At different times he was a cobbler's helper, a printer's apprentice, a clerk in a small dry-goods store. In the last-named capacity he sold a bolt of goods for the price of a yard, and this ended his career as a dry-goods clerk. The work that he found most congenial, and apparently stayed with longest, was that of a clerk in a shipping house on the waterfront.[20]

A vivid account of the wanderer's return survives—in a letter Morgan Grace wrote his brother in 1894:

"John and I were on our way to school passing through Love Lane to the Circular road—A dark grimy figure dressed in longitudinally striped cotton trousers and a blue woven sea shirt hove in sight and gazed at us intensely. I shuddered and said to John—That is William. He scoffed and we passed on. About 4 o'clock the same summer's evening John and I were playing at the end of the garden. The same man jumped the stream leaped over a small hedge picked up a cabbage took a bit[e] out of it, then ran to the house. We followed and were welcomed with sounds of weeping. Lucy Fingleton had fallen on your neck and wept aloud. Down came your Mother, calm and self-possessed. I am glad you have come back William— Lucy get ready a great tub of warm water. He must be washed and made tidy. The Master will be home soon after four o'clock

"Tubbed you were and fresh dressed. Dear me what a great boy he has grown, quoth your Mother. A fine fellow he always was.

"Soon in came your Father. I can see him now—a straight active man [in a] very clean white shirt, dark sort of frock coat, light trousers—James (our man) at whose head the same Father had often cast his boots down stairs because the wrinkles did not shine enough, was polishing your sea boots—Ho, ho, William is that you—I thought you would come back—

"And so the incident ended."[21]

∼ In normal times, Dublin presented contrasting scenes of splendor and wretchedness. In 1848, the year of William's reappearance, the aftermath of famine intensified the wretchedness. Still, the boy's family lived comfortably enough in Brooklawn, a large house in Love Lane (south), since renamed Donore Avenue. The returned runaway was sent to school at Belvedere House, now Belvedere College. It is doubtful if the pupil displayed much interest in logic, metaphysics, or natural philosophy. Greek and Latin probably had less appeal than the universal language of business, bookkeeping, which was also a part of the curriculum.[22]

During his two years in the world, William had outgrown classrooms. His mind was much on America, where he said he had felt "the breath of opportunity" as soon as he landed. Without having been there, other Irishmen felt it, too, and the great exodus from that unhappy island continued. This spelled opportunity for young Grace, who in New York had learned something about shipping matters. It is not surprising, therefore, to find that by 1850 he had left school for business. The surprising thing is that this business should have borne the name of an eighteen-year-old boy: William Russell Grace & Co., head office in Liverpool, with an agency in Dublin. A silent partner, described only as "a man of means," had put up the money.[23]

William Russell Grace & Co. were passage brokers, that is, middlemen between the prospective emigrant and the charterers or owners of the ships that were to carry him to the promised land across the ocean. A passage broker's business was speculative. He guaranteed the emigrant passage at a certain price on a certain ship sailing on a certain date. Actually, the cost of passage fluctuated according to the demand. In 1850, when young Grace was in business, the range was between £3 and £4 for steerage. It is doubtful if many of Grace's clients could afford any other accommodations. Grace would make a contract at a fixed price, taking £1 down to seal the bargain. When the emigrant went on board he paid the rest. If in the meantime the price had risen above that named in the contract, Grace made up the difference. If the price had fallen, he was the gainer.[24]

William Russell Grace & Co. seem to have dealt only with the White Cross line of packet ships. Of twenty-six voyages of record with which Grace was concerned eleven were to New York, eleven to New Orleans, and two each to Quebec and to St. John, New Brunswick.[25]

Young Grace advertised rather extensively in *The Nation,* which in addition to being his favorite newspaper was also the publication most widely read by prospective emigrants. A sample advertisement:

LAST SHIP THIS SEASON FOR QUEBEC.

———

WHITE CROSS
LINE OF PACKET SHIPS
SAILING FROM LIVERPOOL.

———

FOR QUEBEC,
THE 3rd OF AUGUST, 1850
To Sail on her appointed day, the magnificent first-class
New Packet Ship,
COLONIST,
BURTHEN, 1,800 TONS,
J. SINNOTT, COMMANDER.

———

This fine Packet Ship is coppered and copper-fastened, built under the particular inspection of the owners, and fitted up with all the modern improvements so conducive to the health and comfort of the Passengers. The 'tween decks are of enormous height and handsomely fitted up for the accommodations of Steerage Passengers, who will be taken at the lowest possible price consistent with due regard to their comfort, and the following quantity of provisions will be given to each adult for the voyage, viz.:—25lbs. of Biscuits, 10lbs. Flour, 50lbs. Oatmeal, 20lbs. Rice, 5lbs. Sugar, 5lbs. Molasses, $1\frac{1}{4}$lbs. Tea, and 10lbs. Beef or Pork, also Vinegar, Water, Cooking Range and Ovens.

As this line of Packets sail under the inspection of the Government Emigrant Officers, Passengers may depend upon justice being done them.

Parties may secure best Berths by remitting £1 each. As this is the last Ship for Quebec this Season, early application should be made to

WILLIAM RUSSELL GRACE & CO.,
120, WATERLOO-ROAD,
LIVERPOOL;
or to
PATRICK O'NEIL, Agent,
6, NORTH WALL,
DUBLIN.[26]

A later advertisement contained the note:

"Friends of the Passengers by the Colonist to Quebec are informed that she made her passage in Thirty-four Days—Passengers all in good health."[27]

That William Russell Grace & Co. may have done fairly well at collecting emigrants is indicated by the fact that one vessel in which they were interested—"the well known and celebrated 'White Cross' Line Packet Ship 'LORD SANDON' "—sailed direct from Dublin. This was very unusual. Ordinarily Irish emigrants had to cross to Liverpool for a ship. Liverpool was full of Irish who had gone there to try to find work to pay for their passage the rest of the way to a distant new home.[28]

~ James Grace himself got the emigration fever; and he backed a novel idea. The United States was the destination of eight out of ten of the thousands of Irishmen who sailed away every month. Most of the others went to Canada. Although South Africa and Australia held out special inducements, they were at the foot of the list. Probably one factor in favor of the United States was that the British flag did not fly there. James Grace's attention was attracted to none of these places, however. His eyes were on Peru.

A former navy surgeon named John Gallagher had spent his inheritance on land near the port of Callao, in Peru, which he planned to develop into a sugar plantation. Needing dependable labor, he gazed hopefully on his emigrating countrymen. Doctor Gallagher was also an Irish patriot who wished to do something for his people. His mind conjured up a small Irish utopia in distant Peru. Gallagher got in touch with James Grace, who late in 1850 began rounding up prospective colonists. His young businessman son took a keen interest in the enterprise and, in the end, thought highly enough of it to close the firm of William Russell Grace & Co. and prepare to go along. But not necessarily as a part of the sugar plantation scheme. William's inclinations were for commerce rather than farming. He would go as a free agent, ready to take advantage of the best chance for fortune that the fabled land of the Incas might present.[29]

James Grace gathered a party of one hundred and eighty, including women and children. There was a young physician from Belfast to look after the health of the colonists; also Marcella and Eliza Lawler, attractive young cousins of the head of the expedition. Mrs. Grace, however, remained behind, with four of their seven offspring. Only the second daughter, Ellen, twenty years old, and the baby of the family, Michael, seven, accompanied William and their father. At London the emigrants boarded the "fine ship" *Louisa*—1,033 tons, A-1 at Lloyd's. On April 9, 1851, the vessel weighed anchor under a cloudy sky, dropped down the Thames in the face of a northwest wind, and began the long passage toward the Strait of Magellan.[30]

The fact that the *Louisa* was the first Irish emigrant ship bound for Peru raised the incident above the commonplace. As the vessel apparently was not spoken en route, news of her arrival did not reach Ireland until the following October. Then the Waterford *Chronicle* told of the receipt of "letters from some of the emigrants who sailed for Callao, South America . . . under the superintendence of James Grace, late Supervisor of Inland Revenue." The letters described "a most pleasant voyage" of one hundred and one days. That was good time for a sailing vessel. So, on July 20, the *Louisa* had dropped anchor in Callao harbor. Published references to the journey made no mention of the icy beat around the gale-swept Horn, in the roughest and most dangerous reach of water on the face of the globe. "The news they contain," pursued the *Chronicle,* speaking of the travelers' letters, "is most cheering, and three weeks of experience of the climate has made a most favorable impression. One of the letters concludes by saying,—'We have nothing to complain of but the absence of our friends and the ignorance of the language, but we will soon overcome such difficulties.' "[31]

The London *Times* deemed the item of sufficient interest to reprint it.

The climate of coastal Peru, which the immigrants were able to praise on such short acquaintance, has no equal in any other part of the inhabited earth. Though July is a midwinter month south of the Equator, the Irish people found the air bland and pleasant. A profusion of vivid flowers colored and scented the scene. Geraniums stood as high as a man, for the growing season is all year round. With luck the newcomers may have seen the sun twice in those first three weeks. The low gray clouds seemed to threaten a downpour at any minute. Certainly the strangers must have found it hard to believe that in the neighborhood of Callao there is a shower about once in ten years, but never a day of hard rain. All the growing things that met the eye were the products of irrigation, from the waters of the Rímac River. The lands of Doctor Gallagher bordered that stream.

Other aspects of the climate being so agreeable, newcomers to the coast of Peru usually do not miss the sun during the first of their stay. But when sunless weeks have stretched into months—the clouds sometimes resting on the ground and enveloping everything in a mist—the situation gets on the nerves of outlanders. This cloudy period lasts through eight months of the year. Then, in November, summer comes with a brilliant sun out all day long. Yet few days are as oppressively hot as they are likely to be almost anyplace in the United States in July.

Bearing in mind Irish weather, the Gallagher-Grace colonists were doubtless sincere in their early praise of the Peruvian climate. Perhaps they took as a good sign the stories they heard of the absence of rain—feeling as Michael Grace still felt, twenty-two years afterward, when he wrote to John, the last of the Grace brothers to quit the land of his birth: "My private opinion always has been that about any place would be an improvement on Ireland. All I remember clearly of the Old Country is that it rained over half the year and that everything was misery around us."[32]

2~A Youthful Trader in the Land of the Incas

~ The lands that Doctor John Gallagher hoped James Grace's colonists would convert into a sugar plantation and second Eden lay in the fertile Rímac valley, on the north side of the white, dusty cart road from Callao to Lima, the capital of Peru, eight miles inland. The fair hopes that the rainless skies of coastal Peru had helped to engender in the breasts of these travelers were not destined to be realized, however. Before their labors were well started nearly the whole colony came down with malaria and dysentery.

Of little avail were the combined skills of the ex-naval surgeon and of James Ainsworth, the young physician James Grace had brought from Ireland. The disillusioned survivors began to scatter. Some went to California, where the gold excitement was drawing adventurers from the ends of the earth; some to Australia. None, however, did better than the Lawler sisters, who stayed where they were and got excellent husbands. Eliza's was John O'Connor, a fellow countryman engaged in the merchandising business in Peru, and Marcella's a Frenchman named Louis Loiseau, who kept the select school in Lima that young Michael attended. James Grace stuck it out for three years and, in 1854, sailed for Ireland with Ellen and Michael.[1]

Also staying was twenty-two-year-old William Russell Grace, late of William Russell Grace & Co., Liverpool and Dublin. William had fared as well in the New World as his father's colonization scheme had fared badly. He had had nothing to do with the sugar enterprise. Straight off he had gone to work for John Bryce & Co., ship chandlers of Callao, and by 1854 was a partner in that old and respectable firm. In the firm's letter books, communications began to appear addressed to "El Sr. Dn. Guillermo Grace."

The times favored commercial expansion. After twenty-five years of virtual anarchy following its successful war for independence of Spain,

Peru had a stable government. The state's revenues were ample. Though the mines from which had come the gold and silver the Spanish conquerors shipped by the ton were flooded as a consequence of clumsy operation, Peru had a new source of wealth: guano. The mines lay beyond the summits of the Andes. To get the precious metal to the coast was an almost superhuman task. The Spaniards had killed Indians by the thousands doing it. On the other hand, whole islands of guano lay just off the shores of Peru. To load it into ships was a comparatively simple matter.

Guano was bird dung whose extraordinary value as fertilizer had been discovered by the world at large about ten years before the arrival of the Graces. Mountains of this treasure had been accumulating on the barren little islands for centuries. The Peruvian government took possession of it, controlled the sale, and found the proceeds sufficient to meet nearly all the expenses of the state. Peru became the only nation in history without internal taxation.[2]

The guano windfall enabled Peruvian officialdom to live about as sumptuously as its Spanish predecessors. The American chargé d'affaires in Lima reported the salary of the president to be "$40,000 besides $10,000 perquisites, to say nothing of licensed frauds."[3] The president of the United States' salary at the time was $25,000 a year. Still, Peru had plenty of money left for other uses. A railroad—the first in South America—connected Callao and Lima, a telegraph line was projected, and other public and private improvements got under way. Among these were irrigation schemes, such as formed a part of the luckless Gallagher-Grace undertaking.

Though the principal maritime nations were represented by ships that crowded Callao harbor, the flag of the United States outnumbered all others. The merchant marine of the young American nation was the largest in the world. It had displaced Great Britain by reason of merit: superior seaworthiness of ships—superior competence of captains and crews. Particularly did Yankee ships excel on the Cape Horn route. No other vessels withstood so well the pounding antarctic gales.

To Peru, which manufactured next to nothing, these ships brought the produce of the world. They took away guano—and a few other items. Nearly all the large commercial houses in Peru were British, like John Bryce & Co. Naturally they favored British goods and British ships. But John Bryce's brash young partner preferred American goods and American ships: William Grace's stay in New York had left its mark.

In addition to the ships of all nations that the guano trade attracted to Peru, American whalers would put into Callao for refitting and provisioning. In the 1850s there were in the Pacific seven hundred Yankee whalers, mostly out of New Bedford and Nantucket. A single voyage might last four or five years. Callao was also a way station on the busy route between the Eastern seaboard of the United States and California. As an ex-seaman, William Grace must have gloried in the sight of the queenly California clippers, the fleetest and most graceful craft that have ever touched saltwater. They would bang into Callao seventy days from New York, against an average of a hundred-odd for other American ships, which were faster on the whole than almost anything in sail John Bull had on the ocean. The *Andrew Jackson* made a passage between Callao and New York in sixty-one days. Several of her passages to California were under a hundred days, and one was eighty-nine: this against a nonclipper average between New York and San Francisco of about a hundred and fifty days.

Grace, the ship chandler, was glad to see the clippers for another reason. They came in with sails ripped to shreds, with tackle, spars, or mizzenmasts gone. Their captains never haggled over prices. A speedy refitting was all they asked. Speed was the clippers' reason for being, and they set records for sailing craft which stand today. They required twice the crew of a down-easter from the state of Maine, and had less cargo space to show for it. Thus it cost money to run a clipper, but in California in the fifties, money was a ready commodity.[4]

The establishment of John Bryce & Co. was such as a sea captain would feel at home in. The interior of the first floor had been largely constructed of the bones of wrecked ships. The crossbeams and pillars supporting the ceiling were stanchions and yards, the latter still retaining the iron jackstays to which sails had been attached. On the outside the first floor was adobe, the second floor cane plastered with mud and whitewashed, the roof cane with an overlay of plaster. From the jackstays hung ships' blocks of many sizes and designs. There were coils of rope and bales of oakum; barrels of pitch and tar; tanks of odorous turpentine, colza oil, kerosene, boiled and raw linseed oil; boxes of nails. There were salt provisions and hard bread. There were shelves of hemp canvas from Scotland, but no cotton canvas from the U.S.A. Behind a counter a glass case exhibited bottled liquors and "all kinds of things in use on sailing vessels from a sail-needle to a marlinspike." Toward the rear were the firm's offices—two rooms. Back of the offices was the fresh meat and vegetable department.

What a caller saw on view were merely samples. John Bryce & Co.'s main supply of goods was in a warehouse. The store employed sixteen persons, and it was the junior partner's duty to be on hand when the doors opened for business at six o'clock in the morning.

This establishment was older than Peruvian independence, and formerly was known as the "Almacen de Articulos Navales de Pablo Romero." A handsome six-foot young Scotsman from Leith named John Bryce had gone to work there as a clerk, married Pablo Romero's daughter, and inherited his business. The first partner John Bryce took into the firm was his brother Francis; the second, young William Grace.[5]

~ When Grace went to work there, very little of the store's trade was with Peruvians. Yet William lost no time making the acquaintance of the native people and starting to learn Spanish, which one day he was to use as readily as English. Before long the Bryce firm was the main supplier of the little Peruvian navy.

The patchwork appearance of the store building was not out of keeping with the general aspect of Callao. The best contemporary description of that port is from the pen of George W. Peck, more widely known as the author of *Peck's Bad Boy*. He landed in 1853, two years after Grace, and found the place "not imposing." As there was no dock, passengers and cargo were discharged in lighters and small boats. "Half a dozen rods [from the landing steps in the sea wall]," continued Mr. Peck, "you come to a ship-chandler's shop (Velasquez & Lyons) all open to the street, where there are usually a group of captains sitting on old chairs. . . . Opposite, on the right hand corner, is another similar shop and group of sitters (Bryce's)."

Had Mr. Peck looked past the visiting captains he might have seen young Guillermo Grace, mounted on a high stool, busy with the firm's accounts.

Packs of scavenging dogs roamed the dirty streets and snapped at the heels of donkeys pulling creaking carts over the uneven paving stones. Yet, of late, guano money had constructed some presentable buildings. It had ornamented with fountains and beds of flowering tropical plants the plazas, in one of which a band played on certain evenings.

Callao was a lively town, too, with suitable provision for the entertainment of visiting seamen. Mr. Peck noted "a succession of parties of Jack-tars who are never all sober at once . . . making merry after their fashion ashore." In houses "open to the street and to strangers . . . Spanish Quadroons" offered the solace of feminine companionship. The charms of these ladies were not easy to resist: "Their eyes are burning coals, and in their complexions you may see the volcanic fires raging under the skin. They look like bronze Venuses."

His tour of the city took our observer to a seaman's boardinghouse. The proprietor, "a sharp Yankee, [is] swinging in a hammock and smoking a paper cigar, while in a rocking chair sits [his wife,] an Afro-Spanish woman with bright eyes and small hands." The proprietor turned out to be an ex-mate, "an old hand, worthy to compete with our sailor boarding houses in New York." Mr. Peck's implication is that the ex-mate was a crimp. Owing to the number of seamen who deserted their ships in California to dig gold, the shanghaiing, or crimping, of hands from one ship to man another was a recognized profession in Callao, as in most of the large ports of the United States.[6]

Callao's outdoor places of recreation were cock-fighting pits and a racecourse. Young Grace appears to have attended the races and to have been quite well informed on turf affairs in Peru. To see a bull-fight, Don Guillermo would have to go to Lima, the twin towers of whose cathedral, with the hazy blue summits of the Andes in the background, were visible from Callao. Lima had the most commodious bull-ring in South America. The former viceroy's box was reserved for the president of the republic, and, as at the theater, the largest attendance was on Sundays.[7]

Pizarro had laid out the city of Lima in January (1535), a month of sunshine. Limenians still tell the story, for what it is worth, that the Spaniard had consulted the Incas about the climate. By then the Incas had seen enough of Pizarro to wish him no good. So they said that the climate of the projected capital was fine. By the time the clouds and mists came Pizarro was too far along with his city to move it. Had he chosen a site twenty miles farther up the Rímax he would have had sun all the year. In Grace's day wealthy Peruvian and foreign residents of Lima were beginning to send their families on sojourns to Chosica to break the monotony of Lima's dark, damp weather during two-thirds of the year.

One of the oldest cities in the New World and once the richest, Lima was divided into two parts by the Rímac River, and partly surrounded by the ruins of a military wall erected in 1680. Though the town had its splendid edifices, most of them were of sun-dried brick, cunningly and often tastefully covered with plaster. One still hears in wet parts of Peru that a good rain would wash half of Lima away. As it never rains, the town stands—its adobe and plaster construction resisting earthquakes better than rigid granite. Then as now, Lima possessed skilled woodworkers.

They lavished a wealth of talent on the projecting Moorish balconies which nearly met over the noisy narrow streets and footways.

The heart of the town was the Plaza de Armas, dominated by the cathedral begun by Pizarro in 1535. The structure Grace saw was completed in 1758, after the original building had been shaken down by an earthquake. Altogether, one was struck by the number of edifices the Spanish conquerors, with so much to atone for, had raised to religion. Their bells seemed always ringing. One side of the Plaza de Armas was filled by the presidential palace, formerly the residence of the viceroys who, under Spain, had ruled not only Peru but nearly all South America. Off the square were some good French shops and a café. There was also the Grand Hotel Maury, opened by a Frenchman in 1845. Its table and its gilt-framed mirrors would have done credit to Paris. The streets, paved with round stones hard on the feet of man and beast, were a little cleaner than those in Callao; the atmosphere somewhat more decorous; the prices lower.

Though not so overrun with foreigners as the busy seaport, a colorful and varied scene animated the streets of Lima, with its forty thousand people. They were a mixture of races. The dominant white race, the ruling class socially and politically (but not commercially), was of Spanish descent. Next came the *Mestizos,* a mixture of Spanish and Indian. The social line between them and the Spanish was indefinite. Laborers and servants were *Cholos* (Indians), Negroes (freed from slavery in 1854), and Chinese. The last-named were introduced under a form of contract that was slavery except in name. You did not speak of "hiring" a Chinaman, but of "buying" one.

The women of the lower class whom one saw on the streets were usually smoking what Mr. Peck called "paper cigars"—that is, cigarettes. Most of their aristocratic sisters also smoked, though not in public. When a Peruvian lady left her house she wore a *manto,* a black hooded shawl, covering the figure and the face, except the eyes. "It has been argued, and with perfect truth," wrote a New York newspaper correspondent, "that the manto is often made a cloak for vile deception and base intrigue, a man not recognizing his own wife so disguised." Though the journalist exaggerated the efficacy of the manto as an instrument for masking the identity, one did begin to hear favorable mention of candid English bonnets.[8]

In his early tours of exploration about Callao and Lima, doubtless on the back of a good horse, William Grace was the young man of business; but he was not *all* business. Letters exchanged through the rest of his life with members of Peruvian families and with sea captains he had met during his early years in South America show that Grace placed a high value on social intercourse and friendship. Years later an Irish shipmaster, then retired from the sea, wrote that "our old friendship on the West Coast has not died out I am glad to say. . . . When I look back and see what a number of fellows have gone off the books, I think those who have weathered it out are lucky. Most men led a hard reckless life on the Coast. You were always an exception."[9] Young Grace drank only claret, and he did not use tobacco.

On the lookout to expand the scope of his firm, Don Guillermo saw a chance for them to act as commission merchants, as intermediaries, in the importation of goods outside the line of ships' stores. Persuading John Bryce to let him make a trip to Guayaquil, Ecuador, Grace came back with a number of orders to be filled in the British and American markets. This was the beginning of a profitable relationship. When W. R. Grace died, his firm had accounts in Guayaquil dating from that first visit.[10]

During the Crimean War (1854–56), John Bryce & Co. provisioned both British and Russian warships. A story was later published of how young Grace took care of the Russian vessels very promptly, but procrastinated with the British so that they never caught up with the Russians. The object of the account was to establish William's anti-British sympathies. Granting that the young Irishman could be a pretty independent junior partner, the story, as related, makes him too high-handed for credibility. Still, it may have some basis in fact.[11]

If in this matter William displeased the head of the firm, who was thoroughly pro-British, he made up for it with the greatest stroke of his early career. It seems a simple thing, really, as profitable innovations often do in the light of hindsight. The guano trade was growing fast. A great fleet lay constantly off the Chincha Islands, one hundred and twenty miles south of Callao. These islands contained the richest of the guano deposits, and the only ones the Peruvian government had opened to commerce. Costly features of the guano business were the delays in loading and the long water hauls necessary between the points of origin and consumption. Anything that could shorten those voyages, even by a matter of days, would be helpful. William proposed that, to save the captains the time consumed in reprovisioning and refitting at Callao, John Bryce & Co. maintain a storeship at the islands. Accordingly, an old hull was stocked and taken to the islands, with William Grace in charge. Like nearly everything connected with the guano trade, the storeship proved a bonanza.

~ The floating commercial emporium at the Chincha Islands placed perceptive, young William R. Grace in touch with the vitals of Peru's financial, political, and social life. In ten years' time the miracle of guano had raised Peru from a condition almost as bad as it had endured under Spanish rule to that of a solvent nation with excellent credit. The combined foreign and domestic debt, under $31 million in 1850, had been consolidated in bonds bearing an interest rate of 3 percent, which was lower than the yield of obligations of the United States. Money to service this debt was hardly missed from the golden guano stream.

This tempted the Peruvian administration to increase the expenditures of the government. Year by year the budget went up. It went up faster than income. More money was borrowed. This rise in the national debt could not be explained by the construction of a railroad and telegraph lines, the erection of handsome new public buildings, the paving of streets, or the hiring of bands to play in the plazas. Toward the national revenues, officials of the Peruvian republic had inherited an attitude of their colonial predecessors: they treated them much as they would their private property. From President Castilla to the lowliest official in an Andean village accessible by mule track, guano money found its way. No one retired from public service in Peru poorer than he entered it.

In some respects this made for a loyal administration. It also increased the number of aspirants to office. Ramón Castilla, a good man who had done much for Peru, was always having to contend against rivals who claimed they could do better. In 1851, when he had been president for six years, Castilla managed the elections so that a successor of his personal choice, named Echenique, came in. General Echenique proved so immoderately corrupt that two years later Castilla went after him with an army, and resumed the presidency. Still, Castilla had to keep his army in the field, fighting off other candidates, in particular an obstinate one named Vivanco.[12]

Easy wealth also began to unsettle Peru's foreign relations. International diplomatic intrigues, power politics, and financial buccaneering swirled about it, with the United States, the new Pacific power, making its presence felt. Difficult for weak Peru to defend or administer, the guano islands became more than an ever-present incitement to the cupidity of foreign financiers and traders, as often as not backed by their governments. They became a threat to Peruvian independence.

At different times there were moves that looked as if Britain, France, and neighboring New Granada (now Colombia) had designs on some of the treasure islands. On another occasion the British helped capture two armed steamers with which Vivanco, the revolutionary, had put to sea to seize the Chinchas. General Echenique, whom Castilla had put in and out of the presidency, also was busy—trying to get back. He teamed up with the two Lomer brothers, German Jews who falsely claimed to be American citizens. The Lomers agreed to supply the presidential aspirant with a steamer and five hundred armed Americans—for a price, payable in guano. The capture of one Lomer with incriminating papers ended the episode.[13]

When William Grace expressed his admiration for the United States, he was espousing a particularly unpopular cause in South America. Though we were the original inspiration to South American independence, our annexation of Texas and California and the conquest of Nicaragua by Walker, the filibuster, had all the Latin countries scared of us. The envy of Britain and France, who formerly had had the commerce of the Pacific pretty much to themselves, also failed to enhance the esteem in which Americans were held south of the Rio Grande. It took the Lobos Islands incident in 1852, however, to confirm the worst that had been said of the Yankees.[14]

Since the 1840s the United States had been a heavy importer of guano, particularly in the South, where prodigal farming methods were impoverishing the soil. Delivered to an American farm, guano cost $50 a ton. Though we thought this too much, little could be done about it. Peru was the only source of supply; and Peru did not handle the distribution. That was a monopoly of Gibbs & Co., an English house, which paid the Peruvian government $15 a ton. When Gibbs's contract to supply the United States was about to expire, an American firm offered Peru $20 a ton for guano, which it expected to sell here for less than $50. The offer was refused in favor of one from F. Barreda & Brother, a Spanish-Peruvian concern. It was useless to protest that the American bid had been higher than the Barredas': too many Peruvian officials were interested in the Barreda firm.[15]

As this would keep up the price of guano, the United States government took a hand in the matter. The way things happened smells of pre-arrangement. A sea captain named Jewett wrote and apparently delivered in person a letter to Secretary of State Daniel Webster, inquiring whether guano might be taken from the Lobos Islands by Americans. The Lobos lay off the coast of Peru north of Callao and constituted part of Peru's reserve supply. Though ill and in the last summer of his life, Webster responded promptly and vigorously to this obscure captain's communication. He contended that Peru had no title to the Lobos, either by discovery or occupancy, but that an American captain named Morrell was their "probable" discoverer, in 1823. Webster said this gave Americans the right to take guano as they pleased. He added the navy would back them up.[16]

Then it developed that Jewett had a partner, a New York speculator named Benson, who had long had his mind on guano. Benson advertised in the newspapers for ships, promising naval protection. He dreamed of selling guano for $30 and making a fortune. These activities sent the Peruvian minister hotfoot to assure Webster that the Lobos had been recognized for centuries as part of Peru. Webster stood pat. Peru prepared to defend the islands. Then John Randolph Clay, American minister to Peru, in a series of straightforward communications, shot the ground from under his superior's feet. He showed that the islands had been Peruvian since the days of the Incas; and that they had no more been discovered by Morrell than by Webster. The secretary of state had to reverse himself. He admitted, though not to the Peruvians, that he had fallen for a scheming sea captain's tall tales.[17]

By this time twenty or thirty American ships were on their way to the Lobos. Lima was feverish with excitement. Bloodshed seemed unavoidable until word came of Webster's backdown. John Randolph Clay, whose emphatic stand had saved the good name of the United States, asked an American naval vessel then in Callao harbor to proceed to the islands and keep American ships' crews from making trouble. Benson and Jewett got the reverse of what they deserved. So relieved was Peru over the outcome that it footed the bill for the fraud that had been practiced on the State Department. Ship charterers were paid for their bootless voyage, and guano equipment they had purchased was taken off their hands.[18]

~ The Chincha Islands, to which William R. Grace repaired with the storeship in 1855 or '56, were three in number and lay twelve miles off the mainland opposite the small port of Pisco. Their names were North, Middle, and South Island. Isla del Norte, a little larger than the others, was about three-quarters of a mile long by a third of a mile wide. Operations had begun on that island. By the time Grace got there sufficient guano had been removed to level off enough ground to accommodate a little settlement. There was the residence of the Peruvian governor of the islands; a British consulate; offices and quarters for the personnel of

Gibbs & Co., who controlled the export of the product to most of the world outside the United States; the same for Zaracondegui & Co., who, with other Peruvian interests, succeeded the Barredas in 1857 as exporters to the United States. There were huts and a cemetery for the laborers, principally Peruvian convicts and Chinese. There were barracks for guards and for the brutal Negro taskmasters of the Chinese. In the settlement the Chinese, who got $3.80 a month, could buy opium; and seamen, liquor. Overlooking the scene, swarms of marine birds would appear, screaming their resentment of human intrusion.[19]

The rock bases of the islands rose straight from the water, more than a hundred feet in places. At tide level the action of the waves had cut great seaweed-hung caves. In and out of these caverns would "sport and splash . . . short, fat sea monsters, weighing about a thousand pounds each and called sea-lions, from their huge heads resembling a Newfoundland dog's." On top of the rocks, guano lay two hundred feet deep in places. The impressions this made on observers vary. One found the islands "perfectly white, which a spectator would pronounce to be snow"; another spoke of "bold, brown heads, tall and erect, standing out of the sea like living things"; another saw colors ranging from "dark red . . . to a light yellow which approaches white." All were correct. The color of the untouched surface was dark red; other hues were uncovered lower down. Visitors were in agreement, however, about the pungency of the smell the islands gave off, particularly when the reddish crust was disturbed. The dominant odor was of ammonia. When the workmen struck a particularly strong ammonia pocket, the stench was "so powerful at times as to nearly stifle one, and penetrating through the very sides of the ship."[20]

The inhabitants of the North Island settlement formed only a part of the Chincha community. Riding at anchor was a fleet of a hundred to a hundred and fifty ships. In the midst of this floating town, Grace anchored his storeship. This vessel had stubs of masts but no sails or other means of locomotion. It had come in tow the hundred-odd miles from Callao. But it glistened from a coat of new paint, and the sides bore the legend: JOHN BRYCE & CO. The ship carried about what the Bryce store in Callao carried. Fresh fruit, meat, and vegetables were brought out daily from Pisco. As the medium of exchange in the Chinchas was captains' drafts on their owners and the gold and silver of many nations, the storeship was furnished with a formidable iron safe.

William's quarters in the stern of the vessel were roomy and comfortable—a wise provision because his position called for a good deal of entertaining. First off, of course, was the ceremonial exchange of calls with the governor. That dignitary lost no time recommending a nephew for a post on the storeship. The request caused Grace to hesitate. His success as a merchant in Peru had been based on the somewhat novel idea, in that part of the world, of selling honest goods at honest prices, and, to boot, having on hand what his patrons wanted.

Peruvians being noted neither for their industry nor their skill in commerce, when an official asked a job for a relative the thing usually boiled down to a bookkeeping entry: another name on the payroll. William had never granted accommodations of this kind; and he had no room for a sinecure on board the storeship. Still, with misgivings, he employed the nephew, whose name was Manuel Llaguno. To Grace's relief and surprise, Manuel Llaguno proved a hard worker and a good one. Before long he had charge of the floating store's books.[21]

Ships were loaded from barges piled with guano—a dirty, smelly, long-drawn-out affair. Three months were required to fill the average hold. These long stays meant good business for the storeship. They made for acquaintance among the ships' officers, who entertained in turn. The fleet was made up of vessels from the principal seagoing nations, in about this order: American, British, French, German, Scandinavian, Dutch. Young Grace particularly liked to exchange courtesies with American captains—because he liked the United States and moreover because American shipmasters often brought their wives and families with them. This was especially true of the "down-easters" from the state of Maine, where men in the same families had gone to sea for generations and carried their womenfolk along. William met young ladies who had spent most of their lives at sea, and had been, of course, all over the world. They must have found him an agreeable, well-mannered, fun-loving Irishman, who was enchanted by music, liked to dance, and to hear and to tell a story. On board the down-easters was usually music, sometimes a piano. Though all agreed there were more pleasant places to anchor for three months than the Chinchas, seagoing people learn to make the best of an environment. Every Saturday night there was a "frolic" somewhere in the fleet.

Afloat and ashore William Grace had been thrown with seafaring men long enough to know something of the nature of their worldwide fellowship. A rendezvous like the Chinchas was a great clearinghouse for personal marine intelligence. A captain arriving from the Sandwich Islands, or from China, say, would be days imparting the news about the shipmasters he had met with in that part of the world. In the fleet he would meet a score of men he had long known and with whom he had shared varied fortunes. Each of them would have something to tell in exchange. Captains in from Bristol, Antwerp, the Baltic Sea, New Orleans, or Boston would have gossip to swap from those quarters: tales of fair weather and foul; of prosperous voyages; of mutiny, shipwreck, and death. When the long work of loading was done at the Chinchas, the hatches battened, the ship refitted and provisioned for a long voyage—anyplace where the guano went being a long way from Peru—the officers, on the morning of sailing, would serve a more-or-less formal breakfast for their friends in the fleet. Guests would come with messages and letters for delivery at the ship's destination; depart with wishes for a "pleasant voyage and godspeed."[22]

All in all, the Chincha experience was imparting to young Grace something he was to carry through a long life: respect for a shipmaster's calling. He would have agreed with the British merchant-marine historian who wrote that "the masters of American vessels were, as a rule, greatly superior to those who held similar positions in English ships." The preeminence of Yankee seamanship—"cracking on" sail and "carrying hard" being marks of skill and not of recklessness—was not all that attracted young Grace to the Yankee skippers. Their "good characters and fair manners" enabled them, as the English writer noted, to be "received into the best mercantile circles on shore." And their earnings permitted them "to live like gentlemen."

For that matter, many American captains were gentlemen. Some of New England's best families—Starbuck, Nason, Watts, Macy—sent their sons to sea. "American shipowners," continued the Englishman, "required of their masters not merely a knowledge of navigation and seamanship but of commercial pursuits, the nature of exchange, the art of correspondence and a sufficient knowledge of business . . . to represent the interests of their employers to advantage with merchants abroad."[23] Young Grace was aware of the excellent reason that impelled Yankee captains to a zealous discharge of their manifold responsibilities. In many cases they were partners in the enterprise at hand, being part owners of the vessels they sailed. On top of that, sometimes they had a proprietary interest in the cargo.[23]

3 ~ A Courtship at Sea

~ The prospering storeship kept trader Grace on the go. Stocks were cleared out with gratifying speed. This meant trips to Callao, carrying to the parent house the captains' drafts and the gold and silver that accumulated in the iron safe on the ship; trips back, with fresh goods. Inventories were increased, new lines added. The preference, particularly among Americans, for Yankee goods enabled young Grace to convince senior partner Bryce to stock more American-made items. When the ship could no longer accommodate all Grace brought to the islands to sell, a branch store was set up in the growing settlement on North Island. Grace was happy over the way Manuel Llaguno was turning out. The Peruvian took a good deal off the busy young man, and during Grace's absences on the mainland he was in charge of the Chincha establishments.

On one of his visits to Callao, William encountered a stranger who was having difficulty making himself understood in English. Like Grace himself, the stranger was below middle height; and he had a strong, keen face dominated by a large nose. Doubtless, William recognized him as an American; and perhaps as a mariner, though ships' officers rarely wore uniforms on shore. For that matter, a visored blue cap was usually the only badge of authority worn afloat.

When William asked if he could be of help, the stranger said he was looking for the United States consulate. He introduced himself as Captain Gilchrest of the American ship *Rochambeau*, newly from Liverpool. As a reward for the young man's politeness the captain asked William aboard the *Rochambeau* for tea.

And tea it was. The *Rochambeau* was a "temperance ship," and her master a personal teetotaler. The two did not always go together. Some closefisted Yankee captains kept a generous supply of the hard stuff for themselves, but, giving economy the guise of morality, denied it to their crews, who would have appreciated a rum ration while beating a stormy winter passage 'round the Horn—standing watch for days and nights without relief, and sleeping in snatches in their cold wet clothes.

Captain Gilchrest's party was largely attended. Whatever other guests may have thought, William Grace did not mind the absence of anything stronger than tea. And had there been no tea and cakes the young trader would have enjoyed himself all the same. The attraction was the captain's daughter.

Lillius Gilchrest was seventeen, slender, and about as tall as William. She had good features, a good complexion, violet eyes, and lots of wavy brown hair. She met her father's guests easily and, though not a talkative girl, knew the correct thing to say, and said it without shyness. Having gone to sea the first time when she was six, Lillius had no reason to expect this tea party to be different from the entertainments she had been used to on board her father's ships in all parts of the world. The talkative one was Lillius's mother—a large, warm-hearted woman taller than her husband; and you did not have to look twice to suspect that Mary Jane Gilchrest had a mind of her own. Less self-contained than her daughter, she must have found the loneliness of long voyages hard to bear. But in the sociability of ports she blossomed, and made herself a center of interest.

Nor was there anything about the gathering on board the *Rochambeau* with which William Grace was unfamiliar. At similar functions he had met, danced with, and probably flirted with, a good many American captains' daughters. But matters had never gone further than that. Twenty-four-year-old William Grace was, at bottom, a serious chap, inordinately ambitious to get on. "I'm not a marrying man," was his way of dismissing the graver aspects of the woman question. Moreover, young Grace did not, for an instant, lack confidence in himself. After the *Rochambeau* party he mentioned Lillius Gilchrest to a friend. "She is the girl I am going to marry," he added, as if that settled it.[1]

~ The *Rochambeau*'s three months' stay off the Chinchas, loading guano, gave William a fair chance to make progress in the direction of his brassy assumption—a fair chance and no more. In the guano fleet there must have been potential rivals: young mates from New England whom Lillius had met in other ports; possibly home boys from Tenants Harbor or Thomaston, Maine, whom she had known all her life. Any of these youngsters might expect to marry a shipmaster's daughter as a matter of course.

With a population of six thousand, Thomaston was the home of a hundred sea captains, twenty-five of them members of the Watts family, who also owned a shipbuilding yard in which Captain Gilchrest had an interest. Captain Edwin Watts (later lost off the Horn) commanded the *L. B. Gilchrist*, which may have been christened for a member of Lillius's father's family. (They spelled it both Gilchr*est* and Gilchr*ist*.) The *Rochambeau* had been built in the Watts yard. She was, then, a down-easter, sometimes called a modified, or medium, clipper. "The Down East ships were very beautiful," loyally wrote Lillius in a memoir of the seagoing time of her life. "The clippers were faster, but," added the sea captain's practical daughter, "[they] could not in proportion to their tonnage carry as much cargo." At this period no true clippers were in the guano trade. On the China and the California runs those ocean greyhounds found cleaner work that paid as well or better.[2]

In the quest for the hand of Lillius, one thing on William's side was the good impression he made on the girl's parents, who were of dissimilar temperaments. A hard, shrewd little Yankee, George W. Gilchrest was puritanical to the core, and a rather persistent moralizer. At seventeen he had composed and signed a pledge "never . . . to drink any kind of strident spirits nor chew [nothing said about smoking] tobacco. . . . i know some folks say spirits is good in its place but that cant be for it Kills more than it cures. . . . Some say a little dont hurt anybody but a little drinking brings on a gooddeal."[3] The captain also denied himself other indulgences. He would not attend a theater or a dance, or permit dancing on board his ship. According to female gossip, he would not let his wife or daughter trim their undergarments with lace. Yet, all in all, the captain was a less forbidding personage than this behavior suggests.

Though the first Gilchrests in America were landsmen in southwestern New Hampshire, George was born on the Maine coast. Like most of the boys he grew up with, he went to sea. At twenty-one he was master of a brig in the coastwise trade. When Grace met him, in 1856, Captain Gilchrest was a well-to-do man: part owner of the vessel he sailed, as well as of the Watts shipbuilding yard in Thomaston. His wife, Mary Jane Smalley, of a Massachusetts-Maine seafaring family, had less trouble keeping on good terms with her conscience. Mrs. Gilchrest liked the theater and, when opportunity presented, she attended—with Lillius, who was the Gilchrests' only child. Mother and daughter accepted invitations to some of the dances that were held every week on the deck of a vessel of the fleet. Doubtless, William Russell Grace never missed a chance to be their escort.[4]

William's first present to his admired was a *silvador,* or musical jug. The musical jug had two necks. When water was poured into one, the air coming out of the other whistled like the notes of a tropical bird. The gift must have been selected before William learned that Lillius was tone deaf. Despite his love of music, this discovery did not slacken the courtship— which seems to have benefited by the friendly attitude of the mother. At any rate, when William gave Lillius an engagement ring, he also presented a ring to his mother-in-law-to-be. Nor did the young trader spare his purse in this matter. Lillius's ring was set with a cluster of diamonds; Mrs. Gilchrest's with a diamond solitaire.

One account says that the engagement these gifts symbolized took place before Captain Gilchrest gave his farewell breakfast and the *Rochambeau* weighed anchor for the British Isles. Another says it came later, by correspondence. In any event, when they left the Chinchas, Captain and Mrs. Gilchrest were sufficiently concerned to call on William's parents the next time the *Rochambeau* was in Dublin.[5]

To keep abreast of the affairs of the world, William read the *Herald* and the *Courier & Enquirer* of New York. After Lillius's departure he asked his American agent to enter a subscription for "one Thomaston, Maine, paper"—in which, perchance, he might learn something of the doings of his betrothed, whom he was not to see again for three years. Then they met in Tenants Harbor, near Thomaston, whither William had gone to claim his bride. They were married in the Baptist church at that place on September 11, 1859. Lillius was twenty years old; William, twenty-seven.[6]

~ *O*n June 11, 1860, their first baby, named Alice Gertrude, was born on the storeship. Three months later Captain and Mrs. Gilchrest arrived in the *S. Cushing,* loaded a $60,000 cargo of guano, and cleared for Melbourne, Australia.[7] In September 1861 the second baby, Florence Ellen, was born.

Though Alice probably was not the first, and it is certain that Florence was not the last, baby to see its first light off the Chincha Islands, visits of the stork to that region were exceptional events. The fleet must have been combed for presents suitable for infants, and William kept busy passing out punch and cigars. Visitors found the young mother's surroundings as comfortable as they could be made in the circumstances. The living quarters on the storeship were expensively furnished. There was a staff of servants, and a nurse for the babies. Michael Grace, William's youngest brother, was now a member of the storeship family. He had returned to Peru some time before, attended school in Lima for a while, and entered the employ of John Bryce & Co.

About the Chinchas, life flowed as before. If anything, the place was busier than when Grace had first come. Lillius recalled "many parties among the ships of the fleet. Once a week there would be a ball." A passing newspaper correspondent found "educated and accomplished women" aboard some of the ships, and noted that "singing, dancing and feasting is the order of the night." While ships' officers and their ladies entertained on board their vessels, forecastle hands had a place of recreation on North Island, no longer a man's world entirely. "The sable sisters on the Island," wrote the correspondent, "[contend with] bitter envy and jealousy" for the favor of the seamen. "There are drunken frolics and sprees, and wranglings and debates, and affairs of nation and State discussed *pro* and *con*."[8]

William was proud of his beautiful wife, and boasted that she could do anything—even make her husband a suit of clothes. When a Maine man offered to bet that Lillius could not make a suit of clothes, William took him up. Though rather floored by her husband's wager, Lillius set out to win it for him. Ripping apart an old suit, she made a pattern. As she had no sewing machine, every stitch on the new garments was done by hand. In two or three months the suit was finished. The Maine man had paid his bet, but could not resist pointing out that Lillius had put all the buttons on the left side.[9]

Affairs of the nation and state were discussed not only by seamen over their grog on North Island. They were discussed on board the storeship, and everywhere men foregathered. The overshadowing international event was the Civil War in America. British, French, and Peruvian sentiment was for the Confederacy, which was winning the early battles. William Grace was for the Union, and not afraid to express his opinion. Yet William must have had his work cut out defending his favorite country in the *Lizzie Thompson-Georgiana* incident which, just before the war began, had resulted in a rupture of official relations between the United States and Peru.

The revolutionary activities of Castilla's old rival, Vivanco, had reached a periodic climax. Vivanco issued licenses to the American ship *Lizzie Thompson* and the bark *Georgiana* to load guano at islands the government of Peru had declared excluded from commerce. While thus engaged, the vessels were seized by a Peruvian warship, and confiscated.

The United States made a loud protest, demanding return of the ships, with an indemnity. Peru declined to comply, but proposed a reasonable compromise. We rejected it, and diplomatic intercourse came to an end—to the delight of England and France, whose men of money had their own designs on the riches of Peru.[10]

Although the life had its agreeable features, on the whole Lillius does not appear to have carried away many happy memories of the Chinchas. The day was to come when, with her children growing up, she could impart a lively zest to tales of her earlier years at sea with her father: the waterspout in the Indian Ocean that had nearly swamped the ship; the time the grain in the hold shifted during a storm and laid the vessel on its side; the time the *Rochambeau* came under fire in the Black Sea, carrying supplies to the British during the Crimean War. A cannonball struck a spar on a ship so near that splinters showered the *Rochambeau*'s deck.[11] A grim tone, however, pervades her recollections of the Chinchas, set down when Lillius was a grandmother: the perpetual stench of the guano ("If one stood over the hatch of a vessel carrying guano the fumes were almost overcoming"); the convicts and Chinese, worked to a point where death was a welcome release. ("These Chinese . . . would take enough opium to kill, dig a grave and lie in it. It was not uncommon to see a Chinaman lying in an open grave, still alive. When discovered they were revived.")

How could such things be? Lillius Grace had the answer: "The guano business . . . paid very well."[12]

It paid so well that her husband was a rich man at thirty. In 1862, William left the local management of the business to others and established a residence in Callao. William had worked hard for his money—too hard. One day he came home to say that on a physician's advice he was giving up business altogether and taking his family to Ireland. They sailed almost immediately.

~ Eleven years before, William had been glad enough to get away from Ireland. When he should outgrow Peru it had seemed inevitable that he would head for "the States"; and surely Lillius looked forward to rearing her family there. Only lately William had given proof of his regard for his wife's native land, and his faith in the Union. Two American naval corvettes had put into Callao out of supplies. The war news had been bad for the North. After the American paymaster had appealed vainly to banks and merchants to honor his drafts, Grace took them and gave the corvettes what they needed.[13]

But Ireland it was—indicating that William Grace was low in spirit as well as in body. With all its drawbacks, Ireland was the place William Grace's heart called home; and the Catholic Church was still the true church. Since going to South America, and especially since his marriage to a Protestant, William had been neglectful of his duties to religion. On receipt of the doctor's verdict in Callao he began to repair that neglect. The doctor had said that William had Bright's disease; that rest must be part of his treatment; and that, in any event, he might not live long.[14]

The Graces remained abroad for a year or a little more, traveling considerably, in England as well as in Ireland. The good part of the pilgrimage was that William recovered his health. The sad part was the death of little Florence, and of a third baby girl, born in Ireland. These infants were buried in the Grace plot at Arless, leaving Lillius and William with only their first-born, Alice.

During this sojourn, William took his place as the eldest, and most successful, son of the Ballylinan family, making provision of money and opportunity for those who needed it. A few years later we find James and Ellen Grace in receipt of an allowance from their son, which may date from 1863. Assistance to them was also assistance to Alice, William's eldest sister, who had married a poor provider named John Eyre. Alice and her children spent a good deal of time under the parental roof. The youngest sister, Sarah, still at home, was soon to marry. Michael was in Peru; Morgan, an army surgeon in New Zealand. That left crippled John, and Ellen Mary. John wanted to be a farmer and William set him up, buying, in his own name, a fine place called Fernville, near Rathdowney, thirty-some miles from the homestead at Ballylinan. Though the place was run down, William paid £3,800 for Fernville. John began to rehabilitate the estate, and to establish a reputation as a model landlord and employer.[15]

Ellen Mary, a year older than William and never to marry, had embarked on her life's work as a doer of good deeds, with Brother William footing the bills. Ellen dispensed charity wisely, sometimes making quite businesslike arrangements. In 1863 she touched William for £600 to pay the passage of seventy Irish families emigrating to the United States, and to give them something to start on in the land of freedom. Ellen obtained from each head of family a receipt for his share of the money advanced, and impressed upon him that it was a loan. Before long, William Grace was surprised to receive the first repayment. Thirty years later, in 1893, he received the last, canceling the indebtedness entirely. The final payment came from a granddaughter of the original emigrant. Mr. Grace turned over that money, as he had done the rest, to a Catholic charity.[16]

~ What William R. Grace thought good for the seventy families he must have thought good for his own also. So, when he left Ireland late in 1863, it seems that Peru was to be only a way station on the road to the United States. Anyway, that's how it worked out, though two eventful years elapsed before the goal was attained.

The Graces returned to Peru by way of New York, where they stayed for a while with Captain and Mrs. Gilchrest in Brooklyn. Though the tide of the Civil War had turned at Gettysburg, this was not clearly perceived at the time. The spirit of the North was low, and nowhere lower than in shipping circles. The navy had drawn off forty thousand seamen. The depredations of Confederate commerce raiders like the *Alabama* had hoisted marine insurance rates to such figures that a fourth of the great Yankee merchant fleet had been "sold foreign." All the same, in his yard at Thomaston, Maine, Edward O'Brien, a celebrated builder of down-easters, was putting the finishing touches to a fine new vessel bearing the name of the builder and owner. The maiden voyage of the *Edward O'Brien* would be to San Francisco. Scorning the paralyzing rates quoted by Lloyd's, O'Brien intended to send her without insurance, and trust to luck and to the skill of the captain to outwit the Confederate raiders. The captain chosen for this undertaking was George Gilchrest.[17]

Late in 1863, Mr. and Mrs. Grace took a steamer for Panama on the last leg of their journey to Peru. Sometime later Mrs. Gilchrest followed with little Alice. In March 1864 they received word that the Captain had put to sea in the *Edward O'Brien*.

As John Bryce was in England, Grace relieved Francis Bryce as the actual, if not the titular, head of the firm. Finding business only fair, he devoted his energies to its improvement. The Graces lived in Callao, but William was frequently at the Chincha Islands, where the Bryce interests were in charge of an American named Edwin R. Kirtley. Though Callao was a more sightly and a more seemly community than her husband had first seen in 1851, Lillius Grace did not like the place. She attended one bullfight but didn't enjoy it. A series of small earthquakes, which did no more than slop water from pitchers and tinkle the crystals of the chandeliers, got on her nerves. So early in April, Lillius and a Miss Metcalf journeyed to the Chinchas to rest and visit with the captains' families in the fleet. The understanding was that William would follow shortly.[18]

At the time a Spanish naval squadron was cruising the Pacific, ostensibly on a scientific mission. But, as Spain had not acknowledged the independence of Peru or of the rest of South America, the presence of the warships caused a certain amount of uneasiness. W. R. Grace was not among those who shared these apprehensions; and in this he was badly mistaken. On April 14, 1864, when Mrs. Grace and Miss Metcalf were relaxing on board the storeship, and William was still in Callao, the Spanish men-of-war sailed up to the Chinchas and landed soldiers on North Island. The Peruvian flag was hauled down and that of Spain run up. The Spaniards herded the Peruvian convict laborers on board a vessel and took them to the nearest mainland port, Pisco. That evening one of the Spanish ships caught fire and ammunition on board exploded all night.

The next morning Kirtley was able to place Mrs. Grace and her friend on board a vessel bound for Callao. The vessel put in at Pisco, where it took on board one hundred and sixty-five guano convicts and twelve soldiers to guard them. Mrs. Grace and Miss Metcalf were eating lunch when the convicts fell upon their guards and disarmed them. Lillius looked out and saw the captain on the bridge surrounded by armed felons. The captain managed to signal a government launch and, while Mrs. Grace and her companion remained in their locked stateroom, the prisoners were overpowered and taken off.

Later, in Callao, Lillius witnessed the termination of the Spanish incident. President Pezet of Peru agreed to pay an indemnity to recover the Chinchas. The Spanish admiral and his staff went to Lima and some of the sailors were given shore leave in Callao. Pezet's action did not set well with the Peruvian populace. A mob tore up the railroad track between Lima and the port so the admiral could not get back. Then it turned its attention to the Spanish sailors. One was killed on the balcony of the Grace house where he had climbed in search of safety.[19]

In the fall of 1864, Lillius had another exciting time off the Chinchas. Her father had safely completed the voyage to San Francisco and was loading the *Edward O'Brien* with guano. Mrs. Grace and her mother went down from Callao for a visit. One evening the vessel anchored next to the *Edward O'Brien* caught fire and burned to the water's edge. Captain Gilchrest and his crew worked through the night, pumping water on the decks, spars, and rigging of the *O'Brien*. "Not one cent of insurance on Capt. G. ship," wrote Grace in a report of the incident. "If there had been any wind nothing could have saved him."[20]

~ In all, the year 1864 was a full one for William Grace. His grasp of the complex minutiae of business, his punctual performance of promises, and, above all, his ability to make friends among the sea captains made themselves felt in the house of Bryce. On one occasion Grace was obliged to write a tactful apology for Francis Bryce, who had left a captain feeling that Bryce considered shipmasters "beneath him" socially. Certainly, Grace entertained no such illusion. Captains were always visiting at his house in Callao. Lillius and William would return the calls on board ship with genuine relish. Mrs. Grace would voyage to the Chincha Islands on one ship and back on another to keep the captains' wives company.[21]

Instinctively, mariners in difficulty turned to Grace. When Captain Ryan of the ship *Commodore* fell ill, it was Grace who saw that he was comfortably installed in the "best hotel" in Callao. It was Grace who engaged doctors and day and night nurses. When the captain died, Grace collected the deceased's belongings and wrote to the *Commodore*'s owners in Boston:

"I am very sorry to have the melancholy news to communicate to you of the death of Captain A. Ryan. . . . He died last night @ about one o'clock and we are now getting his body ready to be sent home on the next steamer of the 13th March . . . [accompanied by] Capt Mayo late ship 'Golden Rule.' . . . Captain Ryan died of Heart disease and was attended by the first Doctors of this town and the city of Lima. . . . The lady members of the writer's family and Mr Starrett ship 'J I Southard' called and prayed with Capt Ryan on two occasions before his death. Captains Blair, 'Atalanta,' Torey, 'Marshfield,' French, 'Wm Tell', Mayo, late 'Golden Rule' & others sat up nightly with him."

With a list of the late captain's possessions was enclosed a lock of his hair for presentation to the widow of Captain Ryan.[22]

Along with endless day-to-day details there were larger aspects of the situation for Grace to consider. These affected the future of Peru as a whole.

The country was approaching a turning point in its history. The fantastic guano era could not go on forever, sustained by public corruption and prodigal expenditure which poured unearned wealth into the laps of the few while the lot of nineteen-twentieths of the people went from bad to worse. The suspension of internal taxes had been far from a blessing to the common people of Peru. It encouraged indolence and improvidence. Nearly every natural resource that could have built up the country, and made for a thrifty, industrious, enterprising middle and working class, was neglected.

Peruvians who should have taken the lead in developing those resources pursued the guano bonanza, which, amid a rain of gold, was ruining their country. A sign anyone could read was the mounting national debt. Peru was living on its capital.

Even the guano supply was not inexhaustible. Half the surface of the Chincha Islands was down to bare rock. At the rate it was going, a few years would finish off the rest. As to the other deposits Peru had spoken of so expansively, the product seemed definitely of poorer quality; and there was a wide diversity of estimates as to the amount on hand. Should the lower estimates turn out to be correct, Peru had no time to waste looking for other sources of income.

There were plenty of them though, unlike guano, their development required work, imagination, capital, and the cooperation and discipline of a large part of the Peruvian population. Yet one had only to glance at what the Incas had accomplished to know that, gone about the right way, this could be done in time.

Though an hereditary despotism in which every detail of an individual's life, from birth to death, was, in theory at least, regulated by the state, the ancient Incan society had much to recommend it to the common man. He was better off materially than his counterpart in most of the nations of feudal Europe. The greatest of the Incas' many great achievements was in agriculture, enabling the mass of the people to live on a scale that amazed the Spanish invaders. Arid coastal valleys were irrigated and fertilized with guano, which the Incas regarded as a national treasure to be conserved and perpetuated. Strict laws governed the taking of it from the islands, and birds were not molested in mating season. In the Andean foothills and the intermountain valleys, where there is rain, the precipitous slopes were terraced for cultivation. Some of those terraces exist to this day.

Among the Incas was no poverty and no idleness. Loafing, when work was to be done, and begging were punishable offenses. Taxes were paid in grain, woolen and cotton cloth, hides, and labor. The fields of widows, absent soldiers, the sick and the aged, were tilled by others. Public granaries tided the populace over winter seasons and lean years. Gold and silver were used not as mediums of exchange but for ornament. The Incas were not avid miners of these precious metals. The immense stores the Spaniards found had been accumulated over centuries.

A system of roads knit together the Incan empire, facilitating the passage of troops and the circulation of commerce. The Incas' only beast of burden being the llama, which can carry about a hundred pounds, these roads were merely trails. As architects and builders the Incas were not far behind the Egyptians.[23]

This culture the Spaniards had wiped out, in the bloodiest fashion imaginable. Neither they nor, as yet, the Peruvians of the republic had put in its place anything that was as good.

In ruins was the Incan agricultural system, which had supported as many people as lived in Peru in 1864—that is, two and a half million. True, a revival, largely foreign-inspired, was meeting with some success in the coastal valleys where John Gallagher and James Grace had failed. An export business in sugar was developing. But on the whole Peru did not feed itself. Nearly half a million bushels of wheat were brought in each year from Chile at a cost of $2 million. In the inter-Andean valleys great ranges were ideal for grazing cattle and sheep, in addition to the native llama, alpaca, and vicuña. Hides and wool were carried down mountain trails on muleback for export, but the trade was nothing to what could be made of it; and no woolen cloth was produced in Peru except by hand.

Since the flooding of the Cerro de Pasco mines, minerals had been neglected. With coal fields of its own locked in the mountains eighty miles from Lima, Peru spent $3 million a year to bring two hundred thousand tons across five thousand miles of ocean. A Peruvian official informed the American minister at Lima that the British-owned Pacific Steam Navigation Co. "exercised great influence on the Peruvian Government by the force of selling or with-holding coals for the Peruvian Navy." Also neglected were copper, iron, zinc, and lead. The one mineral activity of any moment was in the coastal deserts of the extreme south, where nitrate beds were being opened by Chileans using British capital.[24]

To convert the Peruvian economy from guano to something more diversified and lasting, one requisite was railroads. The iron horse was the miracle of the age. The British Isles, Europe, even distant India, were caught by the railroad-building craze: and until the Civil War halted the work, tracks were going down in the United States faster than anyplace else in the world. In South America, Chile held the spotlight. The Valparaiso-Santiago line was completed in 1863—the personal triumph of a remarkable American named Henry Meiggs. After other contractors had spent nine years building a third of the line and then given up, Meiggs finished the remaining two thirds in two years. Straightaway, Chile put him to work on other roads. Already native products, hitherto unmarketable, were moving over the newly laid rails—to the enhancement of Chile's foreign credit. Though the nitrate beds within Chile's national borders were not nearly as extensive as those of Peru, Chilean revenue from nitrate was on its way to equaling Peru's guano profits.[25]

These activities prompted the Peruvian government to begin some preliminary railroad surveys. When nothing more was done, a young man named Manuel Pardo sought to arouse the country to a realization of the danger. Though only twenty-eight years old, Manuel Pardo had an unusual history. Aristocratically born, and educated in Europe, he had disdained the traditional callings of his class—the army, law, or politics—and had plunged into business, amassing a fortune as a partner in an importing concern and the proprietor of a large farm.

In 1862, Pardo published a penetrating pamphlet on the subject of Peru's national economy. He showed that, guano aside, the total of Peruvian exports had not increased since 1845; and some items had disappeared from the world market entirely. Meantime the country went more deeply into debt each year. What would happen when the guano ran out? Pardo detailed the wealth that Peru had in its mountains and mountain valleys—wealth enough to supply all domestic needs and to provide sufficient exports to redress the alarming adverse balance of trade. He suggested a series of railways to tap those valleys. A note of urgency ran through the writing of Señor Pardo.[26]

Not long after the appearance of the Pardo brochure, Henry Meiggs had a conversation with Juan Manuel Polar, Peruvian minister to Chile. The American offered to construct one of the roads Pardo had mentioned. Henry Meiggs made a good impression on Polar, as he did, at first sight, on almost everyone. Reporting the matter to Lima, Polar recommended Meiggs as the man to realize Peru's railroad dream, and assure that country's "happy future."[27]

Though nothing immediate came of the matter, Peru did not forget Meiggs; nor Meiggs, Peru. It could hardly have been otherwise, for Henry Meiggs and Peru seemed made for each other.

The country wanted railroads. Meiggs wanted railroad contracts, and had demonstrated an ability to fulfill them. The country still could raise great sums for the enterprise contemplated. Meiggs did not come cheap; he required great sums. As a matter of course, Peruvian officialdom expected to line its pockets with funds earmarked for railroad building. That would be all right with Henry Meiggs, who desired above all harmonious relations with his official collaborators.

~ $\mathcal{S}$uch was the situation of Peru at the beginning of 1865: pregnant with great possibilities.

But William Grace had worked too hard again. His old ailment returned, along with that curse of the tropics from which no one bred in a temperate zone seems to escape—dysentery. A month's rest in the congenial society of sea captains off the Chinchas having failed to restore his health, early in 1865, Grace prepared to quit Peru for good. The decision could not have been unwelcome to his wife.

On March 28, the family, including Mary Jane Gilchrest, whose husband still must have been at sea, sailed for Ireland by way of New York. By the end of the summer William, feeling better, was poking about England looking into odds and ends of business for the Bryce firm. At the suggestion of Francis Bryce he bought, for an establishment in Peru referred to only as the Compañía Marítima, the ship *Red Rose*. The price was £12,000, which William considered such a bargain that he offered to take the vessel himself should the owners be dissatisfied. He saw the *Red Rose* manned and loaded with cargo for Hong Kong, from whence she would proceed to Callao.[28]

In late 1865 or early '66 the Grace family sailed for the United States. Mary Jane Gilchrest seems to have preceded them. Exhilarating prospects for business beckoned from that quarter. The war over, peace had let loose a flood of productive enterprise such as the world had seldom seen. Should Peru be in earnest about developing its great store of dormant resources, that would mean more business for the United States. Grace meant to get some of it. Incidentally, William's father-in-law had retired from the sea, taken a house in Brooklyn, and opened a ship-chandlery store on the lower end of Wall Street in Manhattan, near the East River docks.

William had done so well for the Bryce firm that he could retire from active participation about on his own terms. It is not known what these were, except that he withdrew his capital. In any event, the Grace influence in the firm remained the vital influence. Michael was presently to become managing clerk. James Eyre, a nephew, had come over from Ireland to begin his apprenticeship. At the same time, William was free to embark independently of John Bryce & Co. on business ventures of his own in New York; and Michael was free to act as William's Peru agent.

4 ~ The Threshold of Large Events

~ The family moved into a house that Mr. Grace bought in the village of Parkville, just beyond the southern boundary of Brooklyn and about three miles from Coney Island. Though beginning to get a reputation as a seaside picnicking ground, Coney Island was then, in fact, an island, whose permanent inhabitants were largely oystermen residing in shacks. In Parkville, Mrs. Grace got out the curtains of Irish lace her Ballylinan in-laws had given her as a going-away present in 1863. In Peru they had not been unpacked.

The curtains did not stay in Parkville long. Mr. Grace made a quick sale of the house to a man who wanted a place in short order so he could give his daughter a birthday party. That was the way things went in those flush times. The Graces moved to Brooklyn Heights, in the city proper, and into the seafaring circle of which Captain Gilchrest's house was a center. The Heights was a substantial quarter, the home of a number of prosperous sea captains, active and retired. A neighbor of Gilchrest's was Benjamin Flint, of Chapman & Flint, the largest shipbuilders on the Maine coast.

Both the captain's and his son-in-law's homes were seldom without visitors. Many a ship's officer who had spent the war in the navy had little else to do, being without civilian employment. The wave of prosperity which had engulfed almost all other lines of endeavor was tardy, to say the least, in getting around to the merchant marine.[1]

As W. R. Grace's business plans all had to do with seagoing trade, in which he contemplated using vessels under the American flag, the situation called for caution. He took desk room in his father-in-law's ship chandlery at 110 Wall Street and felt his way carefully.

Captain Gilchrest had not located his ship chandlery on Wall Street to be close to the masters of finance, but to the masters of ships. He was only fifty steps from teeming South Street which paralleled the East River and faced the busy wharves. A generation ago the money changers, one by one, had moved to the upper end of Wall Street, in the shadow of the beautiful spire of Trinity Church in whose yard, fittingly, reposes the body of Alexander Hamilton. The migration of these Hamiltonian captains of finance, who touched nothing more tangible than symbolic paper, left the lower end of the street to the toilers among the actual articles and instruments of our ocean-borne commerce.

For all that, Captain Gilchrest came to work in a silk hat. William Grace donned the stately Prince Albert coat that was a mark of the man of property. He let his beard grow, and it turned out to be a striking reddish-brown. The captain did a thriving business, for our foreign trade was booming, the harbor was crowded, and ships' stores were in demand. The fly in the ointment was that the captain's business was not always the kind he would have chosen to do: too many of his customers, foreign ship-masters; too many of his friends idling in the sociable "captains' room" of his establishment with no ships to buy for. The reason for this state of affairs was plain to see: in 1860 more than 65 percent of our exports and imports had moved in American bottoms; in 1866, 28 percent.

Lower Wall Street went to work earlier than upper. At 7:30 each morning William Grace and his father-in-law stepped from the Brooklyn ferry that docked at the foot of Wall. They could look down noisy South Street, note the swift changes and perchance read forewarnings of the shape of things to come. Foreign steamships—squat, ugly things that they were—had begun to crowd in where exquisite clippers, capable down-easters, and packets had lately monopolized the wharves, their slender masts and naked spars making a veritable forest, and their bowsprits thrusting halfway across the street. With the scent of spice and sandalwood from the Orient, and of coffee roasting in nearby ovens, was mingled the acrid smell of coal smoke and steam. And most of the sailing vessels, though they may have been built in Maine or Massachusetts and sailed for years by Yankees, were now under alien flags.

Longshoremen prospered, for never before had there been such cargoes to unload and to stow; but battered old salts—"shellbacks" from the clippers and the down-east Cape Horners—found berths harder to get. The more fortunate drifted into coastwise runs or short trips to the West Indies for sugar and rum. More than ever the jargon of foreign tongues rendered incomprehensible the day-and-night din issuing from groggeries, dance houses, and other recreational retreats of deepwater men on nearby Water and Cherry Streets.

Small sailcraft darted about the harbor, their numbers still increasing, though here also steam had intruded in the form of stubby, chugging little tugboats. The towing masters, like the harbor pilots before them, developed an uncanny ability to sense the arrival of a ship. The schooner-yachts of the pilots racing to sea to snare a prize and bring her in had always provided the harbor with excitement. Now there was a new thrill for the idlers, watching the tugs battle one another for the privilege of docking some lumbering iron-hulled steamer. Catering to the resented newcomers, strange establishments began to take their places among the shipwrights, ship chandlers, blockmakers, sail lofts, warehouses, and commission merchants of South Street: coal yards, steamfitters, boilermakers, machine shops.[2]

In 1861 the American merchant marine was in first place with 2,496,000 tons. In 1866 the British were in first place and the Americans in fourth, with 1,387,000 tons. Confederate commerce raiders and a series of other causes were responsible. In the captains' room at Gilchrest's you could hear many a yarn about Semmes and his *Alabama*. Even Yankees rated him a gentleman. The raiders had sunk or captured 110,000 tons. A worse blow was the rise in insurance rates, resulting, by the end of the war, in the sale to foreign interests of a third of the whole fleet at bankruptcy prices.

A number of factors worked against the anticipated peacetime revival. The reign of the clipper was drawing to an end because that costly form of transportation was a luxury few shippers could longer afford. The opening of a railroad to California took away the last profitable route. That left, of course, the more practical and more numerous down-easters, on which the postwar hopes of American shipbuilders had been based. Those hopes were disappointed when it developed that no longer was there free competition on the ocean. Foreign steam had the benefit of heavy government subsidies. Though the Confederate raiders were gone, foreign sail continued to enjoy the advantage of favorable underwriting rates at Lloyd's of London which controlled the marine insurance market. Besides that, American shipbuilders were handicapped by higher taxation, introduced during the war and still in force; American operators, by higher wages and other costs. As for American steam, it had ceased to give foreigners serious competition when the United States virtually withdrew its subsidies in 1858.[3]

A further reason for the failure of the American merchant marine to come back was our preoccupation with other things. American eyes and energies turned from the sea frontier on which the nation's economic independence had been won and maintained for three-quarters of the century. They turned inland—to the building of railroads, which was resumed on a prodigious scale; to the erection of steel mills, the opening of oil fields and mines, the settlement of the great Western plains. Coastwise shipping, a domestic concern entirely, remained within the orbit of popular interest. Protected by law from foreign competition, it revived at once and throve.

~ Yet, in 1866, steam had by no means superseded sail, which, competing subsidies notwithstanding, was cheaper for long hauls. And, despite handicaps, American sail could still make money in competition with foreign sail. But this took management. In 1869 the captain of a ship of which W. R. Grace was the operator and part owner complained somewhat tartly that Grace was running the vessel "on the cheap." She was the old clipper *Nereus* which Grace had degraded into a carrier of coal, guano, cotton, or whatever could be picked up in the way of cargo. Grace was no skinflint by nature and he had something on his side. With all running costs higher, the American operator who did not watch every dollar and demand the utmost of the still superior skill of American masters would be pushed to the wall. Prudence in the matter of expenditures was one of the factors that enabled W. R. Grace to rise steadily as a shipping man in a period that saw the disintegration of once-great American merchant fleets, such as those of A. A. Low and of Grinnell, Minturn & Co.[4]

Because his American correspondence prior to 1867 has not been preserved, it is not clear just how Grace went about launching his New York business. In general, however, we know that he was an operator, charterer, and part owner of ships. He was also concerned with cargo, which sometimes he shipped for sale on his own account. More often, however, he merely made purchases on commission for foreign dealers, principally in South America. Though this cargo usually went out in ships that were under his own management, it might go in other vessels, notably those of Fabbri & Chauncey, proprietors of the only line—sail, of course—between New York and the west coast of South America. Gradually, Grace worked out agreements with representatives in San Francisco, the British Isles, the continent of Europe, and South America. In Callao, naturally, he had his brother Michael.

Grace's acquaintance among sea captains was very useful. He knew the ones to select for their qualities as businessmen as well as for their qualities as mariners. Though usually Grace used old ships, he also had new vessels, apparently built to his order. There was still some activity in

New England shipyards. Even foreign shipowners patronized them, on the theory that the excellence of American design and craftsmanship made up for the higher cost. The new ships were of the down-easter model and, though called modified, or medium, clippers, they owed more to the chunky, broad-beamed packet of the twenties and thirties than to the true clipper.

While yet in Peru, Grace had taken an interest in ship design. There is a tradition in the Grace family and company that before he came to New York, William Grace was able to persuade Edward O'Brien to construct larger vessels for the Cape Horn route. It may be that Grace made this suggestion, though others had the same idea at the same time and O'Brien was not the only builder to adopt it. Ships began to bear the names of members of the Grace family. In 1867, Mr. Grace appears as one-fourth owner of the *Lillius.* That same year another daughter, Agnes Isadora, was born to the Graces. In 1869 the barkentine *Agnes I. Grace* was christened at Thomaston, Maine. The father of the young lady thus honored owned a sixteenth interest in the vessel. Her master was Captain George C. Smalley, a cousin of William's mother-in-law.[5]

~ The earliest fragment of a book of accounts indicating the nature and extent of W. R. Grace's business during his first years in New York bears on transactions in Peru which went through Michael's hands. On August 21, 1867, when the record opens, Michael held a balance in W. R.'s favor of $15,880.90. On February 11, 1868, when the record ends, W. R. owed Michael $9,665.59. Interest at 10 percent per annum ran on the accounts between the brothers. The total transactions for the period amounted to $61,179.13. Michael collected and paid out money on his brother's account; sold or saw to the delivery of goods W. R. shipped on his own account or on commission; acted for W. R. in the performance of business favors for Captain Gilchrest and for E. R. Kirtley, whose assistance to Mrs. Grace at the time of the Spanish descent on the Chinchas her husband never forgot. The two largest items concern the *Nereus,* a part of whose cargo was lumber W. R. had shipped on his own account. Michael disposed of the lumber for $10,080.76. On the way back the *Nereus* carried guano, and Michael obtained an advance of $10,520.54 on the freight.[6]

Besides attending to his brother's affairs in Peru, Michael was carrying the burden of John Bryce & Co. John Bryce himself was in England much of the time. Francis Bryce, lazy and incompetent, was devoting to a sugar plantation and refinery such of his time as he could induce himself to give to work. Though Francis offered to increase Michael's salary, Michael held out for a partnership. Francis feared Michael's headstrong, speculative ways too much to receive him into the firm—oblivious to the fact that if Michael left there would soon be no firm. At this juncture, John O'Connor, who had married the Grace brothers' cousin Eliza Lawler, offered Michael a partnership in the O'Connor merchandising business. When William learned how the land lay, he hurried over to London to see John Bryce. The senior partner knew what the loss of Michael would mean. He was eager to draw W. R. Grace, also, more actively into the business. "Francis cannot control Michael," he said, "but you can." He proposed a new partnership to be called Bryce, Grace & Co.

This came about on July 1, 1867. The two Bryces each left $50,000 in the business and William supplied a like amount. Michael put in no capital but, in consideration for his services, he was to have a fourth of the profits, the same as the other partners. Each partner drew $4,000 a year salary. By the terms of the agreement the Bryces retired from active management.[7]

In less than two years the Bryces were disturbed by the speculative proclivities of William R. Grace, not Michael. The truth is that William had done a daring thing. He had launched a scratched-up sailing-ship line to Chile and Peru in competition with Fabbri & Chauncey. It looks as if one of his motives was to throw a scare into Fabbri & Chauncey and get from them better terms and better service as a shipper.

He succeeded in scaring the Bryces as well. Michael wrote that they regarded the line as "a speculative business and risky." He complained that they were "opposed to everything where they risk a cent." It would be necessary to double the capital of the house to make the line a success, and to this the Bryces would not consent. Another possibility Michael considered was the acquisition of a partnership in Fabbri & Chauncey, but this seemed an unlikely prospect. Fabbri & Chauncey probably would not agree to it, and Grace was not strong enough financially to force their hand. Therefore, much as the idea of a line of sailing vessels appealed to him, Michael advised his brother to abandon it: "You established the line for a purpose and that purpose is gained, much to our advantage." Fabbri & Chauncey seem to have listened to reason.[8]

Though the fledgling enterprise was given up, the thought of a line of ships under Grace management remained in the mind of William, who observed carefully the struggle of Fabbri & Chauncey to maintain themselves in the face of foreign competition. Independently of Bryce, Grace

& Co., William continued as an individual operator of ships, and added steadily to the number of vessels under his control.

In one way, Michael had been unjust to his partners. In 1860 the Bryces were taking plenty of chances with their money. Francis was going deeper into sugar. And old John was splurging for fair. In London he had blossomed out as an international banker under the style of the General South American Co. To live up to his position he rebuilt Marley, his country seat in Devonshire, and acquired "a nice house" in Paris—"a Hotel as they call it." To meet the outlays occasioned by these undertakings, all the Bryces wanted from the Callao firm was quick, sure profits and no nonsense.[9]

~ In the meantime the political kaleidoscope in Peru had been changing a little more rapidly than usual. President Pezet's act in ransoming the Chinchas from the Spanish fleet had cost him his office. Pezet's successor was a general named Mariano Ignacio Prado who did a great deal to enhance the prestige of Peru abroad. He sought the friendship of the United States. One of Lincoln's last acts had been to restore diplomatic relations with Peru. Alvin P. Hovey, a former general in the Civil War, was sent down as minister. He met Prado more than halfway in the effort to remove the unfavorable opinion many Peruvians, for good reasons, held of our country.

Though it had quit the Chinchas, the Spanish fleet hovered off the coast. In March 1866, it bombarded Valparaiso, in Chile, laying much of the city waste. Then the Spaniards sailed northward and promised Callao the same treatment. So confident of success was Nuñez, the Spanish admiral, that he named the day of his attack—May 2—and warned neutrals and noncombatants to leave. That put things up to Prado, who had evicted Pezet for not being tougher with the Spaniards. The people rallied behind him—women, children, and some foreigners assisting in the preparations for resistance. The frowning old Spanish-built fortress, which stood four hundred yards from *Casa* Bryce, was placed in a state of defense. Closer than that to the Bryce establishment, guns were mounted on the sea wall.

On May 1, President Prado asked General Hovey for advice, which the American gave "as a friend" and "not as a diplomat." This disclaimer did not prevent Hovey's action from being a breach of neutrality. Fortunately, Spain did not hear about it at the time. Hovey said that, despite all that had been done, if Peru tried to fight the Spaniards at close range they would be beaten in fifteen minutes, and Callao destroyed. He suggested that the harbor be mined to keep the attackers at a safe distance.

That night forty barrels of powder, connected by wires to an electric battery on shore, were sunk in the bay. It seems, however, that other members of the diplomatic corps in Lima were not observing strict neutrality. "The French," Hovey wrote to the State Department, "informed the Spanish fleet . . . and before morning nearly every wire was cut."

Shortly before noon the next day the Spanish fleet bore in, firing. Its guns greatly outnumbered those of the defenders. Several hits were scored on the shore batteries in whose crews were a few Americans. Though the defenders, too, scored hits, the attackers came on. Two wires leading to underwater mines remained intact. The Peruvians exploded these home-made torpedoes, throwing columns of water a hundred and fifty feet in the air. The fleet put about, and all day long stood off at ineffective range exchanging shots with the defenders. In the night the Spaniards sailed away. Callao had been saved—not so much by Hovey's torpedoes as by the valor of the Peruvian cannoneers and the timidity of Admiral Nuñez. Ever since, *El Dos de Mayo* has been a Peruvian holiday.[10]

In a further effort to sustain the independence of Peru, Hovey did away with the right of asylum in the United States legation, and vainly endeavored to get other powers to follow. This privilege had been scandalously abused. Foreigners in the toils of Peruvian law frequently needed only to flee to the legation of their country, where they could hole up in safety, sometimes for months at a stretch. Worse than that, the legations sheltered Peruvian revolutionaries who, in the heart of Lima, plotted the overthrow of existing governments.[11]

By no means did Prado rely solely on the good offices of his friend the American minister. On his own he launched a program for the rehabilitation of Peru that was as farseeing as anything since the days of Bolivar, the liberator. He struck at the root of Peru's troubles. He tried to do away with the intricate system of graft by which foreign nations and foreign financiers, preying on the weakness of Peruvian politicians, kept the nation in a condition of economic vassalage. He reinstituted internal taxation. He challenged the authority of the church in governmental affairs. His instrument, and perhaps his inspiration, in the fiscal reforms was the man he had made minister of finance, Manuel Pardo, author of the railroad pamphlet.

El Dos de Mayo had made a great hero of Prado. Much of this prestige melted, however, when Prado showed that he meant business in the matter of domestic reform. Hysterical opposition defeated him completely on the clerical issue. The attempt at internal taxation proved a failure. But graft was cut down. Hereditary pensions were abolished, ending a drain on the national income in which, according to the American minister, "nearly every white family" had participated. The new policy practically balanced the budget for the first time in fifteen years.[12]

Manuel Pardo, the minister of finance, had not forgotten his railroad projects. But he was sagacious enough, first, to try to put his country in a condition to finance their building, and, second, to make a beginning at a new political and industrial order which would be necessary if Peru, like Chile, was to realize the economic benefits the railroads were expected to bring.

The depradations of foreign powers, of which Spain's had been merely the baldest, also was an object lesson to President Prado. Determining to build up Peru's navy, he opened negotiations for the purchase of two American ironclads, left over from the Civil War, and two unarmored steamers to serve as tenders. José Antonio García y García came to the United States as envoy extraordinary to finish the deal and get the vessels to Peru. García went to W. R. Grace, a friend to whom he could write: "If you and your wife are not using the open carriage, please let me have it at two in the afternoon."[13]

The monitors, impressive-looking craft two hundred and thirty-four feet long, were purchased from a private contractor for the excessive sum of $2 million. This was more than the vessels had cost new. Though Grace had nothing to do with that transaction, he seems to have taken care of nearly everything else García was charged with: the recruiting of crews and the supplying of the warships with provisions and ammunition; the purchase of the auxiliary steamers; the reconditioning, manning, and provisioning of them for the voyage to Peru. Though financial records are lacking, all this must have run into money. If customary practice was followed, the commission of Bryce, Grace & Co. was 5 percent of the amount expended.[14]

The work took two years and was attended by various mishaps and perplexities. The two supply steamers left New York to join the ironclads at Southwest Pass at the mouth of the Mississippi. Captain Gilchrest, who never before had commanded a steamer, was in charge of one of the vessels, renamed *Maranon*. A gale off the New Jersey coast sent the *Maranon*'s consort, the *Reyes,* into the Delaware breakwater for repairs. Gilchrest made the rendezvous with the *Maranon*'s boiler tubes ruined. Then his crew left him. García sent Grace a letter sharply critical of

Gilchrest. Though the old mariner was green at steam, there appear to have been mitigating circumstances. The boiler trouble was due to poor coal and a drunken engineer; the departure of the crew to the fact that not until the ship reached the rendezvous were the seamen informed that, to continue the voyage, they would have to serve for two years in the Peruvian navy.

Eventually on its way, the squadron of four vessels ran into a storm off Cuba in which an ironclad rammed and sank the *Reyes,* with a loss of seven lives. There were other incidents and alarms as the remaining vessels proceeded down the east coast of South America toward the dreaded Horn. Though the ironclads were not built for the heavy weather usually encountered off the tip of the continent, apparently the passage was made without difficulty. In the fall of 1869, after a voyage of eight months, the ironclads and the *Maranon* reached Callao. Captain Gilchrest's first command in steam was his last—a circumstance he had no cause to regret.[15]

A year later the American minister wrote from Lima: "Peru has unquestionably the finest navy on the western coast of South America, and that fact alone, in my opinion, has compelled peace with some of her sister republics."[16]

Captain Aurelio García of the Peruvian navy, a brother of José, wrote Grace that the monitors were "the object of general admiration." "May I," he continued, "take advantage of our friendship to impose on you . . . [for] two dozen white shirts and two dozen separate collars . . . of extra good quality. . . . The latter must be of the latest fashion in cut. The shirt bosoms English style, no buttons."[17]

~ Mariano Prado, who had inaugurated the transaction for the monitors, was no longer president of Peru when the vessels arrived.

Inasmuch as it touched their pocketbooks, the Prado-Pardo program had proved unpopular with most of the country's powerful figures. Two revolutions got under way. The first dissenter to reach Lima with the aid of an army was Diez Canseco. Though Canseco lasted as head of the Peruvian government only seven months, that was long enough to do away with Prado's reforms and start the railroad ball rolling without benefit of the preliminaries Manuel Pardo had deemed prudent.

Three weeks after Canseco had established himself in the presidential palace, Henry Meiggs showed up in Lima. For all the millions he had made in Chile, the free-spending Meiggs was hard up for money, and for some time had been angling to bring himself to the notice of the Peruvian railroad planners. Besides that, John G. Meiggs, Henry's brother and business manager, was in the United States trying to scare up money-making projects with a Latin American aspect. Though John lacked Henry's soaring imagination and magnetic qualities of personality, he had a firmer grip on the realities of finance. One of the things John tried to get his brother into was the Peruvian monitor transaction.

While John Meiggs was away, and three months before the Canseco revolution triumphed, so anxious was Henry Meiggs about the Peruvian railroad situation that he contemplated a trip there to try his luck with Prado. The growing force of the Canseco rebellion seems to have caused a postponement of this excursion, for surely Meiggs would have preferred to do business with Canseco. This preference doubtless explains Meiggs's remarkably prompt appearance once Canseco was in power.[18]

Naturally, Manuel Pardo had departed from office with his vanquished chieftain. Diez Canseco had given the ministry of finance to Juan Manuel Polar. This was another fortunate circumstance for Meiggs. As minister to Chile, Polar had been talking railroads with the American since 1862, and seems to have been completely under his spell. Meiggs used Polar to pilot through the intricacies of official procedure the first railroad contract that Meiggs signed in Peru. No time was lost in that matter either. On April 30, 1868, ninety days after Meiggs's arrival in Lima, the Canseco government published a decree approving the contract.

Had the Canseco regime known Meiggs's financial straits, it probably could have obtained better terms for Peru—if that is what it wanted. In any event, the agreement called for the construction of a road in southern Peru, one hundred and five miles in length, from the port of Mollendo to Arequipa, the second city of the republic. The cost was put at $11.4 million.[19] This was $1.9 million more than had been reckoned on by Peruvian state engineers, themselves no niggardly estimators. So, at the outset of his career in Peru, Henry Meiggs upheld his reputation for doing things in a large way. Meiggs kept a "green book" in which he cryptically recorded certain nonconstruction expenditures, totaling $1.235 million. At the head of the list was a "gratuity" to "C" of $270,000. The American minister, General Hovey, merely remarks that President Canseco is said to have been "enriched." A son of Canseco later declared that his father had returned Meiggs's gift.[20]

Three months after the ratification of the contract, General Canseco retired from public life in an unusual manner, that is, peaceably. Colonel

José Balta assumed the presidency. Though Canseco had proved coopera-
tive enough, Balta was the man Meiggs is supposed to have really wanted.
"Much money" is said to have changed hands during the election at which
Balta was voted in.[21]

One can understand the preference of "Don Enrique" Meiggs and of
the Peruvian aristocracy for this resolute soldier. Even Hovey had to admire
the way Balta walked the streets of Lima without a bodyguard—the first
president of Peru to do so since old Castilla. Balta could be relied on to
inaugurate a rule brooking no opposition to his ideas. Those ideas were
completely reactionary. Balta would build the railroads, of course, for
guano was indeed running out. But he would build them without recourse
to the socialistic heresies of Prado and Pardo. Like guano's golden stream,
the rewards of the new economic order to be ushered in overnight by the
railroads would be reserved for the few.

One railroad contract quickly followed another until Henry Meiggs's
engagements with Peru aggregated more than $100 million; and Don
Enrique was not the man to forget his presidential benefactor.

"We have the *whole of Peru Boots and Breeches*." This modest
appraisal appeared in a letter from John G. Meiggs to E. P. Fabbri of the
Fabbri & Chauncey line.[22]

5 ~ Dealing with Don Enrique

~ Peru swelled with pride when Don Enrique Meiggs took over the spending of millions the country raised on guano and on the prospects of the commercial greatness Meiggs's railroads would surely bring. There were those in Chile who had been loath to lose Don Enrique, and Peru dearly loved to score a point against her progressive neighbor. Now, Chile had two reasons to envy Peru: possession of the best nitrate fields on earth, *and* possession of the costly talents of the railroad-building genius.

In 1868, Henry Meiggs had a widespread reputation, for the railroad craze still held the world in its grip. The United States was the only country where enthusiasm for that magic transformer of latent resources equaled Peru's. With one transcontinental track just about completed we were planning three others. Because Meiggs was an American our citizens took a naïve pride in his professional achievements and his fabulous way of living. All but forgiven was the dark chapter that had sent Henry Meiggs from our shores a fugitive from justice whose bankruptcy in the amount of $800,000 was complicated by forgery. In the first place, Meiggs had repaid much of what he owed. In the second place, the very size and audacity of his unfortunate operations appealed to an American's love of big things.

In 1849, Meiggs had disposed of his lumberyard in the Williamsburg suburb of Brooklyn for enough to load a packet with lumber and sail for San Francisco. The $50,000 cleared on that venture started a career of real-estate speculation that ended in failure and in flight. In Chile an order for his arrest and extradition was suppressed in a way that suggests the use of money in a fashion that Henry Meiggs was to make a fine art. The charm of Meiggs's personality also probably had much to do with it. The governor of California who had initiated the proceedings against Meiggs presently went to Chile as United States minister. He and Henry Meiggs became bosom friends.

Henry Meiggs did more for Chile than run useful railroads through mountains where European engineers had failed. He gave that country a needed example of social justice. Certainly for the first time on any large scale in Latin America, day laborers received decent treatment and pay. Meiggs's work camps were models of sanitation; food was plentiful, well prepared, and just what the men wanted—mostly beans; there were entertainments and other incentives to good work. At a celebration marking the completion of one of his roads, Meiggs made a pointed speech. He reminded the most exalted dignitaries of the republic that he had got from native labor results no one had dreamed possible because "I have treated them like men and not like dogs." That, he said, was the way of life in the United States, where a workingman, given ability, could rise to the highest positions. "In Chile I should like to see the same thing."

When Henry Meiggs began to build in Santiago a residential palace that a viceroy might have coveted, his old railroad men flocked there to work for nothing. More, probably, than any other man of his time, Henry Meiggs captured the imagination of all Chile, *peon* and *hidalgo* alike.[1]

When he arrived in Lima the railroad builder was fifty-six years old. An American newspaper correspondent told what he looked like: "He was about five feet, eight inches in height, broad-shouldered, muscular, weighed about 225 pounds and had the biggest fists and the largest head in South America. His eyes were gray, deep set, piercing, and kindly in expression. He had a square jaw and chin, a big nose, a large mouth, and firm-closed lips. His countenance bore the impress of power."[2]

Such was the man William R. Grace tried to size up from the vantage point of a desk in the ship chandlery at 110 Wall Street. His opinion seems to have been about as favorable as the impressions of those who were exposed to Meiggs's personality at closer range. Michael Grace had written his brother: "Meiggs is the great RR man here and his connection is most valuable." An American friend of William's early days in Callao wrote: "Peru promises to be a great country if they can only keep free of revolutions for a half dozen years. The railroad fever is very strong and I hope will continue long enough to open up the country to the interior." The American minister wrote to the secretary of state: "No American on this coast is more popular, and he richly deserves the praise which is universally bestowed upon him."[3]

A friend in San Francisco sent W. R. Grace for collection two notes of Henry Meiggs's aggregating $9,750. They were relics of the California collapse, unoutlawed by the passage of time because of Meiggs's flight.

William sent the notes to Michael, saying that, though a liberal commission had been offered for their collection, Michael probably would not wish to "quarrel with Meiggs." Therefore he had better put the notes in other hands.[4]

A word from John Bryce seems the only exception to the chorus of praise for Meiggs. The senior partner wrote from Paris: "They are going mad in Peru over ferrocarriles—anything can be overdone, and it is so in Lima, at present."[5]

Both Grace brothers went to work on the Bryces, in an effort to make their partners realize and prepare for the business Meiggs's undertakings could bring to Bryce, Grace & Co. Michael also asked William to "get J. Bryce to go to New York" and help arrange for "large credits [there] & good bankers in London." John Bryce did not make the trip, and Michael kept after William to form better banking connections in London than those offered by Bryce's General South American Co. Bryce's bank was altogether too close with its credit to Bryce, Grace & Co.—because John Bryce wanted that company to take no chances. "How would Baring Bros. & Co. do or . . . J. P. Morgan & Co.?" persisted Michael. "I would prefer paying a commission than to be in constant fear to draw a thousand pounds or so over." For credit there were many possible uses. "Meiggs no doubt is a little hard up at times and requires to borrow say £20,000 from you. . . . Not a bad idea." Such an accommodation would repay itself many times in the business Meiggs could throw in the way of Bryce, Grace & Co.[6]

Michael asked William to look up Joseph S. Spinney, Meiggs's purchasing agent in New York. William did so, and soon the families were visiting back and forth. Spinney lived at Great Neck, Long Island. Grace became fond of Spinney personally, but did not regard him too highly as a businessman. Momentarily, Michael played with the thought that the Graces might make such a superior impression on Henry Meiggs, his brother John G., and others in the Meiggs organization "that Spinney might some day be left out in the cold by Don Enrique."[7]

∼ As Don Enrique did not leave Spinney out in the cold, Grace continued to work with him. Grace's first large purchases for Meiggs were of lumber and ties. He bought in Maine, where his wife's relations were of help; in Canada, along the St. Lawrence; in New Brunswick; in North Carolina and in Georgia; in Oregon and in California. Grace's agent along the St. Lawrence was a young man named James R.

Cushier: Grace himself went to New Brunswick and the South. Cushier accompanied a shipload of timber to Peru, scouted Meiggs's requirements, and returned to take another consignment down.[8]

Expanding business obliged Grace to take over more space in his father-in-law's store. He went about the neighborhood pricing second-hand office furniture, and engaged a couple of clerks. One of these employees was nineteen-year-old Charles R. Flint, the shrewd son of a shrewd father, Benjamin Flint of Chapman & Flint, shipbuilders. Charley Flint offered to work for the experience, realizing that this was not much of a concession as "my wage would have been quite near nothing anyway." The young man had a head for business. Before long, when Mr. Grace was away, Charley was in charge of the office, and winning encomiums from his employer: "You talked right to Yates P & Co we can afford to let them sweat it out. . . . Try & Collect from Elwell. . . . If Petroleum is 26¢ . . . buy 5000 Gals."

In 1870, Grace felt that he needed a place of his own, and while absent on a lumber trip, he asked Charley to look for one. He did not, however, approve the young man's recommendation. "Dearborns old office is too dear for me. If I go off Wall I think it might suit as well to go to Beaver or some other cheap street." Quarters were found at 62 South Street, and presently Captain Gilchrest moved his establishment two doors away to Number 66. A year later Grace decided to move again and, on his departure for Peru, left to Flint the choice of a location. The young man took two rooms at 47 Exchange Place—"a splendid, light, cool office."[9]

A handicap to Grace's buying operations was John Bryce's closeness with credit. With Grace practicing every economy and putting into the business all he could rake and scrape, Bryce's refrain was: "Do not draw on me just yet." On top of this came the Franco–Prussian War, upsetting the international money market. John G. Meiggs wrote that it "has cost us at least a million." When Napoleon III surrendered at Sedan, John Bryce was furious because the French did not give up at once. Wish fathering the thought, he wrote to Grace: "Paris will surrender in 15 days more and no mistake." Old John seems to have been concerned for the security of his new house on the Rue Lisbonne. Though Paris held out sixty days longer, John found his "hotel" unharmed. "The Boulevards are almost as full as ever, the restaurants also," he reported somewhat later. "Not so many carriages yet [horses having been eaten during the siege], but people from all parts arriving daily."

Still, John Bryce kept his purse strings tight: "You must not think I do not wish to help the House. . . . You must consider me too poor at present." In response to promptings from Grace, the old Scot did offer to entertain Don Enrique's son Manfred, who was abroad with his tutor.[10]

In the meantime, Meiggs was drawing a willing Peru deeper into his net. "H. Meiggs," the Callao house informed Grace, "has procured two [additional] contracts for railroads, one from Callao to Oroya . . . for S/27,600,000, and the other from Arequipa to Puno for S/32,000,000—in all 59 millions 6 hundred thousand soles [$56,620,000] in Peruvian bonds. This will bring our N. Y. friend [Spinney] plenty of business and us, too. Mr. M. has promised us a sleeper contract."[11]

The line to Puno presented good possibilities in the way of opening up the country industrially. It was to be an extension of the road from Mollendo, on the coast, to Arequipa. Although a range of the Andes would have to be crossed at 14,660 feet, the engineering problems on the whole were simpler than those already overcome on the Mollendo-Arequipa line. Puno stands on the shore of Lake Titicaca, one hundred and thirty-eight miles long, sixty-nine miles wide, and 12,644 feet above the sea. The Titicaca basin was the cradle of the Incas' civilization. As the lake is on the boundary between Peru and Bolivia, the Puno road would give the uplands of that country, also, an outlet to the sea.

The Oroya road was a horse of another color. This line was to surmount the Andes northeast of Lima and penetrate the valley that led to the flooded Cerro de Pasco mines. It seems to have been undertaken in something of a spirit of bravado, as if in substantiation of Meiggs's quoted boast that "anywhere the llama goes, I can take a train." When an engineer protested to Meiggs that "we can't run a railroad along there," the builder is said to have replied: "Well, young man, that's where she's got to go, and if you can't find room for her on the ground, we'll hang her from balloons." However that may have been, Don Enrique found that for once he had underestimated a contract: the Oroya road stood to cost him money.[12]

Grace's man Cushier circulated among Meiggs's engineers and superintendents of construction, discovering their requirements and taking orders. Soon Meiggs's men were writing Grace direct, giving him business hints that were often helpful, and requesting personal favors, usually having to do with their families at home. W. R. Grace had a positive talent for discharging obligations of that nature. It shows in his relations with many, many persons with whom he did business. He treated Charley Flint like a son, and Lydia Cushier, very lonely during the long absences of her husband, something like a daughter. Thus, Grace bound people to him by strong ties. This was good business, of course, but the conviction grows that the main reason Grace did these things was because he liked to.[13]

"I am much obliged to you for the trouble you have taken about my affair with Millan," wrote S. L. Crosby, chief engineer of the Mollendo-Arequipa line which was on the point of completion. "We are wanting all kinds of lumber for the Arequipa Station and any quantity of large lumber, say 12×12 and from 35 to 50 ft. long for the long bridge at this place [Arequipa]." Crosby closed by saying that Arequipa presented a good market "for what they call American chairs," and for black walnut lumber for the manufacture of furniture.[14]

When Crosby took charge of the Puno extension, he wrote to ask of Grace another favor, and added a useful piece of inside information: "The Puno road . . . is without doubt the best contract Meiggs has got. We have taken a good deal of pains in locating the line and so far have got a very economical one. . . . Meiggs ought to make eight or ten millions of dollars on this road." On a contract price of $30,400,000 that would be a satisfactory profit. "But according to all accounts," continued Crosby, "[he] will require it all to build the Oroya."[15]

For some time, Grace had been trying to get to Peru and see for himself how things were. His ideas of the future of Meiggs and his schemes seemed to be undergoing a change. At any rate, in response to a letter of inquiry which has not survived, the Callao house wrote to Grace: "Henry Meiggs—we do not fear any trouble with him, more especially now that the war is finished. However, our sales were cash and we will take care to collect them."[16]

Don Enrique was on a cash basis with Bryce, Grace & Co. Surely that was something different from Michael's open-handed suggestion of sixteen months before that the firm might advance Meiggs $100,000 as an evidence of goodwill.

In the spring of 1871, Grace sailed for Peru, taking the quick route via Panama, which one crossed by rail.

~ When William Grace landed at Callao, he saw his brother Michael for the first time in six years—destined to be the longest period the brothers were ever separated, though the international nature of their business usually kept an ocean between them. A genuine fraternal feeling united these men, who supplemented each other well. William was thirty-nine at the time; Michael, ten years younger. William had the gift of leadership, the sounder judgment, the greater foresight. In making a decision, he bore in mind more factors. Though William fought it, the hot temper of his boyhood could still assert itself. He would blow up at Michael in a stiff letter; then apologize for his language, though not his opinion. The younger brother would write that no apology was necessary.

Michael had an Irishman's impulsiveness, enthusiasm, and never-failing optimism. People liked him. He could conduct a specific transaction brilliantly, close it out, and pass on to something else. His mind might perceive little relationship between transactions A and B. On the other hand, W. R. Grace was ever relating, tying in one transaction to another—building an integrated business structure.

It had become distinctly a family business, supporting any number of Graces in two hemispheres. The voluminous correspondence that passed between the brothers was interspersed with domestic matters, bits of clan and personal gossip. There was news from Ireland where their father had lately died; where sister Ellen continued her good works; where brother John's agricultural experiments cost William money. There was news from New Zealand where brother Morgan, the doctor, had left the army and was becoming a man of mark in professional and public life. There was family news even from Callao: Michael had married a Scottish girl there; Jim Eyre, sister Alice's son, who had come out a few years before to work under Michael, was dead of yellow fever, and his place taken by a second Eyre boy, Edward.

So, during his sojourn, William made the acquaintance of his new sister-in-law, Margarita; renewed the acquaintance of his nephew Ned Eyre, who had landed in Peru as a seaman from William's old clipper *Nereus*. Bryce, Grace & Co. were now housed in a new building. For that matter, a good deal of Callao was new to William, much of the town having been destroyed by a fire that followed the disastrous earthquake of 1868. The old ark of Pablo Romero had been replaced deliberately, however.[17]

The first thing William Grace had to do in Peru concerned the continuation of the Bryce, Grace & Co. partnership, whose existing agreement would soon expire. Michael, and perhaps William, too, would have liked to dispense with the Bryces. An attempt to draw Joseph S. Spinney and E. P. Fabbri into the firm having failed, however, the Graces needed the $100,000 the Bryce brothers had in the business. Michael, on whom the major responsibility for the Peruvian affairs of the firm devolved, demanded a larger share of the profits. He had been getting 25 percent. To this John Bryce, writing from Devonshire, agreed, acknowledging that

Michael "has done very well." So the partners remained as before, and the capital was increased to $280,000. There is no record as to who put up the additional $130,000 though, judging from John Bryce's pleas of poverty, the Graces must have contributed most of it.

Grace offered Charley Flint a share in the profits if he would go to Callao, but Flint preferred to remain in New York. The shrewd young man profited by this decision when, later in the year, Grace expanded his New York business into a partnership—W. R. Grace & Co.—and gave Flint a 25 and Michael a 10 percent interest. To provide Michael with the help he sorely needed in Callao, William made an arrangement with Sylvan D. Hazen, whom Fabbri & Chauncey were paying the excellent salary of $6,000 a year. E. P. Fabbri agreed to giving up Hazen because of the "close & confidential" relations existing between the Grace and the Fabbri & Chauncey interests.[18]

~ And now what of Henry Meiggs?

The first road undertaken, from Mollendo to Arequipa, had been finished in true Meiggs style, ahead of schedule. Leaving other difficulties aside and considering only the *mañana* tradition of Latin America, where a day's work done in two days spells promptitude, Meiggs had performed a remarkable feat. As usual he had been well paid for it, profits for less than three years' work running just under $4 million. Yet things had not gone so smoothly as in the Chilean operations. There were labor troubles. The Peruvian *peon*, accustomed to an idle, irresponsible life, made an extremely poor workman. Hundreds of Meiggs's old *Chilenos* had followed him to Peru voluntarily, and advertisements brought thousands of others. Bolivian Indians, accustomed to the thin air of lofty altitudes, also were employed. The three nationalities did not get along well together. There were complaints about pay, food, and sanitation. The Chilean government stirred up trouble, animated, in part, by jealousy. These tribulations were accentuated by the weakness of the local Peruvian administration.

All difficulties were lost sight of, however, at the fete Meiggs got up to mark the completion of the road. President Balta, his cabinet, and the rest of Don Enrique's eight hundred guests left Callao in three steamers. The desert port of Mollendo, without a green leaf in sight, was smothered under flags and bunting. A bishop blessed the six locomotives that pulled the party to Arequipa for eight days and nights of feasting, dancing, orating, and political conniving. The concluding banquet alone was said to have cost Meiggs $200,000—certainly an exaggeration, as probably was the story that Don Enrique provided champagne baths for the ladies of his entourage. Nevertheless, it must have been quite a dinner.[19]

At the same time, Meiggs was building three other roads, and reaching for still more contracts. One reason for this dispersion of his energies seems to have been to get money to repair the losses he was in for on the Oroya line, the most grandiose of all the projects of Henry Meiggs.

A correspondent for *Scribner's Monthly,* visiting the scene and making what seems a conscious effort at restraint in language, called it "this truly Cyclopean undertaking." The title of his article was "A Railroad in the Clouds." Though W. R. Grace's first impressions are not on record, they appear to have accorded with his later view that "Mr. Meiggs was a visionary man." Of the one hundred and thirty-eight miles of track Meiggs was to have in full operation in six years, twenty-odd had been laid in a year and a half. This was track any builder could have got down. It ran from Callao, through Lima and beyond, over gently rising ground into the belt of perpetual sunshine.

Ahead lay the savage Andes, rising to peaks clad in perpetual snow. Engineers were lowered by ropes down the sides of sheer cliffs to mark the route of the railroad. Laborers were lowered to cut standing places from which to begin their work. Some of the rock was so hard that only diamond drills could make holes for blasting. One stretch of fifteen miles called for twenty-two tunnels.[20]

Though not himself an engineer, Meiggs was a great inspirer of engineers. The chief technician of the Oroya project, responsible for laying out the line, was Polish-born Ernesto Malinowski, who had been in the employ of Peru before the advent of Meiggs. One of Malinowski's most gifted assistants was a Maine man named William H. Cilley whom Grace had long known and possibly had introduced into the Meiggs organization.

While the problems of construction, as great as any railroad builder had ever encountered, were costing an enormous amount of money, Meiggs's main difficulty was with labor. A disease that got the name of "Oroya fever" swept the camps with epidemic force, and hundreds died. Other hundreds abandoned the works and roamed the countryside in formidable bands, plundering and killing. The Peruvian government sent a detachment of cavalry to return deserters to the labor camps. The Chilean government made heated protests, this time with considerable justification.[21]

An adventurer must keep up appearances. Meiggs's Lima house of seventy rooms continued to be the scene of entertainments "rivalling

Imperial feasts." When no guests had been invited, places for thirty were set at dinner, and usually filled by casual callers. According to the custom of the Peruvian aristocracy, this meal started at ten in the evening. Officers from visiting American warships were always welcome. Food left over went to the city's poor. Meiggs's charities were lavish. Despite his own losses in the earthquake of 1868, he gave to the sufferers $50,000 and the services of an army of workmen.

His country place, a modest residence of a dozen rooms, William Grace knew well. It was the manor of the hacienda of Villegas, scene of the Gallagher-Grace sugar venture.

With Peruvian politicians, "outs" as well as "ins," Don Enrique maintained good terms by an intricate system of bribery.[22]

William R. Grace had the faculty of making himself inconspicuous when he wanted to. No record exists that he even met Henry Meiggs on this trip, though undoubtedly he did. It is certain that he saw a good deal of the man's brother, John G., who laid himself out to make a good impression for the prospects of the Meiggs enterprises. In this, John failed. Before sailing for New York, William Grace gave instructions to continue to sell to Meiggs for cash only.

~ Michael Grace was dead against his brother on this. "Meiggs is not to be feared as you imagine," he wrote, and announced his intention to "keep in" with Don Enrique.

He appears to have done so. Addressing W. R. Grace as "Dear Friend," John G. Meiggs wrote that Henry had landed another railroad contract and was about to land a second: terms, $46,550,000. "I have made a contract with your house here for ties . . . and shall probably also give them a large order for lumber." When William did not budge, Michael continued his remonstrance: "We [in Peru] ought to know pretty well how Meiggs is situated. So long as the Government is good we fear nothing and [I] cannot think of treating a man with[out] confidence who has acted so liberally toward us. . . . We must make hay while the sun shines."[23]

When Michael spoke of a "good" government, he meant one friendly to Henry Meiggs. In October 1871 balloting would take place for electors to choose a president to succeed Balta, constitutionally ineligible for a second consecutive term. In September, Michael wrote William: "Pardo is the people's choice, Echenique Government's choice." Michael thought Echenique would win, a logical assumption, for not since 1833 had a government candidate for president lost an election.[24]

It may be recalled that Echenique had been president before. Should he get in again, everything would be all right for at least a while. It was equally certain that the election of Manuel Pardo would bring reforms calculated to interfere with Don Enrique's business methods. This pioneer advocate of railroads was still for honesty and economy in their construction.

William Grace was another who believed that Peru could not continue to pour borrowed millions into Meiggs's hands without ruining its credit. While on his recent visit to Peru, a national loan in the amount of $70,250,000 had been contracted for. The bonds would be offered the following year, 1872. William made with John G. Meiggs three separate bets, each for a suit of clothes, that the bonds could not be sold at advantageous prices. If this loan went through, it would raise Peru's borrowings, since the inception of the railroad craze, to $153 million. As security, Peru had pledged about everything it possessed—guano, customs receipts, and railroads, built and building.

In these matters, Peru had placed itself without reservation in the hands of the French banking house of Dreyfus Frères. To begin with, Dreyfus took complete charge of the handling of guano. Except that it opened the door to reckless borrowing, this was an improvement on the old guano arrangement. W. R. Grace's shipping interests also benefited by the new guano contract, as Dreyfus engaged numerous Grace vessels to transport the fertilizer. In 1870, Dreyfus had disposed of an issue of Peruvian bonds in the amount of $56,090,000, luckily offered a month before the outbreak of the European war, and almost immediately oversubscribed four times. The brilliant success of this loan prompted the larger offering, scheduled for 1872.[25]

The October elections resulted in a triumph for Pardo, who won a majority of the electors. The electors would not meet, however, until the following July (1872) to ballot for a president to be inaugurated in August. Balta got busy at once. He put forward a brand-new candidate—Antonio Arenas—for the final act of election, and coolly asked the other candidate to withdraw. Naturally, Echenique did so. Pardo refused. Then Balta began to mobilize the powers of the government to persuade electors to switch to Arenas. From a Peruvian friend, W. R. Grace received an idea of the nature of those persuasions: "War has been declared against me by the present Pres. Balta & his ministers because I am a friend of Manuel Pardo."

Michael strove to allay his brother's apprehensions about Meiggs. Don Enrique's labor troubles would soon be mended. "Meiggs has just purchased from F^co [Francis] Bryce S/180,000 Chinamen at six months, has contracted for 5000 with Carnevo & Co." The step went against Meiggs's humanitarianism; but his situation was growing critical. In this affair, Francis Bryce acted on his own, and not as a partner of Bryce, Grace & Co.

"Still," continued Michael, "you seem to think he [Meiggs] is not safe. You allow Mr. Pope [Grace's California agent] to talk old times and old prejudices to you. Meiggs has paid all his debts in San Francisco and has certainly acted fairly to everyone. He holds good railroad contracts and altho he has thrown money away by the shovelfulls . . . unless Peru comes to the ground we cannot see that Meiggs is going to fall." Michael defined what he meant by "fall." Meiggs would simply suspend operations and retire with his pockets full of government bonds. "We mention all this because we do not fear trouble and want you to feel safe." On the next day, Michael wrote that he believed Meiggs "will make 20 millions on his roads."[26]

These assurances got nowhere with William, who attempted to "undo" a contract Michael had made for ties for one of the new Meiggs roads. But John G. Meiggs would not allow it. "Don't be afraid," he cajoled, "you will make money out of it sure."[27]

Meiggs was not building all the railroads under construction in Peru. Two were in the hands of native talent: José Antonio García y García and others, in one case; in the other, Federico Blume, a former Peruvian state engineer who had made some of the pre-Meiggs railroad surveys. Bryce, Grace & Co. were rather heavily involved with orders for rails, rolling stock, and timber for the Blume road. While urging financial leniency with Meiggs, Michael advised a tight rein on Blume. So much for Don Enrique's persuasive personality.[28]

John Bryce's credit policy continued to be more than an annoyance. "You have drawn," he wrote William from Paris, "first for £1000 and again for £500 on the General S American Company when Bryce Grace & Co have no credit with Said Company, they having exhausted the one they had. . . . It is not your fault I know . . . but you blow him [Michael] up." A little later the old man softened: "Your brother is doing a big business, and in his place I would . . . [overdraw] as he has done. . . . Though none of you believe it . . . [only a lack of funds has] prevented me from doing my part."[29]

~ *J*n January 1872 a sobering blow fell when Dreyfus Frères cut its credit to Henry Meiggs and to the Peruvian government at one swoop.

This house was banker to Don Enrique's multiplying enterprises, as well as virtual manager of the foreign debt of Peru. The French financiers refused to honor Peruvian government orders for funds for Meiggs until there should be money in hand from the 1872 loan of $70 million. The first word as to the fortunes of the prospective bond issue was far from encouraging. Previous issues had been largely taken in Britain. But at the moment, Britain and the United States were at loggerheads over the *Alabama* claims, growing out of the depredations of Confederate commerce raiders built in British yards. There was even talk of hostilities between the two countries. In France, investors had their hands full with the domestic loan necessary to pay the indemnity to Germany growing out of the recent war. Besides all this, a second large loan within two years to a country like Peru warranted scrutiny on its merits.[30]

Meiggs put up a confident front, John G. writing Grace: "Don Miguel [Michael] showed me a telegram from John Bryce saying that the new Peruvian Loan could not be placed at present. All I can say is that your friend is not posted . . . I bet you one suit of clothing that the bonds would sell at 74, one suit at 76, and a final one at 78%. I abide by my bet."

Reports on the loan were contradictory. At one stage, it seemed to be going so well, at 77.5, that Grace, figuring he had lost two bets and won one, ordered a suit for John Meiggs. By the time John Meiggs learned of this, however, the loan news was so bad that John had to tell Grace he had been too quick about the suit. Auguste Dreyfus worked hard in Paris and in London. Perhaps to give an appearance of health to Peru's financial situation, he resumed the honoring of Meiggs's drafts on that government. Yet, as S. D. Hazen reported from Callao, "the loan hangs, and casts a gloom over matters generally." Well it might: by the middle of the year only $20 of the $70 million had been subscribed, and of this about $19 million was taken by the house of Dreyfus itself.[31]

Michael Grace changed his tune. In May 1872 he wrote his brother: "I note your alarm about the Loan and think you may be right. . . . We have on our shoulders all we can carry . . . considering how pushed we are for money." A month later came a frank confession: "I have been ambitious to show good results to the patrons of the house, and certainly [have] lacked experience. . . . One thing is certain, your advice has made me conservative and has turned my every efforts to consolidating outstanding a/cts and business."[32]

With the financial skies darkening, still another threat menaced the tranquillity of the railroad builders and their suppliers. The failure of the loan was a boon to the candidacy of Manuel Pardo. This impelled Balta to stouter efforts to see that Arenas should be chosen when the presidential electors would ballot in Lima in July. A fearless and cruel Army officer named Tomás Gutiérrez was made minister of war. The army was increased by forced enlistment, and Gutiérrez's two brothers were given important commands.

These preparations heartened Federico Blume, who begged Grace to fill an order for rails and "try" to get the money from Dreyfus. "The opinion here," added Blume, "is that Balta continues as 'Presidente Provisiono' for at least two years more." Three weeks later Blume's optimism rested on different grounds: "Politics all right. Arenas president . . . what I tell you is sure. Pardo—no chance."[33]

Also pulling for Arenas was Michael, who called almost daily on Balta at the presidential palace. Yet he had few illusions as to the future. The best he could write William was: "I think if the new government [Arenas] is established and no revolution on the part of Pardo, things will come out all right for a little while." Efforts were bent to build up business that would survive a railroad collapse. Hazen went south to look into nitrates. He reported good possibilities. As to politics, Hazen regarded victory for Pardo as a foregone conclusion. Otherwise there would be a revolution in the south, at least.

On July 12, Federico Blume chatted for a moment with Michael, who was on his way to the "palacio." "I noticed him either tired or melancholy, which generally he is not. Perhaps he has experienced some disappointment in some business matter. I didn't like to ask."[34]

Any number of things could have been on Michael's mind. With the electoral meeting less than a fortnight off, no one knew for certain what Balta intended to do should the result go against his man.

6 ~ In a Tight Place

~ As if Henry Meiggs did not have enough to do in Peru, he contracted to build an ocean-to-ocean railroad across the republic of Costa Rica. This occurred while W. R. Grace was on the way home from his Peruvian visit. The line would be some hundred and thirty miles long, for which Meiggs was to receive £1.6 million, or about $8 million; $750,000 was paid on the signing of the contract. The rest was to come along in monthly installments.

Don Enrique handed over the whole project to his nephew, Henry Meiggs Keith, thirty-one years old, who had been working on the Oroya line. Grace had hardly time to turn around in the new office in Exchange Place when letters about the venture began to arrive. Keith wrote with a precipitation and sweep that would have done credit to his distinguished uncle: "I . . . have decided upon appointing you my agent in N. Y. for purchases of all materials . . . [you] being exactly the person I need with me. . . . One of the first things I shall require is a barque of 4 or 500 tons burthen with hatches sufficiently large to admit engines [locomotives]." This would be merely a start. "I propose placing a Monthly Line of Sailing Packets between Limon and N. Y. . . . Your brother dined with me yesterday and we had a long talk, the purport of same he will doubtless advise you. . . . I shall want things to move lively."

Michael advised that Keith's plans went further than building the railroad. He meant to "control all copper, indigo, cedar etc. in Costa Rica," and wished Grace to share in these monopolies. Moreover, $375,000 would soon be in William's hands for purchases.

Orders streamed in: "1300 tons of rails with necessary fish-plates, bolts, nuts, spikes, etc., which will give me say 20 miles of track"; also three locomotives and equipment for a hospital. Though the initial credit turned out to be $165,000, when it came, Grace showed that he could act as energetically as any of the Meiggs clan.[1]

In September 1871, Keith started for New York, and John G. Meiggs sent Grace a letter marked "private": "I beg for him your kindest attention, and that you will supply him with the only thing he lacks, which is 'ballast' and 'economy.' He will require to purchase furniture for his house in Costa Rica, and on this point . . . I hope you will persuade him 'to be modest' and remember that if he attempts to make a splurge the people will say 'That fellow is doing that with our cash.'76

This actually occurred in Chile with Don Enrique."

On his way north, Keith stopped off for a view of the scene of his future labors. Costa Ricans received him rapturously. "They postponed their Independence Day until I arrived here. What would the great American people say to having their Fourth of July postponed?" The American minister to Costa Rica shared this enthusiasm. "The name of Henry Meiggs to the contract is a sufficient guarantee that the road will be constructed." He sketched what this would mean to Costa Rica, whose only export was coffee. At present this product went by ox cart to Puntarenas on the Pacific side, and thence around the Horn at $1.25 a quintal for carrying charges. With the railroad it could go to Limón on the Atlantic, and on to New York for $.50. He might have added that the line would give shippers another short link between the two oceans, the only one then being the immensely profitable railroad across Panama.[2]

On this leg of his journey, Keith was accompanied by his brother, Minor C., twenty-two years old, who had his own prospective role in the development of Costa Rica. He intended to form a commercial company which would act as commissary for the railroad gangs, and expand into other lines as the country opened up. The brothers went from Puntarenas to San José, the capital, roughly midway between the oceans. Though the seasonal rains were on, they hired mules and with a guide set out to traverse the rest of the route of the railroad, to Limón, on the Atlantic. Perhaps already the Keiths had been in Costa Rica long enough to hear that a white man who made this journey during the wet season was a hero; but that if he made it more than once he was a fool. Descending from the high central plain, the road diminished to a jungle trail. Jungle gave way to swamps, which even Indians avoided.

Henry Keith had landed in Costa Rica suffering from ague and dysentery, contracted in Peru, for which he dosed himself with the sovereign remedies of the day, quinine and whisky. He was probably feeling no better when he reached the miserable little settlement of Limón, standing on a fringe of solid ground, with the sea in front and swamps behind. There the railroad would begin. There Grace's supplies would be landed. As no roads inland existed, even casual trading vessels shunned that pestilential region, which was known as the Mosquito Coast. So, first off, Keith must provide landing and storage facilities; and, in the absence of adequate maritime charts, furnish Grace with navigating directions to the anchorage.[3]

~ Henry M. Keith reached New York shaking with ague, but dreaming big dreams. A letter from John C. Meiggs warned Grace to watch out for the dreams, and added significantly: "You have now to deal entirely with Mr. Keith as our responsibility has ended." How much Grace was able to accomplish on the head of personal economy seems a question. "I want to make a marriage present to my sister," the visitor scribbled in a hotel room where he was laid up, "and would like say $1200 currency." A school in Connecticut drew on Grace for board and tuition for a brother of Keith's.[4]

With a skeleton crew of engineers on the job at Limón, Keith and technical men of the Meiggs organization in New York gave Grace enough orders to keep him busy for months. Then Keith sailed for London, where he penned extensive reports of his activities. They were a mixture of self-importance, friendliness, and naïveté: "Dined with some of the heaviest bankers in the city last night." "Bischoffsheim [of Bischoffsheim & Goldschmidt, financial agents for Costa Rica in Europe] has behaved first rate. . . . I hope to be home in time for Fannie's wedding." "I send a fine haunch of royal venison for yourself and good wife and two silk dresses, one for [my sister-in-law] Emily Jarvis and the other for my sister Fannie." "I give a dinner tonight to Bischoffsheim . . . and shall arrange . . . for £2,000,000 net over and above what already has been contracted for. . . . Draw on Bischoffsheim for all monies you need and ship specie to Limón to the rate of say $40,000 per month. Yours in haste . . . as I have but ten minutes to dress."[5]

Though Mr. Keith's casual mention was an oversimplification of the manner in which the Bischoffsheim credit was obtained, and £2 million a wild e xaggeration of the amount, funds, nevertheless, were forthcoming to Grace.

Grace was also hearing from Costa Rica. President Guardia had interposed as a sort of liaison officer between Keith and himself a methodical, competent German named Guillermo Nanne. Nanne reported a state of confusion. "This engineer corps which came out from N Y is a complete failure," principally owing to the members' addiction to liquor. Grace was asked to send sober engineers.[6]

He did so, and kept on with orders for excavating tools, bridges, cars, locomotives. "Will you kindly favor us," requested a builder of cars, "with the correct Spanish words for Baggage and Smoking?" When Keith returned to Costa Rica in March 1872, he was enthusiastic over the progress that had been made: "I shall commence laying track next week." This would be done on the easiest section of the line, the inland plain, rails and all other material being carried by oxen from the Pacific port of Puntarenas. "I wish you would send me some Offenbach music written for brass bands . . . [also] Yankee Doodle . . . for the coming 4th July."

At malarial Limón, things went slowly. Nanne reported "sickness still cleaning out our files. . . . I made a contract for 600 Jamaica niggers." The Jamaicans were to stand the climate better than any others. Keith also brought in six hundred and fifty-four Chinese, thirty-five having died en route. And he brought in opium.[7]

In London, Keith had purchased a steamer. He renamed the vessel *Juan G. Meiggs* and spun a web of plans about her. Grace, who knew something about the shipping business, advised that the *Meiggs* be sold at once. Instead, Henry Keith turned her over to his brother Minor for use in connection with the commercial enterprises launched under the name of M. C. Keith & Co. Grace having declined to invest $20,000 in this undertaking, Henry Keith took a certain satisfaction in delineating Minor's agreeable prospects.

He had a monopoly on the importation of liquor, estimated to clear $500,000, "as rum . . . costs 15¢ bottle and . . . [sells for] 45 to 75¢. . . . Minor will also start a Saw Mill near Limon . . . [and] ship two or three cargoes monthly . . . of cedar, mahogany & still more valuable timber. . . . He is buying up all the Rubber, Sarsaparilla, Tortoise Shell, Balsams &c he can. . . . Minor needs 30 or 40 head of Beef per Week [for the railroad workers] and the Steamer can do a profitable business from Texas."

Minor was not afraid to try new things. From Panama he shipped thirteen hundred bunches of bananas to New Orleans. That fruit was almost unknown in the United States. The venture was so successful that Minor took banana plants to Costa Rica and set them out. In other ways the amateur ship operator was less fortunate. With experienced professionals being forced from the sea by foreign competition, Minor Keith found himself in a maze of costly difficulties. Grace appealed to John G. Meiggs to get Keith to sell the vessel. After a year of operation the German Nanne stepped in. Bound for New York with a cargo of cedar and coconuts, the *Meiggs* was then $175,000 in the hole. Nanne asked Grace to take charge of the ship and sell her.[8]

~ The progress of railroad affairs in Costa Rica was beginning to resemble that of the *Juan G. Meiggs*. Still hanging fire was the Bischoffsheim loan that Keith had spoken airily of arranging over a dinner table. The London banker was becoming weary of paying the bills that poured in from Keith, Grace, and others.

In this situation, Henry Meiggs Keith took a leaf from the book of his uncle and namesake. Pressed from one quarter, he sought to draw attention to prospects that lay in other directions. Neighboring Salvador wanted a railroad, and Keith had agreed to send engineers. Not to be outdone, Costa Rica had accorded Keith and associates an enormous grant of land. In this deal was Judge J. P. O'Sullivan, a political fixer and promoter who had access to Ulysses S. Grant. He seems a fair representative of one clique that had the ear of the gullible president. In Keith's opinion the only thing needed to "make this country another California" was a loan of "£1,000,000 to be floated in England" for the development of the granted land.

As to railroad money, that would be taken care of by President Tomás Guardia, who was going to London. On the way, he would stop off in New York. Guardia had asked O'Sullivan to arrange an audience with Grant. "I want him [Guardia]," Keith instructed Grace, "entirely under the management of yourself & O'Sullivan. . . . Keep him aloof from American speculators & politicians," excepting, of course, those of O'Sullivan's choosing. One of the party would be an American named McKay, charged with buying "arms, military telegraph etc for this govt. Make what you can out of him & divide."[9]

At the last moment, Keith decided to come along and do some managing himself. The reception arrangements, however, devolved upon Grace, whose unspectacular program betrayed the hand of a novice. Through Collector of the Port Chester A. Arthur, Grace obtained a revenue cutter to meet Guardia's steamer. Then there was a tour of the financial district, with look-ins at the Stock, Gold, and Produce Exchanges; also a view of American justice at work in the shape of the court presided over by Grace's Brooklyn neighbor and friend, Judge Calvin E. Pratt of the state supreme bench.

The advent of Tomás Guardia failed to impress New York. The *Herald* gave it two sticks of type in which Keith was referred to as "Mr. Henry M. Heist, nephew of the celebrated Henry Meiggs of Peru," and Grace as "Mr. R. S. Grave." Chagrined by such skimpy and slipshod notice, "Mr. Grave" dashed off a line to Charley Flint: "I will send you tomorrow a photograph of General Guardia & a sketch of his life even tho' it cost us 500$ we must get it in Harpers and/or Frank Leslies."

As a result of this activity, *Harper's* ran a "personal"—so brief and colorless that, more than anything else, it served to emphasize the visitor's insignificance.

President Grant did better, and received General Guardia at the executive's summer residence at Long Branch, New Jersey. There was also a sojourn at Grace's country house at Great Neck, Long Island, during which the host wrote: "I am half tired of these chaps already." But he wasn't rid of them. Grace took the party to Saratoga, cautioning Flint en route: "Don't make any heavy cash advances to Keith."[10]

At different times a member of the traveling delegation was another confidant of Grant, a North Carolina Republican named Thomas Settle. With Settle, Keith discussed affairs of state, and tried to get a mail subsidy for the *Juan G. Meiggs*. As a result the *Meiggs* carried letters on one trip between New York and Jamaica, and Grace received an order on the Post Office Department for $18.20. Before sailing for Europe with Guardia, Keith told Grace to give a watch to Settle's secretary, Robert M. Douglas, a son of the late Stephen A. Douglas, the senator from Illinois and one of Lincoln's rivals for the presidency.

When Grace asked Douglas the kind of watch he would like, a reply came from Washington on stationery that no one fails to notice: the private writing paper of the White House. Mr. Douglas said that Grace's letter had upset him: "You know not my sensitiveness to receiving presents of any value." In New York, he had refused "a suit of clothes from Mr. Keith." Still, he did not wish to give offense by declining "a genuine token of friendship." Grace's own "sense of propriety" must decide the matter; and Grace could also select the watch. On any stationery, the letter was worthy of preservation.[11]

As Grant was running for reelection that year (1872), Douglas, Settle, and O'Sullivan were busy with campaign chores. They, or somebody, made a reluctant convert of the newly naturalized Grace, who couldn't "stomach Greeley." Consequently, Grace's first presidential vote was cast for Grant. In the light of what was to follow, this was a strange beginning in politics for W. R. Grace.[12]

~ With Guardia and Keith away, Grace's letters from Guillermo Nanne began to take on a confidential tone. The German felt the need to speak freely to one whose judgment he valued. Nanne's particular worry was money, for the European expedition of Guardia and Keith was not being crowned with the success so confidently expected by them.

Yet Keith, with some effort, kept up his optimistic chatter to Grace. What if Costa Rican bonds were down? "Such things are to be expected and cannot last. . . . Costa Rica is the star of the tropics. . . . The reelection of Pres. Grant augurs well for Costa Rica."[13]

Eventually some money was raised, at ruinous rates.

"I am afraid," Grace told Nanne, "they have made a regular mess of the loan in England. . . . It is the Peruvian loan over again. . . . This whole difficulty over funds is becoming very serious. . . . If it were not for your energy & push the whole thing would have gone under. . . . If Govt. dfts. are no avail and go to protest what can we hope for? You were formerly much discouraged. I am so now, & anxiously await the appearance of Mr. Keith."

Keith returned to New York alone, Guardia having gone direct to Costa Rica. H. D. B. Norris, chief engineer of the road, also came up to New York. Though Grace had lost faith in Keith—"he has committed too many 'disparatos' [inconsistencies]"—he retained confidence in Norris. Perhaps the engineer and Nanne might pull things through. This hope was dampened when, unable to agree on procedure, each of the two men wrote Grace he would like to resign. Moreover, Grace was now entirely without money except his own, and he had put in about $65,000 of that.

At this juncture, Guardia took a hand. Though beyond his depth in engineering and financial matters, the president of Costa Rica was a man of some force and decision. He and Grace had got on well together. While Keith talked of millions, Guardia actually produced $37,500 and begged Grace not to delay shipments of material. "Again I feel impelled to repeat to you what I have so often said in N. Y. . . . If ever . . . you may have momentarily to supply some cash you will never be caused any financial loss."[14]

~ W. R. Grace was unable to devote his full energies to the Costa Rica railroad because he had other irons in the fire. In particular, certain events in Peru impinged upon his notice.

July 12, 1872, was the date Michael Grace drove to the presidential palace in Lima with a worried look on his usually sunny countenance. On that day the presidential situation in Peru was this: Three sets of electors claimed the right to name Balta's successor. One group was for Pardo, whom Michael Grace knew to be the people's choice; one group for another independent candidate, Ureta; one group was for Balta's candidate, Arenas. Congress, which had assembled on July 1, was in the process of deciding which electors had been legally chosen. Already it was clear that the decision of Congress would be to seat a majority of the Pardo electors.

In Lima, excitement ran high. What would Balta do? Would he yield, or would he defy the constitution and the Congress and try to retain power? Minister of War Tomás Gutiérrez was urging him to retain power.

After much hesitation, on July 22, Balta summoned Gutiérrez to the palace and announced his intention to bow to the will of the electors. This meant that if constitutional courses were followed, Manuel Pardo would assume the presidency on August 2.

Only conjecture supports the assumption that, of late, Michael had argued in favor of Balta's retirement. That conjecture is strengthened, however, by the fact that Henry Meiggs is known to have argued for it. Meiggs preferred to take his chances with Pardo, rather than face the consequences of a country torn by armed rebellion. Michael preferred likewise, and, on July 20, the Callao house informed William that Balta was "talking" of stepping down. "This on the whole is good news. . . . Some roads will be stopped to a certainty but some will be finished."[15]

Henry Meiggs, Michael Grace, and, for that matter, Balta, reckoned without the man of violence Balta had made minister of war. When the president broke the news of his intended retirement, Tomás Gutiérrez had acted like lightning. There was "h–ll to pay generally," as the American consul at Callao expressed it in a private dispatch to W. R. Grace. The consul did not exaggerate. Gutiérrez had arrested the president, dispersed the Congress, and proclaimed himself "supreme chief." Pardo and his principal adherents had escaped seizure only by fleeing to legations or to vessels of the Peruvian navy.

After his first swift stroke, however, the supreme chief ran into difficulties. The diplomatic corps refused to recognize his government. Banks and business houses closed their doors and ignored his demands for money. Under Captain Aurelio García y García, W. R. Grace's friend with a passion for fashionable shirts, the fleet espoused Pardo's cause and cleared for action.

On July 26—while W. R. Grace was en route to Saratoga with his Costa Rican guests—armed citizens attacked Gutiérrez's troops in the fort at Callao. When Silvestre Gutiérrez, the dictator's brother, started to take reinforcements to the garrison, he was shot to death in the Lima railroad station. In retaliation, Marceliano Gutiérrez, another brother, murdered the imprisoned Balta. Then Marceliano led troops to Callao and marched through the streets firing indiscriminately.

At this point Michael Grace, his wife, and baby daughter—all British subjects—took refuge on one of Her Majesty's warships. The American gunboat *Pensacola,* a French and a German man-of-war, and sundry merchant vessels also were speedily filled with noncombatants. "This was very fortunate," Hazen wrote of Michael's prudent conduct, "as during the night his house was pierced by cannonballs. One went clear through, destroying a bedstead." During the same night, Marceliano Gutiérrez was killed in Callao, and the supreme chief nearly hacked to pieces while trying to escape from Lima. Daybreak revealed the bodies of Tomás and Silvestre Gutiérrez swinging, one from each of the twin towers of the cathedral.

With these preliminaries, Manuel Pardo took the oath as president of Peru.[16]

Like most of the local commercial community, which originally had hoped for a continuation of the Balta regime, Michael Grace was quick to jump on the Pardo bandwagon. "The present administration," he wrote during the week of Pardo's inauguration, "promises economy, increase of receipts and moderation. It is generally believed that all [except one railroad] contract commenced will be carried into effect. Meiggs we think will be all right." He asked William for two cargoes of ties.

William could not agree with his brother: "I can't see how the Govt. can go on with the roads." Yet he sent the ties. "Meiggs I leave to you . . . [having] made up my mind after due reflection . . . 'tis better you should "paddle your own canoe.' "[17]

President Pardo, also, had a canoe to paddle in this, his second attempt to rehabilitate Peru. The first attempt, as Prado's minister of finance, had failed, though, notwithstanding a generation of extravagance, Peru's foreign debt was then manageable and its credit good. Those very factors had contributed to the failure of reform. Neither the governing class nor Henry Meiggs saw any necessity for a change.

Consequently an entirely different, and more immediately perilous, set of circumstances confronted the aspirations of Manuel Pardo in 1872. As Hazen wrote on August 26, when the new president had been in office twenty-four days: "Meiggs . . . is pushing the railroads with a firm hand, leaving the administration no excuse to abandon or break any of the contracts. . . . The people of this section want the Oroya line." The same held elsewhere, for each road had been laid out with an eye to local pride almost as much as anything else. Everyone was saying: "Stop any road except ours." "Consequently," pursued Hazen, "I fail to see how any of them can be renounced without breeding trouble."[18]

Nor could Pardo himself; and so he told the Congress in language almost as blunt as Hazen's. Yet to finish the roads, Peru must have money. That meant putting through by some means the languishing loan of 1872. This would bring Peru's indebtedness to a figure that would require the total receipts from guano to pay the interest. Even then, some $28.5 million more would be required to finish the roads. Where would it come from?

Pardo suggested an export tax on nitrates and an increase in customs dues. He also suggested local taxes, both as a measure for raising revenue and for awakening the energies of the mass of the Peruvian people, whose habitual idleness had necessitated the importation of railroad labor, starting a fresh cycle of problems. As another means of elevating the condition of the masses, Pardo recommended the establishment of public schools. Still, the president did not quite relinquish the one really sane solution—that of giving up or deferring construction of certain roads. As many another executive has done, Pardo tossed this hot potato into the lap of Congress. In all, it was a mixed and desperate program.

Some money must be had very soon, for Peru was scraping the bottom of the barrel, and Meiggs was using his private funds and credit to keep the railroad work going. And for once Don Enrique was practicing personal economies.

Oddly, the man to whom both Pardo and Meiggs looked in their straits—Auguste Dreyfus—was in Peru. John Bryce suspected he had set out from Paris to try to help perpetuate Balta's political regime. However that may have been, Monsieur Dreyfus had landed just in time to witness the bloody scenes that eventuated in the triumph of Pardo. As these were enough to try any banker's nerves, Dreyfus proved hard to deal with. Nevertheless, he promised Peru some money, available the following year. But as Peru had to have cash before that, a stopgap loan of nearly $6 million was arranged with the Providencia Bank of Lima.[19]

~ Through all this Michael sent encouraging reports, of which William was skeptical. "I hope your prediction for the future may be realized. I have not as much faith. . . . Goodbye old fellow, love to Margarita." On the last day of December 1872, William began a letter by wishing his brother "a happy & prosperous New Year." In the next sentence he got down to business. Twice W. R. Grace & Co. had been obliged to make remittances to John Bryce's London bank to cover Michael's drawings. "We have borrowed from Chapman & Flint all they have here and in London. . . . I don't care to close many old years in so tight a place, & if any trouble comes of it you will be entirely responsible. . . . Is it not time to think whether you are overtrading? . . . Ponder these matters over in the new year & never apply to us again to remit money for you." When William learned of the Providencia loan to Peru, he sold his stock in that bank.[20]

The gravity of the situation dawned on the sanguine Michael. Dreyfus and the government fell out over details of the emergency loan. "Meiggs may have to stop his roads as the Government owe him S/4,000,000. . . . Quien sabe como salta el Lievre hoy [Who knows how the hare will jump today]?" John G. Meiggs, too, dropped his confident manner. Unless the government could raise "a temporary loan," Henry would be forced to close down. "I owe your brother a small sum, but shall take care of him in any and all cases." And if anything was lacking to complete the unpleasant picture, Michael supplied it with the word to "keep back all shipments and I will see BG&Co out of Meiggs all OK."[21]

By the time news of these disclosures was on its way to New York, William already knew how the land lay. Among other things he knew the size of the "small sum" Henry Meiggs owed—despite William's repeated injunction that Don Enrique pay cash on the nail. These unpleasant facts appeared in the end-of-year statement of the Callao house's affairs. When the elder brother read this document, his temper got the better of him. To use a phrase of Michael's, he "blew up."

"Now I foolishly flattered myself when you wrote me a long letter acknowledging the wisdom of my advice &c that you were since then on the conservative tack. This balance sheet shows no such thing. . . . If you dont think as I do in this respect & in regard to business in general then as a friend & a brother I ask you to finally let me out of the concern . . . as I cant see any safety in the present mode of carrying the business on. . . .

"H^y *Meiggs* owes \$178983.52 truly I w^d never have believed this had I not the papers before me. . . . And yet besides this, coal and Sleepers on the way to a goodly amount. . . . If Meiggs goes *you cant* get clear for a loss of 250,000\$. . . . Men who know Meiggs well here & in Cal^a [California], his own agent here [Spinney] included, would not . . . trust him for 50,000\$. This I have tried to hammer into you."

William commented on other items in the statement:

"*O'Conner & Co* the risk taken by you for the percentage gained . . . is gambling for a very small margin.

"*Wm Seymour* what new claim has he on us that he owes the sum of 6290\$52 . . .

"*E Llona* if he cant pay the amo: now due 12137\$71 I cant see the safety in our buying so largely for his Hacienda.

"*Wholey Brothers* you promised me should never owe you again.

"*William Lewis* owed 13900\$ May 31/71 & then you wrote he should pay off gradually. . . . Now he owes 4000\$ more."

And so on, name after name.

William went into the matter of assets and liabilities:

"You have a capital of		\$280,000.00
and have due to you by Sundries	845,000.00	
less J Bryce & W&R	153,000.00	
	\$692,000.00	

this is not a healthy state of affairs in any country & infinitely less so in Peru.

"You owe *on call* by your own books

To the 3 Banks	\$242,978.00
Comp^a Sud Am^a	102,746.00
Callao dock Witt & Comp Ligna	75,946.00
Moore Bro^s & P&T	78,468.00
WRGrace & Co	157,354.00
	\$657,492.00

besides to OExpress [*Ocean Express*] &

other vessels	\$121,867.00
Sundry creditors	51,303.00
	\$173,170.00

"Where are the funds to meet these demands. Stock will not pay them when required, & no house can be prosperously, not to say safely, managed on any such principles of business. this is as certain as death."

Michael had been proud of the fact that in eighteen months' time the profits of the firm had exceeded its capital. William called those profits illusory. "They are all in amounts due . . . [and] I very much fear Mr Meiggs & . . . others too will [not pay]. . . .

"So now you have my remarks & honest opinion & . . . if it does you as little good as my past advice has it will not affect you very much, I fear, so good bye for the present."

Within a few days, William repented his hasty words. He asked Michael not to let them offend him. But he continued his earnest counsel. Should his conclusions be correct, Bryce, Grace & Co. were headed for "failure." Such a failure "would make no difference in my feelings toward you as a brother." The world, however, would judge the case differently. "For no matter what your past record has been, just make a heavy loss by Meiggs & others, use up the capital in your hands, and you will learn the bitter lesson of what it is to fail as a business man."[22]

Grace was speaking from close observation. The great postwar boom in the United States, in which railroad building was the bellwether, had reached its zenith. The year just past—1872—had witnessed a narrowing of credit and the collapse of four thousand overextended firms owing $121 million. Like many another house, W. R. Grace & Co. had closed the year in a "tight place." And like many another businessman, Grace braced himself for even harder going in 1873.

~ Though the two crowded rooms that constituted the offices of W. R. Grace & Co. at 47 Exchange Place were as busy as a hive, a casual visitor might have been misled as to the firm's standing in the commercial world. The secondhand furniture could be mistaken for more than an evidence of frugality, or a disinclination on the part of the principal partner to put on the dog. And the brisk, cordial, brown-bearded little man whose desk was nearest the main entrance, and who called clerks by their first names and asked questions about their families: could he, indeed, be Mr. Grace?

The visitor might also find it difficult to believe Mr. Grace the possessor of a personal fortune of half to three quarters of a million dollars—that is, at the inflated prices prevailing at the beginning of 1873. Probably half of the sum was tied up in the New York and Callao establishments. The rest was in other investments, largely real estate. These holdings were scattered from Connecticut to the outskirts of Brooklyn. Buying and selling constantly, Grace had made a good deal of money in the rising market of the past few years. Three or four times he had sold homes in Brooklyn over his family's heads. The itinerant life precipitated by these transactions came to a halt in 1872 when Grace bought a farm on Great Neck, Long Island. The following year, Brooklyn was forsaken and the Graces established their city residence in a three-story brownstone house at 108 East Seventeenth Street, Manhattan.

Grace had his desk by the office door because he said he liked to be handy to callers. Interruptions did not trouble him. More secluded spots were reserved for the resident junior partners, of whom there were two when Horace J. Moody was taken into the firm in '73. That Grace gave his partners latitude appears in the fact that Moody invested some of the firm's surplus in stocks that Grace did not approve of. In a tactful note he suggested that Moody consider switching to something safer: "I take wild cats . . . [only when] I can afford to make a total loss and not feel at all badly about it."[23]

A visitor proceeding from Mr. Grace's place of business to one of his homes would have been struck by the change. There nearly everything was of the best. All about was evidence of money used with good sense and good taste. Consequently, the family lived without much show. There was not a hint of aspiration to cultivate the "right" people. Yet "right" people, entering a Grace house, would have recognized many things as "correct"—though the atmosphere of informality might have been a little disturbing. Servants were well-trained and competent. Grace made that clear in a statement of requirements for a waitress, adding: "Protestant or Catholic, indifferent." Time off for church in either event. "14$ or even 15$ [monthly] if a very extra woman." From the first Grace had kept a pair of fast-driving horses—a real luxury in a city—and he might spend a thousand dollars for a carriage.

Grace houses were gay—overrun with company; something always going on. Ships' officers and seafaring relatives of Mrs. Grace preserved the maritime flavor. Visitors from Peru, notable and otherwise, were in and out all the time. Through Judge Pratt, one of Brooklyn's leading citizens, Grace met men of some distinction in public affairs. The homes were enlivened by Mr. and Mrs. Grace's fondness for young people and dancing, and by Grace's love of music—anything from an Irish jig tune to the productions of classical composers. He was a frequent attendant at the opera in Manhattan, to which his tone-deaf wife dutifully accompanied him. Every summer they made a pilgrimage to Lillius's old home in Maine, and to fashionable Saratoga. As William was a sufferer from hay fever, at the season for that affliction the couple would try to get away to the White Mountains.[24]

The purchase of the farm at Great Neck was, as Grace intended, a milestone in the history of the family. The inspiration burgeoned from an inherited attachment to the land: a feeling that a family should have its roots in the soil. Significantly, he named the place Gracefield—for the historic seat in Ireland, which William as a boy probably never saw the inside of. Though Grace had his jest about ancestor-worshiping families—"they're like potatoes, the best of them underground"—he could not escape the impact of eight centuries of landed gentry behind him.

Gradually the Gracefield property was expanded from ninety-two to a hundred and forty-four acres. Carrying a pair of pruning shears, Mr. Grace would tramp over it, note and order the improvement of sites where he hoped his sons and daughters might someday build their homes.[25]

For the original property, Grace paid $30,000. The house, a large, rambling white-shingle homestead, looked comfortable and well used. It stood on a promontory overlooking Manhasset Bay of Long Island Sound. You entered a broad hall, on the right of which was a big living room, and on the left a dining room of equal size. Back of the main dining room was the children's. Though he never got through working on the grounds, Mr. Grace did little to the house beyond eventually adding a billiard room and opening bedrooms on the third, or attic, floor.

A dirt road ran past the house, and across the road was a collection of buildings that could have been mistaken for a small village—carriage house, stables, barns, an ice house, the farmer's house, and so on. Mr. Grace was always building or altering something there.

Immediately he stocked the place with driving horses, saddle ponies, cows, and sheep, all imported from Ireland. John Grace made the selections. He sent them over in charge of Pat Delaney, whose father had worked on the Grace place at Ballylinan. "The ponies," William wrote his brother, "turned out better than ever. The bay horse is still lame, but the vet thinks he will be all right. . . . The blacks are in fine order & shine like a new dollar." Pat Delaney was put in charge of a farm Grace owned across the Sound in Connecticut. Pat's reports on things there were spelled phonetically, with some regard for an Irish ear: "The bull his waight is Twenty hundred Nointy Ponds. His Hayth is 15 hands 1 quarter."

The blacks worked well in harness. Tom McGovern, the coachman, would bring them around in time for the drive of two miles to the landing in Little Neck Bay to meet the commuting steamer *Sewanhaka* at eight in the morning. Grace himself would take the reins, and rarely was he passed on the road.[26]

When the family went to Gracefield, there were two children—Alice, nearly twelve, born at sea off the Chinchas, and Agnes, five. After Agnes there had been two babies who failed to survive their second year. Shortly after the move to the new place, Mrs. Grace gave birth to their first son, christened Joseph S. Spinney Peter Grace. This was a compliment to the father's business associate and Great Neck neighbor, and to St. Peter. Before the young man was old enough to recognize his long name, it was clipped to Joseph Peter—a result of the far-reaching tribulations bearing down upon Henry Meiggs. They had caused strained relations between J. S. Spinney and W. R. Grace.[27]

~ The money Grace spent in the interest of charity and friendship is nothing to dwell on particularly. Money provides the easiest means for a rich man to meet such obligations. It is the amount of time and considerate attention Grace gave to these things that is worthy of mention.

Grace was a devout, but by no means a narrow, Catholic. "A man's mind is his kingdom," he wrote Sylvan Hazen—on the subject of choosing a wife, but the remark expressed Grace's views on religion as well. Nevertheless, his work for the Church was unending. It may have been on one of his excursions to the White Mountains that he made the acquaintance of the mother superior of the Convent of Our Lady of Mercy at Manchester, New Hampshire. In any event, when six young sisters were going from that institution to California, the mother superior asked Mr. Grace if he would see that they got on the proper train in New York. There were many details to attend to. Grace himself met the sisters. He did all that was asked, and more. He saw that a business friend—a former sea captain and a Protestant—helped the nuns to make their change of trains in Chicago.

Time and again on brief meetings, W. R. Grace left lasting and favorable impressions—as in the case of the traveling sisters. The word was passed around in Church circles, with the result that, a few months later, Grace took care of another party of nuns going from an Eastern convent to the Far West.[28]

The wives of absent men appealed to Grace for about everything. Edna Norris sent a photograph of herself to be framed "in a plain mahogany or black walnut" and forwarded to her engineer husband in Costa Rica. Lillie Keith and her sister Emily Jarvis were almost as persistent in their requests as the Church. Two Latin American boys—one from Costa Rica and one from Peru—were sent to Grace to be put in school. He selected the schools, saw that the boys were properly shod and clad for the climate, and patiently dealt with all the other problems schoolboys can pose for a guardian. During vacations he received them into his home. One lad was diligent and grateful, making it a pleasure to help him. The other was the opposite. Though he never said so, Grace must have been relieved when this boy returned to Peru because the school would not serve him beefsteak three times a day.[29]

There was also the question of the future of William's crippled and sensitive brother John, who was blue over the lack of success of his farming operations in Ireland. Dreaming of getting out in the world, as all the other Grace boys had done, John wrote to his brother Morgan about pioneering in New Zealand. The picture Morgan painted seemed designed to dishearten: "Settlers . . . separate themselves from all civilized society. . . . [Their] wives drive cattle, cook sometimes for 10 or 15 men, wash, mind children." It was too much for a man who could not walk without crutches. So John turned his thoughts toward America.

William warmly encouraged him. On a trip to California, he wrote long descriptions of the country. They fired John's mind. "My head is so full of the Western States of America . . . I can scarcely think of anything else." He thought in terms of farming or stock raising, never having done anything else. Poring over maps and handbooks, John asked for more light on Minnesota, Colorado, Texas, and the Blue Ridge region of Virginia.

All along, William appears to have had other plans for his lame brother, but he wished the decision to seem to be John's. Grace was doing so much business on the Pacific Coast that he wanted a branch house there. He arranged for James F. Chapman, a sea captain who knew the Coast and had business experience on shore, to call on John. The two hit it off. John sold, at a heavy loss, William's Irish farm of Fernville and brought his family to New York, still undecided between business and farming. Privately, Michael came forward with a brotherly proposal. Should William want John in New York, Michael would cede, without consideration, his 10 percent interest in the New York house. Though William did not press John, he had Chapman on hand to talk up the business possibilities of the Pacific Coast. The captain was an uncle of Charley Flint. Three months later, in April 1873, with Chapman as a partner and guide, J. W. Grace & Co. opened its doors in San Francisco.[30]

7 ~ Mutiny on the Florella

~ As W. R. Grace contemplated the fact that railroad building in Peru and in Costa Rica had been managed with something less than the wisdom of Solomon, he could congratulate himself that not all his eggs were in one basket.

In addition to his part in the soaring schemes of Meiggs and of Keith, where the risks were great and the profits, when there were any, large, Grace clung to his original and unspectacular role of trader. Suppose all the railroads that had been started should not be completed. On the west coast of South America, life would still go on. There would be a market for such articles as cotton goods, petroleum, lard, rice, sewing needles, padlocks, and brooms. Not even in the heyday of the railroad business, when all looked rosy, did Grace lose sight of this humble commerce in "notions." He contrived to expand it, and to spread the reputation of Bryce, Grace & Co. as purveyors of dependable merchandise.

Whether locomotives and bridges or padlocks and brooms, everything moved to its destination over many thousand miles of blue water. So Grace kept his hand in shipping. This was ticklish work. By 1870 hope for a grand revival of the American merchant marine had begun to die. There was a special significance to the chantey sailors sang at the end of a long voyage when, with sails clewed up, they manned the capstan to walk a ship up to the wharf:

> O, the times are hard and the wages low,
> *Leave her, Johnny, leave her;*
> I'll pack my bag and go below,
> *It's time for us to leave her.*[1]

Definitely, steam was the coming thing. Without subsidies worthy of the name, American steam could not challenge foreign rivals. The Suez

90

Canal cut thirty-four hundred miles off the route between New York and Bombay, and three thousand off that between New York and Canton: one more advantage to steam, because the absence of regular winds prevented sail from using the Red Sea.

Besides that, our sailing vessels were getting old. Their captains were getting old. Merchant captains of the prewar days, who had sustained the prestige of the Stars and Stripes on every ocean, were, like George Gilchrest and James Chapman, finding more profitable employment on shore. In other cases they were simply retiring to their solid white New England houses, where the widows' walks were of no further use to the women of the family. The new captains had not "come through the cabin window," to be sure. They were good navigators, and tough, capable seamen; but not the equal of their predecessors at business, or at correspondence, as Grace may have reflected as he deciphered their misspelled letters.

Good mates, however, were getting to be a problem because so little officer material was found in the forecastles. The reverse had been true during America's golden age on deep water. In those days, forecastles were nautical academies. Many a lad from the New England and the Chesapeake coastal towns went to sea for the good reason that his father had done so. He went with every expectation of a mate's or a master's ticket one day—the former nearly always and the latter very often before he was twenty-one. Boys from the hinterland farms went to sea because the pay was good. This type of seaman saved his pay. On top of that, from China or the Spice Islands a foremast hand might, as a private speculation, bring back in his sea chest enough to net a profit the equal of a year's wages on a farm. A couple of such voyages could provide the wherewithal to return to his inland hills, take a wife, and settle down.

The California gold strike and the postwar rush for Western homesteads conspired with other circumstances to make the land more attractive than the sea. In the fifties our forecastles had begun to fill with foreigners, particularly British and Scandinavian, content, or at any rate resigned, to serve out their lives before the mast, never dreaming of an officer's berth. Even then, crimping, or shanghaiing, to fill up crews was extensively practiced. More and more, Americans who clung to the sea came, by a process of elimination, to be a hard lot, unsuited to grasp the larger opportunities that lay on shore. Discipline at sea had always been harsh. To handle the latter-day type of crew it became, not infrequently, brutal. With their flogging, tricing up, and meeting-the-gunner's-daughter, the "bully" captain and the "bucko" mate were bywords in the Yankee service. At nearly every port he touched, a master lost men by desertion. At sea, mutiny was often in the back of some resentful seaman's mind. These conditions were worse in sail than in steam.[2]

Yet Grace stayed with sail. There was no need of Minor Keith's fiasco with the *Juan G. Meiggs* to remind him of the hazards in the path of a novice trying to operate in steam without government help. Grace stayed with sail because he had been in it from boyhood; because he knew and understood the men who were destined to go from youth to old age or to sudden death in that ancient service of the sea; and because he had confidence in his judgment.

It may be that other factors entered in, namely pride of accomplishment and sentiment. Not only to make a living in sail, but to build up a paying fleet while all over the world, and especially in the United States, the sailing ship was on its way out, was an achievement that should have given any man satisfaction. As for sentiment, they say it has no place in business. Though W. R. Grace could see a dollar farther than most, and think of more ways of getting it, he was not devoid of sentiment in business. It shows in all his relationships, particularly those having to do with the operation of ships.

Hard-bitten and oft misused, the men who worked those ships had pride in their calling. Shellbacks held themselves several cuts above their colleagues in steam. "Soogi-moogi" and "paint passer," meaning steam sailor, were terms of disparagement. Certainly, in this dying era of sail, the men who kept canvas plying the oceans could boast of skills and perils unknown to those in ships propelled by machinery. An ordinary seaman was expected "to hand, reef and steer . . . set a topgallant or royal studding-sail gear out of the top . . . and perhaps also to send down or cross a royal yard." Of an able seaman much more was required. "His calling was the most dangerous in the world. It took strength, skill and courage to furl topsails on a great clipper ship, with its masts and eighty-foot yards bending like whalebone in a River Plate *pampero*, great blocks beating about like flails, and . . . sails slatting with enough force to crush a man's ribs." So wrote an eminent American maritime historian, himself a seaman.[3]

~ Across Grace's desk by the door moved a correspondence that Conrad would have relished. Unfortunately, except in rare instances, no copies of Grace's replies were kept. Yet the one side that has been preserved treats of matters as varied as the sea itself. Captains regularly reported their whereabouts, their adventures, their disbursements. Disbursements were minutely detailed. A desperate fight with a gale might be mentioned only to account for a delay or for expenditures for repairs. The death of a crewman in performance of his duty might get a line, though a mutiny would be gone into more fully. Endlessly they passed on trade information and personal gossip. And if in a port of call a captain ran across a length of silk that took his eye, he might purchase it as a gift to Mrs. Grace for a dress. When an infant, born at sea, was named for William R. Grace or for his wife, probably more than one obliging correspondent would report the occurrence. One of the Grace babies who had died—Annie—had been named for the wife of a sea captain.

Grace was included in the freemasonry of fellowship and assistance among men who followed the sea. By no means all captains made fortunes plying their trade. So when pinches came it was natural for a retired master to write to his friend. W. R. Grace received many communications that in another field of commerce might be called begging letters. "My dear wife died suddenly yesterday, and I have not the means to give her a respectable burial. Will you . . . let me have $150.00 and greatly relieve and oblige." Captain Stevens could write so bald a request with a clear conscience. Grace scribbled at the foot of the letter, "Sent check $150.00." "I want you to do me a favor," wrote Captain Brown. "I want to buy half of a Fishing vessell and I would like to hire Five Hundred dolars for a couple of Years."[4]

The Grace establishments in New York, Callao, and San Francisco served as unofficial post offices through which the families of mariners sought to maintain contacts, uncertain and tenuous at best, with their men at sea.

"My Dearest Husband,

"I am writing this few lines to you to let you know that we are quite well and we was verey glad to hear in your letter witch I Received to day that you was well and Dear James you say that will be the last letter you will send. Dear James I cant think what is the Matter you dont get my letters. I wrote one in answer to the last I had from Callao and I wrote answers to the one before this one. Dear James you must not Fret about me to go away with another Man. I am not tired of the one I have so you can put your mind easy about me."

There followed two pages of domestic news from a suburban village near Liverpool: doings of the children; how the family spent Christmas (1875); the affairs of the Baptist Chapel and of the Temperance Society.

"With my kind love to you Many times over, your loving Wife if you think I can Call myself so

MARY WATKINS

in hopes we shall see one another Soon Please God to Spare us."

First Officer Watkins of the bark *Toronto* failed to receive that letter, too. With other uncalled-for seamen's mail it was found in 1947 in the files of the Callao house where it had lain unopened for seventy-one years.[5]

The fame of the "bronze Venuses" of Callao had spread far. A Boston maiden advised her brother to resort to prayer before going on shore. The Belgian bride of an American mate, writing in unaccustomed English from Antwerp, kept the matter between her man and herself. "I know you like the females . . . [and] they told me how there is good looking womans in Callao. . . . So be on your *gard,* for if I hear anything of news not agreeable you need not think to com to the *nest* of your Marie."[6]

When fears and yearnings grew too intense for passive endurance, wives, widows, and mothers sometimes wrote W. R. Grace direct. "Has . . . the Ship Gensecole of Liverpool from the Brazills . . . arrived at New York. . . . My son Christopher Hall is a seaman onboard of her. . . . If you will be kind enough to write it will be a great consolation to a troubled Widow." "Is Tom Kelly comeing home or is he getting better. . . . You will please excuse a troubled Mother." Those letters were from Ireland.[7]

From Staten Island, New York, came one from the wife of Captain Weymouth. This lady had been the recipient of gossip to the effect that in Callao her husband "was half crazed" and had behaved as a "beast." If that was not enough, Mrs. Weymouth's informant had added that "half had not been told." The captain's wife wrote to Grace for the facts: "And if this is true I will say this for my husband, he was never guilty of it before, and he is now forty-four (44) years of age." Though almost a teetotaler, Grace was tolerant of the great weakness of seamen when on shore. A mariner in need of a dram never went thirsty in the Grace household. Mr. Grace sought to assure Mrs. Weymouth, and still keep within the bounds of credibility. There had been, he said, no report from Callao against her husband—merely a notation that "Captain W. was a little sick from causes supposed to be liquor, but . . . [he has] entirely reformed."[8]

Captain Baker was upbraided for failing to pay the Graces a visit while he was in Brooklyn. Baker confessed an indisposition for social life. Since the death of his "good wife," and his own retirement, he had stuck very close to his home in Kingston, Ontario. The prospect of blundering about Brooklyn's perilous streets was too much for a grieving man. However, he was grateful for a hammock Michael Grace had sent from Peru: "It is a splendid one & I anticipate many a good *Siesta* in it next summer." Three months later a change had come over the old sea dog. Wives, he said, were to be had with "no difficulty." But wives "such that can, & will, take the part of a *good* Mother are hard to find." With this observant preamble, Captain Baker announced that he was going to marry his housekeeper. There was new vigor in every line the old fellow penned. "I may come on . . . to New York . . . [and if I do] . . . will endeavor to be a better Boy than last time."[9]

There was also the case of the Widow Godfrey, who was with her husband when he died in Mobile, Alabama. Grace was one of the first persons to whom Mrs. Godfrey wrote, prostrate from grief—and annoyance: "I never knew a man tie his property up in such a fearful manner." Moreover, the manner of the captain's death—he had committed suicide while afflicted with delirium tremens—rendered it impossible to realize from his life insurance more than the $1,100 paid in premiums. Mrs. Godfrey protested that she was nearly penniless. What was the chance of raising something on the two vessels in which the late captain had owned a sixteenth interest each? Would Mr. Grace be kind enough to see about it, and keep wind of these assets from Mrs. Godfrey's creditors? It was a charming letter, the Widow Godfrey being, indeed, a charmer.

The years ensuing disclose traces of her passage. W. R. Grace and H. D. B. Norris, chief engineer of the Costa Rica railroad, were only two of her admirers. These irreproachable husbands had their private little joke about being rivals for her favor. Alone one night before a wood fire in his office, Grace concluded a dreary business letter to Norris with a brightening allusion to the "joyous merry widow." Norris replied from fever-ridden Limón. With enough railroad troubles to drive a saint to distraction, he sprinkled poetry through a paragraph in praise of the heartbreaker. "If Mormonism were only universal, wouldn't you and I have 'a gay old time' fighting for that widow?"

After four years of widowhood, Mrs. Godfrey landed spry and well-fixed old Captain Hamilton, whom Grace called "always one of my best friends." Retired from the sea these ten years, Captain Hamilton lived in the country near New York. Grace's letter congratulating the bridegroom contained a proper show of envy.[10]

~ At sea a shipmaster's life was an austere one. In the clippers his solitary dignity was awesome to behold and, one would think, rather hard on the captain himself at times. He ate alone. No one spoke to him unless spoken to. Entire voyages would pass without the exchange of a word, even with his officers, except in the line of duty. In lesser vessels there might be some unbending, yet, always, the captain's word was law. He possessed, literally, the power of life and death over his men.

On shore a captain might be another man: approachable, affable, even talkative—the yarn-spinning seaman of fact as well as fable. But just as often he retained his habits of remoteness and taciturnity except with his own kind. Among this select company was W. R. Grace. Captains unburdened themselves to him. The words that passed between them in friendly talks in Grace's office or in his home have been lost. Only letters survive. They were safety valves by which men compelled to silence and aloofness by the traditions and the necessities of their calling could relieve their minds on personal as well as professional matters.

At sea a captain was so used to having his way that when he ran into a despot on shore who got the better of him the result was trying on the disposition. Such a czar was the harbormaster at Savannah, a Mr. Finney. Captain W. A. Lord wrote of his experience with Finney. Lord's troubles began when he refused to accept the stevedores Finney had recommended. Immediately it became difficult to get lighters. The anchorage assigned to Lord was a poor one for so large a vessel: "There is nothing to lay against and very little to make fast to and often at low water the ship would list over, sometimes very badly." Just outside Lord's mooring, Mr. Finney put a bark which was loading timber from rafts. The rafts broke Lord's mooring lines. Even after the bark was loaded, Finney kept her there in Lord's way. "If ever you catch me in Savannah again . . . you may laugh at me and call this all talk."[11]

An English captain, Burgess Wingate, commanding an English ship, the *Wiltshire,* found shore officials of his own country every whit as unreasonable as W. A. Lord had found Harbormaster Finney. Wingate described his departure from New York in February 1872. The harbor was filled with drifting ice. The *Wiltshire*'s two tugs lost control of the ship. Wingate feared she would ground on Governor's Island. By a lucky accident a third tug came past and turned to, and, after three hours' struggle, the *Wiltshire* got safely clear of the harbor.

The "various changes"—storms, ice floes—incidental to a winter crossing of the North Atlantic, Captain Wingate passed over casually. Not until he was in contact with land again, at Liverpool, did a real problem arise: "You will doubtless remember the little fracas between my new mate and crew." The difficulty referred to, which had taken place on an earlier voyage, seems to have been something Wingate had mentioned to Grace in New York. The fact that the *Wiltshire* was not a Grace-operated ship shows that captains outside the employ of W. R. Grace & Co. sometimes talked freely to the head of that house.

This triviality, this "little fracas," had been made a pretext to hound a ship captain who had done no more than his duty. "Your humble servant is to be pulled up on the red tape system by the Board of Trade"—the body in the United Kingdom that had power to review the disciplinary actions captains had taken on the high seas. Wingate was unaware of the exact charges he would have to meet, but surmised they would have to do with "insulting the sailors": "Owners seem to have a leniency toward the poor sailors rather than be troubled to support those in charge." As a general proposition this assumption was one with which neither seamen nor neutral observers would agree. Therefore, inasmuch as Captain Wingate anticipated losing his command, the chances are that his offense had been rather grievous.

At all events, the captain was "disgusted . . . heartily sick of the sea; and ask you, Grace, seriously, not as a friend of yesterday but as one of long standing, can you in any way possible point out any line where a moderate living might be insured. . . . New York or any other York [will do], all places or countries being . . . pretty much alike."[12]

The ship captain weary of the sea was no phenomenon. F. A. Soule let himself go in long letters to Charley Flint which the junior partner passed on to his senior: "When you get this just think of us poor devils off Cape Horn, half froze. [Other seamen have related how fire froze off the Horn.] I hope we won't have such a hard time as we did coming out, though it will be the middle of winter—night most of the time and the season . . . for Easterly winds." You had to know Captain Soule to understand that this was no plea for sympathy. The captain had a sense of humor, and his complaints were half in jest. He said he was carrying the smelliest lot of guano ever loaded. While fleas and lizards stayed around guano by choice, Yankees associated with it only out of financial necessity.

Captain Soule had brought railroad materials to the Peruvian port of Ancón, which he described as consisting of a depot and thirty or forty bamboo huts. The railroad laborers were making things lively, though. Looking for gold ornaments, they had dug up an Indian graveyard, which the Peruvians had preserved for four hundred years. Callao was a discreditable place. "Bribing is the regular system. Any man can be bought for a small sum." It may be that selling oneself cheap constituted, in the New Englander's eyes, the more damning offense of the two. Bryce, Grace & Co., Soule reported, did the biggest business in the port: "brokers, ship chandlers, butchers, grocers, importers, everything." That was the type of business a railroad collapse would not ruin.

Charley Flint seems to have been talking of going into business for himself; and, before getting an interest in the firm, he did leave Grace for a year for a partnership in Captain Gilchrest's store. "Going to sea is about the meanest thing a man can do," continued Soule. "I expect you will be going into some kind of business soon. When you do, perhaps you will give me a situation as a clerk."[13]

When captains did retire they often found life on shore as vexatious as life at sea. From an old fellow in the decaying maritime town of Searsport, Maine: "As I have benn at home some 3 months I am begining to think I must go to sea soon. If you should see or hear of an opening would you please let me know of it. . . . A new [ship] I am thin[kin]g of going into but if you should see a good second handed one."[14]

C. K. Limstrong yielded to a common longing of sea captains. He purchased a farm—near Manassas, in Prince William County, Virginia. It was a pretty place with a small and varied orchard. Once there, Limstrong found the life less idyllic than he had dreamed during long and lonely watches on the quarterdeck. True, he was within thirty miles of the District of Columbia; but Washington was not a commercial port. "The greatest fault I have at present is that I am so far from salt water and old friends. . . . I never thought that land labour was so bad to mannage as I have found it here. I think I would sooner mannage a rough ship's company than the poco-poco farming labourer here."[15]

~ *J*n the seventies, Grace operated many more ships than he owned. And I have yet to find a vessel he owned the whole of at this period. Grace preferred owning a quarter interest in four ships to owning one ship entirely. For the same reason many shippers preferred to distribute a valuable cargo among three or four ships. The Grace vessels were of all kinds—large and small, that is, ships, brigs, barks, and schooners. They were old and new, but mostly old.

During the seventies, however, Chapman & Flint built in their Maine yard three splendid down-easters, the *W. R. Grace,* the *M. P. Grace,* and the *Manuel Llaguno.* Manuel Llaguno, the young Peruvian Grace had employed with misgivings off the Chinchas, became a partner in the Callao house sometime after its reorganization in 1876. The naming of these ships by Chapman & Flint, who also owned them, indicates a community of interest, a Flint and a Chapman being partners in Grace houses. In the case of the *M. P. Grace,* not all the advertising the Grace houses received from the ship was favorable. The conduct of a Captain De Winter got the *M. P. Grace* blacklisted, for mistreatment of sailors, by a primitive seamen's union in San Francisco.[16]

Though the *Manuel Llaguno* made two trips from New York to San Francisco in a hundred and two days and one to Singapore in a hundred days, by and large spectacular performances by sailing vessels were a thing of the past. Voyages were rated merely as successful or unsuccessful. Like peaceful nations, a consistently successful sailing ship had no history outside of ledger entries that would gladden the heart of an owner.

Sometimes seamen spoke of "unlucky" ships, in the firm belief that certain vessels could by no means shake themselves free of misfortune. Such a ship seems to have been the *Nereus,* a clipper formerly called the *Elwood Walter.* Yet she had made at least one profitable round voyage to Callao—on which Grace cleared perhaps $10,000. The event gets two lines in a book of accounts. That was in 1867, before Grace had a proprietary interest in her. To relate all that the Grace correspondence tells of the *Nereus's* ill luck would fill this chapter.[17]

The correspondence tells more than that. It tells of expedients to keep down expenses; the improvisations by which worn-out ships were nursed and jury-rigged through their last voyages.

Let us pick up the *Nereus,* H. M. Nickels master, as she enters the estuary of the River Plate, late in September 1868, from Cardiff for Montevideo with coal. Owing to "verry light winds" it had been a sixty-nine-day passage. On docking, the first news Captain Nickels received was that Grace had bought a five-eighths interest in the old hooker. "I am well satisfied," Nickels wrote, "to have you to sail for." The captain himself owned the rest of the ship. He reckoned to discharge the cargo in fifty-odd days. The great trouble would be to keep his crew, so effective was the crimping practiced in Montevideo: a sailor invited into a waterfront groggery would wake up at sea on another ship. Some incoming vessels had lost all their hands, but, so far, Nickels had "only lost two Boys." "As soon as I get discharged . . . [I will] let you know the amount of my disbursements. My wife and boy are well and wish to be remembered."[18]

Nickels came down with "the Bloody dysentery," and, though sailing was delayed until mid-December, he was too ill to go. The first mate, A. N.

Miller, was promoted to the command. By this time the crew had nearly all disappeared, but Miller bested the crimps by getting out of jail some seamen who were willing to work for three dollars a month and freedom. This seems to have been Miller's first command and he strove to make a good impression. He cracked on sail and drove the *Nereus* in a rapid passage around Cape Stiff, a name sailors have for the Horn, and in twenty-seven days reached Juan Fernandez Island, of Robinson Crusoe fame, in the Pacific. Hope for a record passage went glimmering, however, when the southeast trades failed Miller, and he came into Callao forty-five days from the Plate, an average run. At Callao, Miller held onto his crew by the expedient of putting "the doubtfull ones in irons."

He reported the condition of the ship: "The metal [covering the underwater portion of the hull] put on 18 months in N. Y. is wore thin as paper and off in many places. The ship is wormed from 17 ft. up, some of the plank in waist is rotten . . . one upper deck beam and some of the hanging knees tween decks are rotten. . . . Some of the backstays are bad, and the fore rigging is fearfully bad." The lifeboat was unfit "to trust the ships company in."

At this juncture, Miller received news of the death of Captain Nickels. Grace promised that should Miller give satisfaction on the forthcoming voyage to England he would be confirmed in command. "That one sentence," replied Miller, "has given me renewed encouragement." He bought a lifeboat and made some repairs, justifying the expense with the statement that Nickels, intending to sell out of the *Nereus*, had let the ship run down.[19]

Off the Chinchas the *Nereus* loaded and got away ahead of some of her competitors. While running his easting preparatory to rounding the Horn, Miller encountered a tremendous gale. Giant graybeards, rising to heights of sixty feet, moved in on the ship like mountains. Some of the crew were at the pumps, the others aloft taking in sail. Still, water in the hold gained four inches an hour and several tons of guano were damaged.

The winds carried the vessel into the Antarctic. Crossing the longitude of the Horn and turning northward, Miller ran into fog and ice fields. Then a "snorter," a fierce sudden storm, hit the ship. Sailors tell of a man who opened his mouth in a snorter; the wind blew him inside out. Scudding before the storm, the *Nereus* shipped a sea that stove in the after house, filled the cabin, and spoiled nearly all the bread, flour, and small stores. Refusing to put into port to replenish, Miller placed the crew on short allowance and, a hundred and twenty-six days from the Chinchas, dropped anchor in the Cove of Cork, in Ireland.[20]

Grace decided to sell the ship, if he could get £3,000. Miller, and others, had recommended this course. But no one would give "anything like" that amount. As the vessel was unfit for another voyage round the Horn, Grace ordered her in ballast to Tybee Island, at the mouth of the Savannah River, for cotton. With her top sides caulked and other superficial repairs, the *Nereus* was ready to sail from Plymouth, England, where she had discharged the guano, when a gale swept into the Channel. It was a wild night. Several ships in the harbor went on the rocks, and the captain of one committed suicide. Miller saved the *Nereus*, but, as he wrote Grace, "If I had known the old tub had been well insured," he would not have risked his life to do so. Patched up again, the old tub was on her way.[21]

In the South on a lumber trip, Grace visited the *Nereus* at Savannah. "Ship looks well. I think Miller does not think as well of ship as she deserves." He asked Captain Gilchrest to find "a first class man to take $\frac{1}{4}$ of her and go in her." Also, would Gilchrest "examine closely" Miller's accounts? Grace's father-in-law found no man; and apparently he discovered nothing wrong with Miller's accounts. At any rate, Miller retained the command. Ill luck, however, continued to pursue the ship. While the *Nereus* was lying in the river, another vessel rammed its stern. In a storm en route to Liverpool, she lost sails and forerigging and sprang a leak. The cotton, which Miller had carefully stowed, was badly damaged: another Jonah voyage.[22]

In Liverpool, Grace's agents dug up Captain Thomas R. Herbert, described as "a shrewd old chap." He paid $7,500 for Mrs. Nickel's interest and took command of the *Nereus*. Grace paid Miller's return fare on a steamer. In New York, he got another berth and was lost at sea.

Captain Herbert justified the claim to shrewdness by helping handle the insurance claim arising from the damaged cotton. The underwriters at first declined to pay, on the mistaken assumption that there was water in the *Nereus*'s hold when she left Savannah. Otherwise it does not appear that the captain was very smart. Examining the ship *after* he had paid his money, he found her in about the state Miller had complained of. But whereas Miller had apologetically laid out a hundred or so dollars now and then, old Herbert put the *Nereus* in dry dock and spent $8,000 on her.[23]

Herbert brought the rejuvenated ship to New York with a cargo of iron—a profitable voyage. Grace reloaded her for the west coast of South

America, and in fine spirits the old seaman headed for the Horn with a good breeze of wind behind him. One hundred and two days later, when the *Nereus* dropped anchor in Callao harbor, Captain Herbert reported that en route "the crew all [had] mutinied."[24]

Grace was fed up. A brutal captain might be undesirable; but a weak one was worse. Grace offered the *Nereus* for sale at a figure that threw Herbert into a panic. It would be "ruinous to me. . . . I trust you will let me down easy, for I am not young like you . . . and able to stand the torrent of misfortune."[25]

Taking pity on the old man, Grace arranged for the *Nereus* to trade along the west coast of South America. When in Peru a few weeks later, Grace himself looked into the situation. It was hopeless. "If the Capt. was a different man" he might have done a profitable coastwise business; "but he is old, dissatisfied, crabbed and disappointing."

Grace had been saddled with the *Nereus* for nearly four years. On his return to the States he offered her to a South Street firm, and closed the account with a line in a letter to Michael:

"Nereus is sold—she fetched $21,000. Good riddance."[26]

~ *O*ne would like a clearer picture of the "mutiny" on the *Nereus* during her last voyage around the Horn under Grace management. What measures did the men take? What measures did old Herbert take? How was it that he regained, or was handed back, his authority? The Callao house, reporting the incident to W. R. Grace, touched on none of these details, and, moreover, frankly indicated a belief that the captain's story was fishy. The fact that Michael Grace did not write personally, but entrusted the task to a clerk, appears to confirm this. To Callao the affair seemed mainly to establish the ineptitude of the superannuated captain and the fact that none of his officers was "worth a cent." The Callao house gave Herbert a new crew, but apparently took no steps toward the punishment of the alleged mutineers.[27]

An idea of what may happen in a case of sure-enough mutiny is provided by Captain Law of the *Great Pacific*, though he does not throw much light on the cause of the affair. A mutiny might be due to several causes. As intimated before, seamen of the period were a rough lot, often rebellious by nature; and the life they lived was little calculated to bring out the kindlier side of their characters. One Cape Horn skipper (not in the Grace employ) advised a mate that it would be unwise to strike a man on the temple with a belaying pin. And, once a man was down, he should be kicked only on the legs or above the short ribs, it being a waste of money to disable a seaman completely.

More than other parts of the world, the region of Cape Horn seemed to impregnate the minds of sailors with mutinous thoughts, and small wonder. The log of a down-easter described a scene off the Horn in language few professional stylists could improve: "The force of the wind was so great that the ocean smoked, and one could not see the jibboom for spume, which flew through the air like steam." A phosphorescent quality of the misty atmosphere sometimes would make the rigging glow, producing an eerie effect: and seamen are superstitious people. Snow, sleet, beds of slush seven feet deep, and howling gales were ordinary features of a winter passage. Even during calms a deep swell gave the ocean the appearance of frothing oil. Many ships were lost in those dangerous calms.[28]

In a letter written at Valparaiso to Michael Grace, Captain Law described his difficulties:

"The mutiny of my crew compelled me to bear for this port. I anchored here last night & have sent my crew to prison. . . .

"[When the trouble started] we were in 97.45 W & 37 S 14 days out from Callao. . . . I had only about 2 charges of gun powder which I divided into 5 and not having balls broke up a patent sheave and took the rollers to put in my horse pistols." A sheave is the wheel in a block; the "rollers" the captain speaks of were roller-bearings. Law thus prepared to force the issue only after the four officers, unaided, had sailed the ship for twenty-four hours. Law himself seems to have kept two of the weapons, capable, as they were, of firing only one shot each. The other three pistols he handed to the three mates. Then, continues the captain: "Gave the mutineers 2 hours to consider the matter."

Before that time was up "a terrific squall struck us. . . . [The officers] were not sufficient in number to heave the ship & put her on the port tack, the sea running too high. We were under two lower topsails & fore mast stay-sail. The wind shifted with the squall, carried away my foretop [and] the staysail. The ship broached too and was only saved [from being dismasted] by the men and I coming to terms instantly." The ex-mutineers squared the main yard, bringing the ship under control.

An indication that the men had not been wholly at fault in the first instance appears in Law's statement that his officers were "unfit for their positions." As soon as competent mates could be found, Law said he would get his crew out of jail and proceed to New York.

"Kindly remember me to Mrs. Grace & all enquiring friends."[29]

~ Jf anything, Captain Law overdoes the literary virtue of succinctness—a failing not evident in the communications of R. C. Mears, master of the ship *Florella*, of which Grace was part owner. As nearly as I can, and still be clear, I shall relate Captain Mears's adventures in the captain's own language, so that you may get the story somewhat as Grace got it at his desk in New York. You will observe that Captain Mears was no scholar; but he was a brave man, cool and resourceful in the face of danger. You may note also that here again some of a captain's troubles were due to incompetent mates—and, in one instance, to a mate who was a villain to boot.

Captain Mears took command of the *Florella* at San Francisco and loaded her with railroad timbers for Chimbote, Peru. His instructions then were to take a cargo of guano to Charleston, South Carolina.

At sea on May 25, 1872, he wrote his employer an account of the voyage to that time:

"I sailed from San Francisco on the 22nd of April after waiting . . . one week for a crew." Because inducements for seamen to desert in California were still strong, San Francisco was a notorious port for crimping. That some of the *Florella*'s crew may have come on board involuntarily is intimated by their subsequent behavior. "On the 1st of May," the master continued, "we were in Lat 17°13' N, Long 115°27' W. Thar we lost the N. E. trades & took the doldrums or light airs & rain squalls from South to SW, which continued until the 19th. Lat 49°29' N, Long 108° W we took the S. E. trades and crossed the Equator on the 22nd."

Thus, as he wrote, the *Florella* was approximately abreast her destination, though some sixteen hundred miles offshore. In making this wide arc, Mears had followed the customary tack for sailing vessels, taking advantage of favorable winds and currents. The captain touched on the condition of the ship:

"[She] is pretty tight . . . [though] I am sorry to say . . . in a worse condition aloft than I had expected. One of the main topmast crosstrees is broken, fore trusseltrees are all rotten & jibboom rotten and sprang. . . . The topmast backstays & lower riging . . . [are bad]. . . . Hoping you are enjoying good health, I remain with respect."[30]

On August 25, Mears was ready to leave Chimbote, and not sorry for it. The *Florella* carried only two officers besides the captain, and the uneventful run down from San Francisco had proved the worthlessness of both. Mears paid them off at Chimbote. This was not all that happened to the ship's company in Chimbote. "The cook & 6 salors stole the boat &

run away. It cost me 40 soles to get the boat back . . . & I have [only] 3 men & the steward left of the old crew. My carpenter fell down the hold yesterday. . . . He was [disabled and] verry near being killed. . . . I am verry sorry because he was a verry handy man & I need him." Any ship, let alone an old one, had need for a carpenter every day.

Michael Grace sent two mates and five Indians to help work the ship to Callao where fresh crew material was taken on board.[31]

In late November or early December the *Florella* raised anchor at the Chincha Islands and stood on a course for the Horn. Not until February 19, 1873, did Mears have an opportunity to write his employer again. He was then on the opposite side of the continent, in the Atlantic, seven degrees north of the Equator. As he had much to tell, and many other burdens on his hands, Captain Mears did not finish his writing until the following day.

"I thought," he began, "that before this I shold have bin to Charleston, but every thing has worked against my makeing a passage. . . . Out of my crew that I got in Callao 2 of them were sick & have bin no use to me. 3 of the other men that I got thar were almost useless as regards working of a ship as they cold not splice or steer & did not know one roop [rope] from another. . . . Cook . . . did not no enough to boil beef & pork & when I have not cooked myself I have had pretty hard fair. . . . The 2nd officer was worse than none for an officer."

Captain Mears's remarks are almost positive evidence of shanghaiing to fill out the *Florella*'s crew. No shipmaster would have taken such men. Paid so much a head, crimps did not care what they drugged and dragged on board. As a young seaman, Herman Melville tells of a dead man carried by a Liverpool crimp into the forecastle of the ship in which Melville was serving.[32]

"On the 7th of Decr," continued Captain Mears, "1 man fell from the fore topsailyard overboard, his head hitting the channels, killing him instantly. That made me pretty short handed with an old ship whear I had to be verry careful. . . . On the 7th of this month one of . . . [the sick men] died."

Still, thanks to decent weather for that part of the world, and favoring winds, Mears made a good passage of Cape Horn. Then the elements turned against him. From the latitude of the Horn almost to the Equator he had to beat against contrary winds, including a twelve-hour gale.

During the northward beat "on the 15th of Janr. the 2nd officer [Silvester by name], being neither of use or ornament aft, I sent him & his lugage forward whear it seemed that he wold be of more use." That is, Silvester was demoted to seaman. Fortunately, the first mate was "a live stiring fellow" who gave excellent satisfaction. Mears let him keep the day watch and the captain took the second mate's watch at night. Nearing the Equator "the wr. was warm & pleasant & we let them [crewmen not on duty] sleep on deck nights. . . . Things seemed to go on well but, . . . from his [Silvester's] first being turned forward, . . . [the mate and I] observed that there was a difference in the deportment of the men . . . but nothing that we cold take in hand."

On the night the sick seaman died—February 7—the captain noticed a number of crewmen, Silvester among them, lying on deck near the hatch house, but thought nothing of it. On being relieved by the mate early in the morning, Captain Mears turned in, leaving a call for eight A.M. so he could perform the traditional duty of reading the service consigning to the deep the body of Able Seaman J. W. Cromwell. The captain, however, found himself awakened at seven o'clock, by Winnenger, the steward. Winnenger said that he had just told the mate what he, Winnenger, had heard and seen during the night. The mate had said the captain should have the story without delay.

"The steward [said] he was in the main hatch house. . . . [On the deck outside] he hird a earnest conversation in rather a loud whisper going on, so he crept as near them as he cold without attracting thar attention to hear what they were talking about. It was about murdering the mate & myself. . . . [A little later] Silvester . . . knife in hand, . . . com aft to the forward entry of the cabin & to the mates door where he was asleep. But his cowardly heart seems to have failed him thear, & then he com up the starboard side of the poop & aft to look for me. But it seems that at that time I had gon below, as the steward stood up & looked but cold not see me. Silvester went back to the men & told them thar was no chance now. . . . They concluded then to let it go for the present, but took an oath to stick together & murder us before we got to Charleston."

When the steward had finished his account, it was time to call all hands for the last rites for Cromwell. Nothing was omitted from the ceremony sanctioned by custom: "Backed the main topsail, set collors $\frac{1}{2}$ mast, had funeral sirvises & burryed the dead, filled away main yard & stood on our cours." With the entire ship's company on deck and knowledge of how many of them Silvester had contaminated, the two officers must have experienced some anxious moments.

The captain slept no more that day, which was Sunday. He and the mate talked things over, but could settle on no plan for taking the plotters. The only men of whose loyalty they were sure were the steward, the carpenter (happily recovered from his fall at Chimbote), and an aged seaman named William Thompson who had been beaten because he would not join the mutineers. "So I told the mate I wold stand wach as usual & we wold show no signs of surspicion—that things might go until Monday, when we cold form a plan to take & secure them. . . .

"Evry thing passed off through the night as usual except a little more stiring around on the deck & talking together. . . . At breckfast I told the mate that . . . by noon I would decide on some plan." By noon Mears had it figured out. "I told the mate . . . to send the men . . . except the sail maker & Wm. Thompson, . . . below to restow salt provisions & clear up the fore peak. . . . The sail maker [George Wissen] we wanted first of all . . . [deeming] him the most guilty of all except Silvester.

"The men being turned too forward, I had the carpenter work on a door in the cabin. All things now being ready, I called the sail maker in the cabin & told him to look in the room and get som canvis. The mate came in rite behind him & shut the cabin door. The mate drew his revolver & I stood by with the irons [and] told him the least nois or one word we wold blow his brains out."

It seemed incredible that Wissen should escape from this trap, but he did.

"His movements were so sudden & unexpected," continued the captain, "that he made a bolt by us & got out on deck, we after him. My pistol missed fire 3 times & the mates also 2 or 3 times. He got to the hatch & give the alarm, but I was so cloas to him that he had to keep on runing. He went around the forward house & . . . made out on the jib boom."

After sending two shots, which missed, after the fleeing sailmaker, the captain dashed aft toward the hatch, for the critical moment was at hand. Should Silvester succeed in leading a charge from the hatch it was altogether possible that the mutineers would carry the day. But the mate, with pistol drawn, and the carpenter had reached the hatch in time. They had the mutineers at bay, and the mate was threatening to shoot the first man to show himself.

Up came Silvester, shouting to the others to follow. The mate let him have it, and the ex-officer tumbled back down the hatch. Somewhat surprisingly, a moment later his arms were thrust up in token of surrender.

When irons were clamped on them, Silvester was hauled on deck—only slightly wounded.

The others submitted without resistance, though George Wissen, the nerviest man of the lot, stayed on the jibboom for twenty-eight hours. By that time, Mears had questioned all the other men separately and had pretty well traced out the history of the conspiracy. As a result, Silvester, Wissen, and two others were locked below in double irons. Mears, and his mate had been in danger almost from the moment Silvester had been sent forward. Perhaps the thing that had saved them was the distrust of some of the mutineers of Silvester's abilities as a navigator.

"This affair of having to confine 4 men tells sadly on the looks of the ship. I was in hopes to have her in good order when we got in. . . . All that I have is the mate & carpenter, cook & steward, Thompson, 2 youngsters & Alfred Jacobs who is sick & I doubt if he will live . . . but I hope in time to bring Charleston all rite."[33]

~ Mutinies had become so common that in 1872, Congress passed the Shipping Act, aimed at freeing sailors from evils that were a principal cause of unrest at sea. W. R. Grace had no part in the agitation that brought about this reform. But in 1876, at any rate, he was sufficiently interested to obtain a copy of the official report of the results of the act's operation in the port of New York. Years after that, when Mr. Grace was in politics on the reform side, he recommended as shipping commissioner for New York a man calculated to discharge his duties zealously.

The report of the commissioner for the year 1875 begins with a review of earlier conditions:

"As the Port of New York was the great centre of the worst abuses perpetrated upon the sailor before the law was enacted, so it has been the great battle-ground in its enforcement. Opposition and obstructions have been encountered here, such as have been unknown elsewhere. A large and powerful combination of sailors' landlords and shipping masters existed which not only dictated to shipowners the seamen they should employ and the rates of wages they should pay, but, at one time, offended by the administration of the Shipping Law, resisted its operation openly and by force. . . .

"The number of ship owners in this port is comparatively small, while the number of ship agents representing . . . vessels visiting this port is very large, and for this reason, any united action on the part of ship owners to resist the pretentions of this combination would have been impracticable. . . .

"When seamen were scarce 'shanghaeing' prevailed. . . . Men from the country, mechanics of every kind, merchants even, would be met in the streets of the city, induced to drink, drugged, boated off to a waiting vessel, represented as good sailors, and while their captors . . . would secure the advance wages of these victims, they would be carried to sea, . . . utterly unfitted for any duty."

Bona fide seamen, too, were the prey of crimps—"shipped while drunk . . . told perhaps that it was to Charleston, and carried to Liverpool or the East Indies. . . . Once at sea and sober . . . it is little wonder that these men were often dissatisfied, insubordinate, and mutinous, and that captains and officers were tyrannical and abusive."

Crimps operated in cahoots with seamen's boardinghouses and other waterfront dives. Often they were the proprietors of such places. Certain shipping masters, shipping agents, and ship captains were parts of the ring, so that from one year's end to another a seaman might see hardly anything of his earnings. Landing with little or no money due him, he could obtain "advance wages" on his next voyage. The advance would be paid to a boardinghouse keeper. "The landlord's interest lay in keeping sailors drunk . . . and this interest was not neglected." When there were more seamen than berths, landlords took "blood money" from sailors for getting them jobs. When seamen were scarce, the landlords held up the shipowners or captains.

After three and a half years of the operation of the Shipping Act, the commissioner claimed that "shanghaeing, fraudulent shipments, fraud in paying seamen their advances or in paying them off have ceased to exist. Seamen of bad character, mutinous and insubordinate, have to a great extent been weeded out. . . .

"Ill treatment of seamen on shipboard is of rare occurrence.

"Captains may see and thoroughly examine seamen before engaging them.

"Seamen are . . . questioned as to the fairness of their settlement by their landlords, and every injustice that is shown is corrected on the spot. . . .

"The mutinies, riots and fighting which prevailed under the old system are now unknown."

The commissioner admitted a few shortcomings:

"Blood, or bonus, money is still surreptitiously demanded and received by certain ship agents, owners and masters. . . .

"The system of advance wages . . . exists . . . in part. Steamships have almost entirely abandoned it; and there seems no good reason why the owners of sailing vessels may not follow an example so wise."[34]

Though the commissioner painted things in too bright colors, progress had been made. Accounts of mutinies were much rarer. I have seen no reference to one in a Grace ship, after the *Florella* trouble. The Shipping Act had no force outside the jurisdiction of the United States. Conditions remained bad, particularly in South American and Far Eastern ports. For more than a generation to come, a seaman had no bed of roses.

8 ~ Riding Out the Storm

~ At the beginning of 1873 the financial skies looked dark in every quarter. To meet its engagements, W. R. Grace & Co. was dipping into surplus and into the private funds of the senior partner. The crisis in Peru, brought on by railroad financing, had embarrassed entirely solvent customers there. The tightening of the money market at home and in Europe had its effect. John Bryce's London bank, never much help, was of even less assistance now. "Don't draw on me," was the familiar refrain. Yet the Bryces, particularly Francis, did not hesitate to draw on Bryce, Grace & Co. in Callao, which in turn drew on W. R. Grace & Co. in New York.

All told, demands on the New York house were heavier than ever. Capital had to be found for the new San Francisco branch, J. W. Grace & Co. In Costa Rica, Keith and Guardia begged for more credit. And the worst offender against the rules of prudence was Michael, in charge of the Callao house—or so W. R. Grace reasoned before he was to ferret out the truth about John Bryce and his bank. The Callao house owed the New York house $157,000. Altogether Callao owed $830,000, and had $692,000 owing it. Those were the figures as of December 31, 1872. A considerable amount of Callao's debts W. R. Grace believed uncollectable, particularly $178,000 due from Henry Meiggs.[1]

Such was the situation that had prompted William's stiff letter to Michael on learning of the year-end condition of the Callao house.[2]

Perhaps the letter did Michael some good, though he seems to have bettered his situation before it arrived. In any event by April 12, 1873, he had improved matters considerably with reference to Meiggs, whose account was the one William feared most. On that date the railroad builder's unsecured indebtedness to the house was down to 89,000 *soles*—at normal exchange about $84,500. Meiggs kept pleading with Grace not to desert him: "I shall look out for Michael in all circumstances." As time passed William began to feel easier about Meiggs, and continued to send down railroad materials. "Meiggs just paid us £5000 on a/c," wrote Michael in August '73, trying to keep his brother cheerful.[3]

In their relations with Meiggs the Grace houses found involuntary but useful allies in President Pardo of Peru and in Dreyfus Frères of Paris. This was not because the Peruvian government or its French bankers were partial to Grace. It was because they had a bear by the tail and dared not turn loose. If Meiggs went, about everything in Peru would go. To throw out of work the twenty thousand men employed on the railroads, to stop their pay amounting to a million *soles* monthly, would precipitate a new economic crisis and probably a political revolution. So it was up to Pardo and Dreyfus to keep Meiggs afloat as long as they could, hoping that some turn of events would point a way out.

The Callao house was far more deeply involved with Peru's new sugar industry than with Meiggs. In his commentary on the 1872 statement, William had alluded critically to the fact that Francis Bryce and Emiliano Llona owed $132,000. The money had been advanced to get under way their sugar plantation and grinding mill at Santa Clara, in the Lima region. Other sugar estates financed by Bryce, Grace & Co. were those of Alzamora at Cartavio, and of Canaval at Paramonga, both in the north of Peru. Wha' these two owed early in '73 does not appear but, with Michael extending credit constantly, it had grown to nearly $600,000 by August of 1874.

Michael had great faith in the future of sugar in Peru, and this appears to have been shared to some extent by William. In 1873, Michael wrote his brother an optimistic account of the prospects. The bulk of the crop was exported to England. Some of the machinery Grace was buying for the planters and refiners came from there; the rest, from Belgium and the United States. Michael thought this trade enough to warrant the establishment of a Grace house in London or Liverpool. He, himself, hoped to be able to do this when the present partnership agreement with the Bryces in the Callao house would expire in 1876. At that time the Graces expected to dispense with those unhelpful partners.

Michael seemed right about the sugar business, which, with nitrates, presented the only moderately bright spot in the troubled economy of Peru. Though the government was preparing to take over the nitrate industry to replace fading guano, sugar remained in private hands. Within three years' time it had grown from almost nothing to the third export of Peru. The product was of superior quality. Production costs were low, once the heavy initial expense of getting machinery on the ground was out of the way. Plantations and mills were manned by Chinese contract laborers who received next to nothing in the way of pay.[4]

Notwithstanding somewhat favorable prospects, Michael's continued advances to the sugar people made things all the harder for William, who was holding the bag in New York.

～ ℐn September came the calamity that for years was to hold the world in the grip of hard times: the panic of '73. The match to the fuse was the failure of Jay Cooke & Co. of Philadelphia, dragged under by efforts to finance the construction of the Northern Pacific Railroad.

The first reverberation of the crash to reach Peru toppled the banking house of Bianchi Brothers. The principal partner fled to Ecuador. Michael reported his house's loss not "worth mentioning," and correctly predicted the action that averted financial chaos. "The Banks, Government, Dreyfus, Meiggs and all the commercial houses well connected in London are too much interested to allow everyone to come down." Banding together, they gave Peru's financial structure an appearance of solvency, which was better than nothing.

A month later the usually sanguine Michael wrote that his life was a "nightmare." What troubled him deepest was William's critical situation in New York, for which Michael knew himself to be largely responsible. "The fact is no documents can be turned into cash at this moment, and altho we have abundance of all sorts of documents we cannot raise funds. Every house in Peru is so placed. . . . Consequently . . . our efforts to remit largely and to assist you have been in vain." Michael promised to "stop everything . . . until we pay you." "On no consideration" would he draw on his brother for "another cent, . . . [and] I won't sleep sound until I can relieve you. . . . Margarita has been very sick. I have taken her to Chosica."

Touched by his brother's distress, William wrote not to be "so blue tho' I doubt not there is great & serious cause for it." He said that the New York house had survived the first and worst shock of the panic. "We are out of all danger & have to thank our friends here and the Bank. . . . Notwithstanding that independent of Llonas a/c . . . B. G. & Co owe us today at least Two hundred and ten thousand dollars . . . we will try & be as light as we can on you in the immediate future."[5]

William's version of the fight to raise cash for his engagements was modest. Mortgages on Gracefield and the town house were details he failed to mention.

Early in 1874, W. R. Grace sent Charley Flint to Costa Rica to extract some money from President Guardia which Grace had advanced as a personal loan. From there Flint proceeded to Peru, and reported on various matters. All that the government and the big bankers were able to do had failed to stay the financial paralysis that was creeping over the world. Despite a virtual moratorium on private debts, one Lima house after another was closing. What the government, Dreyfus, and others did do, however, was to keep Meiggs going by a succession of financial improvisations. And Meiggs sustained the government. Pardo was able to put down an armed rebellion headed by Nicolás de Piérola, the cabinet officer under Balta who had worked closest with Meiggs. Had Don Enrique lifted his hand, as some had counted on, the insurrection might easily have triumphed.

"Bryce Grace & Co As far as I can see will not lose anything by Meiggs," wrote Flint. And later: "Meiggs owes the house today only S/38,000."[6]

Whatever his failings, Don Enrique was no fair-weather sailor. Disaster did not daunt him. One would have to read his most private correspondence to know how near the brink he had been since late in 1872, for it could not have been guessed by the face he displayed to the world. It is not too much to believe that but for Henry Meiggs's fortitude, Pardo and Dreyfus would have thrown in the sponge long ago. In the light of hindsight that would have been the sensible thing. One can follow a forlorn hope too far.

An old device of the hard-pressed financial adventurer is to bring a new rabbit out of the hat. In the spring of '74, Meiggs launched the Compañía de Obras Publicas y Fomento del Peru. One of the objects of the Public Works Co. was to make over the city of Lima. Since Grace had gone there in 1851, the capital of Peru had more than doubled in population. It was the home of a hundred thousand people. The city had overrun the old military wall and spread haphazardly down the valley to the Rímac. Meiggs visualized a planned and ordered city, with magnificent through boulevards, streetcars, gaslights, sewage and waterworks systems, and up-to-date homes for working people. Don Enrique said that he would live to see the day when Lima, with five million population, would be the metropolis of the Pacific.[7]

The technical head of the new enterprise was William H. Cilley, then also superintendent of the Oroya railroad. Charley Flint, who had known Cilley in Maine, landed the American agency for Obras Públicas for W. R.

Grace & Co. Spinney had expected it, and that was the beginning of the rift between him and Grace. It is strange how this fantastic scheme revived drooping spirits in Peru. The infectious charm and force of personality of Don Enrique penetrated even the hard hide of Charley Flint. "Meiggs will throw his whole future into this Co." which "is run differently" from the railroads. "Don Enrique with all his good heart . . . does not make his decisions according to his feelings, but as his judgment dictates." Nor did Grace's shrewd young negotiator give way to sentiment entirely: "I however do not advocate giving credit to this company at present. . . . Conditions will be cash in N. Y. before shipment."[8]

How Meiggs managed to pay cash is not known. At the time the Public Works Co. was inaugurated, the Peruvian government managed a new guano contract with Dreyfus under which the bankers would service the country's foreign debt for another fifteen months. Though a connection between those two events is unlikely, the debt arrangement was a breather for all concerned in Peru.

The Public Works Co. contract was good news. Yet obviously it could not amount to enough to rescue the Grace houses from a situation that grew progressively worse due to the deepening of the worldwide depression, the uncooperative attitude of John Bryce, and Michael's credit policies. Despite the promise not to draw another cent on New York, the indebtedness of the Callao house steadily increased. Michael was too deeply involved in sugar to cease his advances. Thus, in June 1874, Callao owed New York $258,000, exclusive of the Llona-Bryce sugar account—by this time reduced to $110,000—which William had taken over.

This could not go on. William's own need for liquid funds once more was acute. New York banks which had come to the aid of W. R. Grace & Co. in 1873 could not be depended on forever. William wrote his brother a serious and solemn letter:

"The sum you owe my house in New York is unjust to them & entirely disproportionate to the capital of the N. Y. house. . . . A time has now come when they must refuse to execute orders or make payments for their lack of funds. . . . In actual self defense, that a/c must be reduced to 50 to 100 thousand dollars." William gave explicit instructions as to how this should be done. "All your energies must be concentrated to collect monies in & . . . realize debts even at a loss." The Callao warehouses contained goods valued at $336,000. "Sell merchandise for cash without profit, dispose of all municipal bonds, dock shares etc. and get cash in hand."[9]

~ Before ordering Michael to go to work digging himself out, William had provided a safeguard for Callao in the form of a credit for £60,000 on the great English bankers, Baring Brothers. This was for emergency use only. Before the Baring credit should be broken into to any extent, William determined that John Bryce, for once, should lend a helping hand.

When times were flush and the Callao house was making a profit of 100 percent a year on its capital, John Bryce had scooped up his share and spent it on luxurious living in Europe. When the squeeze came in 1873, the Grace brothers had been obliged to put a good deal of their own profits back into the business. The Bryces had put nothing back. Francis Bryce had drawn on the house to pay private debts he owed his brother John. It seemed to William that the Bryces were using the house as too much of a personal convenience. Callao owed New York $368,000—and for practical purposes New York meant W. R. Grace. As partners in the Callao firm, the Bryces were responsible for their share of that debt. Francis Bryce was too deep in sugar to help. But, judging by his scale of living, John was differently situated. So William went after John in earnest.

"Now is the time to take hold and do something," he wrote, after reciting what the New York house had done. William asked that John Bryce's General South American Co. place £20,000 to Callao's credit and obtain another £15,000 from some other source. At the same time, William wrote Michael to stop "helping Francis to pay off John."[10]

John Bryce refused to advance anything until the Callao house should cover drafts on the Bryce bank, totaling £40,000, which would fall due at different periods within the next sixty days. William wrote again, more urgently. When no satisfactory answer to this came, Grace and his wife took a steamer for England.[11]

On October 14, 1874, the Graces arrived at Marley, the Bryce estate in Devonshire, where William received a surprise. Grace had calculated that motives of selfishness, mainly, had been responsible for John Bryce's attitude. Now it appeared that the old man was in reality strapped for funds. He apologized for the tone of his recent letters, saying that they had been "written under great mental pressure." To this Mrs. Bryce added that her husband had been "partly out of his head." The banker exhibited a list of assets, aggregating £180,000, which he said were tied up by the depression. After another talk, it developed that John was not too hard up to help. At any rate, Grace got his partner to promise credit of £20,000 on the General South American Co. and one for £15,000 on himself personally.

Thus, Grace thought his mission completed: "BG&Co should be able to get on nicely & comfortably."[12]

Next day a word dropped by Mrs. Bryce aroused Grace's suspicion that he had not got to the bottom of the matter after all. There followed another session with Bryce in which Grace drew forth an appalling story. The bank was in worse shape than the banker. In fact, the General South American Co. was little more than a shell. "They are living from steamer to str under heavy discount & liable at any time to fall." Nearly all the bank's business was with South America. So depleted were its ready funds that the institution's fate from day to day virtually depended on whether a ship brought more remittances to collect than drafts to pay. Thus, Bryce's reiterated plea for Callao to remit and not to draw.[13]

Painstakingly, William went into the bank's condition, which was in every way desperate. The main cause for this had to do with backing speculative enterprises in South America, such as William had long urged Michael, without too much success, to keep clear of. Another factor was the frozen condition of good assets in the hands of South American clients. Finally, there was the stupidity, and worse, of John Bryce and other directors of the bank. The bank had paid prodigious dividends that had not been earned. Some insiders had thus been able to sell their shares at fancy prices and get out. John Bryce lived on a scale of $100,000 a year. He had transferred to his sons assets worth $600,000.[14]

Such a bank deserved to fail, and if the failure had been on Bryce's head solely perhaps William Grace might not have concerned himself a great deal about it. But the blow would not fall on Bryce alone, for Bryce was a partner, nominally the senior partner, of Bryce, Grace & Co. of Callao. Thus, Callao's credit would be seriously impaired. Very probably the Barings would withdraw their support. Should Callao go under, what would happen to Callao's chief creditor, W. R. Grace & Co. in New York? The possibilities were not agreeable to contemplate.

In the most critical situation of his life, W. R. Grace turned first to measures calculated to save the threatened bank, or, at any rate, postpone and diminish the shock of its end. After going over the figures with Bryce, he urged several steps. One was that the stockholders be assembled at once and heavily assessed. Old Bryce was so shaken that it was hard to get him to do anything. Particularly he shrank from a revelation of the bank's condition to the shareholders. But at length he consented, and seemed somewhat relieved to have Grace's steady hand and clear head working for him. Perhaps in consideration of this, he allowed to stand the two Grace credits, aggregating £35,000 that had been promised the day before.[15]

Over a period of nearly three weeks, meetings were held in Paris and in London to get the stockholders to "pony up," as Grace put it, £80,000 to support the bank. During that time, Grace underwent the deepest anxieties of his business career. Hope rose and fell. There were times when he thought the measures he had set in motion might save the bank permanently. In that case all would pull through—in London, Paris, Callao, New York, and San Francisco. It was now necessary to include San Francisco in the picture, for, as if in proof of the adage that trouble never comes singly, word had been received of John Grace's involvement there. At other times, things looked so black that the only chance of salvaging anything seemed to lie in strengthening the New York house and letting the rest go. All along, Grace was getting new light on the operations of John Bryce. In Grace's opinion, the nature of these affairs entitled Bryce to no sympathy and no help. When John Bryce had seen his bank going down, he had coldly drawn on Callao, which was obliged, in turn, to draw on New York.

With considerable difficulty, Grace kept up an appearance of friendly personal relations with the banker, and pretended not to be offended by what had gone on. In this way, Grace stood a better chance to work off Bryce, Grace & Co.'s debt to the New York house, and prepare that house to survive a catastrophe. Writing in the Hotel du Louvre in Paris, between frantic bank meetings—"I am inclined, with the crowd that surrounds me, to be half demoralized myself"—Grace sent out his instructions. Michael was to cease his remittances to London, and remit to New York instead. Both Callao and New York were to draw on London. "My plan . . . is to secure WRG&Co anyhow and BG&Co too if we possibly can." If only New York could be saved, Michael could go there and make "a new start." "We must lean on ourselves alone."

Flint and Moody in New York were urged to conserve the firm's funds, and to do no business except for cash. Grace also took steps to put what was left of his personal estate in order. It had been impossible to keep some of the bad news from Mrs. Grace, who wrote her mother to "economise." Reporting his health "fair, I may say good," Grace added that "this trouble has taken the flesh off my wife's bones."[16]

With the bank propped up temporarily, at least, Mr. and Mrs. Grace took a week off to visit Grace's sisters in Nice. "The sun shines brightly and things look charmingly," he wrote Moody, "but I have no special pleasure in them as my mind is half the time turned to matters in Peru."[17]

How well had Michael performed the tasks delegated to him? Grace sailed for Peru to find out. At Panama three days before Christmas 1874, he received a large bundle of mail. The news it contained was better than he had dared to hope. Michael had come through in fine style.

Callao's debt to New York had been cut from $368,000 to $155,620. The completion of pending transactions would bring it to $23,120.

Bryce, Grace & Co. would be out of the General South American Co.'s hands by January. Failure of the bank after that date would involve the Callao house only in the way of prestige, the Bryces being partners. Steps to minimize that had been taken by arrangements to preserve the good name of Grace with Baring Brothers.

Michael had moved to protect the Grace interests in the matter of Francis Bryce's indebtedness, by obtaining mortgages on Francis's property.[18]

William spent three months in Peru finishing what Michael had started and, in general, putting the Callao house to rights. In April, while William was on his way to New York, the General South American Co. went into voluntary liquidation. Most of the losses were borne by those who deserved to bear them—an outcome much better, even for them, than the scandalous crash that had seemed inevitable before Grace had tackled the problem six months earlier. Sustained by the Baring credit, the Callao and New York houses were scarcely affected. The following year, 1876, the partnership agreement of Bryce, Grace & Co. expired. The Bryces were dropped from the firm, which took the title of Grace Brothers & Co.

~ The Grace houses still had their problems, the thorniest of which were bound up with the state of affairs in Peru. Though these grew worse by the day, as long as Henry Meiggs kept going there was a spark of business life. The question was, how long could Meiggs last?

His shot-in-the-arm Public Works Co. was fizzling out. "Doing no profitable business here & is not likely to do any," was the way W. R. Grace sized it up before he left the scene.

Grace would have liked to help Meiggs—but how? While a guest at Meiggs's seventy-room residence in Lima, Grace came down with dysentery. He remained until he had recovered, obviously touched by the warm human qualities of his host. "I write from the house of Don Enrique Meiggs & the ladies of the family desire special love & regards to Mr. Flint."

But to business. "The position of our friends to M's is very critical. They leave their men unpaid today, Saturday, for the first time, although they have in hand . . . an acceptance of Dreyfus at 6 months for 25,000$ [which] can't be discounted at any price, . . . another of F. B. [Francis Bryce] for 12,000$ & 300,000$ Treasury Bonds, yet they can't borrow 60,000$ to tide them over this week. They telegraph MPG to come up & help them. . . . They believe him to be the Grand Financier."[19]

Whether Michael was able to thaw money out of the frozen banks on the strength of Meiggs's collateral does not appear. Yet the men were paid something and the railroad work went on after a fashion. The Peruvian government, however, was getting to the end of the last strand of its rope. The question of recognizing the inevitable and ordering a stoppage of Meiggs's operations was seriously discussed in the Congress. Meanwhile, Meiggs, and all he could gather about him, dreamed up various schemes. The "grand financier," Michael, sat in at some of the sessions. He submitted to William one proposal, calculated to raise 6 million *soles,* no less, "all to continue Meiggs Rail Roads."[20]

Ninety days later, in August 1875, the government suspended the work. The railroads that were to bring forth in realizable form the great natural riches of Peru had bankrupted the country.

With Dreyfus declining to come to the rescue again, in January 1876, Peru defaulted interest on its foreign debt. A year later payment was suspended on some of the domestic debt.

With most business in a state of coma, the Peruvian sugar industry made encouraging strides. In 1875 exports were double those of the year before. The plantations were keeping up interest on their debts and beginning to pare down the principal. Thus, in the matter in which the Graces had the most at stake in Peru, the tide seemed to have turned. They held mortgages on the three estates with which they were involved: Canaval, Alzamora, and Llona-Bryce. Through an *interventor,* they virtually operated the Alzamora property. In August 1875, Canaval began reducing its indebtedness of $258,000 by monthly payments. The Alzamora account already had been scaled from $458,000 to $343,000. Though having the hardest time of the three, Llona-Bryce had reduced its load from $110,000 to $101,000.[21]

In 1876, President Manuel Pardo went out of office broken and beaten. At one time this man had been the hope of Peru, with a truly enlightened economic policy based on the construction of railroads. But he had come into power too late. His successor, Mariano Prado, will be remembered as having been president before, and, as such, the sponsor of Manuel Pardo's ineffectual attempts at reform in the sixties.

With the country embarked on a regime of printing-press currency, worth 10 percent of par, what could Mariano Prado do now?

For one thing, he could listen to Henry Meiggs, who was contriving his last cast for fortune.

Simply stated, Meiggs's project was to put Peru on its feet financially: enable it to resume service on the debt and to redeem the flood of paper in coin. The copper and silver to do this lay in the Cerro de Pasco mines, flooded and inaccessible for purposes of large-scale operation. Meiggs's engineer Cilley reported $70 million in silver available above the water line—and he was probably correct. Meiggs would complete the Oroya road to the mines; pump out the mines; work them. And he would meet all, or nearly all, the costs himself. To Michael Grace the old gambler spoke vaguely of capital "from London & California." John G. Meiggs was abroad looking for money. He had taken his wife's savings to make the trip.[22]

Sixty-six years of age and in poor health, Henry Meiggs drew on his dwindling strength and means to promote the scheme in his old style. There were bribes for editors and public men. A contract was signed with the Peruvian government in February 1877.

Work started on a small scale and the workmen were paid with a new kind of currency called *billetes de Meiggs*—Don Enrique's private money. By the same means some work was resumed on the railroads. An outcry by bankers and merchants went up against the *billetes*, though they were supported to some extent by government bonds that Meiggs owned.

Michael Grace, however, was not taking this brand of money on the Meiggs account, which he kept close to a cash basis. This irritated young Charles Watson, who had succeeded J. G. Meiggs as Don Enrique's business manager. Watson was married to a niece of his patron. Watson's letters to J. S. Spinney exuded complaints: "I expect the Graces have had something to do with [injuring] Don Enrique's credit in New York." "I expect your neighbors W R Grace & Co will make the most . . . of our misfortunes. We have however paid *them every thing* they could scrape up against us."[23]

By this time, interest in the health of Don Enrique began to overshadow that in his monetary problems. Shortly before the signing of the Cerro de Pasco contract, Michael had reported Henry "sick again." His heart was giving way. But he worked on: infusing hope in those about him; painting dazzling pictures of the wealth that one day would flood down from the mountains. Early in August, he had a sharp attack. Propped against pillows, unable to sleep, and fighting for breath, Meiggs pondered the question of the *billetes*. Five hundred thousand *soles* in the right hands produced a government decree making his money legal—within the limit of S/5,333,333.[24]

Eleven days after the legalization of the *billetes,* Michael informed his brother: "Meiggs has been reported below remedy. I trust not." Nearly all Peru, including those who saw his faults more clearly than Michael, trusted not. On September 13, Michael reported: "Meiggs still lives but it is thought that he cannot recover." On the 21st: "Meiggs cannot recover." In the dark hours of the morning of September 30, church bells tolled. The street in front of the seventy-room house filled with people until one could hardly get through. Mostly they were laboring people, come to mourn the passing of one they believed had been their disinterested friend.[25]

~ While events were running their course in Peru, W. R. Grace had the Costa Rica railroad on his hands. Full of wind and whisky, Henry Meiggs Keith had proved an utter fool—with all the weaknesses of his uncle, and none of the talents. Any chance of finishing the road seemed to depend on Guillermo Nanne, the German general manager, and H. D. B. Norris, the American chief engineer—each of whom reported confidentially to Grace.

In June 1873, Grace wrote Michael that the first step should be to get rid of Henry Keith. A month later this was done, with the approval of the Meiggses in Peru. Keith appeared in New York, the picture of importance and indignation, and went on to London to raise millions of pounds and redeem everything. Grace's love of family life was always involving him in the domestic affairs of those who surrounded him. Keith had left his wife and a new baby in Brooklyn. Mrs. Grace and Mrs. John G. Meiggs, who was visiting in New York, did what they could to make them comfortable while Grace looked after the young mother's finances. After keeping pleasantly tight in England for nearly a year, Keith rattled about New York for another year, and then died. "[Though] I can't help feeling sorry for him," Grace wrote, "his wife, I fancy, thinks it a great relief."[26]

By this time (1875), Costa Rica was a mess for fair. After Keith had been dispensed with, Nanne and Norris kept the work going and President Guardia provided funds. These were so limited that it was a fight for anyone to get paid—a fight that Grace, for his part, usually won. The government defaulted on its early bond issues because, as Nanne assured Grace, it had been "fearfully swindled" by usurious English bankers. Grace rather agreed with Nanne on that point, and complimented Guardia on his ability to continue the work without recourse to paper money, as in Peru. Grace still had some confidence in Nanne, and promised to keep materials going forward as long as Guardia could raise money to pay for them.[27]

The thin ice on which the whole business rested broke in 1876. Guardia retired from the presidency with half a million dollars, leaving the new administration in such a fix that with difficulty it borrowed $50,000 at 18 percent per annum. Norris and Nanne quit or were discharged, and Grace's connection as a supplier for the railroad came to an end.

At the same time, Grace was dealing with the younger Keith brother, Minor C. It may be recalled that M. C. Keith & Co. held the commissary concession for the railroad. Properly managed, such concessions were always profitable. In addition, Minor had branched out in trade on his own. He was one of the early exporters of bananas, for which Americans as yet had had insufficient opportunity to cultivate a taste.

In the early days it was difficult to separate the activities of the Keith brothers. In his grandiloquent way, Henry did the talking for both. Thus, Grace formed a poor opinion of Minor Keith, who had gone to Costa Rica as a youth of twenty-two, devoid of business experience and over-shadowed by his incompetent brother. Credit was extended sparingly to M. C. Keith & Co. To cover a debt, Minor turned over to Grace an interest in a Texas cattle ranch. Time and again Minor insisted that his house and the railroad were distinct concerns. His letters were one long plea, mostly in vain, for more credit. Grace wrote in 1875: "Minor Keith, I have not a spec of faith in him."[28]

Early in 1876, when Grace was getting out of the Costa Rica rail-road, he sent Arthur K. Brown to Central America to report on several matters. Brown sensed from the atmosphere of the New York house that nothing very favorable was expected in connection with Minor Keith. In Panama, Brown reported Keith in heavy trouble, due to unpaid accounts with the railroad—Keith not being as good a collector as W. R. Grace. Nevertheless, added Brown, "M. C. Keith & Co. have the confidence of everybody with whom I have spoken."

After his first look about in Limón, Brown still wrote with reserve. Keith paid his debts. Brown had talked to some of the laborers who were cutting railroad ties for Keith. Their wages might get four months behind, but Mr. Keith always paid up; and they liked him. Brown found the books of Keith's firm "clear and in good order."

A week later Brown had learned more about his man: "He is not only the pillar of the place [Limón], but the *place itself*; without him . . . [it] would cease to exist in a week." He sustained the railroad, feeding its workers and supplying materials. A washwoman could bring to his store a bill against someone in the railroad camp, and Keith would have it collected. On one occasion, Keith "at his own expense" had saved the Negro railroad workers "from starvation." This was a part of a long record that made Keith more powerful than the authorities. When a fire threatened Keith's store and warehouses, the workmen had turned out in force and saved them.

At the end of two months the investigator was Keith's open champion: "I cannot conceive it possible for a man to live within ten miles of Minor C. Keith & not be impressed by his honesty & business capacity. . . . I have written my opinions . . . [knowing that I am] running the risk of being . . . positively censored in your office."[29]

Mr. Brown was not censored; nor was his advice heeded. W. R. Grace & Co. cut off its credit to Minor Keith and let his drafts for $10,000 go to protest. In the face of this crushing blow Keith, then only twenty-six, wrote with manly restraint: "We do not think it w as right to dishonor our name, especially when we would have had remittances to more than cover all our deficiency inside of three months. . . . If we were *not sound* we would frankly let you know it."[30]

Six months later Norris, on a trip for Grace, saw Keith in Limón. "Poor fellow I pity him, he has shown such pluck in holding on and trying to pull through."[31] He did pull through, making his name a subject for legend. Keith took over the railroad and finished it; turned the malarial swamps back of Limón into a banana plantation; expanded all over Central America; and built up the largest business institution in that part of the world—the United Fruit Co.

The throwing over of Minor C. Keith seems W. R. Grace's greatest error of judgment in business.

9 ~ The Pacific War

~ At one time or another in the lean years from 1873 to '78, the shadow of bankruptcy was across the paths of most business-men. "I do feel uneasy about it," W. R. Grace confessed, "especially when I see stronger & better houses that have had to succumb." But once Grace had the Meiggs business on a footing so that its inevitable collapse would not drag down the Callao house as it dragged down nearly everything else with which it was concerned, and once the Bryce bank failure had been weathered, the Grace firms did very well.[1]

This was due to the sagacity of the senior partner, who, in the easy days of railroad and guano money, had broadened the base of his opera-tions by establishing in articles of everyday use a commerce that would survive the boom. He sent Hazen, Ned Eyre, and even Michael, up and down the coast and into the interior to find out what people wanted and could afford. He had Charley Flint go over the ground with a fresh eye and a more intimate knowledge of the resources of the American market. Par-ticularly he desired a foothold in Chile, where trade opportunities were ahead of those in Peru, and where imports had been virtually cornered by the English.

In this way, Grace introduced Singer sewing machines, McCormick reapers, and Fairbanks scales to the west coast of South America. Eventu-ally he established a considerable business in household furniture, though in the desert nitrate port of Iquique, at any rate, this was slow work. Flint found a local retailer overstocked with hat racks which he could not give away: "[Iquique] is not up to such improvements." Nevertheless, Hazen landed a contract for a theater to adorn "that lovely place." Grace agreed to supply a building—complete with "stage, scenery, curtains, etc., dressing and waiting rooms, store and barrooms," and seats for twelve hundred. Almost any roof would do, Hazen said, because it never rained in Iquique.[2]

125

Grace sold more lumber than anything else. Most of it was Oregon pine. He had made his contacts with the sources of supply during the railroad heydey, and apparently could underbid anyone else doing business on the coast. Within a few years, Grace had nearly $400,000 tied up in lumber alone.

Yet the strength of this trade lay in its variety. One almost interminable letter of Flint's not only mentioned but discussed above a hundred items. It read like a dissertation on the inventory of a country store: lard, tallow, fish, canned goods, crackers, kerosene, lamps, pails, tubs, shoe pegs, brooms, tobacco, nails, cotton cloth, butter, cookstoves, condensed milk, saddles for mules, pitch, tar, rope, resin, "small hardware." English competition was stiff all along the line. Among other things, Flint called their hams, paint, codfish, nails, rope, oilcloth, and cement "better" or "cheaper" than ours. There were suggestions for packing, branding, and stowing. To meet English competition, crackers should be in five-pound tins. Buckets should have three hoops; and brooms, painted handles.[3]

The building of such a diversified business represented hard, close work, and much disagreeable travel. It was one thing to sit in comfortable offices in Callao; another, to put up with the accommodations for transients found elsewhere on that coast, Valparaiso excepted. Once a market had been carefully studied, the Grace method was to select a local agent. In Peru's second city, beautiful Arequipa, Flint lined up H. W. Harmson & Co., the leading mercantile house. In the Peruvian nitrate port of Pisagua the agent was the mayor, who had the un-Spanish name of J. D. Campbell. Mr. Campbell was also a merchant and banker.

After having formed these excellent connections, Flint's reception in Santiago de Chile was a shock: "Of course in Peru . . . [we] are one of the powers that be. . . . Here . . . [we] have no position. . . . I have met a number of the merchants of this city, and I have only found one who had ever heard of the house." Flint did what he could to correct that condition. He recommended a change of agents, and went over the market with a fine-tooth comb. Before long Grace was shipping lumber, and plenty of it, into the Chilean capital under the noses of his English rivals.[4]

It should be borne in mind that these achievements were against a background of unusual economic circumstances—in Peru, that is: Chile's finances and general economy were in good shape, conditions considered. Before the death of Henry Meiggs, Peru had been in desperate straits so long that the condition was accepted as almost normal. With the passing of Don Enrique the state of affairs became chaotic. Yet, if hope is the most easily acquired of the virtues, Latin Americans are exceptionally virtuous people. In a country as naturally rich as Peru, it can never be so dark that there is no gleam somewhere.

The "discovery" of great new guano deposits was announced. About all it amounted to was the tapping of Peru's last reserves. Still, interest revived in guano, and Grace Brothers & Co. attempted to obtain the agency for the United States, with the backing of the Barings. When the British bankers declined to cooperate, the matter was dropped rather abruptly, for Grace was contemplating a much more important deal in which he wished the aid of the Barings.[5]

～ This concerned nitrate, long regarded as Peru's great untouched legacy and the ultimate successor of guano as a standby in the way of revenue. The world's largest natural source of nitrate lay between the coastal hills and the Andes, in a forty-mile-wide plain that stretched six hundred miles north and south. The whole region was a desert as barren as the mountains of the moon. The northern half, in the province of Tarapacá, belonged to Peru. The next province, Atacama, was part of Bolivia. The southernmost quarter only was Chilean territory.

During the guano El Dorado, Peru had no incentive to undergo the hardships of developing its nitrate holdings. Bolivia was too backward to attend to its share. The work fell to progressive Chile, whose explorers had been the first to grasp the reality of this latent wealth. Chileans and Peruvians were quite different peoples. Chile's population was of almost solid European stock—Spanish predominating, with an influential mixture of British and German. The country had been sparsely populated by Indians, whom the colonial settlers mostly killed off. The climate had been unfavorable to Negro slavery. Compared with Peru, the country was poor: a man had to work for a living. The result was a hardy, nationalistic, enterprising, aggressive race that has been likened to pioneers of the United States.

Chileans pushed into the forbidding and neglected Bolivian and Peruvian nitrate country. With the help of English capital and technical skill, they began to turn the desert wastes into money. On Bolivian territory, they founded the port of Antofagasta, and brought life to Peruvian Iquique and Pisagua. Lima let these things go on, in fact encouraged them by refraining from taxing the foreign exploiters and populators of the southern part of Peru. At the same time, Peru reckoned on some day reaping financial benefit from Anglo-Chilean enterprise, though it did nothing until

1873 when a law was passed granting to the state a monopoly of the nitrate of Tarapacá. Two years later Peru exercised its sovereignty to the full, with a law calling for the expropriation of the nitrate properties. In view of the country's financial plight, there seemed nothing else to do. To pay the private owners, Peru tried to float a new loan, and, failing, took the properties anyhow, promising to pay later. Of course this did not set well with the aggressive Chileans, or with their English partners.

Peru made other preparations for the imposition of de facto rule over her part of the nitrate country. In 1873, the year the nitrate monopoly was nominally established, a secret military alliance was entered into with Bolivia. Though Chile was to make much of this pact later on, it was a natural act on the parts of the contracting nations. Piérola's revolt against Pardo in 1874 was supplied with money and arms from Anglo-Chilean sources. Hazen informed W. R. Grace that Chile encouraged Piérola to create a "pretext for . . . wresting the province of Tarapacá from Peru."[6]

Michael Grace had long had an eye on the nitrate situation. When the expropriation took place, the Peruvian government made an arrangement for handling the product with the American firm of Olyphant & Co., which went bankrupt due, in some measure, to unexpected demands by the hard-pressed Peruvian government. Late in 1878, Michael Grace came forward with an offer for the nitrate concession. W. R. Grace saw S. G. Ward, American representative of the Barings, about banking support. Much impressed, Ward suggested that Grace go to London and talk to the principal partners. "It is more costly to do this business by credits from Barings than by securing it here," William wrote his brother, "but . . . it is much more secure, as no matter what condition the money market is in we have every assurance that we should never be called on for our credit but would be allowed to renew it continuously."

William sailed on short notice in January 1879, and was completely successful. Baring Brothers & Co. cabled Callao a credit of £65,000 to back Michael's proposal. The combination of Grace and Baring was enough. Grace Brothers & Co. obtained for four years the sole agency for shipping Peruvian nitrate of soda, the distribution in Europe to be managed by Baring Brothers and in the United States by W. R. Grace & Co.[7]

Grace had substantial reasons for self-congratulations. Peru was embarked on a course that should, in the fullness of time, bring that country out of its financial troubles. As an instrument to that end, the Grace houses stood to clear more than $1 million during the life of the four-year contract.

While Mr. Grace was relaxing in Ireland, a cloud darkened these agreeable prospects. Without warning, Chilean troops landed on Bolivian soil at Antofagasta and took possession. Peru proposed that they withdraw pending mediation. When this was refused, Bolivia declared war. Grace started home. A few days after he arrived, Chile declared war on Peru.

"The bombshell exploded," wrote Grace, "as it always does in such cases—when least expected."[8]

~ Instead of devoting the spring of 1879 to the profitable export of nitrate, the Grace organization was obliged to turn its attention to war, the prime object of which would be the defense of its interests in Peru's nitrate territory. On the news of the surprise seizure of Antofagasta, Peru hastily embarked troops for the neighboring province of Tarapacá. Michael cabled and wrote the New York house to attend to orders placed by the Peruvian government. So far was war from Grace's calculations that the house cable code contained few words for military materials.

In the absence of the senior partner, Charley Flint had responded on the instant to press reports of the seizure of Antofagasta. When the first order came from Michael, a thousand rifles, billed as "agricultural machinery," were at sea, and Flint was rounding up all the small arms and ammunition in sight.

The Chilean attack caused great patriotic manifestations in Peru. Large amounts of money, good money, came out of hiding—offered by citizens in the defense of their country. Always the optimist, Michael wrote his brother that Peru would not be easy to defeat. William replied that he wished he could believe it. He went further. In case of a Chilean victory would not Peru have to meet an indemnity? Would this not come "out of the immediate products of nitrate and guano"? And would not this play hob with the Grace nitrate contract?

W. R. Grace received many appeals from Peruvian leaders. In response to one from President Pardo, he reaffirmed his support and uttered the predictions of victory required by good usage, though without exhausting the possibilities of the Spanish language in that particular. Very soberly Mr. Grace added that the longer the war went on the greater would be the destruction, no matter who won. "There should be," he said, "a means of solving the quarrel pacifically," by mediation. He promised to work to that end.[9]

Nothing came of the efforts of Grace, or of more eminent would-be peacemakers, for the reason that Chile was determined upon a decisive victory. This aspect of the case swung the sentiment of the rest of Latin America and of the United States in favor of Peru and Bolivia—the United States conveniently overlooking that Chile's action constituted an extension of what we, in our push to the Pacific, had called "manifest destiny." Like us, Chile could claim provocation. Had not Daza, the foolhardy adventurer currently ruling Bolivia, ordered the confiscation of the properties of the English-owned Chilean Nitrate Co. of Antofagasta?

With less than half the population of Peru and Bolivia, Chile was much better prepared for war. Its finances were in order, its foreign credit excellent. Its army, though smaller than those of the allies, was more efficiently trained and equipped. Chile was also superior on the sea. The new English-built *Almirante Cochrane* and *Blanco Encalada* were three times the size of Peru's best fighting ship, the *Huáscar*. Peru had fit for high-sea duty only one other ironclad, the *Independencia*. The two monitors Grace had been instrumental in acquiring in the United States were all but laid up on account of worn-out boilers.

Chile had need for its naval superiority. Once the invaders lost command of the sea, they lost everything. Although, before declaring war on Peru, Chile had forehandedly thrown an army into Bolivian Atacama, of which Antofagasta was the principal port, that army could not be supplied or used to overrun Tarapacá, Tacna, and Arica unless Chile controlled the sea, long overland desert marches being impossible for troops. Conversely, if Peru was to stand any chance of winning, its inferior navy must be employed with skill and daring. Grace's first commentary on the war was to point out the importance of the Peruvian naval command. Not until one or two of the Chilean ironclads were done away with would Peru have an easy moment.[10]

Therefore, war work fell into two parts: one, the equipping and supplying of the armies Peru and Bolivia were building up in the threatened Peruvian provinces of Tarapacá and Tacna; and, two, a search for some means by which a quick and crippling blow might be delivered against the Chilean navy, without too much risk to Peru's inferior fleet.[11]

~ The torpedo, a new thing, was then the only David weapon against seagoing Goliaths. In the American Civil War, marine torpedoes had been used on several occasions, and once with a result of great military value. That was the destruction of the Confederate ironclad *Albemarle* in the Roanoke River. A young Union naval engineer named John Louis Lay made what was known as a spar torpedo, that is, an explosive charge on the end of a spar, or pole, twenty or thirty feet long. Lieutenant William B. Cushing volunteered to command a foray putting Lay's torpedo to test. With a small crew, Cushing took a little steam launch through the Confederate defenses in the night. The *Albemarle* was surrounded by a cordon of logs. Discovered, and under heavy fire, Cushing pushed the torpedo over the logs and exploded it. His launch sank with the *Albemarle*. Of the launch's crew only Cushing and Lay escaped death or capture.

Since the war, Lay had become a torpedo manufacturer, and at the moment was in Russia, where an instrument of destruction of his invention had been adopted by that government. It was a great deal more destructive than the improvised bomb that had sunk the *Albemarle*, and could be used with less risk to the users. The new Lay torpedo could be sent against a target a mile away. The weapon was controlled by two electric wires a mile in length—one wire to propel and guide it, the other to explode the charge at the right time. Thus the torpedo could be launched from shore, from a large warship, or from a small boat if it proved unfeasible to take a large ship within striking distance of the target.

The United States Torpedo Co. manufactured a somewhat similar instrument, which was directed and exploded by one wire instead of two.

There was also the spar torpedo, which took a daredevil to handle. The naval torpedo station at Newport, Rhode Island, still thought well of this short-range instrument, as Flint learned by talking to a number of naval officers, including Admiral Porter. The navy men discussed the subject of launches from which the torpedoes could be fired—torpedo boats, they called them. Although the Lay and the U. S. Torpedo Co. products could be directed from land or from large craft, small boats presented the best means of getting within range of a target. Each of these companies made boats for that purpose. Navy officers, however, favored a torpedo boat made by the famous shipbuilding firm of Herreshoff of Bristol, Rhode Island. Though larger and more expensive than the others, Admiral Porter offered the opinion that a Herreshoff boat presented the "surest way of disposing of the enemy fleet."[12]

This complicated things a little. Grace, acting as Peruvian agent, had already bought several torpedoes and torpedo boats from the Lay and the U. S. Torpedo people. He had dispatched them on the way to Peru, along with experts from the two companies who were supposed to show Peruvians how everything worked. The Lay company suspended work on Russian orders to expedite matters for Peru. The first Lay torpedo, with boat and two men, had gone April 10, five days after Chile's declaration of war on Peru. To make matters doubly sure, W. W. Rowley of the Lay company went down "to direct the proposed plans." Being well known in torpedo circles, Mr. Rowley took passage under the name of H. J. Patchen.[13]

This precaution was rendered advisable by the presence of Chilean agents and sympathizers in Panama—in Callao, even, among the English colony. The Chileans, too, were trying to buy torpedoes in the United States. Until the war started, Charley Flint had been the Chilean consul at New York. A little later a telegraph company employee, not knowing that Flint had resigned his consular post, offered to reveal, for pay, telegraph files disclosing the activities of one C. R. Flint as a munitions agent for Peru. After that, Flint was more careful of his telegrams.[14]

On the west side of the Isthmus, to ensure speedy delivery, it was necessary to transship to vessels of the British-owned Pacific Steam Navigation Co. Though carrying a stream of war goods to Chile by way of Magellan, P. S. N. C. would not handle munitions for Peru—if it openly knew it.

Meantime, Grace had been requested to study the Herreshoff boat, an almost noiseless craft whose presence would be difficult to detect on a dark night. After a trip on one in Long Island Sound, Grace took the advice of our naval officers and bought it for $18,500. This craft was fifty feet long, and difficult to disguise. With no concealment of the fact that he was shipping a steam launch, Grace billed the craft to the Compañía Cargadora del Peru, guano dealers of Callao. The Pacific Steam Navigation Co. refused to accept the launch at Panama. Grace protested to the line's agent there. What call had he to hold up an item of commerce which the guano company wished to use in the regular course of its affairs? The agent wrote back that he had held it up because the launch could be used for purposes quite alien to guano. After thanking the agent for his diligence, Mr. Grace implied that he would have to rebuke Grace Brothers & Co. and the Compañía Cargadora del Peru for involving W. R. Grace & Co. in a transaction of so suspicious a nature.[15]

A flexible code governed some who profited by small wars in those days. For example, that Herreshoff boat and five others reached Callao. The Pacific Steam Navigation Co. did not carry them. That company merely sold two steamers to a party who turned out to be the Peruvian government. The offer was too attractive for a faithful servant of the stockholders to disregard. If the Peruvian government employed these steamers to carry war materials to be used against Chile, P. S. N. C. could act perfectly innocent.

~ While these things were going on, news from the theater of war made it imperative, from Peru's point of view, that some of the torpedoes get into action against the Chilean fleet.

The *Huáscar* and the *Independencia*—inferior vessels, really, but Peru's only ironclads capable of going to sea—steamed up to the roadstead of Iquique to lift the Chilean blockade of that port. The two blockading craft were wooden corvettes, no match for the ironclads. Speedily the *Huáscar* sank one. When the other fled, the *Independencia* went after it, ran into a submerged reef, and was lost.

For practical purposes the engagement left Peru to face the Chilean navy with one ship. That ship, the *Huáscar*, was in the hands of a good man, Miguel Grau. To this day, Chile respects him as a brave and generous adversary. Admiral Grau remained at sea, defying the entire enemy fleet and upsetting all of Chile's hostile plans. Grau captured an armed transport with a thousand troops. He took two laden supply ships. He exchanged shots with enemy ironclads, but wisely declined battle with a superior force. This sort of thing could not last forever. Grace was pressed for torpedoes.[16]

For some time the idea had been considered of finding an American adventurer who would be willing to operate these engines of war. The first man interviewed was a merchant captain and Civil War veteran named Griffin. He would "agree to sink the 'Almirante Cochrane' or 'Blanco Encalada' . . . for a consideration." The consideration Griffin mentioned was $1 million.

Griffin declined to lower his price enough, and W. R. Grace wrote that he would try to "get men out of the Navy or the Confederate side." He also suggested that Michael broach the matter to some of the American torpedo men then in Peru, or to William H. Cilley, still in Peru trying to salvage something from the wreck of Meiggs's fortunes. "I am now persuaded that the only thing to save Peru are torpedo launches."[17]

With the approval of Peruvian authorities, W. R. Grace got in touch with Charles W. Read, late of the Confederate navy, whose feats of valor in that service equaled those of Cushing and Lay on the Union side. After Appomattox, Read had served in the Colombian navy, and so knew the Spanish language and temperament. United States naval officers spoke highly of the Southerner. During the Civil War, with the whole coast in a state of alarm because of his depredations, Read had sailed a captured Yankee fishing schooner into the crowded harbor of Portland, Maine, seized a revenue cutter that was anchored there, and put to sea again.[18] Captain Read was thirty-nine years old—a small, quietly spoken man of undistinguished appearance who had been graduated from Annapolis in 1860. To Flint he did not look like a hero. After a visit to the Herreshoff yard, Read said that he would undertake the mission. He would need only one other man, an engineer for the torpedo boat.

Read's terms were modest beside Griffin's, but when he left New York, they were not definitely fixed. With an engineer named John H. Smith, Read sailed on August 20, 1879. Grau was still at sea, baffling the Chilean fleet and keeping its army tied down to Atacama. The lifting of the blockade at Iquique had enabled Grace to get out some valuable nitrate cargoes. Five days after Read sailed, Grace wrote his first optimistic letter on the subject of the war: "To date, Peru has done well. . . . I believe with the new elements of defense that Peru can protect its ports."[19]

~ Grace had no occasion to write in that vein again. Before Read reached Callao, an attempt to sink one of the small Chilean vessels with a Lay torpedo resulted in a fiasco. The trial was made from Grau's *Huáscar* by an employee of the Lay company named Stephen Chester. After starting in the direction of the target, something went wrong with the torpedo. It turned in the water and headed back toward the *Huáscar*. The wires were cut and the ship cleared out to avoid being blown up.[20]

Read was commissioned a commander in the Peruvian navy. The *Almirante Cochrane* and the *Blanco Encalada* were undergoing repairs at Valparaiso. Read said this favored a torpedo project. As the harbor of Valparaiso could be easily entered, he hoped to achieve a surprise. But when the word leaked that, in event of success, the new commander was to receive a large sum in prize money, a loud protest went up. A number of Peruvian naval officers volunteered to fire the torpedo for nothing. A one-legged army colonel volunteered. The trouble was that none of them "knew a torpedo from a Chinese stinkpot." Or such was the expressed opinion of one American—not, however, the reticent Read.

Peruvian officers, who almost invariably have good manners, must have recognized Read as a gentleman. Yet the newcomer appears to have inherited a certain prejudice that had grown up against American torpedo specialists who had preceded him to the scene. There were three sets of them—the Lay, the U. S. Torpedo Co., and the Herreshoff men. For the most part they seem to have been a rowdy, hard-drinking lot. With the rest of Peru living on depreciated paper currency, the Americans drew their pay in gold and cut a wide swath with the ladies of Callao's waterfront. The sober members of the contingent, who tried to get something done, were divided with jealousies. Ford Snyder, a U. S. Torpedo Co. man, called Read and Smith "the biggest blockheads since Rowley & Chester. Smith claims to have been a chief engineer in the U. S. Navy. He is a dilapidated old Scotchman who never came nearer being a chief in the Navy than Sitting Bull did being President. . . . Read claims to have been in charge of the Confederate torpedo service, which is all bosh."[21]

After the fizzle by Chester, this sort of talk did not elevate Read in the eyes of Peruvians. So, while Peruvians and Americans alike talked and quarreled, the *Almirante Cochrane* and the *Blanco Encalada* completed their repairs and stood to sea. On October 8 the lifting of a morning mist off the lifeless coast of Atacama revealed the *Huáscar* to the *Cochrane* and two other Chilean warships. In less than two hours the *Huáscar* was a wreck, with Grau and most of his crew dead.

That was the end of Peru's navy as a fighting force. Torpedoes were its last and only hope. On his record, which included more than one success against seemingly impossible odds, Read would appear to have been the best naval man available at that stage of the war. He offered to patch up one of the monitors and take it against the Chileans as a torpedo carrier. The chief engineer of the Peruvian navy said that would be too risky. When the naval commandant of Callao informed Read that, in any event, no prize money would be forthcoming, the quiet Southerner packed his bags and caught a steamer for the United States. An offer by Snyder to use his U. S. torpedoes against the enemy was accepted. Snyder sailed for the south, but he did no harm to the Chilean navy.[22]

With the *Huáscar* out of the way the Chileans lost no time. On the next day, ten thousand troops embarked at Antofagasta for the Peruvian coast of Tarapacá. Landing at Pisagua, in bitter battles they defeated the numerically superior Peruvians and Bolivians, completing their conquest of the province in seventy days. Remnants of the allied army retired northward into Arica and Tacna. These reverses swept the presidents of Bolivia and Peru out of office. In Peru, Nicolás de Piérola took the helm. Ostensibly to purchase munitions, ex-President Prado sailed for New York, where he arrived without authority and without money. "[He] has not, as was supposed in Lima, walked off with a goodly swag." Grace felt sorry for the exile, showed him certain courtesies, and shunted him off to Europe.[23]

Grace was sick of the war, and resigned to Peru's defeat. He thought he had done his duty to Peru in the matter of supplying fighting materials for land and sea, and that inexcusably poor use had been made of the weapons, particularly on the sea. "The return to this country of Read . . . has so disgusted me with the management of Peruvian affairs that I have lost faith in their future." To his sister Ellen he jested about his "conceit," but meant every word when he said: "If *I* had had the management of this war . . . the road . . . [would have been] an easy one to travel; & yet all has gone wrong. It will probably destroy all our [South American] business; yet it is probably all for the best."[24]

~ With the fate of the west coast of South America in the balance, it was obvious that whichever way the cat jumped Grace interests would be seriously affected. To cope with the situation, W. R. Grace occupied himself with several lines of action, some more clearly defined than others.

Peru still had a chance, though not much of one, to reverse the tide of military disaster. Piérola showed energy in reorganizing and reequipping the beaten troops of his country and of Bolivia that had taken refuge in Tacna and Arica. W. R. Grace & Co. continued to act as purchasing agent, though the senior partner no longer gave the matter his first attention. That fell mostly to Flint. Among other things, Flint's search for a miracle weapon brought him in contact with Swedish-born old John Ericsson of *Monitor* fame, who had lately completed a torpedo of revolutionary design.[25]

When Grace wrote his sister that an end to his South American business might be "for the best," he was thinking of the opportunities that existed in the United States, where the long depression had worn itself out. A military debacle on top of the national bankruptcy caused by the railroad building spree would render Peru a poor field for business for years to come. As too valuable to waste on Peru, Michael Grace was ordered to New York, leaving Grace Brothers & Co. in the hands of Manuel Llanguno, nephew Ned Eyre, and John W. Grace.

Rather unpredictably, John had lately turned up in Callao. He had not made much of a success of the family's San Francisco house, J. W. Grace & Co. For this it would be unjust to blame John and his partner too much, and William did not blame them at all; the times had been very hard. Still, crippled, mercurial John was not at heart a businessman. He was a farmer. On the subjects of agriculture and stockraising his California letters fairly glowed. When William was looking for a foothold in Chile, there had been some mention of sending the discontented John there. The war put that prospect on the shelf. It did not, however, prevent John, early in 1879, from pulling up stakes in San Francisco and going to New York, with a notion of visiting Peru to see how he might like it. William sent him down. Despite the war, John decided to stay.

Always tolerant of John's shortcomings, William painstakingly answered an "amusing" letter in which the newcomer had aired his impressions of the Peruvian people.

"For myself," William wrote, "I like the Peruvians; I always enjoyed their society & I never looked upon them as more deceitful than [other] people. . . . The English in foreign lands, I never liked; they are, in my experience, presumptuous & self-opinionated; . . . yet in England, I have met very many pleasant good fellows, but I confess I think the Peruvians are pleasanter company & more kindly & benevolent in their character.

"Foreigners as a rule talk as you write. . . . Insensibly this feeling becomes manifest to those about you & you are put down as a hater of the people amongst whom you live . . . whereas if you educate your mind . . . to think kindly of the people of the country & to sympathise with them, you are received & treated as a friend. . . . I know houses in Peru that were in my time hated as haters of Peru. The policy of our [Lima] house has always been to be a Peruvian house. This may be well worth bearing in mind."[26]

At the same time he put out a feeler to Baring Brothers, in an effort to hang on to some of the nitrate business in the altogether likely event that the deposits, or most of them, should be lost to Peru.

For the most part, English financial and industrial interests had supported Chile vigorously. The eminent house of Baring belonged to a minority that, like the Pacific Steam Navigation Co. in the sale of the steamers, had not permitted its left hand to know what its right hand was doing. Though financial agents in London for Chile, Baring had helped Grace to purchase Krupp and Armstrong guns destined for use by Peru against Chile. Grace showed his appreciation by sending Thomas Baring a hamper of canvasback ducks from Maryland.

After the conquest of Tarapacá, Grace wrote the British bankers a frank letter: "Our . . . interests during this war, as you know, have been entirely with Peru." The time had come, however, to face the "possibility of the whole of the nitrate business of that country falling ultimately into the hands of Chile. . . . We think it possible, however, if you desire it, once peace is concluded, that Mr. J. W. Grace or perhaps Mr. M. P. Grace, might undertake [a trip to Chile] to procure for you all the necessary information in regard to the future of this business, on its new basis."[27]

As soon as Michael Grace reached New York, William sent him to London to keep the nitrate question alive with the Barings.

That, on one hand. On the other, Grace was prepared to reduce his operations on the west coast of South America to a fraction of their former scope. To compensate for this, he had entered the rubber business on the east coast, in Brazil. But it was the United States that loomed largest in Grace's plans and desires. There he saw enough opportunity for any man.

"All things are booming & the flood of prosperity is overwhelming," he wrote to his brother Morgan in New Zealand. "Stocks and bonds of all kinds are away up. . . . Manufacturers are making money. Products of farms are up 20 to 80 pr ct. Lands, houses etc. are improved in value & the Amr. Eagle's scream of joy is heard in all directions. We have not participated much in the grand boom of advancing prices, but have benefits flowing from this cause. I sold out nearly all my stocks when I needed capital to cover the nitrate & rubber business. . . . However, we never were doing a better business than now. The Chilean Peruv. War alone mars the outlook."[28]

Still another factor in William's plans for the future was the personal freedom he felt at having virtually discharged his obligations as the head of the Grace family. He had seen his sisters married or provided for, and was helping several of their children. Of his brothers, Michael was a rich man. John seemed taken care of. William preserved John's interest in the San Francisco house, still called J. W. Grace & Co. John's successor there, George Duval, was making that interest quite valuable. The other brother, Morgan, the scholar of the family, was in ways the most fortunate of the Grace boys. He had a philosophy that raised him above the rivalries of commerce. Yet, Morgan had supplemented the practice of medicine with a venture in New Zealand wool. Caught in a squeeze after '73, he had appealed to William. It was at the time the Bryce bank failure threatened to wipe out the Grace business. William sent Morgan $10,000.

Long letters, unique among Grace's correspondence in that they contained comparatively little of business, passed between William and Morgan. In 1875, Morgan visited New York, and charmed the whole family at Gracefield. On his return, Morgan wrote that the visit "filled up a blank in my life." Rambling on in his characteristic way, he began to dissect his brother's personality:

"The gothic structure of your eccentricities has reached my heart. A more thoroughly illogical man when angry or excited I don't know. A more humble minded rational citizen when 'compos mentis' I never met. . . .

Who so liberal as you but my dear old Father who is dead; who so economical but Uncle William. You are a regular bundle of incongruities, and I never met a man I would rather be quizzing, bullying and coaxing, chiefly because there is always an element of danger in the pursuit. As for Lillius, I can give no reason for it, she is amiable, patient, grateful, good natured, intelligent, quick witted and loyal to the backbone. Any other woman would hate your family. . . . I almost believe if I had not a copper in the world and not a shred of character that I would go to your house for shelter and that is saying no little thing."

Morgan went on to pay his respects to one of his favorite aversions, the too avid pursuit of the dollar:

"After all, what does business matter with Lillius bright and happy, Alice growing amiable, Agnes bright & loving, Joe well & strong, Lillie affectionate and the baby bawling. We are all too solicitous about business. . . . If it does not remit about forty, man is likely to become a slave to it. John is established. Mick can . . . accumulate wealth. Then why should you persist in being a slave? By all this, I mean to advise you to ease off. Your children are growing up and they and your wife require a great deal of your attention and will repay it. I propose following this course myself."[29]

Morgan Grace did ease off from his medical practice, with the result that he was elected to the upper house of the New Zealand parliament, a distinction of which William was inordinately proud.

Early in 1880, William was writing again to Morgan about the American boom: "I am myself lately interested in a big scheme here—the Ontario & Western RR. . . . Altho my associates are amongst the sharpest, keenest & some of the most unscrupulous men in the community I . . . will try & play my cards well, & if I do there will be a great deal of money in the thing. . . . Many wise people think that it is between 45 & 55 a man can realize the result of his life's labors and amass a fortune if he so desires." At forty-seven, William was a millionaire. Was that not fortune enough? Morgan must have smiled as he read: "I often think to myself 'Is the prize worth the effort we make for it?'. . . . I am often weary of my labors & yet I have a foolish ambition to see this house grow. Possibly Michl may make up his mind to take hold [of it]."

William wanted to spend more time at Gracefield with his family, his horses, and his trees. "Lillius is fat, fair, forty & . . . never better in her life. . . . Our last baby is the handsomest one of the lot!!" Carolina Sophia was just a year old—the eleventh, and last, child born to Lillius and William Grace, and the seventh surviving. Alice was nineteen, with plenty of beaux; Agnes; eleven; Joe, eight; Lilias, six; Louise, four; William Russell, Jr., two.[30]

There was something besides repose that W. R. Grace wanted in that spring of 1880. He wanted an activity that had nothing to do with making money, and nothing with the War of the Pacific, which dragged on to Peru's ruin.

An opportunity presented itself. There had been another crop failure in Ireland. Coupled with a changeover to paying rents in coin instead of in kind, it had resulted in distress reminiscent of the forties, which Grace remembered so well. A lecture tour by Charles Stewart Parnell, the Irish nationalist leader, had brought a disappointing response in the United States—perhaps because he laid too much emphasis on the political situation in his country and not enough on the economic.

In February, James Gordon Bennett's New York *Herald* took hold of the situation in dramatic fashion. It devoted a full page to a tabulation of counties and towns most in need and printed a stirring letter from Ireland which contained the words, "For God's sake give us money or food." The *Herald* opened a subscription with a contribution of $100,000.[31]

W. R. Grace had been sending donations privately, and filling the purse of his charitable sister Ellen. In accord with long practice, Mr. Grace had done this without publicity. In fact, he had striven to avoid publicity in the matter. Now, for almost the first time in his life, he departed from that course. He offered to place at the disposal of the *Herald* the Chapman & Flint-owned and Grace-operated square-rigger *W. R. Grace* and to donate one-quarter of the cost of the cargo, whatever that might be.

The *Herald* naturally hailed this generous offer, which Grace made more than good. Although the United States government supplied the ship—the historic *Constellation*—Grace put his own force to work purchasing, crating, labeling, and stowing the cargo. Gradually Mr. Grace himself took virtual charge of the campaign. The *Herald* sang his praises and Grace became a hero to thousands who had never heard of him before. The work brought him in contact with a variety of persons whom he had previously known slightly if at all. Among them were John Kelly, the head of Tammany Hall; Levi P. Morton, banker and Republican leader; Henry L. Hoguet; and T. B. Connery. In something over a month's time, $300,000 were raised and the *Constellation* loaded to the hatches.[32]

With the *Constellation* on her way, Mr. Grace did not return to business. The taste of public service afforded by his work for Irish relief had created a desire to continue that form of endeavor. This time he decided that the United States should be the beneficiary of his efforts.

The more Grace had seen of the rest of the world the deeper had become his regard for the land of his adoption, its institutions and its people. Yet, like most businessmen of his class at the time, Grace had been too intent upon his own concerns to take an interest in the public affairs of his country. His letters indicate a greater familiarity with political intricacies in South America. Possibly it occurred to Grace that this was not a good thing. Possibly Morgan's elevation to the New Zealand parliament had something to do with it. Possibly he merely wished to help a friend, an honorable and able man, who aspired to a high public office. We do not know, though the last assumption seems the most likely. What we do know is that of several possible courses of action W. R. Grace was turning over in his mind early in 1880 was a project calling for his entry into public life—that is to say, politics.

We know this because it is what he did; and never again, for long, was Mr. Grace primarily concerned with the making of money.

10 ~ Apprenticeship in Politics

~ In 1880, when W. R. Grace decided to take a hand in politics, he entered a field that was virgin to him. If he had previously so much as attended a precinct caucus, there is no record of it. This is not to say that Mr. Grace did not know a few politicians. One was the most powerful politician in the city of New York, "Honest John" Kelly, the chieftain of Tammany Hall. Even before the Irish relief campaign, Kelly had been an occasional caller at the Grace town house on Seventeenth Street. A common interest in Catholic charities may have brought them together.

Grace called himself an independent Democrat, as did his closest and most admired friend in public life, his old Brooklyn neighbor Judge Calvin E. Pratt of the New York Supreme Court. Grace was not alone in his admiration of Judge Pratt. The jurist's record on the bench was distinguished; his conduct so far above faction and above party that at the most recent election no Republican had been nominated to oppose him—a rare tribute in those days before the nonpartisan judiciary.

Friendship with Pratt may have had something to do with a change that had taken place in Grace's political inclinations. When he came to the United States in 1866, Grace leaned toward the Republicans, because they were the party of Lincoln whose cause young Grace had espoused when it was not a popular cause in Peru. Grace also was an admirer of Grant, as a military leader. Enough of that admiration lasted to induce the lately naturalized citizen to cast his first presidential ballot for Grant in 1872.

Thereafter, the corruption in the Republican party, from the president's circle down, became too much for Grace. Yet in the state of New York, the Democrats, under Tweed, were even more crooked, until a courageous leader, Samuel J. Tilden, cleaned house. Grace joined the Democrats and voted for Tilden, who became governor in '74. Though a reformer, Mr.

Tilden was a party man who believed in a party machine. He encouraged Honest John Kelly, a lieutenant in the Tweed fight, to reorganize Tammany. Honest John's reorganization turned out to be different from what Tilden had in mind. Where graft had been brazen under Tweed, Kelly screened it with a decent show of privacy.

Consequently, Mr. Tilden and Mr. Kelly fell out; but this did not keep Tilden from winning the presidential nomination in 1876, and winning the election, though the Republican nominee, Rutherford B. Hayes, became president. This was achieved by counting all doubtful states—including South Carolina, Louisiana, and Florida—in the Republican column. That gave Mr. Hayes a majority of one electoral vote, though Tilden's popular majority was 250,000.

Public reaction to this proceeding made Tilden a hero, and would have guaranteed him the nomination in 1880, except for two things: Mr. Tilden's illness, and the unsleeping enmity of John Kelly. Rather than see a pro-Tilden slate victorious in the state election of 1879, Kelly bolted the ticket and nominated himself for governor in opposition to the regular Democratic candidate. Thus, Kelly succeeded in diminishing Tilden's prestige, and sending a Republican, Alonzo Cornell, to Albany.[1]

Up to this time, W. R. Grace's name had appeared just once outside the role of an ordinary voter. In 1878, Kelly was looking for a respectable Democrat of no political experience to run for mayor of New York as a blind for Tammany. Grace was mentioned—though the mention scarcely achieved the volume of a whisper—and there were one or two brief newspaper notices. Kelly may have had nothing to do with this, but, in the light of what was to come, it looks suspicious. The nomination went to Edward Cooper, millionaire merchant, man of goodwill, and son of the revered Peter Cooper. The good-government people turned out to help elect Cooper. The new mayor strove in the cause of reform; but John Kelly and Tammany carried on much as before.[2]

Though the public never heard of it, the following year Grace did take a small and positive part in a political matter. A member of the Board of Education named Pomeroy was seeking reappointment. The story was going the rounds of Catholic voters that Mr. Pomeroy, an Episcopalian, had prejudices against the Roman faith. To a local Democratic leader, Grace wrote that he had known Pomeroy for years, that the story about him was untrue, that Pomeroy was an excellent school trustee, and that he deserved to be continued in that post. Considering what was to happen before the year 1880 was out, this action by Grace is of interest.[3]

Such was the nature of the Democratic political arena in 1880; and such, the political background of W. R. Grace, who had decided to enter that arena. A modest man in most things, it would seem that, as a beginner, Mr. Grace might have been content with a minor role. That was not the case. Mr. Grace began his political career at a point most politicians spend a lifetime working up to. He started out to win the presidential nomination for his friend Judge Calvin E. Pratt of Brooklyn.

~ The idea was by no means preposterous. Comparative unknowns had won presidential nominations before, for example, Abraham Lincoln.

Elements in the situation in 1880 favored a dark horse. Tilden, the titular head of the party and the hero of 1876, had literally dropped out of sight. Arthritic attacks had lost him the use of his left arm; his face was discolored and unhealthy-looking: his voice could hardly be raised above a whisper. Able to make but few public appearances, and those hardly to his advantage, he sought to keep his hold on the public by issuing statements from the depths of his silent mansion facing Gramercy Park in New York. To maintain, against such handicaps, a grip on the popular imagination requires a very exceptional man. Mr. Tilden's star was descending.

One of the first requisites for a presidential candidate is the ability to carry his home state—especially if that state is New York. Mr. Kelly had shown that Mr. Tilden could not do this in 1879. The public forgot, and politicians overlooked, Mr. Kelly's motives. The remembered fact was that Mr. Tilden's ticket had failed to carry New York just a year ago.

Though his motivations were different from Kelly's, W. R. Grace was one who believed that, to stand the best chance of winning, the Democrats should pass over the ill and old Tilden, who would, indeed, make a sorry figure on the stump. He thought the candidate should be a new, vigorous, magnetic figure, capable of waging a whirlwind campaign. Judge Pratt had these qualifications.

Still, the supplanting of the veteran crusader, who was no novice at the game of politics, would not be a walkover.

Nevertheless, in May 1880, with a month or six weeks of the practice of applied politics behind him, W. R. Grace could write hopefully to a friend, Dr. George Crosby, of New Hampshire:

"If you have never before been an 'astute politician,' take a hand in now, and you will make one easily. The delegates from this State are on the surface for Tilden, but they all know that Tilden could not possibly carry this State, and they are at heart for some other man. . . . The plan is to induce Tilden, after a show for himself, to go for Pratt. . . . Now we want some States like yours to hold out against Tilden, and later, we want some strong man from your State to be in our confidence."[4]

When Grace assured the doctor of the ease with which the political science could be mastered, he imagined himself speaking in the light of personal experience: to the enthusiastic amateur many things seem simpler than they are. Yet, allowing for the exaggeration that is part of the craft of politics, Grace's diagnosis of the New York situation was accurate.

A progressive Democrat, with a large independent following and even some Republican support, Pratt was also in a singularly fortunate position geographically. His judicial district, embracing Brooklyn, was important and doubtful territory. Possibly, Pratt was the only Democrat who could carry it.

Moreover, Kings County, in which Brooklyn is situated, would occupy a strategic position in the nominating convention. The seventy members of the New York delegation had been instructed to vote as a unit. The balance was such that the Kings County vote would be almost certain to decide the way the state would go. Since it was conceded that victory in November would turn largely on New York, the wishes of the Kings delegation would carry weight at the convention. Within the Democratic organization, Brooklyn was a Tilden stronghold. Grace felt Pratt the man to take Kings from the old leader.[5]

The fitting of Calvin Pratt so neatly into the New York scheme called for political acumen above amateur rating. Possibly, Grace was responsible—with some help from John Kelly and from Hugh McLaughlin, the Democratic boss of Brooklyn. But if the judge was to make an impression on the national nominating convention, other states besides New York must be considered. Here a quality of W. R. Grace's mind came in handy: there was nothing insular about his thinking. In business the world was Grace's field. Without loss of motion he could gather up from two or three continents scattered details of a problem and bring them together for solution.

A problem confined within the boundaries of the United States Grace was apt to regard as simple, in one respect: he could write a letter to California and get back an answer in two weeks, against two months in the case of Peru. Armed with a list of states—East, West, North, South—where there seemed a chance for missionary work for a dark horse, Grace began to write letters. Some went to friends or business associates who wielded political influence, or who, like Doctor Crosby, Grace thought might do so if they tried. Other letters went to friends of Judge Pratt; to politicos recommended by the judge's partisans; to individuals culled from the list of convention delegates. Grace's ability to write a good letter had played its part in the success of his business. The letters he wrote on behalf of Calvin Pratt were good ones, too.

~ To one whose allegiance was undetermined, Grace would be casual, or cautious: "I think it might be of some importance to talk over the matter of the Maine Delegates to the Democratic National Convention."

Or he might simply request a roster of a state delegation and "any special points in regards to the delegates, so that in case any of them are personal friends of yours, I might write you at length as to what my future objects and views are."[6]

Grace wanted to keep Pratt out of the newspapers, and do nothing that might nullify the surprise value of his name at the convention. As a result, until their fidelity was assured, recipients of campaign letters were likely to find themselves in a peculiar position. They were told about the candidate's record as a soldier and a jurist, about his achievements and personality. They knew his stand on important matters, and who was supporting him—everything, in short, except the name of the man they would be asked to vote for "at the proper time."[7]

Meanwhile, Grace kept an interested eye on the struggle between Tilden and Kelly. He seemed to be confident of his hold on the Tammany boss. "If we can even neutralize Tilden," he wrote, "you know I can neutralize Kelly." And again: "I may add that besides Judge Pratt being a Tilden man, we have personal friends interested in this matter who count positively on the assistance and endorsement of the Kelly faction at the proper time."[8]

In any case it was to Pratt's advantage that Tilden and Kelly stay at each other's throats. The more evenly divided the sentiment in the rest of the state, the better would be Brooklyn's chance of swinging the entire delegation to Pratt. The same principle held true for the country at large. Grace urged his correspondents in other states to boom their local aspirants strongly before the convention.[9]

As the convention approached, Grace must have been delighted at his success in keeping his candidate out of the papers. The appearance of Judge Pratt's name as a member-at-large of the New York delegation attracted no notice whatever. This was only natural, there being little about Pratt to draw the attention of the editorial writers who were indulging in the usual speculations. He had twice distinguished himself: in the war, in which he had been severely wounded in battle; and on the bench of the state supreme court. Neither of these were achievements that would mark him, on the surface, as presidential timber. Nevertheless, Grace was able to line up influential supporters in all the important states, carry on a voluminous correspondence, and lay out an elaborate plan for nomination without the newspapers getting wind of it. It spoke well for the good faith of the men who had committed themselves to Pratt.[10]

Notwithstanding these accomplishments, Grace did not make the mistake of underestimating his opposition: "Tilden is an old fox, & it may be hard to beat him." In all, the novice was making progress. He was learning the ropes.[11]

The Republican convention ended in Chicago ten days before the Democrats were to assemble in Cincinnati. The result of the Chicago meeting must have pleased Grace. After passing over Grant, who wanted a third term, the Republicans had refused to give the nomination to James G. Blaine, whose faction occupied a place roughly similar to that of Tammany in the Democratic scheme. The independent wing of the party had brought about the selection of a little-known compromise candidate, James A. Garfield of Ohio.

Mr. Garfield had the good fortune to be born in a log cabin, and to have worked as a towpath boy on a canal. He had served with considerable distinction in the army. His record in Congress was progressive and good. Thus, Candidate Garfield was a slightly more eminent prototype of Calvin Pratt. In short, the Republicans had reacted as Grace hoped the Democrats would to a comparable situation.[12]

After obtaining railroad passes for himself and a servant, Grace reserved several rooms and a parlor at the Emery House in Cincinnati. On June 16, he left New York in an amiable frame of mind. "I am off to the land of pork to see how they will manage the Convention. The next President will not be your friend, Grant. Now if he should be my friend—"

And there he left it.[13]

～ The work of the amateur strategist faced the severest test known to American politics: the intricate manipulations that are the core of a national nominating convention. In the business at hand—an attempt to put over a dark horse—W. R. Grace had one thing, at least, in his favor: the cloak of anonymity, a garment that the rise and fall of Enrique Meiggs and the gunrunning operations of the Peruvian war showed that Grace could wear to advantage. Outside the small circle he had taken into his confidence, no one seems to have entertained the remotest idea that Grace was interested in the forthcoming convention. Indeed, if the politicians converging upon Cincinnati had been asked point-blank who W. R. Grace was, the most accurate answer received probably would have been something about that New York fellow who had had a hand in the Irish relief.

Mr. Grace arrived in Cincinnati on Friday morning, June 18. The convention would open on the Tuesday following. By then Grace hoped to have the Pratt nomination cinched, or next to it. To this end he had gathered about him a mixed entourage, different members of whom would be persona grata with varying shades of party opinion. There were men from the New York Democracy and other anti-Tammany clubs. Tammany, also, was represented. These objectives had at their disposal the Grace block of rooms at the Emery, and the Grace charge account. In an atmosphere of cigar smoke, tobacco juice, and whisky, began the 'round-the-clock conferences and confabs, with their airs of conspiracy, their discreet feelers, tentative promises, swapping, and switching.

Mr. Grace and his co-workers at the Emery did not constitute the sole agency that was striving to put the finishing touches to the Pratt boom. Staying at other hotels but quite aware of what went on at the Emery were four men who had forgotten more politics than W. R. Grace knew: John Kelly, Hugh McLaughlin, William C. Kingsley, and John C. Jacobs. Kingsley was a wealthy Brooklyn contractor whose business had not suffered from his political alliance with Boss McLaughlin. Jacobs, a state senator, had been selected to direct the fight for Pratt in the caucuses of the New York delegation.

Though Grace had doubtless consulted with some of these personages during the course of his preconvention activities, that work seems to have been largely his own doing. And the professionals must have been pleased with it. Grace's activity at the Emery also was very important—not the least of its functions being to preserve the spontaneous, nonprofessional, independent aspect of the Pratt movement. It could hardly have been by accident that none of the five hundred Tammany rooters John Kelly had brought to Cincinnati were billeted at the Emery House.[14]

One by one Grace met the men with whom he had been corresponding. Through them he enlarged his acquaintance among the members of the state delegations he had been working on by mail. At the same time, Kelly and McLaughlin were busy with the most delicate part of the plan—the winning of New York. At first it had been supposed that Tilden would make a real fight for his home delegation. The scheme of the Pratt men was to deadlock the delegation and to slide in the judge as soon as it became clear that Tilden could not command a majority.

But Tilden was, as Grace had remarked, "an old fox." From the beginning there had been a rumor that he might refuse to let his name go before the convention, and, instead, try to throw his support to Henry B. Payne of Ohio. The rumor was enough to disturb the New York delegation and imperil the task that had been entrusted to Jacobs. Naturally the Pratt group tried to use the report of Tilden's possible withdrawal to strengthen the cause of their man. Kelly publicly announced that he had come to Cincinnati with only one object: to defeat Tilden. On the other hand, Tilden's emissary, William C. Whitney, New York City's elegant young corporation counsel, was very much in evidence—smoothly turning aside questions about Tilden's intentions. Tilden's choice of Whitney to represent him seemed significant, for the lawyer was Payne's son-in-law.[15]

On Sunday a letter from Tilden materialized. Ostensibly a declination, it was phrased to suggest that the veteran would accept a nomination by acclaim. If Tilden was being foxy, he overdid it. A nomination by acclamation was out of the question. At a hastily called caucus of the New York delegation, Jacobs scored a smacking triumph. To the dismay of the old leader's followers in and out of New York, Tilden's withdrawal was taken at face value. Then, with the aid of anti-Tilden independents, the Pratt men defeated a resolution to switch New York's vote to Payne.[16]

The moment had come to bring the Pratt boom into the open, making, in all, a busy Sunday. The stage for the newly declared candidate's initial personal appearance was well chosen—the Grace suite at the Emery. Delegates and political managers were herded thither. They were wined, dined, and introduced to the judge, whose bearing and manner impressed everyone favorably. The correspondent for the New York *Herald* telegraphed to his paper:

"Judge Pratt was in the Emery House this evening, and involuntarily held quite a reception. He is apparently fifty years of age, handsome, dignified, . . . and self-possessed. He has a good legal past, a first-rate war record, and a war reminder in the guise of a rebel bullet in his head yet, and a surprisingly good judicial record. He plays a good game of draw, is a staunch friend . . . [and] never bolts a ticket."[17]

The Pratt people had not overlooked the item of newspaper mention of their man—at the right time. That time was now, and the Grace staff worked hard to get the boom across in the Monday morning papers in Cincinnati where it would impress the delegates and visitors. This effort met with only moderate success. Though Tilden and a few minor hopefuls were out of it, Payne remained very much in the race—as did Bayard of Delaware, Field of California, Hendricks of Indiana, and Hancock of Pennsylvania.

On Monday, however, Pratt made observable gains. At sundown, Grace felt pretty confident—perhaps more so than the experienced politicians in the Pratt camp. Though the rank and file of delegates and onlookers might inquire, as reported by the New York *Times* correspondent, "Who the Devil is Pratt?" leaders seemed to be making tracks for the bandwagon. With the convention set to open the following morning, thirty-eight of the New York delegates were pledged to the judge. Though a bare majority, it was enough to invoke the unit rule. North Carolina, New Hampshire, and some other states had pledged themselves in advance to switch to Pratt as soon as his candidacy was announced. Spokesmen for southern states announced that they would vote as New York did. Delegates from Pennsylvania, Maryland, and Illinois, who had declined to pledge themselves by correspondence, met the presentable candidate—with results that delighted Pratt's supporters. As Judge Spear of Pennsylvania told newspapermen: "[When] our people come to realize . . . that Randall [the favorite son] can't be nominated, you needn't be surprised to see the fifty-eight votes of Pennsylvania declared for Pratt." Less publicly, the support of delegates from Iowa, Nebraska, Nevada, and Massachusetts was tentatively pledged.

In any event, that was the way Grace sized it up.[18]

Moreover, the Pratt boom had caught on back in New York. The *Evening Post*, the *World*, and the Brooklyn *Eagle* were out for him. Other papers were friendly. "The amount of work that has been done for him, quietly and unostentatiously, is incredible," one journal said, and proved the point by stating: "Mr. Kingsley is leading the fight for Pratt." A Cincinnati paper called Hugh McLaughlin the power behind the Pratt movement. Grace's name was not mentioned in print.[19]

On Monday evening, then, Pratt seemed to have a fair chance. It was during the small hours of Tuesday morning that the blow fell. A rumor was abroad in the hotels and saloons that Pratt had been baptized a Roman Catholic. The gossip reached the ears of newspaper reporters who went in search of more exact information. Along about midnight they came to see W. R. Grace. He emphatically denied the story, and set out to find the candidate so he personally might deny it.

Though the necessity for such an errand doubtless incensed Grace, he performed it willingly. As for Calvin Pratt, the decency and courage with which he met a disgraceful issue entitles him to honorable mention in the footnote to history that is reserved for a legion of disappointed aspirants to the presidency.

When Grace asked Pratt to contradict the charge about the baptism, the judge said that he could not, and told this story. While lying wounded on a battlefield, and fearful that his last hour was near, he had consented to receive the holy water from the hand of a devoted comrade-in-arms, the Catholic chaplain in a regiment under Pratt's command. The priest had long since died; the judge had never practiced the faith; indeed, he had given the matter no thought in years. But he would not deny that the baptism had taken place; nor would he attempt an apology for it. When the implications were made clear to him, Calvin Pratt gave the word to withdraw his name.[20]

Before the convention met, the matter was formalized at a secret caucus of the New York delegation. State Senator Jacobs removed the judge's name from consideration because, as the *Times* explained, he was "not well enough known in the West." "After spending a night on it," commented the Brooklyn *Eagle*, "and looking over the field generally, Judge Pratt reached the conclusion that he did not care to go into the Convention with a bare majority of the delegates behind him"—two-thirds being required to nominate.

The Cincinnati *Enquirer* seems to have been the only newspaper to announce the true cause of the unexpected extinction of the "auspicious" Pratt boom—a fact that Grace overlooked when, a few days later, he wrote to a Democratic leader in California: "We did not deem it wise to let the people know in Cinn. why Pratt retired, but I think you will join me in saying it was wise; no matter what individuals may say or think, this country is not prepared to see an R. C. President."[21]

～ $\mathcal{A}$s Pratt had accepted his disappointment more calmly than might have been expected, there was nothing for Grace to do but to display equal fortitude. At least Grace had the satisfaction of seeing his political judgment vindicated to some extent when General Winfield Scott Hancock, of Pennsylvania, was chosen as a compromise candidate. Like Garfield, and like Pratt, Hancock had never been identified with bossism in his party. Nor was he unacceptable to the bosses as a fire-eating reformer.

Grace at once sent a cordial message to Hancock, and received, as promptly, an equally warm invitation to join the campaign headquarters. He was gratified to find his work for Pratt so readily recognized, but thought it wise not to take too active a part in national politics for a while. "Personally, I did not lose all interest in the canvass," he wrote to Michael in London, "but at the same time, I felt that . . . [I] could not take any steps which would tend to place me in the light of a political manager. . . . I never passed through a more acute period of exhaustion & mental labor than I did during my stay in Cincinnati."[22]

On June 28, 1880, a day or so after her husband's return, Lillius Grace brought their daughters Alice and Agnes from Gracefield to look over the new town house, at 31 East Thirty-eighth Street, that Grace had just purchased. At four o'clock in the afternoon they were joined by Mr. Grace on board the *Sewanhaka*, the lavishly fitted, gilded Long Island Sound commuting steamer. It was a pleasant day, and the ship, capable of carrying six hundred passengers, was not crowded with the three hundred and fifty aboard.

Mr. and Mrs. Grace found seats near the stern and the girls wandered off. An hour later, as the vessel passed Hallets Point, there was an explosion below-decks. Smoke poured from the engine room. The Graces saw flames flash out amidships, cutting off the afterdeck from the bow with a wall of fire. Agnes came running up, crying. Of Alice there was no sign. Grace set out to find her.

Lillius Grace, who had been in peril at sea before, transferred the earrings she had bought that day at Tiffany's from their package to her coat pocket. Then she began to help others. She showed how to get at the life preservers, stowed behind wooden slats overhead. She helped frightened passengers to fasten the clumsy cork belts about them.

Grace returned without Alice, and sought to console his wife with the probability that the girl was forward, on the other side of the fire. It was safer there than aft. The captain had headed the ship for Randalls Island, thus driving the flames toward the stern. Already, hysterical passengers were jumping from the decks. It takes a cool, strong swimmer to breast the tide and current in that stretch of water. Some managed to make the island, but more were drowned. With the flames roaring nearer, Grace and his wife did what they could to stem the spread of panic, and to prevent people from leaping overboard until they were close enough to the island to have a chance in the water. While this was going on, Alice showed up, unharmed.

By sticking to the wheel while the pilot house burned over his head, the captain beached his blazing ship. Passengers on the forward decks were able to walk to safety, but for those who were aft there was nothing to do but leap into the water. Taking a position outside the rail, Grace began to help them over the side while Lillius saw that their life preservers were in order. Afterward both recalled the lady whose girth was as great as her disinclination for the water. It took the two of them to launch her.

The Graces were among the last to jump. In the water, surrounded by frantic people, they had the most fearful time of all. Though he managed to hold on to Agnes, Grace became separated from his wife and Alice. A rescue boat picked up Mrs. Grace barely in time to save her. Alice was piloted to a launch by a young man with whom she had jumped.

Fifty of the three hundred and fifty passengers lost their lives.[23]

～ *G*race had been successful in keeping his part in the unlucky Pratt-for-President movement out of the newspapers. His behavior in the *Sewanhaka* disaster was another matter. Letters of congratulation and commendation came from all quarters of the country—even from abroad. Not since the Irish relief movement had the name of W. R. Grace been so conspicuous in the public print.

Some months after the accident, Mrs. Grace was on a Brooklyn ferry when a gentleman with one arm introduced himself as Henry V. Duryea, and asked if Mrs. Grace remembered him.

"Of course I do," she said, "and I've often wondered if you were saved."

Mr. Duryea told of having advertised in a newspaper for the name of the lady who had helped him into a life jacket.

Mrs. Grace said she had not seen the notice.

"Plenty of others did," Mr. Duryea replied. "Over forty women answered that advertisement."[24]

True to his resolution, Grace contented himself with a minor local role in the Hancock campaign, privately confiding that he found it "a damned nuisance." But when his name began to figure in the speculations as to the choice of a Democratic candidate for mayor of New York, Mr. Grace expressed no annoyance.[25]

The selection of the mayoralty candidate for 1880 would be important for two reasons. First, it would determine whether John Kelly of

Tammany Hall kept his job as city comptroller. Under Mayor Cooper, Kelly had held on to the comptrollership by the skin of his teeth. Not wishing to run such risks again, Kelly turned over in his mind the names of respectable citizens he regarded as safe, in the Tammany view. This brought him to a private audience with Grace. Kelly asked if Mr. Grace would accept a nomination backed by all factions of the party.

Grace said he would, and added: "But, if elected, *I'll* be the mayor, you know."

What boss has not heard that talk? "Sure," said Honest John, "Mr. Grace, *you'll* be the mayor."[26]

The second, and most important, consideration in the municipal campaign was for the Democrats to select a nominee for mayor who would add strength to the national ticket. It was more than possible that the vote of New York City would determine whether Hancock or Garfield should go to the White House.

In September, Tammany leaders met with those of anti-Tammany Irving Hall, the next largest Democratic club in the city. The two groups agreed that each would draw up a list of acceptable candidates, and meet again to choose a nominee from one of the lists. The second meeting was on October 18 at the Monument House on Union Square, just around the corner from Tammany Hall. Kelly and his henchmen kept the Irving Hall people waiting for hours while they held a caucus. What they discussed the newspaper did not report, but there were suspicious editorials when, after the lengthy confab, Kelly acquiesced without hesitation to a name on Irving Hall's—not Tammany's—list. The name was that of William R. Grace.[27]

The Irving Hall list was a notable one. Grace's name appeared in company with eleven others who represented the cream of the reform and liberal movements in the city, among them Peter R. Voorhis, Wheeler H. Peckham, William C. Whitney, Everett P. Wheeler, and Oswald Ottendorfer. The less friendly papers hinted broadly that Irving Hall had been hoodwinked, and that Grace's name had got on its list through some mysterious agency of Honest John Kelly.[28]

Grace put off his letter of acceptance in the hope that the opposition press would disclose its line of attack. He had not long to wait. Next morning the *Times* led off its editorial page with the following:

"So far as we know, Mr. Grace is a perfectly respectable man, of no particular ability or knowledge of public affairs. . . . Though neither his birth nor his religion can be held to be of itself a disqualification for the office of Mayor, there will be a natural desire on the part of reflecting men of both parties to have his position defined on certain public questions. . . . A man's views on the propriety of diverting a portion of the public education fund to the support of Roman Catholic schools become of more than usual importance when he seeks election as Mayor of New York. . . .

"The chief objections to Mr. Grace will, however, arise from the character of the influences which have contributed to his nomination. Mr. Kelly accepted the nomination of Mr. Grace simply because he was the one man on the Irving Hall list who would best serve as a figure-head for the Tammany Boss."[29]

The *Herald*, claiming to speak for "the great mass of Catholics," deplored the nomination, saying that Kelly's decision had been "not the act of a good citizen, nor of a good churchman, nor of a wise politician." The religious issue, it insisted with some foresight, would obscure all other matters. Even the Democratic *World*, and the distinguished and liberal *Evening Post*, were lukewarm. The suspicion was gaining that Irving Hall had been duped into putting forward a Kelly man.[30]

Thus enlightened, Grace composed a letter which he submitted to the press on October 22. He discussed all the mayoral functions, the physical and financial maintenance of the city government. With reference to the public school system Mr. Grace said:

"In any appointments which I may have to make in connection with our school management, I shall not fail to give full and proper recognition to the prevailing American sentiment in this regard. I believe that the common schools established by the people and esteemed as their richest inheritance should be maintained inviolate and I shall favor liberal appropriations for their support."

The letter closed with about as near a repudiation of Tammany as could be made by a Tammany-supported candidate:

"My name was presented for nomination by one of the two principal Democratic organizations of the city, accepted by the other, and approved by other influential political associations. In so far as such considerations may be taken into account I shall not be unjust to any of them; but I shall not forget that I owe my services to the whole public, and shall endeavor to merit the approbation of all citizens whose first concern, irrespective of party considerations, is that the public service be honestly and efficiently conducted. I accept the nomination . . . without pledges to individuals or political associations."[31]

These assurances were not sufficient to dispose of the religious or the Tammany issues. When the Republicans nominated William S. Dowd, the liberal weekly *Nation* remarked: "The City has never had a Catholic mayor, nor, since Colonial times, we believe, one who was not a native, and both these circumstances are likely to be heard from on the local stump."[32]

They were. With victory in the national as well as the city election in view, Republicans neglected nothing in their effort to make Grace unpopular. A good start with independent voters was Grace's association with John Kelly. And Dowd was a strong opponent in any case. A businessman, he was also one of the oldest members, in point of service, of the board of education. Tall, portly, and dignified, his gray hair and beard lent him an air of maturity beyond his fifty-six years. His campaign slogan was "No Dictator for New York City, and Non-Sectarian Public Schools." These remarks of a Dowd speaker were typical:

"It is now proposed that the entire and absolute control of our city government shall be delivered to one sect to the exclusion of all others. . . . It is proposed at the coming election to place these [public] schools under the absolute control of one sect which has for centuries held, and still holds, an indefensible dogma that all education should be sectarian."[33]

Grace's protests were of little use. In the language of one Republican orator: "If Mr. Grace is a good Roman Catholic, he must, in the conscientious discharge of his duty, if elected Mayor, make this City subordinate to that idea of the Holy Father in Rome."[34]

Eight days before the election, the *Times* raised the question of whether the "Tammany-Irving Hall candidate for the Mayoralty" was a citizen of the United States. The newspaper said that a search of court records failed to disclose his name on the list of naturalized citizens. Whether a Catholic mayor could turn over the administration of the public schools to representatives of the pope seemed to be a matter of opinion. But there was no doubting that the election of a British subject as mayor of New York would be invalid. Some confusion in the records was apparent, and by the time Grace was able to produce his naturalization papers, the citizenship issue had been superseded by another that was equally serious for the Democratic candidate.[35]

This attack was launched by the New York *Tribune*, in the lengthy, detailed, impressive statement which assumed to deal with attested facts and not with emotional suppositions such as formed the basis of the objections to Mr. Grace on the ground of religion. The presentation set forth that, in 1865, W. R. Grace was appointed to the Callao agency of the New York Board of Underwriters, a post which he held until 1871. The Board of Underwriters was a clearinghouse maintained by

American marine insurance companies. Among its functions was the examination of claims for losses, the prevention of overpayments and frauds, then common, and, in general, the representation of the interests of marine insurers in foreign ports. As the board's Callao agent, W. R. Grace was charged with mismanagement, diversion of funds, and the rendering of falsified reports.[36]

Immediately, Grace denied everything in so far as the charges related to himself. He pointed out that he had left Peru early in 1865, and had not been back except for three months in 1875; that at no time had he received an appointment as the underwriters' agent in Callao, or had he acted as such; that he had never before heard of the individual instances of irregularity cited by the *Tribune*; and had never owned a dollar's interest in any of the ships involved.[37]

The denial received less attention from the press than the accusations. The accusations had given particulars; and the *Tribune* was no scandal sheet. The greater part of Grace's disclaimer was general, and rested on his unsupported word. On Monday, November 1, the day before the election, a significant if fragmentary piece of corroboration of Grace's story appeared—in the columns of the *Tribune*. Captain Augustus Meyers, surveyor general for American Lloyd's, a marine insurance company, wrote to say that "in the interest of truth and justice . . . Mr. Wm. R. Grace had nothing whatever to do with the matters of the [ships] *Washington*, *Libby* and the *Mary*, which I officially and personally investigated."[38]

So things rested when the polls opened at six o'clock the following morning. Grace was sick at heart. Two weeks of demagogic campaigning had taught him that there was much he did not know about politics when he had accepted the nomination. He regretted that acceptance. Aside from an understandable ambition to head the government of America's largest city, he had hoped to strengthen the national ticket. By now he knew, or should have known, that he had been a drag on that ticket, which needed every vote it could get in New York.[39]

The first tidings from the polling places were more depressing than had been anticipated. Though they did not say so publicly, Republican leaders were prepared to see Grace squeeze in—the efficacy of the combined machinery of Tammany and anti-Tammany Democratic factions being what it was. What the G. O. P. chieftains did expect was a close contest in the city that would take enough votes from Hancock to give Garfield the state—and the presidency. All along, the G. O. P. strategy had been to strike Hancock through Grace.

Early returns indicated that the Republicans might get more than they hoped for. Dowd had a small lead, which increased slowly as the night wore on. Though running far ahead of Grace, Hancock was not doing well enough in the city to carry the state if the rural counties turned in their customary Republican majorities. Mr. Grace went to bed believing himself beaten. He was awakened by a crowd in front of his house cheering him as the next mayor.

Grace had a lead of a thousand votes, not likely to be overcome as the unreported districts were strongly Tammany. They eventually swelled Grace's majority to 2,914, giving rise to reports that he had been "counted in" by Tammany overseers.

The victory was a lonesome one. Though Hancock carried the city by 42,000, he lost New York State by 20,000—and so lost the presidency. In a sad letter, Grace commented on the contest: "Had I known such feelings would have been manifested, I would never have become a candidate. . . . None of you feel more deeply Hancock's defeat than I do. I would have been willing to sacrifice not only my own election but everything that was fairly within the scope of my control for the attainment of the end we all so ardently desired."[40]

Thus ended William R. Grace's swift and uncomfortable apprenticeship in politics. For a beginner he had done marvelously at Cincinnati. That near-success had carried him into the mayoralty race, with consequences that a more seasoned politician should have foreseen. Surely, Kelly must have foreseen them; but all Kelly cared about was the perpetuation of Tammany's influence in the City Hall. To run Grace afforded what the Tammany boss thought to be his only chance.

The mayor-elect addressed himself to three tasks:

1. Active management of W. R. Grace & Co.: turned over to Michael Grace, who had been summoned by cable from London.

2. The inaugural message: Grace intended this document to be the first step in fulfillment of his pledge to give New York City a government that would merit the approval of independent citizens who had gone against him on election day.

3. Vindication of his reputation in the matter of the marine insurance frauds.

Concerning the last issue Grace, at the outset, engaged the sympathetic interest of Whitelaw Reid, the editor of the *Tribune* and sponsor of the charges. Without publicity, Grace sent a mutual friend to Reid to say that Grace was collecting evidence, which he intended to lay before the *Tri-*

bune. Grace would be willing to abide by the verdict of the editor as to whether that evidence acquitted Grace of the irregularities the paper had imputed to him.[41]

An array of documents was obtained in Callao, which Michael Grace reduced to eleven pages of writing, responding to the *Tribune*'s accusations one by one.[42]

Before publicly acknowledging this production, Mr. Reid conducted his own investigation of its trustworthiness. A week after Mr. Grace's inauguration as mayor, the *Tribune*, in a handsome apology, retracted its campaign statements:

"We opposed Mr. Grace, not only on political, but on personal grounds—having brought up against him during the short but heated campaign, the charges concerning marine insurance at Callao. . . . Mr. Grace . . . then labored under the embarrassment of not knowing the full facts in the case himself, his brother, who was the active partner at Callao, being absent, in Europe, and the papers being in Peru."

Mr. Reid adverted to Michael's report, and substantiating documents:

"We have examined them carefully, and have to say that, whatever the Insurance Companies may have thought, these facts overturn any evidence they, or their agents or witnesses have furnished, against either Mr. Grace or his house. We take the more pleasure in stating this conviction, since it is not only agreeable to find that injurious suspicions are not sustained, but since it now concerns the self-respect of our citizens that the Mayor of New York should not rest under them."

The same issue of the *Tribune* carried in full—eight columns—Mr. Grace's inaugural message, with this editorial comment:

"If the performance of the new Mayor shall come up to the promise of his message, the people of this city shall have good ground for satisfaction."[43]

11 ~ The First Term as Mayor

~ There is much in any New York mayoralty that goes beyond the boundaries of the city, much that recurs with the generations and is duplicated everywhere the municipal brand of politics is played. When Grace came to office in 1881, New York had rid itself of Tweed, but not of evil machine rule. The city remained *the* horrible example of municipal government.

This corruption was no surface thing that could be swept away by getting rid of a few crooked officeholders. It was rooted in the lives of too many of the city's people—the laboring poor upon whose votes, in the end, any political organization must depend. Tammany politicians seldom missed a trick when it came to perpetuating themselves in office by bribery, ballot-box stuffing, and blackmail. But their real hold was deep in the hearts of the unenlightened mass of the poor people.

The Tammany method can be illustrated by following a ward heeler of Grace's time through a day's work. The record is furnished by George Washington Plunkitt, a district leader who later published a series of what he called "very plain talks on very practical politics."

In the morning, Mr. Plunkitt was in court, where he bailed out a bartender, secured the discharge of four drunks, and paid the fines of two others. Then he took care of the rent of a family about to be dispossessed, and found jobs for four unemployed men. That afternoon he put in an appearance at an Italian funeral, a Hebrew funeral, a Hebrew confirmation ceremony, and a Catholic church fair. At the fair he bought chances for everything, kissed every baby in sight, flattered the women, treated young girls to ice cream and their fathers to stronger refreshments.

Back at district headquarters he spent ten dollars for tickets to a church excursion, purchased admissions to a neighborhood ball game, and listened to the complaints of a dozen pushcart peddlers. By that time it was evening, and he went to a Jewish wedding, having already sent the bride a present.

The concluding and crowning event of the twenty-four hours was unscheduled—a three A.M. fire. Fires were important, and it was not every day that a district leader got a chance to help at one. "If a family is burned out," Plunkitt explained, "I don't care whether they are Republicans or Democrats, and I don't refer them to the Charity Organization Society. . . . I just get quarters for them, buy clothes for them . . . and fix them up till they get things running again. It's philanthropy, but it's politics—mighty good politics. Who can tell how many votes one of those fires brings me? The poor are the most grateful people in the world, and, let me tell you, they have more friends in their neighborhoods than the rich have in theirs."[1]

In the face of this sort of social service, it is not strange that the slum-dwellers of New York were inclined to ignore high-sounding reformers. It was hard for poorly educated immigrants to think in terms of basic social readjustment when the problem was immediate: a job or a meal or a roof over the children's heads. A hundred dollars spent on the victims of a fire might come from a thousand-dollar bribe, paid to prevent the passage of a law that could have prevented the fire—but this was not easy to understand. What these people did understand was that when they were in trouble, someone from the Hall took care of them—on the spot, without ifs or ands or buts.

In this way, Tammany kept its grip on great masses of people, and kept its politicians in power. The wherewithal for rendering these services, many of them so humane and so needful, came from the spoils of office. It seemed almost futile to point this out—to indicate that for every dollar spent on the indigent, fifty lined the pockets of the philanthropic politicians; that the whole system made for the perpetuation of the misery and ignorance it assumed to relieve. The needy saw only that ready dollar.

Such was the system that W. R. Grace had pledged himself to try to displace. Granting that he meant it, the task would be tremendous. Though far from a figurehead, the mayor of New York possessed definitely limited powers: Tammany had seen to that. Such powers as he did have had become enfeebled by disuse. Something more than right thinking and well-meaning would be necessary for a mayor to get at the innards of the system. Cooper's administration had shown that. The mayor who accomplished anything would have to revitalize the authority of the city's chief magistrate, to attract able and unselfish lieutenants to his standard. Unremitting and often thankless labor would be his lot.

~ *O*n January 1, 1881, when W. R. Grace took office, neither Tammany nor the good-governmenters were sure of him. Good-governmenters, however, were more hopeful than they had been during the campaign when many of their number had come to believe that Honest John Kelly had put one over in getting Irving Hall to sponsor the candidacy of Grace. On the other hand, Mr. Kelly was distinctly less hopeful. Between the election and the inauguration the board of aldermen had voted Kelly out of the city comptrollership, where Kelly had had his hands on the public revenues and a great deal of the city's political patronage. Kelly knew that the office could have been saved for him by the mayor-elect.

It had come about in this way.

Very shortly after the election, Irving Hall had shown its distrust of its recent candidate in a striking manner. Without consulting Grace, it made arrangements with the retiring executive, Cooper, and a majority of the board of aldermen, to pass on to Grace a mayoral cabinet so vigilant in the cause of honest government that should Grace turn out to be a Tammany tool he could do the city a minimum of harm. The chief aim was to eliminate John Kelly as comptroller. Kelly's term, like that of certain other members of the mayor's cabinet, would expire early in December before Grace would take office. Cooper nominated Allan Campbell for the comptrollership. Campbell was a civil engineer who, as commissioner of public works, had done much to clean up that hotbed of graft. For the public works job, Cooper nominated Hubert O. Thompson, an Irving Hall leader. William C. Whitney was renominated as corporation counsel, and Maurice J. Power, of Irving Hall, as a police court justice.

Kelly lost no time organizing a countermove. If he could persuade the aldermen to delay action on the nominations, and particularly Campbell's, until the first of the year, Grace, and not Cooper, would be the mayor. With good reason the Tammany leader felt that he could block approval of the Cooper nominations provided enough aldermen received specific promises of patronage under the Grace regime.

The balance of power in the aldermanic chamber was held by seven Republican members. In the past, Kelly had been able to control Republicans with patronage. To do so in this instance the quid pro quo would have to be a handsome one. The acquiescence of the mayor-elect would be indispensable. Anxiously the anti-Tammany press watched to see what Grace would do. The mayor-elect said what he had said all along: that he had been elected without pledges to anyone. Though it must have galled him to realize that the liberals who had nominated him did not trust him to make decent appointments, it gradually became apparent that Irving Hall's doubts were not pushing Grace into Kelly's arms.[2]

On December 10 the matter was settled. Feeling that Kelly had been unsuccessful in his attempts to influence Grace, the aldermen voted 13 to 8 to accept Mayor Cooper's nominations. The following day John Kelly surrendered his office to Allan Campbell.[3]

There was a perceptible warming of the good-governmenters toward Grace. The *Tribune* reported that it was considered "treason" in the Tammany clubhouses to say a good word for the incoming mayor.[4]

The open break came soon after Grace had taken the oath. Threatened with insurrection in his own ranks, Boss Kelly strove earnestly for some sign of favor from the City Hall. Warily he approached the mayor with a suggestion for a minor appointment. Mr. Grace promised to look into it. "That is," he said, "I shall appoint him if I find he really is, as you say, the right man."

When the appointment was announced, the Tammany boss sought to follow up the advantage he thought he had gained. He made a proposal for a more important post. When, a few days later, he received a note from Grace saying the man was totally unfit for the position, the Tammany leader requested a private interview.

Sensing that this would be the showdown, Grace told his office boy that when Mr. Kelly came there should be no interruptions: "Stay out on those steps and, on your life, don't let anyone in." Kelly arrived, noticeably grim. For a while the mumble of voices within the executive chamber was unintelligible to the guardian of the door. Then they grew more distinct. At length Mayor Grace was heard to say: "No one can dictate to me, Mr. Kelly." A few minutes later a red-faced Tammany boss stalked from the City Hall.[5]

~ Mayor Grace did not dramatize his break with Kelly. He never seems to have alluded to it, publicly. But the fact was soon out, and it brought more good-governmenters into the Grace camp. Shortly thereafter Mr. Grace answered another campaign argument by appointing William Wood, a strict Scotch Presbyterian, to the vacant presidency of the Board of Education. Then came the fight to reorganize the graft-ridden. street-cleaning bureau, and the attack upon another bastion of Tammany's power, the Police Department. This was the battle that brought the remainder of the good-government element to the Grace standard, some of them shamefacedly anxious to atone for their earlier distrust. Had Mr. Grace deliberately arranged the intended snub of the preinauguration nominations, he could hardly have hit upon a better stratagem for consolidating respectable support behind his administration.

At the end of February 1881, after less than two months in office, Mayor Grace was resting from a recurrence of his old tropical ailment of dysentery, and from the rigors of the festivities incident to the dedication of "Cleopatra's Needle" in Central Park. In 1879 the Khedive of Egypt had presented the ninety-foot obelisk to the city, but how to get it across the ocean nobody seemed to know. For nearly two years the gift stayed where it had been for centuries, in the sand beside the Nile. Lieutenant Commander Henry Gorringe, United States Navy, solved the problem by having an old steamer cut in two and rebuilt around its cargo. This engineering feat attracted attention on both sides of the Atlantic. Gorringe was one of the heroes at the ceremonies having to do with the formal installation of the relic in Central Park.

While taking it easy at his newly acquired home in East Thirty-eighth Street, the mayor occupied himself by reading the reports of the street-cleaning bureau during the term of his immediate predecessor in office. The condition of New York's streets was a scandal. The cleaning bureau was under the Police Department. Mayor Cooper had tried to see that the money appropriated for that purpose was used to clean the streets, and to this end had removed certain police commissioners from office. The commissioners had gone to the courts and got their jobs back. The streets remained as filthy as ever.

Mr. Grace addressed a letter to the commissioners responsible. After comparing in detail the steadily rising expenditures of the bureau with the increasingly bad condition of the streets, he wound up:

"These and many other facts appearing from the face of the reports of 1879 and 1880 are unexplained and inexplicable by anything shown in the reports themselves, and they appear to me as being of sufficient moment to call for explanation, which . . . it is undoubtedly in your power to give. . . . I feel it my duty to call upon you to make . . . a further and supplementary report which will explain and justify, if such be possible, the facts hereintofore referred to."[6]

The commissioners said that it was impossible to do any better with the funds available. Grace didn't believe it. He asked Mayor Prince of Boston if he could spare his superintendent of street cleaning long enough for a few days' conference in New York. The talks with the

Boston man convinced Grace that he was right in his estimate of the New York situation.[7]

He acted at once: first, setting in motion the machinery for a bill to the Legislature in Albany, removing the street-cleaning bureau from the Police Department; next, bringing formal charges against three of the police commissioners. Commissioners Joel W. Mason, Stephen B. French, and Sidney P. Nichols were asked to resign or to prepare a defense for a public trial before the mayor within ten days.[8]

Independent political leaders packed Cooper Union for a mass meeting in support of the mayor's action. Joseph H. Choate, a Republican and later the ambassador to Great Britain, concluded a long evening of oratory: "If it is true that the Commissioners cannot clean out the streets, why it is at least possible that we can clean out the Commissioners. . . . By the grace of God—and by that other Grace whom the people of this city have chosen to execute their will—this thing shall be done." To push the matter the meeting selected a Committee of Twenty-One, headed by a public-spirited millionaire ironmonger, Abram S. Hewitt, a brother-in-law of former Mayor Cooper.

The committee backed a bill in the Legislature to set up a separate street-cleaning department. The proposal went quickly enough through the senate and Grace announced that he had asked Commander Henry Gorringe to head the new department. Gorringe had said that he would accept.

John Kelly had an answer to this excellent stroke. At Albany a substitute bill was put forward in the assembly. This measure proposed that the Board of Health and the mayor jointly, and not the mayor alone, should be responsible for appointments to the street-cleaning department. Kelly thought he could control the Board of Health, of which Police Commissioner French was a member.

The Committee of Twenty-One filled the air with protests. Grace's cause was championed by newspapers which had fought him the autumn before. Mass meetings—one sponsored by "physicians and friends of sanitary reform"—championed it. Tammany was worried. A meeting attended by two hundred and fifty of its rebellious spirits raked John Kelly over the coals, and threatened a revolt.[9]

All this was unavailing. On May 24 the substitute bill went through. It was signed by Governor Alonzo B. Cornell, a Republican and a son of the founder of the university of the same name. Mr. Cornell owed his office to Kelly's bolt from the regular Democratic ticket in his feud with Tilden in 1879.

Henry Gorringe refused the appointment. Nevertheless, the public clamor in support of Grace had its effect. The mayor was able to obtain the approval of the Board of Health of the appointment of James Coleman as superintendent of the street-cleaning department. Coleman was a politically obscure young man—not Grace's first choice, and certainly not Kelly's. But with the police commissioners on trial before the mayor, Kelly took him. Mr. Coleman went into office with the gaze of an aroused public upon him. Before long New York's thoroughfares looked better than they had in many years.[10]

Meanwhile the trial of the police commissioners was making headlines. The charges against these officers related to their conduct of the former street-cleaning department, and not of the law-enforcement aspects of the Police Department—which would, indeed, have been a fertile subject for inquiry. Their counsel was Colonel George Bliss, a cagey lawyer and an expert on technicalities. Grace's sharp exchanges with the distinguished pettifogger made good reading. They proved to any reasonable mind the negligence and incompetence of the commissioners. In 1873, Bliss had drafted the charter of the City of New York, which defined, among other things, the powers of the mayor. Knowing this document forward and backward, Bliss challenged every act of the mayor that seemed to approach the narrowest limits of his authority. The public reaction to this exhibition was in favor of Grace.[11]

Through it all, the accused commissioners sat unmoved and confident. They had been through the same thing with Mayor Cooper. The trial ended in July, and on August 22, Grace rendered his decision, removing French, Mason, and Nichols. Still, the commissioners seemed undisturbed. The mayor's verdict was subject to review by Governor Cornell.

Without delay the forces of Tammany went to work on the governor.

Bliss served immediate notice of an appeal to the courts. Cornell rendered this unnecessary by setting aside the mayor's ruling. He did so on technical grounds having nothing to do with the evidence. The governor held that, as the street-cleaning department was no longer under the Police Department, it would be unjust to remove the commissioners for the shortcomings of that agency.[12]

Though the governor's action prevented a thoroughgoing reorganization of the city's corrupt Police Department, Grace was able to do away with some examples of lawbreaking that had become traditional under bluecoat protection. Early in his term he ordered raids on gambling joints. The gamblers lay low for a while and then reopened. Even the now friendly *Herald* chided the mayor about the "flagrant violation of the law." Grace prodded the police again, this time with more success. And before the end of his term he halted, in New York City, the open sale of chances in the nation's most publicized gambling game, the Louisiana lottery.[13]

~ Though the specious nature of Cornell's reasoning in the police commissioners' case did the governor's reputation no good, it was something of a boon to Grace. The mayor rose in the public esteem. Under the leadership of Hewitt the Committee of Twenty-One, created to reinforce Grace in his fight for an independent street-cleaning department, began to assume the aspect of a real reform movement. This development helped Grace in the important fight of his second year as mayor—the elevated railroad case.

In the pursuit of his financial schemes, Jay Gould had been accustomed to "handle" public men as a matter of course, by any means from outright purchase to political pressure. Gould's New York *World* had supported Mr. Grace's candidacy, doubtless for reasons akin to John Kelly's. Grace had been in the City Hall only a few months when, with the help of Cyrus W. Field and Russell Sage, Gould spared enough time from his transcontinental railroad schemes to formulate a plan to take over the elevated lines of New York City. There were three roads. The plan was for Field and Sage each to acquire one of the lesser lines. Gould would buy up the Manhattan Elevated Railway and, finally, combine the three. Gould started by using the *World* to hammer down the price of Manhattan stock.[14]

The aspersions cast by the *World* on that company were not groundless. The Manhattan's finances were shaky. It owed the city a fortune in taxes and had petitioned the mayor for a reduction or a moratorium on the debt. In a communication addressed to all three roads, Mayor Grace, Comptroller Campbell, and Corporation Counsel Whitney served notice of the city's intention to collect the taxes in full. The letter pointed out that if, as the roads claimed, meeting their taxes would render them unable to pay dividends or interest, "the operation of natural laws" would lower the value of the roads' securities. This would open a way eventually to lower taxes by reducing the assessments based on the market value of the property.[15]

For the moment this was just what Gould wanted. A little later Corporation Counsel Whitney won a legal round over the transportation companies when a court sustained the city's right to tax those companies' property as real estate. The *World* praised the decision as a victory for the people of New York City.[16]

But when Gould had acquired control of the Manhattan at bargain rates, his attitude toward taxes underwent a change. He asked for a conference with Grace, looking toward an adjustment of back taxes and a lower assessment in the future. Grace replied that no conference seemed necessary. The roads would have to pay their taxes. Incidentally, Grace himself owned about $40,000 worth of Manhattan stock, purchased some years before. To the mayor's letter, Gould coolly replied that Grace was visiting an injustice upon the companies, which he said were overassessed: "I regret that you have not seen your way to accede to my request to meet you, and in behalf of the elevated companies to settle their taxes. . . . You compel these companies in self defense to submit their case to the Legislature."[17]

Mr. Gould had rarely experienced much trouble getting what he wanted from the Legislature. A bill, written to his order, was promptly passed and sent to Governor Cornell. Grace was determined that the people should know of the governor's responsibility in the matter. He and Comptroller Campbell wrote Cornell the strongest letter they could compose, and sent copies to the newspapers:

"The bill is legislative robbery. . . . It deprives the city of half a million of money now due to it, puts a premium on defiance of the law, and compels every citizen to contribute toward the payment of the taxes of the elevated railroad companies for the year 1880."[18]

Alonzo Cornell was not a slow-witted man; and it would be a mistake to judge his administration by his behavior in the matter of the police commissioners. Moreover, within a few weeks the Republican convention would meet to select the state ticket for 1882. Cornell wanted another term. He vetoed Gould's bill.

With the help of Governor Cornell and the Legislature, Grace won another transportation victory at Albany. A bill pertaining to the surface lines would have granted free franchises to certain existing corporations. Twice, Grace managed to secure bids of $1 million and more for the privileges for which the companies wanted to pay the city nothing. In the face of this evidence of the value of the franchises, the legislators refused to do the bidding of the transportation lobbyists and enact the free bills.[19]

In 1882 a matter came up that concerned Grace neither as merchant nor as mayor, but nevertheless meant much to him. Great Britain inaugurated one of its periodic policies of repression in Ireland. Americans of Irish extraction were incensed, but there was little they could do until British troops imprisoned a number of American citizens in Ireland, on suspicion of illegal activity. Our Department of State protested, without result.

Ireland was grateful to Grace for his famine-relief work. Irish newspapers had chronicled with pride his election as "Lord Mayor" of New York. A "monster meeting" at Cooper Union afforded Grace an opportunity to express his sentiments on the recent developments:

"There now lie in English prisons deprived of their liberty, denied all knowledge of the charges upon which they are held, and refused a trial, a number of American citizens who have been crying pitifully to our American government, in the name of their citizenship, to protect them against this tyrannical action of a foreign state. . . . We are here this evening, gentlemen, according to the words of the call to demand that our Government extend to these men the full protection that their allegiance to it guarantees."

It must have been something of a letdown when the papers announced on the following day that all the prisoners had been released, except three. These preferred jail rather than return to the United States.[20]

Though that closed the matter, Grace was not allowed to forget his Irish birth. The old question of his citizenship was dragged out by a property owner whose mortgage Grace had foreclosed. He claimed that Grace, as an alien, had no right to own real estate. Beginning as a court action, the issue found its way to the New York State Senate. That body declined to act when Grace revealed that his citizenship was doubly established. On the eve of the mayoralty election, when the record of his original naturalization could not be found immediately, Grace without publicity had obtained a second set of papers from a Tammany judge.[21]

~ When James A. Garfield's reputation as an independent Republican cost him his life, a new direction was given to political activity. The president was assassinated by an insane and obscure adherent to the "stalwart" wing of the party. With no show of repentance, Charles Guiteau, the crazy murderer, repeated over and over, "I am a Stalwart of the Stalwarts, and Arthur will be President."[22]

The ascendency of Chester A. Arthur was both a blow and a spur to liberal Republicans. In New York City the hopeful incentive to decent Democrats was the record in office of W. R. Grace. It afforded the rallying point for crusaders for honest government. In October 1881, a month after Garfield's death, when Grace's victory in the street-cleaning department episode and his moral victory in the case of the police commissioners were fresh in the public memory, the old Committee of Twenty-One expanded into a political entity called the County Democracy. The leader and organizer was Abram S. Hewitt, who had such collaborators as Corporation Counsel Whitney, Commissioner of Public Works Hubert Thompson, former Mayor Cooper, Maurice Power, and E. Ellery Anderson.

Though Grace had two members of his cabinet on the new party's board of strategy, and in its ranks political associates going back to the Pratt campaign, he himself resisted importunities to push himself forward in the movement.

"I deem it proper that I should refrain from all active participation in politics during my incumbency of office," he wrote in response to an invitation. "It is my purpose, so far as lies in my power, to keep the office with which the people of this city have honored me entirely apart from all partisan or factional controversies and to administer it upon business principles purely and simply. . . . This I believe to be the true Democratic doctrine, and in the spirit of this doctrine . . . I prefer, as I have said, to take no active participation in politics so long as I shall be Chief Magistrate of the city."[23]

The same objections did not entirely hold with outside activity in the business world. Though Michael Grace ran the family business, with only occasional supervisory assistance from his elder brother, the mayor found time to assist in the organization of the Lincoln National Bank. The name—in honor of the Civil War president—was suggested by Grace. This undertaking showed the growth of Grace's reputation among businessmen as well as among liberal public figures. The president of the new bank, with whom Grace became increasingly close, was Thomas L. James, who had been Garfield's postmaster general. Several representatives of the Vanderbilt interests, and Albert Van Santvoort, head of the Albany Day Line Steamship Co., also were among the organizers.[24]

While Grace was busy with bank matters, the County Democracy scored its first triumph. At the state convention at Albany to select candidates for the Legislature, the new organization won all the seats for Manhattan, completely excluding Mr. Kelly's Tammany Hall delegation. W. R. Grace's aloofness from politics was more apparent than real. Though he did not attend the Albany gathering, he sent a representative—Richard Morrison, late of Tammany, and a member of the intimate Grace circle at the Emery House in Cincinnati—with these instructions:

"I have informed several friends that I would have a Gentleman there who would absolutely represent my views in regard to Candidates &c. I feel pleased to have you go in this capacity as I fully trust both your judgment and prudence, & I authorize you to say that I will endorse and approve of your efforts and recommendations."[25]

Grace approved of the slate evolved at Albany. He shared the feeling of a headline in the *Herald* reporting the mass meeting in New York City at which the ticket was ratified: "NEW BORN DEMOCRACY." Yet he took no visible part in the ensuing campaign. He did not need to. With a stalwart ticket, the Republicans were on the defensive. Grace must have enjoyed their discomfiture when the ready tongue of George Bliss, which had so annoyed Grace at the police trial, got the G. O. P. into deeper trouble.

Bliss was a Republican leader who worked with Tammany when it seemed to pay. To a group of reporters he bragged of the time he had bested Kelly. Giving dates and names, he explained that in a certain election the G. O. P. machine was to throw three thousand votes to a particular Tammany candidate in return for a like number of Wigwam votes for a Republican. "It was all fair," he chuckled. "We got our three thousand votes, but Gumbleton [of Tammany] didn't get his."

What prompted Bliss to make this admission is undiscoverable. When the baneful effects were apparent, he did his best to modify or retract, but there had been too many witnesses.[26]

People were fed up with that sort of thing; the County Democracy swept the field against its Republican opposition.

~ The following year, 1882, with state and city campaigns on the calendar, Grace took a more active part in the affairs of the wing of the party that had been built, in the first instance, on his achievements as mayor. Determined not to be a candidate for reelection, naturally Grace desired a successor who would keep to the path along which he had started. Besides that, thanks to the Republican split, the Democrats had a wide-open chance to annex the governorship. But unless the nominee should be an anti-Tammany man the mayor's hands would be more or less tied, no matter how lofty his intentions.

Though locally in power, it would be no simple thing for the County Democracy to retain authority in the City Hall or extend it to Albany. John Kelly had rarely worked harder. He spurred on his ward and district leaders, his precinct and block captains. The Plunkitts were never busier at weddings, confirmations, fires, and funerals. Honest John in person moved persuasively from one leader to another of Irving Hall and the County Democracy. His earnest plea was for a "united Democracy." This was no time for factionalism. The state of the Republicans should show that. If the Democrats stood together, they could win.

There was something in this talk, as anyone could see. What anyone could not see was that a unified Democracy—before the nominations were achieved—would fall under the sway of Tammany. The Hall had the machinery, and it knew the ropes; the County Democracy did not. The Hall even had two newspapers to din in its arguments—the *Sun* and the *Mail and Express*. John Kelly and his hierarchy made a profession of politics. They worked at it all day long. Grace, Hewitt, Choate, Cooper, Anderson, and the rest were men of large affairs to whom politics was an avocation. That is why so many crusades peter out after one surge, such as the County Democracy's victory in '81. To duplicate that feat in city and state in '82 would require an organization with some full-time workers. In no other way could the right man be nominated. After the nominations would come the election. Here Tammany's hold on the city's laboring masses would be very useful in piling up votes for the reform ticket. So, whatever they thought of him, intelligent reformers did not treat Honest John too cavalierly.

That was the practical politics of the situation in 1882—something Grace, for one, did not overlook.

The mayor was making his influence felt in the counsels of the reform movement. In a little better than a year and a half he had emerged as an arresting figure in the public life of the metropolis. Few public servants had borne the honors of office more modestly. Few had asked less for themselves. His sole public interest was capable and honest government; his sole political desire the regeneration of his party as an instrument to that end.

The nomination for governor would come first. Grace's candidate was the choice of the County Democracy —John Kelly's successor as city comptroller, Allan Campbell. The convention was held in Syracuse in September. Hewitt and Corporation Counsel Whitney, in charge of Campbell's interests, headed the County Democracy delegation. Several other city officials departed for the scene. When the *Sun* heard that Grace, too, had gone, it was disturbed: "Today and for the next few days New York City will be without a Mayor, acting Mayor, or President of the Board of Aldermen."

Grace penned a good-natured note to Charles A. Dana: "I, of course, ask for no retraction of the statement etc., but merely as a personal matter to report myself in N. Y. & with no intention of going to the convention, all of which was well known in the [mayor's] office yesterday."[27]

To a delegate at Syracuse whom Grace felt to be in need of enlightenment the mayor wrote to explain his preference for Campbell. He touched also on what he thought should be the reformers' attitude toward Tammany:

"Allan Campbell . . . would unite all the Conservative elements, irrespective of party; . . . and I hold that we live today in a time *when the best man* & not mere party lines will govern the voters.

"I am, as you know, firmly convinced that, if the Democracy sacrifice principle, show cowardice, or act on the principle of apparent expediency . . . they will indubitably fail. . . . I think that, while Tammany Hall should be treated with the greatest consideration, . . . it would be absolutely suicidal to admit them into the Convention & that the result would be to drive away from the party all men who, in defense of their convictions, stood by Lucius Robinson [the Democratic nominee abandoned by Kelly] in 1879."[28]

Tammany, however, won twenty-four seats on the convention floor—to the County Democracy's thirty-eight, and Irving Hall's ten. The County Democracy voted solidly for Campbell. Kelly's first choice seems to have been Henry V. Slocum of Brooklyn, but his intention was to back the winner, whoever he might prove to be. So on the first ballot, he distributed his votes among four candidates. After two ballots, Campbell had failed to develop strength, and on the third ballot, there was danger of a break to Slocum until Hewitt threw the County Democracy's twenty-four votes to another dark horse, Grover Cleveland of Buffalo. That started the shift that nominated Cleveland.

Grace could not have been too greatly disappointed. Stephen Grover Cleveland had begun adult life as a teacher of the blind; as the convivial bachelor sheriff of Erie County he was called Big Steve in beer-hall circles; as mayor of Buffalo he had dismayed some of his political backers by instituting a reform administration. His veto of a padded street-cleaning contract followed Grace's successful battle in the same field.

Grace also must have observed with some interest the proceedings of the Republican convention. For all his uneven record, Cornell was the hope of the liberals. His support of Grace in the elevated railway tax fight was cited in his favor. But Cornell had against him the personal influence of President Arthur, Jay Gould's money, and the managerial genius of Jay Gould's lawyer, former United States Senator Roscoe Conkling. The outcome was the nomination of Arthur's secretary of the treasury, C. J. Folger, a choice that improved Cleveland's chances.[29]

~ John Kelly had not done very well at Syracuse. He had scrambled on the Cleveland bandwagon at the last minute, after the nomination was assured. Back on his home ground, however, the Tammany chieftain displayed greater finesse in the maneuvers preliminary to the selection of a Democratic candidate for mayor to succeed Grace.

For more than a year, Honest John had been as busy as a beaver, spreading the gospel of party harmony. This bore fruit in the creation of a Conference Committee, representing the three factions of the party, to select the city ticket. From the first Grace was suspicious that Kelly would dominate the deliberations of the committee. He discussed his fears with independent Republicans such as Joseph H. Choate and Carl Schurz; with progressive Democrats like Oswald Ottendorfer. Grace found those gentlemen of like mind.

They waited until the Conference Committee, on October 14, nominated Franklin Edson for mayor. Edson was a successful businessman, with a colorless record on the reform issue. Grace and a number of his supporters feared that in office, Edson would be controlled by Tammany. "He will not be endorsed by us," the *Herald* quoted a member of the old Committee of Twenty-One as saying. "He is next door to a Tammany man." Though the speaker was not identified, he expressed Grace's sentiments.[30]

Yet what were the liberals to do? Their organization. the County Democracy, had participated in the selection of Edson and had endorsed him. To put another candidate in the field would split the reform vote. Hewitt, Anderson, Power, Thompson, and others were willing tacitly to accept Edson, though they did not like him and regarded his selection as a triumph for Kelly. In this Grace did not go along with his liberal colleagues. Grace was for fighting Edson, and he found supporters in such men as Oswald Ottendorfer, Carl Schurz, and Charles Scribner, the publisher. Grace and his friends called a mass meeting, which was held at Cooper Union on October 23.[31]

Mayor Grace presided, and in his introductory remarks brought the name of Allan Campbell before the meeting. In so doing, he defined the attitude toward public office that was to govern the remainder of his own political career:

"My short experience in public life has convinced me that what is needed in the great public offices are men of thorough independence and high standards, and with an absolute determination to serve the People against monopolists, whether they be monopolists of our public franchises or monopolists of political power. . . .

"Tweed became a power through the expenditure of the public moneys. The cohesive power of plunder was the secret of his influence. Today large sums of money require to be expended for the water supply. Shall the politicians spend it wastefully to strengthen their machines or shall the People's representatives spend it wisely for the People's good?"

Though Mr. Grace's administration had been praised by friends of good government in distant parts of the country, Grace personally seldom mentioned his achievements. He departed from that course now, not to glorify himself but to testify to the fitness of Campbell:

"I will tell you a story of the aqueduct bill. . . . In 1881 . . . [it] was passed by both houses [of the Legislature] empowering the Commissioner of Public Works to build an Aqueduct and make other expenditures for the Water Supply of the City of New York, and ordering the Mayor and Comptroller to issue bonds for the payment of such expenditures. As soon as I found that no provision was made for the protection of the City's interest through its proper representatives, the Mayor and Comptroller, I . . . [notified] the Commissioner of Public Works . . . that the bill must be withdrawn immediately or I would . . . denounce the whole enterprise. . . . I telegraphed to the Governor begging him not to give his approval to the bill. . . . After some consultation with the Commissioner of Public Works and Corporation Counsel, an amendment to the bill was agreed on as follows:

" 'The issue of bonds as required from time to time shall be subject to the approval of the Board of Estimate and Apportionment, all work shall be done and material purchased by contract publicly let to the lowest bidder, and no contract shall be made, or lands or water rights purchased, without the approval of at least three members of the Board of Estimate and Apportionment, of whom the Mayor and Comptroller shall be two.'

"Comptroller Campbell and myself then wrote urgent letters to the Governor urging him to sign the bill in its amended shape; but the Governor in his wisdom saw fit to veto it. During the last session of the Legislature various efforts were made to secure the consent of Comptroller Campbell and myself of some bill allowing the work of building the new aqueduct to be put into the hands of a commission. . . . We would agree to no bill for the expenditure of $15,000,000 or $20,000,000 of the people's money . . . [unless] authorized by the . . . Mayor and Comptroller. . . .

"It is in this condition you find the thing today, and you may expect that the next Legislature unless prevented by the veto of the new Governor of this State, will probably pass, in the interest of the politicians, just such a bill as that passed in 1881.

"Now judge for yourself if you want a mayor without experience as a public officer and who has been nominated by a combination of politicians; or a man like Allan Campbell, who is to my knowledge, a thoroughly liberal man . . . a Democrat in State and national matters, and yet in municipal matters convinced that business principle and not party should control the government of a great city like this."[32]

Campbell was duly nominated on what was called the Citizens' Ticket. Grace collected a campaign fund. Campbell also received the endorsement of the Republicans. But neither the Citizens' Committee nor the Republicans had a political machine to compete with Tammany and its allies.

Had there been a straight reform ticket to oppose a straight machine ticket, the Citizens might have fared better. But the Citizens' Ticket was weakened by the inclusion of an old-time spoils politician as candidate for county clerk. Tammany, on the other hand, was running its men on a straight Democratic ticket headed by Grover Cleveland, who had the support of the reform element. Whitney, Anderson, Hewitt, and others remained aloof from Campbell, though they supported Cleveland for governor. Thus the machine won again. The straight Democratic ticket carried the city with a healthy majority of 21,407 votes for Edson.[33]

~ John Kelly aimed a parting shot at the retiring mayor. The *Mail and Express* came out with an indignant story about the condition of the streets below Fourteenth Street. "Reeking with Filth, Traffic Impeded, Foul Gases Polluting the Air," read a headline. "Mr. Coleman's Department and the Million of Dollars Paid to Clean the City—HOW IS THE MONEY SPENT?"

Grace found the charge to be true, and called on Commissioner Coleman to explain. It turned out that the contractor in charge of that district was vacationing in Europe, and that there had been a spell of bad weather. Coleman got the area clean in short order.[34]

Instead of casting a shadow over the last days of his term, the episode served merely as a farewell reminder of Tammany's enmity.

"It is no small praise of a public man in this city to say that he has earned the cordial hatred of Tammany Hall," remarked E. L. Godkin in the

Evening Post, which had opposed Grace in 1880. This achievement alone on the part of one who, before his election, was supposed to be in close alliance with the faction, would account for the popular reaction in favor of Mayor Grace.

"But his claim to public respect and confidence rests on a broader and more positive foundation. The Mayor has used the limited powers with which the charter clothes him in the interest of the whole city rather than of any party."[35]

Wrote Oswald Ottendorfer, editor of the influential *Staats-Zeitung*, which also had fought Grace two years before:

"His successful struggle against the corruption of the Streetcleaning-Department deserves especially very high praise. Mayor Cooper began this struggle like Mr. Grace a few months after his inauguration. . . . But while under Cooper the whole affair subsided into nothing, the energetic beginning of Mr. Grace . . . terminated . . . in a thorough reform, . . . the results of which are now before us."[36]

Whitelaw Reid began an editorial in the *Tribune* with the words: "Mr. Grace retires to private life with the good will and respect of substantial and public-spirited citizens." He closed with: "We thought very ill of him when he was elected; and it gives us the greater pleasure to be able to speak thus of him as he goes out of office."[37]

Finally, came an unintended touch of drama. On December 29 the Board of Estimate assembled for what was expected to be its last meeting under Mayor Grace. When the work was not out of the way at one-thirty, Grace suggested an adjournment until three. An alderman asked, Why not until next morning? "No," replied the Mayor. "We are here now, and tomorrow some of us may have our necks broken."

The next morning Grace was driving on Seventy-second Street with a girlfriend of his daughter Alice. The snorting little steam engine of an elevated train frightened the team. As the horses bolted, a wheel of the carriage struck an "L" pillar, throwing out the occupants. The girl was unhurt, but Grace lay unconscious.

Word reached William M. Ivins, the mayor's secretary, that Grace was dead. A little later a telegram arrived at the City Hall: "Have been thrown from my carriage but not seriously injured. Please send me payrolls and aldermanic papers."

The city's concern over the accident was another indication of the affection New York felt for the man who had given it the best government in a generation.[38]

12 ~ Peace Terms for Peru

~ "Here I am again, my own boss & at my own desk," W. R. Grace wrote in January 1883. The desk was worthy of note. It had been made for John D. Rockefeller, and had a flat, not a roll, top, which measured six by five feet. When the Standard Oil Co. vacated the premises at 192 Pearl Street, into which W. R. Grace & Co. moved in 1882, a few items of furniture were left behind to be sold. In the lot was this desk, which caught Mr. Grace's eye; but he thought $200 too much to pay for it. He asked a young bookkeeper, Maurice Bouvier, to go to Standard Oil's new offices at 26 Broadway, and tell Mr. Rockefeller that Mr. Grace would give $100 for the desk.

Maurice was anxious to make an impression because he had just joined W. R. Grace & Co. Previously he had been the mayor's office boy at the City Hall. In that capacity, Maurice had guarded the mayoral door during the eventful conference with Honest John Kelly. Mr. Rockefeller said that, for Mr. Grace, he would shave the price to $185. Maurice was sent back with an offer of $115. The desk changed ownership for $150. It is still used by the presiding officer of W. R. Grace & Co.[1]

A great deal of water had gone under the bridge in the nearly three years since Mr. Grace last had been in active management of the business. Though invaded, devastated, and disastrously beaten, Peru refused to make peace. Michael Grace, who had taken charge of the Grace interests early in 1880, had thrown his influence behind efforts to bring the war to a formal conclusion on the best terms for Peru that Chile could be brought to agree to. Failing in this, his policy had been to go along with the tide, and cautiously reestablish the activities of the Grace houses in a sphere dominated by the might of the victor. Advised by William from time to time, Michael had played his cards well.

To go back to 1880:

Chile officially showed its hand in October of that year, after the defeat of the Peruvian and Bolivian armies in Tacna and Arica. In response to an attempt by the United States to end the bloodshed, Chile demanded, either by annexation or occupation, all Bolivian and Peruvian nitrate territory, in addition to a $20-million indemnity and other concessions from Peru.

In bitter fury, Peru refused the terms. Chile sent a marauding expedition through the agricultural region north of Lima—on the pattern of Sherman's march through Georgia. Another force moved on Lima. After furious fighting on the outskirts against an improvised Peruvian army, the capitol was occupied in January 1881. Fearing reprisals by the Chileans, Grace had brought Manuel Llaguno and his family to the United States. When Llaguno died here of pneumonia, William and Michael Grace lost a friend to whom they were devoted, and an astute business partner. As a consequence of the blockade of Callao, Grace Brothers & Co. had transferred its offices to Lima. During the fight for the city, John Grace and his nephew Ned Eyre took refuge on a vessel in Callao harbor. Michael Grace rushed down from New York to try to integrate Grace interests with the terms of Peru's capitulation.[2]

Peru did not capitulate. Nicolás de Piérola took to the mountains with remnants of his troops. Chile set up in Lima a rival government under García Calderón, a lawyer who had been identified with Henry Meiggs and other foreign interests in Peru. Chile's object was to have a regime to make peace with. But Calderón, too, refused Chile's harsh terms. In this Calderón had the support of the United States, and the encouragement of Michael Grace.

American popular feeling resented the Chilean terms. James G. Blaine, Garfield's secretary of state, began to shape a long-range policy for composing the differences between Peru and Chile. This policy was pro-Peruvian in that it sought to avert the "dismemberment" of that country. Yet it did not ignore Chile's economic contributions to development of the nitrate country, nor her military victories. While the secretary was thus engaged, and while Michael Grace was still in Lima, I. P. Christiancy, the United States minister there, wrote Blaine a remarkable communication. He said that Chile was out to establish a "provincial" government over Peru which would mean "the ascendency of English over American influence on this coast." He urged that the United States "intervene in compelling a settlement of peace on reasonable terms." If Chile proved unamenable, we should take "control [of] Peru by a protectorate or by annexation." Most Peruvians, he said, would be in favor of either.

Though Michael Grace had too much sense to subscribe to any such jingo claptrap, he did hope that the United States might be able to ameliorate the terms. At the same time Michael cultivated good relations with Admiral Patricio Lynch, head of the Chilean forces of occupation, and landed a certain amount of business in connection with those forces. Lynch had served in the British navy. Though his expedition of destruction in the north had given him a name in Peru similar to Sherman's in our South, Lynch was not a bad man.[3]

Mr. Blaine not only ignored Christiancy's unsolicited suggestion; he recalled the man. Then Blaine got under way a scheme to try to save Peru's nitrate territory. The scene of his operations was Paris, where our minister was the financier, Levi P. Morton. Morton got in touch with French financial interests which represented European holders of Peruvian bonds. A corporation called the Compagnie Financière et Commerciale du Pacifique was formed. The idea was to place "all Peruvian guano & nitrate (including Tarapaca) . . . under Neutral protection of Foreign Powers, including the U. S.," and to administer it through the Compagnie Pacifique. In this way it was intended that Chile should receive a huge indemnity, but would forego annexation of Peruvian territory. W. R. Grace & Co. would be a stockholder in Pacifique and the consignee of all guano and nitrate shipped under that company's contract to the West Indies, Canada, and the United States.

Blaine sent new envoys to Peru and to Chile to work for his plan. Grace established a house in Valparaiso, called Grace & Co. The manager was Noel West, an Englishman formerly with the Pacific Steam Navigation Co., and persona grata with the Chilean government. John Grace went down from Lima for the formal opening of the house, and later took up his residence there. Michael Grace wrote West that Chilean antagonism toward the "*name of Grace*" would die out in time. He said that Chile should appreciate that, in serving Peru, "we acted consistently"—meaning, possibly, that unlike some firms, Grace had not sold arms to both sides. Had the Grace interests been in Chile, "we would have been equally loyal" to that country.[4]

Though Michael Grace went along with the ambitious Blaine-Morton plan, from the beginning he had little faith in it. "I am convinced," he wrote privately, "that Chile won't yield Tarapaca except to superior force and I am satisfied that the U. S. Govt. will not use force. I consider Tarapaca lost to Peru for ever and that the Paris gentlemen are chasing a phantom." The secretary of state, however, was a man of energy. The envoys he sent south backed him up in positive and fairly sensible fashion. Calderón acted bolder and bolder. Chile was beginning to get worried when, in September 1881, President Garfield succumbed to an assassin's bullet. At once it was rumored that Arthur would alter Garfield's foreign policy. Admiral Lynch lost no time. The Calderón government was suppressed and Calderón exiled to Chile.

Michael Grace wrote the Lima house that just when the Chilean minister in Washington had begun to fear that the United States meant business, it looked as if Garfield's death had brought an end to Peruvian hopes. To make certain, Michael took another trip to the capital. President Arthur received the visitor with a politician's smooth courtesy. What he said amounted to exactly nothing. Michael failed to get hold of Blaine, but the secretary's assistants offered little hope for a continuance of a strong policy.

The state of uncertainty did not last long. Blaine was succeeded by former Senator F. T. Frelinghuysen of New Jersey. Mr. Arthur did more than reverse Garfield's policy toward Chile. He attempted to blow it sky-high, by the publication of certain diplomatic correspondence—including Christiancy's crazy letter—which gave an unflattering impression of what Blaine had tried to do. The whole thing was a political stroke, an attempt by the "stalwart" Arthur to discredit the policies of his "half-breed," or liberal, predecessor. Though his program on the whole was decent and enlightened, Blaine had made mistakes in detail. He had been talked into the manifest impropriety of espousing certain shadowy claims, in large amounts, of French (not American) citizens against Peru. He had insisted that Chile honor the claims. The press had a field day over these disclosures. In one way it was fortunate that the constructive features of Blaine's effort were ignored. To have enlarged upon them would have brought in the name of Grace. Any partisan hack could have twisted this to the disadvantage of Mayor William and created a diversion at a time when he was doing good things for the city of New York.[5]

～ The spectacle of a president of the United States making his country ridiculous before the world in the matter of foreign policy in order to gain a local political advantage disgusted Michael Grace, as it did many others. "*Am. Intervention* is all a humbug," he wrote his fellow British subject, Noel West, at Valparaiso. "Uncle Sam has backed down."

To Ned Eyre in Lima, Michael expatiated on the consequences as he foresaw them:

"The United States will be thoroughly hated on the West Coast and will be jeered and laughed at by all the Foreign Legations; made fun of by the Chilean Press, and thoroughly despised by the Peruvian people who will blame them to a very great extent for the present trouble. . . . When the European Powers wanted to interfere some year and a half ago, the United States, riding their hobby of Monroe Doctrine, refused to allow them to interfere and promised to arrange the matter themselves, and now, after raising the hopes of the Government and the people . . . they abandon them to the mercies of the victorious army."[6]

Ten days later Michael called on the new secretary of state, Mr. Frelinghuysen, to whom he probably communicated a milder version of his views. He came away feeling a little better. Before leaving office, Mr. Blaine had sent to Chile William H. Trescot, an experienced international lawyer and diplomat. Frelinghuysen said that his course would depend on what Trescot reported. Michael took this to mean that we might still exert some pressure.

Naturally, Michael was not told that Trescot's instructions had been so modified that he had nothing to back his words except more words. The diplomacy of moral suasion got nowhere with the Chileans. The unhappy Trescot agreed to carry to Peru terms that were so exorbitant that Frelinghuysen repudiated the envoy by cable. Lonesome and blue in Lima, Trescot unburdened himself to John Grace of an account of an interview with the foreign minister of Chile. "Balmaceda actually refused to go in to the matter of Tarapaca at all," John quoted Trescot as saying, "simply said the place is ours now. . . . If the U. S. wants Tarapaca for Peru or anyone else she must first drive us out. . . . What can you answer a man that talks like that? . . . I was not prepared to fight so I had to shift the subject."[7]

As successful in diplomacy as it had been in war, and with nothing to fear from the United States, Chile set out to smother the last spark of belligerence in Peru. "The Chileans stop at nothing. . . . My personal compts. to President Arthur," wrote John Grace, whose Irish had been aroused. An entire railroad was pulled up and shipped to Chile. The treasure vaults in the municipal building in Lima were shipped. Money contributions were forced from citizens and business houses, Grace Brothers & Co., on one occasion at least, getting off very lightly indeed with an assessment of two thousand *soles*, silver. "The Peruvians will soon have to sign any peace laid before them . . . or be utterly ruined."[8]

Frelinghuysen sent a new minister to Peru, James Rudolph Partridge, who was noted for forthright action. Though merely secretary to the governor, Partridge had done as much as any other to avert the secession of Maryland in 1861. About the first thing he did in Peru was to assemble the ministers of Britain, France, and Italy to discuss the peace terms. For this he was ordered home by the next steamer. The New York *Times* said that Partridge had acted with more sense than the State Department. Michael Grace went further. He said that our "dog-in-the-manger" tactics kept Peru helpless before the conqueror: "If a general foreign intervention had been allowed this war would have ended 2 or 3 years ago."[9]

While Michael was working to obtain a reduction of the Chilean demands, he was also trying to induce the die-hard Peruvian leaders to look at things as they were, and agree to the best peace obtainable. A government set up under Miguel Iglesias, one of the defenders of Lima, signed a peace treaty in October 1883. The terms, though hard, were a little milder than those given Trescot. Tarapacá was ceded. The Chilean army would continue to occupy Tacna and Arica, and at the end of ten years the disposition of those provinces would be determined by a plebiscite. The nation thus taking permanent possession would pay the other nation $10 million. Chile had already seized the Lobos Islands, Peru's best remaining guano holding, and had ordered the sale of a million tons of the fertilizer. Chile was to remain in control of the Lobos until the million tons were disposed of, but was to turn over half of the proceeds to creditors of Peru who had a lien on guano.[10]

~ Thus, embittered Peru became the master once more, in name at least, of its destiny. What this destiny held aside from poverty and oppression was hard to see. Peru's plight brought to the mind of W. R. Grace the plight of the late Confederacy following the Civil War, which Grace had first seen on lumber-buying trips four years after Appomattox. Actually, Peru was in a worse situation from our South. Recovery depended on reestablishment to some degree of the national credit. Over the country hung a foreign debt of some £33 million sterling, on which interest had been unpaid since 1876. Though the peace treaty provided for certain remittances by Chile, out of Peruvian pockets, to certain bondholders, no payments were made until many years later. Consequently the bondholders, who were chiefly English, began to band together to see what they could do for themselves. About the only properties left to Peru that were capable of providing revenue were the railroads and the almost unworked mines.

Chile emerged from the war rich and confident, the most likely field in South America for business enterprises. Efforts to create goodwill for the "name of Grace," as represented by the new Valparaiso house, were part of a campaign to get a share of that business. At the same time, Grace did not forget, nor allow his partners to forget, that the Grace fortune had been founded in Peru; that Grace Brothers & Co. was "a Peruvian house," whose support of Peru in the war had gone beyond the ordinary limits of the profit motive. But for his death, Manuel Llaguno would have now been the managing partner. As it was, this post fell to Ned Eyre.

Any prostrate society attracts the vultures of business, with their peculiar talents for profiting from calamity. In this situation, Grace Brothers & Co. became a leader, perhaps the foremost leader, among those who took an opposite course and began to work for the ultimate rehabilitation of the country.

Before the war, Grace had taken over for debt the Cartavio sugar plantation of ten thousand acres. With the restoration of peace, Grace poured money into Cartavio—$75,000 for a grinding mill alone—and prepared to double the working force of two hundred Chinese. The matter of obtaining the additional laborers was taken up with the Chinese minister in Washington. Fair pay and treatment were promised, with the workers under the supervision of the Chinese legation at Lima.[11]

Relatively this was a small thing. The important matter was a settlement with the foreign bondholders. It occurred to Michael Grace that if he could control some of the railroads and mines in Peru the bondholders would have to deal with Grace as well as with the Peruvian government, which was in a poor position to bargain.

Under a contract executed with Henry Meiggs, the numerous Meiggs heirs and a few others owned the operating right to the Oroya railroad, the unfinished line that ran from Callao, through Lima, and almost to the summit of the Andes eighty-seven miles distant. This was the road—probably the most difficult piece of railroad construction ever attempted, costs averaging $200,000 a mile—that had hastened the downfall of the imaginative Meiggs.

In February 1883, William H. Cilley called at the Grace offices in Pearl Street. When construction ceased, Cilley had been the chief engineer of the road. The Graces knew him to be a good man. Cilley said that the road was wastefully operated, used "to support in clover a whole batch of fellows who did little or no good." One was a nephew of Meiggs who drew a yearly salary of £3,000, or more than $15,000. Cilley suggested that Grace take the road out of the hands of the present operators, substitute competent management, and make something of it. Cilley was one of the executors of Henry Meiggs's estate, and the owner of four hundred shares in the operating company. He said he could control two thousand shares, or nearly 25 percent of the stock. As John G. Meiggs and certain heirs were hard up, Cilley did not think it would be difficult for Grace quietly to acquire a majority of the stock.

Cilley saw further than the profitable operation of the unfinished road. He spoke of its extension to the Cerro de Pasco mines, which the Meiggs heirs also controlled; and the operation of those mines to the enrichment of all private parties concerned, and to the considerable financial relief of the Peruvian government.

W. R. Grace did not warm to the suggestion. He thought the rehabilitation of Peru would be a long process, and cited the case of our southern states. He had never taken much stock in the riches of Cerro de Pasco. When the dying Meiggs had acquired the mines in an effort to retrieve his hopeless situation, Grace thought the scheme "about as feasible as the recovery of the buried treasure of the late lamented Captain Kidd."

Even after the elder Grace's return to business in 1883, Peru and Chile remained Michael's special province. Michael favored the Cilley plan, and had his way. The arrangement was that Grace should furnish as much as $40,000 to acquire additional shares in the operating company. This was to be done without the knowledge of the particular heirs who were doing so well from the road as it was. The furtive campaign failed. A year later, 1884, in London, Michael took up the thing openly with Alexander Robertson, a son-in-law of Meiggs. Robertson helped to manage an arrangement whereby the stock in the railroad operating company and in the mine concession was held three-eighths by Grace, three-eighths by Cilley, and two-eighths by Robertson. Like Cilley, Robertson was an executor of Meiggs's estate.

By then the foreign bondholders were pretty well organized, with offices in London and lawyers at work. Michael believed "that it will not be a very long time before the Peruvian Bondholders will turn to the railroads to seek . . . remuneration." Michael would be waiting for them.[12]

~ About the year 1800, the first rubber powder flasks and overshoes were imported from Brazil, where they were made by native workmen. The manufacture of rubberized cloth in 1823 by a Scot named Macintosh gave the world its first raincoat that would really turn away water. For the next seventy-five years, any waterproof coat was called a "mackintosh." Mr. Macintosh's enterprise was the beginning of the rubber industry. The introduction of the solid rubber tire for carriages and bicycles in the early eighties was one of the new uses that were always coming on to increase the demand for the product.

In 1877, W. R. Grace had got into the rubber business. In those days all rubber was "wild" rubber—the uncultivated product of tropical forests. The best variety came from the Amazon valley of Brazil. By 1882, Grace had $200,000 or $300,000 in the business and was prepared to expand. He established two houses, Sears & Co. of Pará (in which the Grace interest was 80 percent), and Scott & Co. of Manáos (Grace interest, 70 percent).

Things were going along well when Mr. Grace found occasion to write Richard F. Sears a fatherly letter. He said that he had heard certain stories about Sears's use of alcohol. "For myself, I fancy . . . you probably have allowed the habits & good fellowship of Pará to grow upon you a little." Mr. Grace suggested that his partner "do as I did in Peru—take nothing neither beer, ale, wine (except claret) or much less spirits; people will wonder and talk for a little while, but they will soon get accustomed to it and it will help your stomach & keep your liver cool & healthy." Grace also looked up Mrs. Sears and arranged for her to join her husband in Brazil.

No one knowing Pará in 1884 could envy Mrs. Sears. The town stood on the bank of the Pará River, one of the mouths of the Amazon, about fifty miles from the sea. It was about the unhealthiest place in the hemisphere. Where the filthy streets did not end at the river, they were stopped by the steaming, impenetrable jungle. During the wet season, it rained nearly all the time, and in the dry season it rained once a day. The temperature never fell below seventy. Aside from a small colony of American and European rubber buyers, the population was a composite of Negro slaves, Indians, and Portuguese. Yet there was a good deal going on in Pará. It was the entrepôt for the fabulous Amazon valley, where river steamers transferred their cargoes to ocean-going vessels. Pará was, in fact, the world's rubber capital; "fine Para" was the trade name for the best grade on the market. There were some smart men among the cosmopolitan and convivial foreign rubber group at Pará, but none smarter than Grace's young Bostonian, Sears, who was getting the name of the shrewdest trader on the river.

Whatever the drawbacks of Pará as a place to live, J. Alvin Scott, resident partner of Scott & Co. of Manáos, must have thought it a paradise.

Manáos was a settlement in a clearing nine hundred miles up the Amazon. It had the advantage of being in the heart of the best rubber jungles on earth. In 1883 the price of rubber was high, the market expanding. Scott & Co. and Sears & Co. were making money fast. Experience has shown that men will put up with a good deal to do that.[13]

Though Grace was unable to land a nitrate contract with the Chileans that would compensate for the Peruvian agreement that had gone up in smoke, employment was found for Grace-operated ships in the nitrate and guano activities under Chilean control. This and other matters, such as rubber, increased the number of vessels under Grace management. While Grace's shipping interests expanded, the United States merchant marine as a whole continued to decline until, by 1880, it was a comparatively small factor in our foreign trade. Steam continued to crowd out sail. Though Grace might charter a steamer for a specific purpose, he remained almost exclusively an operator of sail.

In 1882 he realized a long-cherished ambition and established his own line between New York and the west coast of South America. It was called the Merchants Line. This marked the beginning of the end of a rather unsatisfactory working arrangement with Fabbri & Chauncey, which owned the old line on that route. The Grace vessels undercut F. & C. by 30 or 40 percent on rates to Chile. Once Grace had the upper hand in Chile, the new line was extended to Peru. To survive as long as they had on the toughest route on earth for sailing vessels—Cape Horn—Fabbri & Chauncey could not have been indifferent operators. Yet Grace thought the company loosely run, and the speed with which it collapsed in the face of Grace competition seems to confirm this. In 1883 the Merchants Line absorbed its rival and raised its rates.[14]

W. R. Grace had long been interested in the project of an interoceanic canal across Central America. The idea had been discussed since the early Spanish days. As time went on, various routes, from Panama to the Isthmus of Tehuantepec in Mexico, were explored. Generally, the Nicaragua route seems to have been favored. Though longer than the Panama route, there were not the mountains to contend with. This was one of the various sideline projects with which Henry Meiggs Keith busied himself when he and Grace were associated in the Costa Rica railroad.

When we annexed Texas and began the war with Mexico that was to bring California into the Union, Great Britain moved to get control of the Nicaragua route. The result was a diplomatic tussle ending in the Clayton-Bulwer Treaty of 1850 by which it was agreed that neither the United

States nor Britain should exclusively control, or fortify, a canal. The extent of Britain's victory became clear when the rapid development of California showed the need for a canal under American control. Vainly, Presidents Grant and Hayes endeavored to obtain modifications of the Clayton-Bulwer pact.

While this was going on, Ferdinand de Lesseps, the veteran French promoter responsible for the Suez Canal, obtained a concession to cut a ditch through Panama. The American public was thoroughly aroused. President Hayes declared a canal across Panama would be "virtually a part of the coast line of the United States." The French government promptly disclaimed any connection with the de Lesseps enterprise. Nevertheless, except for Britain's unyielding attitude on the 1850 treaty, our government probably would have taken the contract out of the Frenchman's hands. After a stock-subscription campaign on behalf of de Lesseps's company had met with only moderate success in the United States, the promoter began operations in 1883 largely with private French funds.

W. R. Grace was among a minority of Americans who, like U. S. Grant, supported the French scheme. They held that the thing to do was to get a canal built somehow. Then the United States would find a means of protecting that part of its "coast line," treaty or no treaty. In April 1883, Grace gave a dinner at Delmonico's to Charles de Lesseps, vice president of his father's canal company. An impressive list of guests included General Grant, former Secretary of State William M. Evarts. former Secretary of the Navy Richard W. Thompson, and former Postmaster General Thomas L. James. In the course of the speaking, only de Lesseps referred directly to the controversial aspect of the project, and he was tactful about it. The dinner attracted considerable attention, however, and advertised the strength of canal sentiment in the United States.[15]

At the Chincha Islands off the coast of Peru, the supply boat *John Bryce* sold its wares to ships that came to haul guano, a natural fertilizer, from the islands. *Courtesy W. R. Grace & Co.*

The staff is photographed outside John Bryce's store in Callao, Peru, June 1866. *Courtesy W. R. Grace & Co.*

India House, headquarters of W. R. Grace & Co. from 1885 to 1913. Located on Hanover Square, India House today is a national historical monument, occupying a site in the city associated with the earliest Dutch merchants of New Amsterdam. *Courtesy W. R. Grace & Co.*

The Grace staff at India House, 1885. *Courtesy W. R. Grace & Co.*

L. to R.: Lillius Gilchrest Grace, W. Russell Grace, Jr., Mayor William Russell Grace, Louise Grace, Lilias Grace (Kent), Joseph P. Grace. *Courtesy W. R. Grace & Co.*

13 ~ Mr. Cleveland's Decision

~ Though out of office, W. R. Grace did not neglect his political fences entirely. Sometimes when Governor Cleveland was in the city the Graces entertained him. On one occasion, Mr. Grace asked to be excused from a gubernatorial reception because he had accepted an invitation from the Union League Club for the same evening. Though almost to a man the club's members had voted against Grace in 1880, many had supported him thereafter. As Mr. Grace told the governor, it would be "unwise to be even in the slightest degree discourteous."[1]

For the young Republican assemblyman Theodore Roosevelt, Grace had a warm regard. He worked to secure the passage of Roosevelt's bill circumscribing the powers of the Board of Aldermen. "It is the first step in the direction of real reform in this City & helps to take municipal matters out of the arena of mere politics, State and Federal." Though the Roosevelt bill was defeated, the legislators did enact a law which had in it the seed of a merit system.[2]

On other occasions, Grace raised his voice for honest and economical local government. He drew closer to the enlightened Oswald Ottendorfer of the *Staats-Zeitung*, often asking the editor to bear down on members of the Legislature in the interest of good municipal management. Grace even tried to win over Dana of the *Sun*. He went to the trouble of procuring orchids from Brazil for the editor's collection. It required more than orchids to get Dana to support clean government on a nonpartisan basis.[3]

Still, there was a limit to Grace's interest in politics. "My ambition is all gone," he wrote a friend in June 1884, just before the Democratic national convention. "I have not the heart to go to Chicago, tho I think I could be of some service." He predicted, not so astutely as usual, that "Cleveland will be beaten by Kelly."[4]

New York's governor won the presidential nomination on the second ballot. He pledged himself to dislodge the spoilsmen. He declared the people were entitled to "pure, just and economical rule."

Grace wrote the candidate: "I rejoice exceedingly at your nomination as the triumph of a man who represents the best principles of the Democracy & fearlessly refuses to be made the tool of the bad & designing men of our party. I hail your success as the token of a new era in politics. . . . Tho I know it will take hard work to win, I am certain of success."

But this private opinion was reserved for Charley Flint: "*Politics* look well sentimentally & bad practically for the Democrats."[5]

Various matters combined to keep Grace's mind from public affairs. The saddest of these was the death of his beautiful daughter Agnes, just short of her seventeenth birthday. Day and night the sorrowing parents had sat by the girl's bedside, and William wrote that "her Mother's hair became quite grey in one night on the left side of her head." Four months after Agnes was gone, Grace gave his brother John a touching picture of the parents' grief: "My wife cant get over . . . the loss of our girl. . . . Whenever I see Agnes Photo about the house I kiss my hand to it & say God bless my baby, just as if she were there in person for I cant feel that she is gone."[6]

There were also business worries. The inflationary bubble which had started to swell in 1878 burst in May 1884. W. R. Grace warned his friends to look to their margins and keep as quiet as possible. He himself felt safe, and assured his brother John that, though "surrounded by dynamite," his immediate obligations were small.[7]

Among the more serious failures was that of the Marine Bank. Grace knew James C. Fish, president of the institution. He had had business dealings with Ferdinand Ward, a director of the bank and a partner of the brokerage firm of Grant & Ward. When the Marine Bank went under, Grant & Ward suspended amid a scandal that revealed Ward as a knave of the first water. The crash took Ulysses S. Grant's last dollar, and, before the repercussions were over, caused Grace some anxious moments.

During the boom, one of Grant's sons had gone into partnership with Ward. The general himself entered the firm. The credulous Grants left the management of the business to Ward. Ward borrowed large sums on usurious terms from institutions such as the Marine Bank. He borrowed from wealthy individuals, one of whom was W. R. Grace. Hinting at lucrative but nebulous contracts through General Grant's influence, Ward carried on his confidence game without hindrance from the unsuspecting general. Ward kept up his front by borrowing from new victims to pay "interest" or "dividends" on mines never worked, contracts never awarded, and loans never made.

To try to stave off collapse the general sacrificed his home, his swords of honor, gifts from admirers, and his wife's small fortune. Ward's rascality outraged the nation, but press and public forgave Grant his gullibility. A failure at everything except the art of war, he remained an American folk hero. Grace received a passing note as one of Ward's victims—and there the matter rested for a time.[8]

∼ ℐn mid-September, Grace wrote a long letter to his old political associate, Hubert O. Thompson, now an important Cleveland man. Grace spoke of the municipal situation and the discouraging possibility that Cleveland's backers might combine with Tammany. He made only a conditional promise of active support, saying: "When I see that the Natl. Comtee realize that the best interests of Cleveland dictate a full recognition of the desire of the people to see good administrative reform adopted here as the 'watchword' of the whole campaign, I will gladly go to work." Enclosed was a check for $1,000—a small contribution for Grace.[9]

Later the same month, Grace visited Cleveland in Albany. Possibly he obtained the assurance demanded from Thompson that the nominee would not back Tammany; possibly Cleveland's qualities of statesmanship captured Grace's imagination. In any event, overnight, the former mayor threw himself into the campaign.[10]

He made things hum: supplying and raising funds; organizing meetings; finding speakers; herding people to hear them. This work was aimed at the independents of both parties; and to do it Grace deferred action on the only positive political undertaking he had in mind before the Cleveland interview. This was a "businessmen's meeting," an old-time rally on a big scale, to launch an independent city ticket against Tammany. Now Grace saw wider possibilities for such a ticket: a chance to team it up with the national campaign and put Cleveland on the clean-government side in the inevitable clash with John Kelly.

Having done much to rejuvenate the local Cleveland campaign, Grace turned to his neglected city enterprise. There was not a day to be lost. The election would be on November 4. October 20 was the date selected for the meeting at the Academy of Music. Grace took charge of the multifarious activities necessary to promote its success.[11]

Who would be the candidate for mayor? A citizens' committee asked Grace to run. After earnest consideration, he declined. Grace feared Cleveland would be beaten, and that this would minimize the importance of the mayoralty. He felt also that his business needed him. He tried to find a candidate; offered to put $5,000 behind an acceptable man. Robert B. Roosevelt, George W. Quintard, and others were canvassed in vain. After ten days of fruitless search, Grace consented to run. The Academy of Music meeting would be in the nature of a nominating convention.

Ottendorfer, Frederic R. Coudert, and E. Ellery Anderson were among the speakers. A leader of the American bar, and incidentally attorney for the Grace business, Coudert was at home on a platform. But on this occasion he made what might have proved an unfortunate slip. "It makes little difference to us who may be President," Coudert said. "If we have a good Mayor we can stand almost anyone for President." Grace turned the phrase around, and repeated it again and again during the two-week campaign: "Above and beyond all, I appeal to you to vote for Cleveland. We can stand almost anyone for Mayor if we have a Democratic President."[12]

John Kelly was furious. Grace's acceptance threatened a bargain the Tammany boss had contrived with the New York managers for James G. Blaine, the Republican candidate for president. In this way, Kelly had expected to defeat Cleveland and to retain control of the city government as well. Tammany was to "cut" Cleveland in favor of Blaine. The Republicans were to "cut" their own mayoral candidate in favor of Hugh J. Grant, the Tammany nominee. The name of W. R. Grace on the Cleveland ticket was sure to draw off large numbers of Catholic votes which ordinarily Tammany could control; also, large numbers of Republican votes. Grace's ability to attract good-government Republicans was speedily demonstrated. Getting wind of the Kelly-G. O. P. deal, Theodore Roosevelt came out for Grace.[13]

Kelly struck out with everything Tammany had and managed to throw additional light on the history of Grace's naturalization as an American citizen: He revealed that Grace had not been a citizen when first nominated for mayor, with Mr. Kelly's blessing, in 1880. At that time, Mr. Grace's supposed citizenship had rested on papers taken out in 1867. These papers stated that Grace had come to the United States as a minor. The fact was that he had entered as a seaman, not as a bona fide resident. In any event his long subsequent residence in Peru and in the British Isles had vitiated any right that might have been acquired by that early entry.

The discovery of this during the 1880 campaign had resulted in the secret "midnight naturalization" before a Tammany judge on the eve of the election. Though this ceremony had actually made Grace a citizen, the Tammany press throughout the 1884 campaign referred to him as the "alien candidate." It was further pointed out that though he had previously voted in Long Island, Mr. Grace had not registered and had not voted in the 1880 election which had made him mayor the first time. More surprising than this, Mr. Grace still was not registered and consequently could not vote in New York City in the current 1884 campaign.

Mr. Grace explained his most recent failure to register. On the last day the books were open, he said he had gone to the Lincoln Bank to get his naturalization papers. There he learned that they were in the hands of his attorney, who could not be located in time. It was not the sort of an explanation that would have prevented Kelly's disclosures from damaging the cause of an ordinary candidate. That they did not damage Mr. Grace is proof that Grace was no ordinary candidate. The *Times* called the whole citizenship episode "creditable" to Grace; the *Evening Post* called it a Tammany "farce." The "alien" issue was lost sight of. The larger issues, the vital issues, of the campaign stayed in front, which is something that does not always happen in politics.[14]

Long since, the newspaper cartoonists and sketch artists—this was before the half-tone process for reproducing photographs—had made Grace a familiar figure. The former mayor had got rid of his brown beard, retaining only a mustache and goatee which showed traces of gray. He wore gold-rimmed glasses. His keen blue eyes were naturally friendly, but they could turn hard when there was nothing to be friendly about. Grace kept in trim by riding horseback. His short, compact form did not carry a pound of spare flesh. He moved with a springy step for his fifty-two years, and, in all, created the impression of a man who got things done.

The candidate's air of assurance and the enthusiasm of his supporters rested on Grace's almost invulnerable record as a public servant. The nature of Tammany's attacks on that record constituted its best endorsement. Grace kept the campaign on a high plane. Not for a moment did he lose sight of the fact that on him probably depended the fate of the national ticket. "I am here to talk for Cleveland. . . . As to myself, I am running a local race on my record where people know me. What I want is that all Democrats set aside petty local jealousies and support the national ticket."[15]

Grace was elected by ten thousand votes.

For three days the national contest was in doubt, owing to the close vote in New York. The suspense was prolonged by Jay Gould's Western

Union Telegraph Company, which delayed, when it did not falsify, returns favorable to Cleveland. When it was clear that Cleveland had carried the state by twelve hundred, and thus the nation, Grace felt that he had had something to do with this outcome: "*Pushed* into the fight when no one else could be found, . . . 'tis pretty plain that I held many & brought back many who otherwise would have voted for Blaine."[16]

According to the *Evening Post*, Grace deserved more credit than he gave himself. "Kelly staked everything on the November election and lost. . . . His plans were so well laid, and the 'deal' with the Blaine Republicans was so perfect in all its details, that both they and he . . . would have won but for the nomination of Mr. Grace for mayor. . . . No other man could have done this. . . . So complete was the overthrow of Kelly that even his stolid temperament was affected by it, and the man whose face, figure, and conduct have for so long a time constituted the very personification of obstinacy was confined to his house by an attack of nervous depression."[17]

The mayor-elect turned over the direction of his business to Charley Flint. "Here I am O. K.," he wrote Michael in London, "but looking forward to hard work & small pay after Jany 1st."[18]

~ W. R. Grace's return to the City Hall on January 1, 1885, was the occasion for an ovation of welcome such as perhaps no other incoming mayor of New York has enjoyed. It was a national, as well as a local, event—a triumph for the forces of honest government hailed throughout the land. For this Mr. Grace had his enemies, principally, to thank. To tie the hands of the new mayor, for twenty-one days John Kelly, sick and beside himself with rage, had directed a battle that shocked the country and humiliated decent New Yorkers. Not since the time of Mayor Fernando Wood, who in 1861 attempted to take New York City out of the Union, had the metropolis witnessed such spectacles.

It began with an attempt to pack the city government with last-minute appointees hostile to Grace. This was an old Gotham custom, to which the city charter lent itself. The tenure of certain municipal offices controlling much patronage ended on December 10. The mayor about to retire could fill these places, subject to the approval of the board of aldermen. As we have seen, this had happened in 1880 just before Grace came in the first time. Grace, in turn, had done the same thing, because he did not trust his successor, Edson. The Grace appointees who had especially annoyed Mayor Edson and Mr. Kelly were Commissioner of Public Works Hubert O. Thompson and Corporation Counsel C. H. Lacombe. A power in the County Democracy, Thompson had been very active for Grace in the recent campaign.

Consequently, Edson named two Tammany men to succeed Thompson and Lacombe. Though that sort of thing had been done for years without too much being said about it, the crusading spirit engendered in the late campaign caused an outcry. There were enough Grace Democrats among the aldermen to unite with the Republican members and block confirmation. When it was feared that a combination of pressure and inducements by Kelly might lure away some of the Grace aldermen, a court injunction was obtained restraining the aldermen from transacting business. No sooner had this injunction been dissolved than Theodore Roosevelt obtained another, directed against Mayor Edson. On the last day of his term, Edson threw a heavy police cordon about his office. At five o'clock in the afternoon he disobeyed the injunction and sent the aldermen a fresh nomination for commissioner of public works. The nominee's name was Rollin M. Squire, and that was all anyone seemed to know about him. Mysteriously, there were sufficient desertions from the Grace ranks in the aldermanic chamber to confirm Squire. The enigma deepened when it was whispered that former Commissioner Thompson had something to do with this.[19]

With some difficulty—the policemen did not know him—Mr. Squire got through the lines to the mayor's office, gave the requisite bond, and was sworn in. It was then ten-thirty P.M. Remarking that his term ended at midnight, Mayor Edson put on his hat and coat and made his way through the crowd that had gathered about the City Hall. The crowd, consisting in about equal parts of Grace men and Tammany men, stayed around, feeling that the show was not over. It was right. The president of the aldermanic board, a muscular Fourth Ward saloonkeeper named William P. Kirk, marched into the mayor's office. At twelve o'clock he announced that he was mayor. A Tammany judge was on hand to administer the oath. Under the charter, in the absence of the elected mayor, the duties of that office devolved upon the president of the Council.

Kirk made it clear that he did not intend to challenge Mr. Grace's right to office. Kirk would retire at noon, after a tenure of twelve hours.

"Mayor" Kirk's first official act was to appoint E. T. Wood corporation counsel. Mr. Wood was a brother-in-law of the recent Mayor Edson. Wood gave bond and was sworn in. An act of the Legislature, effective at midnight, had done away with the necessity of aldermanic confirmation of mayoral appointments. But when Kirk asked for the mayor's seal to affix the certificate of Wood's appointment, the custodian of that emblem, a Grace man, refused to give it up or to reveal the combination to the safe in which he had locked it. When Mr. Wood appeared at the office of the corporation counsel to take possession, he found that door locked, too. Inside was Mr. Lacombe and a number of friends, provisioned, and it was said armed, for a long siege.

As "Mayor" Kirk's tenure drew to an end, the interior of the City Hall had an untidy look. As a result of the all-night occupation, it smelled of tobacco, whisky, and onions. At twelve o'clock noon, Kirk walked out, followed by most of his friends. Grace men had been arriving in force for two hours. They filled the building and the grounds outside. A few minutes after Kirk had left, the crowd parted to make way for the Grace carriage. Mr. Grace raised his silk hat in response to the cheers.

The oath taken, the mayor stood beside his desk for four hours shaking hands. It was a composite of New York that streamed past him. A Jewish pushcart peddler might follow a member of the Stock Exchange. "On behalf of the Sullivan Club," a young man said, as he handed over a floral piece in the form of a harp. "Ah," said the mayor, "the Sullivans are a great family." But when one greeter conveyed his congratulations in Gaelic, Mr. Grace responded in English.

When the last hand had been shaken, Mayor Grace formally refused to recognize the appointment of Wood. He reappointed Lacombe and ordered the police to protect the corporation counsel in the discharge of his duties. Squire's appointment was another matter. Grace said it seemed to be legal, and briefly received his new commissioner of public works.

The behavior of the retiring commissioner, Thompson, puzzled everyone. After putting up the stiffest kind of fight to retain his post, all at once he had given in to Squire. Squire himself remained a mystery. Biographical data that the reporters could get hold of was meager. The new commissioner and Franklin Edson had been boys together in New Hampshire; after that, Squire had practiced law in Boston. The nearer one came to the present, however, the less distinct was the career of Rollin M. Squire. He had not been in New York for more than a year or so. He had no law practice to speak of, but he hung out with politicians and was known as "Flynn's friend who tells funny stories." Maurice B. Flynn was a rich, freespending contractor whose firm did a great deal of work for the city. He was a member of the County Democracy and a friend of Hubert O. Thompson. Undoubtedly these facts in some way explained the circumstance that several County Democracy aldermen had voted to confirm

Squire. And Squire's job during the coming two years would be important. In addition to the large amount of patronage the commissioner of public works normally controlled, he was a member of the aqueduct commission which was spending millions on a new water supply for the city.[20]

Yet, in all, New Year's Day, 1885, was one of the great days of W. R. Grace's life. It was entirely too much for John Kelly, who never regained his health. The following year he died.

~ Mayor Grace's inaugural message promised a businesslike, nonpolitical administration. It was well received, as were the initial steps the mayor took to carry it out.

Grace's first and possibly his most important appointment was that of William M. Ivins as city chamberlain. During Grace's first term, Ivins had served as the mayor's private secretary. The next opening was on the Board of Charities and Corrections, whose department was badly organized. The mayor's eye fell upon Louis D. Pillsbury, superintendent of the Tombs prison. He was pleased when Pillsbury accepted only on condition that he "would not be asked to make political appointments." Mr. Grace was the first mayor to appoint a woman to the Board of Education. Grace Dodge more than justified this confidence. She introduced industrial education into New York schools and, seeing the need for better qualified instructors, was instrumental in the founding of Teachers College of Columbia University.

Grace was fortunate in having a man like Everett P. Wheeler at the head of the city Civil Service Commission; and he made a good choice of a private secretary—young Francis M. Scott, later promoted to assistant corporation counsel. In the matter of promotions, Grace received some criticism on the ground that he ignored seniority. The mayor said this was to advance abler men.[21]

In addition to being free of aldermanic review of his appointments, the mayor of New York at this time had the power to remove certain officials without the approval of the governor. Inasmuch as the governor at this juncture was David B. Hill, this power of removal was a good thing for the cause of honest government. In the case of the Board of Tax Assessors, Grace was not slow to use his new authority. After observing their operations for five months, Grace summarily bounced all four members of the board and named new ones.[22]

He was obliged to use different tactics, however, to circumvent the park commissioners, who, according to one critic, didn't know a sugar maple from a cedar of Lebanon. Nevertheless, under a legislative enactment called the new parks law, the commissioners had formulated large plans. They proposed to maintain parks in Westchester County and elsewhere outside the city. Mayor Grace arranged a mass meeting of taxpayers. It happened that another legislative act limited the bonded indebtedness of cities. Having enlisted popular support, Grace used this act to modify the designs of the park commissioners.[23]

The Board of Aldermen had traditionally enjoyed a profitable commerce in street-railway franchises. Though Grace had long contended that franchises should be sold at public auction, he had to watch aldermanic grants pass over his veto for more than a year. Then the Legislature, contrary to its usual practice, agreed with Grace and directed that the franchises go to the highest bidder. From any criticism of the aldermen, Grace excepted the president of that body, Adolph L. Sanger—"an excellent Gent., a Hebrew, . . . [and] a very honorable man."[24]

In 1885, Charles T. Harvey presented the city a bill in the amount of $165,000. The basis for his claim was peculiar. Many years before, the city and state authorities had approved of plans Harvey had drawn for elevated railways. The railways were constructed by private capitalists who, according to Harvey, "froze out" the planner. The Legislature and Governor Hill approved Harvey's claim. Grace refused payment without a legal test, which Harvey never seems to have made.[25]

Early in the summer of 1885 a steamer arrived from France bearing a cargo of great boxes which contained Bartholdi's disassembled statue of Liberty Enlightening the World—a gift of the French people. The statue and the party of Frenchmen who had escorted it across the ocean were welcomed with festivities that lasted for days.

A month after Liberty's arrival, Ulysses S. Grant died of cancer of the throat in the Adirondacks. The nation had been touched by the old soldier's last fight—to stave off death until he could finish his memoirs, in the hope that they would provide for his family. While rain poured from the skies, the body lay for two days in state in the City Hall.

Grace's admiration for Grant went back to the days when the young Irishman was watching the tides of war from Peru. He wrote Mrs. Grant, suggesting that her husband be buried in Riverside Park, overlooking the Hudson. There were other offers. Grace received a telegram from Colonel Frederick Dent Grant: "Mother takes Riverside; temporary tomb had better be at the same place."[26]

President Cleveland, the two former Presidents, Hayes and Arthur, and notables civil and military from all over the Union saw the hero laid to rest. Chester A. Arthur took the nominal chairmanship of a committee to raise funds for a memorial. Grace, however, did most of the work, until differences of opinion divided the committee and donations began to taper off. Grace resigned. Eventually, General Horace Porter took charge. In 1897 the monument was finished and Grant's remains placed in it.[27]

~ An incident in connection with Grant's funeral and temporary burial in 1885 had a surprising sequel: the unmasking of Commissioner of Public Works Rollin M. Squire in the most dramatic and successful battle against corruption of Grace's second term.

Squire had placed among the mourning tributes at the temporary grave some verses that he had written about Grant. Mr. Squire was not a poet, and the newspapers intimated as much. Grace asked Squire to remove the literary effort and the offended author complied.[28]

Though certain that rottenness was at the bottom of it, Grace had not solved the riddle of Squire's appointment and speedy confirmation during the closing hours of the Edson regime. Mr. Grace had asked his city chamberlain, Ivins, to conduct an investigation into Squire's past. What Ivins reported confidentially the whole town knew by the time of the verse incident. In Boston, Squire had been a shady and financially unsuccessful lawyer; he had come to New York soon after the election of his friend Edson as mayor and made a precarious living on the political fringe of that administration. At the time of his appointment as commissioner, Squire hardly had a decent coat to his back. Almost immediately thereafter he acquired a home in the country.

Under Tammany the Department of Public Works had always been an avenue to riches. And in addition to enjoying this potential source of income, Squire was a member of the Aqueduct Commission. That body was responsible for the construction of the new Croton aqueduct to bring the city's water from Westchester. Thirty-three miles long, and calculated to take ten years to build, it was the most costly project yet undertaken by the City of New York. In his first administration, Grace had fought to give the mayor a large say in the financing of the work. This was not done. The mayor was merely one of several members of the Aqueduct Commission. Though thoroughly suspicious of most of his colleagues, and in particular Squire, there was nothing the mayor could put a finger on. He played, therefore, a waiting game.[29]

The incident of Squire's verses, which afforded the newspapers a good deal of amusement, opened a crack in the door. First off, the commissioner wrote Mayor Grace, revoking a previous letter of resignation the particulars of which were not specified. This did not come as a complete surprise. It confirmed what the mayor had already heard and, indeed, what some of the newspapers had intimated, namely, that a letter of resignation, signed by Squire, had been for some time in the hands of someone other than the commissioner. The obvious conclusion, of course, was that this was the price the Boston carpetbagger had paid for his office. The mayor asked Ivins to try to locate the letter.[30]

Ivins located the letter of resignation, but never saw it because its custodian would not give it up. The custodian was the attorney for Maurice B. Flynn, the free-spending contractor who had been a generous contributor to the Grace campaign chest. Ivins did, however, see a copy of a document that was much more damaging to Squire than the letter of resignation. This amazing paper, as brazen as anything in the days of Tweed, told the story of Squire's purchase of his office. Dated December 26, 1884, five days before Squire's surprise nomination, it read:

"Maurice B. Flynn, Esq.:

"Dear Sir: In consideration of your securing not less than four County Democracy Aldermen who shall vote for my confirmation as Commissioner of Public Works . . . I hereby agree to place my resignation as commissioner in your hands . . . and, further, to make no appointments in said office without your approval, and to make such removals therein as you may suggest and request, and to transact the business of said office as you may direct. Very truly yours,

"ROLLIN M. SQUIRE."

This paper incriminated not only Squire. It incriminated Flynn, and probably Hubert O. Thompson, the former commissioner. More than that, it tarnished the reputation of Grace's reform party, the County Democracy.

It was Thompson who had told Ivins of the existence of the Squire bargain letter, and had produced a copy of it. Flynn confirmed the genuineness of the copy, but refused to show the original. Thompson and Flynn wanted Squire out because Squire had played them false, running the office to suit himself. Thompson and Flynn wanted to make a deal with Grace to oust Squire and appoint another of Flynn's friends. Ivins said they would have to see Mr. Grace, and held out no hope that the mayor would accommodate the bargainers. At the same time, however, Ivins kept Grace in the dark about the Squire-Flynn letter while Thompson and Flynn tried to make a deal with the mayor. They told Mr. Grace they could get Squire out, but would not say how. Though Thompson and Flynn, separately and together, saw Grace several times, the mayor refused to make any promises whatsoever. Hoping to get evidence on Squire independently of Thompson and Flynn, Grace asked his commissioner of accounts to go over Squire's books.[31]

All this time, Ivins was trying to get his hands on the original of the Squire letter. After some months he succeeded, owing to a rift between Thompson and Flynn. Thompson placed the document in Ivins's hands on July 19, 1886. Ivins immediately gave it to the mayor. Meanwhile the commissioner of accounts had found doctored payrolls and evidence of civil service violations in Squire's department. The bargain letter, however, was the clincher. On July 28 the mayor preferred formal charges against Squire. The letter was included among the exhibits, and its publication caused a sensation. The executive committee of the County Democracy straightway read Flynn out of the party. Action could not be taken against Thompson, who had died suddenly two days before the charges were made public. It was a timely demise.[32]

After a tempestuous hearing before Mayor Grace, sitting as chief magistrate, Squire was removed from office. The case went to Governor Hill, who had blocked Grace's attempts to remove other undesirable officials. This time Hill sustained the mayor—not because the evidence proved Squire a crook, but because it proved him a fool to have put his bargain in writing.

As Squire's successor, Grace named a distinguished military engineer, General John Newton. Newton cleaned house in the city's Public Works Department, but he could do little to stop the graft in the building of the aqueduct where Hill tools still made up a majority of the commission.

Grace was more fortunate in the Squire case than in that of Alex Shaler, a grafter who was a member of both the armory and the health boards. For more than a year the mayor tried to get rid of this man, who was under indictment for bribery. He desired to appoint Theodore Roosevelt to the health board. Hill steadfastly blocked all attempts to remove Shaler.[33] Scandalous violations of the laws having to do with the sale of liquors prompted Grace to bring charges against the excise commissioners. Again, Hill refused to act. Fortunately the excise commissioners' terms expired before Grace's did and the mayor appointed a new set.[34]

～ It was in 1885 that the Grant & Ward chickens came home to roost.

Two years before, one of the remarkable figures of American newspaper history, Joseph Pulitzer, had come from St. Louis to buy Jay Gould's discredited and languishing *World*. The new owner's first task was to get the ordinary run of people to read his paper, and trust it. For this, Pulitzer had a formula that no publisher of his day could equal: a combination of belligerent political liberalism and yellow journalism. There were gaps in the *World*'s record for idealism. In the 1884 campaign it did not raise its voice in Grace's fight against Tammany. When Cleveland took office, it joined the cry of the spoilsmen for wholesale removals.[35]

Ferdinand Ward and two confederates were in jail, awaiting action by the grand jury. Ward was talking to newspapermen, striking out in every direction to try to help himself by besmirching the character of others. He made accusations against a great many people, among whom were W. R. Grace and Grace's confidential clerk, E. H. Tobey. Ward said that Grace had charged from 300 to 500 percent interest on money advanced to Ward for purposes of speculation.[36]

Though Grace denied Ward's statements, his records of dealings with Ward were not produced at the time and are not available now. Grace's surviving correspondence suggests no double-dealing. Rather, it indicates a growing irritation with Ward. At one time, Grace called Ward sharply to account for treating an extension on a loan from Grace as a sort of indefinite postponement. Again, he wrote: "I want to wind up the loan made you a year ago . . . in connection with the Mexican Southern RR. 'Tis 6 months since we were to have wound this up, and now I am *desirous of positively closing it out.*" No mention of interest or the amount of the principal of any loan appears in this correspondence.[37]

The *World* made the most of Ward's sensational chatter. Editorially, it accused Mayor Grace of having "shared the profits of his [Ward's] rascalities" and having "aided and abetted Ward in wrecking the Marine Bank."[38]

Grace's answer was to sue Pulitzer for libel and ask damages in the amount of $50,000. E. L. Godkin of the *Evening Post*, one of the great liberal editors of his day, applauded the mayor's action. "Nothing has been more scandalous of late in 'journalism' than the way Ward has been allowed to deluge the newspapers from his cell . . . with attacks on the reputations of anybody . . . who ever had dealings with him."[39]

Five days after his libel suit was filed, there began a development that put Grace in a bad light. A grand jury returned indictments against Ferdinand Ward, two confederates, and E. H. Tobey, the confidential clerk of W. R. Grace & Co. Grace had given testimony before the grand jury on Tobey's part in the dealings with Ward. According to the *Tribune* the mayor had sworn that Tobey had "gone it all alone."[40]

Ward was tried and sent to prison. Tobey was never tried. When the case was called in 1886, he did not appear. Later it was learned that he was in Peru, in the Grace employ. Strangely, the newspapers made little of this.[41]

Nor did the Grace versus Pulitzer action ever come to trial. It faded out of the newspapers and no trace of its eventual disposition can be found in existing court records. Whether the action was terminated on the motion of Pulitzer or of Grace is not known. But certainly Grace must have consented to a quiet ending of the suit.[42]

At the same time it should be noted that no proof of Ward's charge that Grace profited by Ward's crooked speculations was ever brought forward. The receiver for Grant & Ward found that when the firm went under, it owed Grace $70,000.[43] Years later Wilson S. Bissell, who had been Cleveland's law partner, disclosed an incident associated with the Grant & Ward case. The Marine Bank had made a loan of $30,000 on Grace's recommendation. When the bank was pulled under by Ward's operations, Grace, though legally free from liability, sent his personal check for $30,000 to the defunct institution's receiver, and took up the loan.[44]

∼ Things began to shape up earlier than usual for the city campaign of 1886. In the beginning it was Grace against the field—if Grace would run. His fight against corruption wherever he found it had won friends everywhere but in the Tammany and Hill camps. Grace's contempt for what the machines might do to him politically—as when he refused to attend a Democratic dinner because Hill would be there—won him friends. The County Democracy urged Grace to run. Theodore Roosevelt and other Republicans offered to support any movement that would nominate Grace. The mayor knew his strength. In his own opinion he would have "a clean walkover"; but he declined to run. He said he had had enough of office, and that his business needed his attention, as indeed it did.[45]

In midsummer the situation took on a new aspect. Henry George, whose *Progress and Poverty* had won him renown as a champion of the oppressed, was asked by a delegation of labor leaders to go out for the mayoralty. He refused, but the George movement did not die. It was a time of strikes and unrest in the ranks of the workers. Richard Croker, who had succeeded to the leadership of Tammany, was alarmed: the George agitation was affecting the Hall's hold on the city's working people. Conservatives were alarmed, fearing a "revolution." Croker got William Ivins to make George the proposition that if he would forget the mayoralty, the

County Democracy and Tammany together would send him to Congress. Leaping to his feet, George said the offer ended his uncertainty. He would run for mayor.

Grace's strength among the laboring people would have made him the ideal candidate to oppose George, but Tammany served notice that it would not accept Grace. Then Croker executed an astonishing tactical surprise. At a Tammany convention he nominated that irascible pillar of incorruptibility, Abram S. Hewitt, and carried his point. That evening, Hewitt had dined at the home of his brother-in-law, former Mayor Cooper. When reporters burst in with the news, Hewitt refused to believe it. After Grace, for one, had strongly urged Hewitt to run, and after the County Democracy, also, had nominated him, Mr. Hewitt consented to enter the contest—with a strict understanding of no promises. Though Croker must have believed the no-promise part, to his mind Hewitt was preferable to Grace or George.

The Republican nominee was Theodore Roosevelt.

That three eminent men should contest for mayor of New York was a tribute to the fear of the labor vote by the conservatives of both parties—and to the administration of W. R. Grace. The canvas was a wild one. Conservative journals like the *Times* and the *Tribune* grew hysterical over the possibility of a labor mayor. Even the liberal *Nation* believed "that nothing has occurred in the history of New York threatening its welfare so seriously as the George movement."

Hewitt polled 90,000 votes; George, 68,000; Roosevelt, 60,000.

Both Hewitt and Grace admitted that the significant thing was the ground swell for George—achieved without money, without newspapers, and without political machinery. As Grace wrote Cleveland, the labor vote represented a "new force in Politics which will not be easy to handle." Ten days after turning his office over to Hewitt, Grace, still thinking about George's race, confided to a friend: "Personally, I am probably stronger with the labor organizations than any other man in New York."[46]

~ Though business took most of Grace's time during the next year and a half, he did not lose sight of public affairs. With Hewitt continuing the war his predecessor had begun on corruption, Grace could center his attention on the looming menace of Hill, already the greatest threat since Tweed to good government in New York.

David B. Hill had risen swiftly. First in the Legislature, then mayor of Elmira, he became lieutenant governor under Cleveland in 1883—the place on the ticket being a concession to the back-room boys. When Cleveland was elected president in '84, Hill moved into the governor's mansion. He had been there ever since. Scholarly and unscrupulous, a master on the chessboard of politics and a bachelor who could give all his time to it, he had built a formidable machine on the basis of corruption.

The main thing that dismayed Grace was the increasing tendency of Cleveland and some of his associates to defer to Hill's power instead of fighting it. Grace's principal complaint was that Cleveland paid too much attention to Tammany and Hill in matters of patronage, and too little to the good-government people. A rift between Cleveland and the uncompromising old Hewitt had opened for the same reason. Hewitt even grew cool toward Grace, thinking Grace did not stand up to the president strongly enough in the matter of patronage.

Grace did stand up to the president, but his criticisms were confined to the White House circle instead of being circulated abroad. In one patronage-soliciting letter to Cleveland's private secretary, Daniel S. Lamont, Grace dryly alluded to the president's usual assurances of "careful consideration": "I write you thusly, hoping that my recommendation in this case may not be too deeply buried in 'careful consideration' as to be lost sight of." With a stiffer attitude toward the machines in mind, he wrote directly to the president: "I am not a radical [a bogey word since the George campaign], but I generally take radical means to cure radical evils & I find that the people like it & applaud the courage displayed."[47]

Despite disappointments, Grace remained genuinely interested in Cleveland's welfare. The alienation of Hewitt disturbed Grace. He warned the president that it could be the cause of much harm. When the mayor returned to the Cleveland fold, Grace was delighted.[48]

The greatest thing that could happen to Cleveland, Grace believed, would be for someone to smash the power of David B. Hill. Since the president himself made no move in that direction, Grace began turning over in his mind the notion of trying it himself. Though no longer a novice at politics, W. R. Grace had contemplated nothing more audacious since his essay to win the presidential nomination for Calvin Pratt. Not that the idea of Grace for governor was new. There had been much speculation about it, particularly following the second victory for mayor. In the spring of 1885 the *Telegram* had estimated Grace's chances for the 1888 nomination better than Hill's. That was before Hill had entrenched himself. Grace's most ardent well-wisher would not have said such a thing in 1887.[49]

Nevertheless, in the spring of that year, the former mayor let it be known, privately, that he was considering the race. He counted on Cleveland's support—rather confidently, it seems: "Cleveland needs me more than I can possibly need him, and consequently I will no doubt hear from him and the national administration later."[50]

Grace went over the situation with his old friend McKelway of the Brooklyn *Eagle*. Grace said his primary interest was the reelection of Cleveland in 1888; this was more important to him than the governorship. The implication, of course, was that Grace at the head of the state ticket would help Cleveland more than Hill could. But if this word reached Cleveland, the president gave no sign. Months went by and, near the end of 1887, Grace took up the subject with Oswald Ottendorfer in a "full and frank" letter: "My idea is to try & get the nomination for Governor next fall. If you sympathize with my ambition & feel that the best interests of the State would be served by me, I would feel indebted for suggestions."[51]

Ottendorfer's response seems to have been favorable, as had been McKelway's. Certainly, the politicians' grapevine had carried word of Grace's ambition to the White House by now. Yet the former mayor heard nothing from the national administration. Perhaps he expected to hear something, though, when Mrs. Grace and he received invitations to attend the president's reception for the justices of the Supreme Court on February 3, 1888. D. Cady Herrick of Albany and several other anti-Hill men were in the capital, ostensibly for social visits. Through their agency, Mr. Grace's gubernatorial ambitions broke into the newspapers. "Ex-Mayor Grace," wrote a Texas correspondent, "recognizes that if he is to be governor at all he must slip in under the tail of Mr. Cleveland's coat."[52]

The Supreme Court dinner was too formal an affair for the discussion of politics. But the Graces stayed on, and dined out every night. They spent a second evening at the White House. This gave rise to a good deal of talk, though the New York *Herald* reported that while the visitors were "charmingly entertained" by the president's young wife, the executive had exchanged hardly a word with Mr. Grace. The *Herald* may have been right. In any event, on his return home, Grace wrote to Lamont that "everyone thinks the Administration is behind Hill." Early in March, Grace's lieutenant Maurice Power went to Washington to try to find out where Cleveland stood. Grace wrote the president that Power was an authorized envoy and repeated that New York liberals feared that Mr. Cleveland hesitated to challenge Hill for reasons of party harmony. Grace ended his letter: "I would be supported by all the independent press of the cities of N. Y. & Brooklyn."[53]

What Cleveland told Power is not known, except that it could not have been anything very favorable to the Grace candidacy. With a national campaign coming up, Cleveland was afraid of Hill. And he may have been impressed by the talk that though Grace would run well in New York City his religion would hurt him upstate. Nevertheless, Grace's friends kept his candidacy in the papers—overdoing it in one instance, when the New York *World* announced that Mr. Cleveland had finally accepted the former mayor. Grace denied this, as he had to; but he went further and said he was not a candidate at all. Then he suddenly departed for Europe. Though a genuine business emergency—the Peruvian debt—obliged him to leave at this critical juncture, some took that excuse with a grain of salt. They thought that Mr. Grace had nothing to stay for.[54]

Grace was still in the fight, though with diminished hope. Before sailing he wrote Cady Herrick: "I leave matters in this Co. [New York] in good condition, & if I don't secure a *United* delegation from the Co., I will not ask my friends to help me." To Hugh McLaughlin, the Brooklyn boss, Grace reiterated that he would be a candidate "*if*" he should get a united delegation from his home county, "and the Administration make no objection, but keep their hands off."[55]

So much for the comedown of Grace's expectations from Mr. Cleveland.

~ After an absence of six weeks, Grace returned from England, on May 6, 1888. In the meantime, Hill had made hay. On May 15 the Democratic state convention met in New York City. Though Cleveland men kept Hill out of absolute control, the governor's influence was strong. A handful of Grace delegates heard their leader's name hissed and saw a Hill satellite, Ed Murphy of Troy, installed as party chairman for the state. On a radiator at the entrance of the convention hall was a stack of pamphlets bearing the title, *A One-Sided History of William R. Grace, the Pirate of Peru*. The author was one Peter Hevner, an American who, over a span of twenty-five years, had mixed in a number of schemes in Peru. His twenty-one pages of scurrility were, despite the title, directed mainly at Michael Grace; and they contained hardly a grain of truth.[56]

The May meeting selected a Cleveland delegation to go to the Democratic national convention in St. Louis. Grace was made a delegate. He regarded it as an empty honor because by then it was obvious that Cleveland would be renominated without opposition. The ex-mayor also was irritated because Cleveland had not broken squarely with Hill. "That crowd will be for anyone & cash," Grace wrote to Lamont. "No man can afford to abandon his friends in politics." The last words were as near as Grace came to alluding to his gubernatorial ambitions, which seemed in pretty poor case.[57]

In July 1888, a month after the St. Louis meeting, affairs in New York took a dramatic turn, and Grace's fading prospects brightened. A slip by Hill led to the exposure of the aqueduct ring, which had defied Mayor Grace for two years. In short order a legislative investigating committee uncovered an almost incredible story of plundering at the hands of Hill and his gang. Through Rollin M. Squire and three other tools on the Aqueduct Commission, the governor had turned the aqueduct job into the most fruitful source of loot in the state. Eight hundred thousand dollars had been paid for excavations never made; for $150,000 the commissioners had overlooked defective work on the part of a contractor; $1 million too much had been spent for fill.[58]

Mayor Hewitt took advantage of these disclosures to force Hill to back a bill, which was speedily enacted, reorganizing the aqueduct board with the mayor of New York in control. Hill hoped this capitulation would stop the investigation. It did not. During the last part of August, W. R. Grace took the stand. After what had gone before, Grace's evidence was not sensational. It served the purpose, however, of refreshing the public's mind as to the ex-mayor's early efforts to put the aqueduct on an honest basis.[59]

When Grace finished his testimony, the state convention was less than three weeks away. Hill had determined to brazen it out, and nominate himself at any cost. To this end, Ed Murphy and "Blue-Eyed Billy" Sheehan of Buffalo, whom Cleveland had once publicly insulted, strengthened the Hill lines upstate and made a deal with Croker for the Tammany vote.

In the face of all this there was something of a public uprising. If the aqueduct scandals had shown anything, they had shown that David B. Hill belonged in jail and not in the governor's chair. Grace made one more effort to induce Cleveland to repudiate the corruptionist. In a blazing letter he summarized Hill's record, concluding: "I am thoroughly & deeply interested in your election but not sufficiently so to induce me to sacrifice my own conscientious convictions. . . . I never belonged to a political gang & . . . I think it only fair to let you know how I feel." Grace enclosed a supporting statement from D. Cady Herrick.[60]

In a revealing and wordy communication, Mr. Cleveland replied at once. He praised the services of Grace and Herrick. But when they suggested that "I ought to control or dictate the nomination in New York State," they asked what was not proper. That was a matter for the party organization. "You are both . . . men of influence in the party, . . . both on the ground near the Democratic people of the State. . . . I am isolated here, full of public duties." Mr. Cleveland refused "absolutely . . . to interfere, or to express an opinion respecting the subject of your letter." Intimating that Mr. Grace should substitute "judgment" for "passion," the president ventured that when the time came, Grace would "be found supporting the . . . [state ticket] even if it should not be in line with your aim."[61]

The presidential tactics of evasion did not still the public clamor against Hill. A mass meeting filled Cooper Union. Then the honest-government people threw away everything by making two mistakes. First, they were unable to agree on a candidate, some being for Grace, some for Hewitt, and others for Smith M. Weed. Second, they put the whole issue up to Cleveland. The president repeated what he had told Grace: that he could not discuss the local contest.

That remark gave Hill the nomination without a fight.

Hill's friends applied to Cleveland for a written endorsement of their candidate. In cold anger at the impudence of the suggestion, Grace wrote the president that such an act "would be more than the Presidency is worth." Others also may have argued the morals of the case, but more confined themselves to the politics of it, as did the Cleveland supporter who used these words: "Of course you endorse him, but why write a letter? . . . Hill is all right and will be elected but you keep *mum*." Mr. Cleveland kept mum.[62]

Infuriated, Hill passed the word to the bosses to "knife" the president at the polls. With the independents estranged by Cleveland's tacit endorsement of Hill, and Hill on the warpath over the president's refusal to go whole hog and put that endorsement into words, the Democratic presidential candidate was in a bad way in New York. Additional errors of judgment kept Cleveland from making the best of his opportunities in some other states.

For these reasons the presidency went to Benjamin Harrison in a close race. Hill carried New York by a comfortable majority, and Cleveland lost it by 13,000. In the city Tammany, with Hugh Grant, triumphed over Abram S. Hewitt—a loss for good government all round. In the opinion of others besides W. R. Grace, it was a loss that could have been avoided.

Discouragement did not ride Grace too long. By the end of December he was writing a London friend: "There is no use denying that we have each had some of our expectations balked and that the end of the year does not find us exactly where, a few months ago, we calculated to be. . . . All this cannot be helped and we must hope for better results in the new year."[63]

14 ~ The Rubber Fight

~ W. R. Grace had turned from business to public affairs because at the moment he was tired of making money, and because there was a strain of idealism in his Celtic nature. Grace loved his adopted country, where, with all its imperfections, he saw greater equality of opportunity than anywhere else on earth. With a degree of unselfishness found among public men of the highest type only, Grace set about to reduce those imperfections. Grace had personal ambitions, to be sure, but the thing is that he was willing to subordinate them to the general good.

Therefore it seems too bad that a man of Grace's instincts should have seen the worst side of Grover Cleveland, who, with all his imperfections, was the best American statesman of his time. Given a free choice, Mr. Cleveland followed Whitney instead of Grace, and countenanced one deal after another with such characters of the political underworld as Hill, Ed Murphy, and Dick Croker.

In this dispensation of affairs it is scarcely surprising that after a go at politics, Grace would draw a long breath and express satisfaction at getting back to business. As Grace did business it was the cleaner sport: this in a day when an argument about the relative morality of business and politics would have been a pot-and-kettle argument.

Aside from the Bryce affair in 1874, none of the meanness, the intrigue, the ingratitude, and the doubtful honesty that Grace found every day in politics did he encounter in his own business—that is, prior to the time of which we are about to speak. By now this business had expanded to six houses and various agencies on three continents. In an era that witnessed the rise of the "trust," these businesses remained unincorporated. They were simple partnerships. With the senior partner busy with other things most of the time the wheels turned smoothly and profitably. It remained a family business, with Michael shuttling from New York to

London to Lima; John at Valparaiso; Ned Eyre at Lima; various other nephews in various places; and presently a son-in-law (Alice's husband), William E. Holloway, at San Francisco. W. R. Grace was head of the family and head of the business. In the midst of public concerns he might pause to hear a problem, and when he gave his decision, that decision was final. But Michael had developed and grown. He had matured in judgment. A matter had to be vital for him to bother William about it when "our senior" was immersed in politics.

Partners who were not of the Grace family—like Sears and Scott in Brazil—were taken into it by adoption. When in New York they stayed at the Grace houses. Grace and Mrs. Grace still busied themselves with the problems of the wives of absent husbands; and the Grace homes were overrun by temporarily orphaned children. Grace himself would have been the first to refuse any credit for this: he loved to do it.

Some of the great of the nation, and a good many others in public life, came to Gracefield and to the Grace town house. They met Grace business associates, Grace partners, Grace employees, and their families. Though the maritime flavor of the Grace households had been diluted by the advent of new people, one still encountered an occasional shipmaster, possibly a little uneasy in such landsman company. Like as not he would be grateful for an opportunity to retire to a corner with his tot of rum to swap yarns with old Captain Gilchrest.

After Michael, the partner next in rank and in competence was Charles R. Flint. With W. R. Grace otherwise engaged and Michael away, Flint had charge of the New York house, which supervised the activities of all the others. No outsider could have been more a member of the Grace family than Charley Flint, who had been with the Grace firm since he was nineteen. In 1885, Charley was thirty-five and on the way to being rich. Successful outside speculations as well as a share of the profits of W. R. Grace & Co. were building up a fortune. Having been about sailing ships all his life, he became a fashionable yachtsman. The Graces smiled over Charley's cultivation of the social elite.

When Charley Flint left his old employer at the end of 1885, it soon developed into more than a termination of friendly business relations. It terminated their personal relations. In a business way, Grace found himself unexpectedly on the defensive against a rival who knew many of the business secrets of W. R. Grace & Co. Hurt and angry, Grace plunged into the bitterest business fight of his career, and the only fight of its kind in which he was ever engaged. At times it made politics seem a tranquil occupation.

~ The Grace-Flint breach came over rubber.

In 1882 the business was booming and the price of "fine Para" touched $1.15. "Our intimate relations," Grace assured his partner R. F. Sears of Sears & Co., the Grace house in Pará, "with such Manfrs as Hotchkiss, Banigan, Converse, Meyer etc, as well as our close relations with Earle Bros, who control so largely the small manufacturers, give us a peculiarly favorable position 'inside the lines,' as it were, enabling us to forecast the future shaping of the market as no other house can."[1]

This advantage demonstrated itself early in 1883 when, in consideration of heavy inventories and the high price of rubber, eight of the largest American manufacturers agreed to close their plants until the price should drop to $.80. Apprised in advance of this move, Sears saved his house heavy losses. In 1884, as a part of the general recession of business activity, the bottom fell out of the crude rubber market. "We are the lucky ones in that business," Grace wrote to his brother John. "Price fine Para a year ago was 108c pr lb today it is 50c. We have been all the time oversold. We were short 300,000 lbs when the thing collapsed."[2]

Charley Flint, who was attending to the details of the New York end of the business, made a trip to Pará in September '84. He turned in an adverse report on Sears. This must have puzzled Grace, who had every reason to feel that Sears had done very well. Indeed, the profits of Sears & Co. had been sufficient to make Sears, owning a fifth interest, a wealthy young man. The report did not change Grace's opinion of Sears. "Alice will be married Octr 18," he wrote his traveling partner. "Your wife is well and apparently waiting with patience. . . . My most true and sincere regards to Sears & lady."[3]

While the price was down, business almost at a standstill, and rubber dealers less fortunate than Grace absorbing their losses, Grace proposed that the leading manufacturers band together to stabilize the situation. Whether as a result of Grace's suggestion or not, this was done. The syndicate included the Boston Rubber Shoe Co. (E. S. Converse), L. Candee & Co. (H. L. Hotchkiss), the East Hampton Rubber Tread Co. (E. T. Sawyer), the New Jersey Rubber Shoe Co. (Christopher Meyer), the National Rubber Co. (A. O. Bourne), and the Woonsocket Rubber Co. (Joseph Banigan). In this way, Grace maintained his "inside" position.[4]

By 1885 good times were back. The price of rubber was up, manufacturers were buying and running their plants full blast. In three years, W. R. Grace & Co. had outgrown the old Standard Oil quarters on Pearl Street. In 1885 it moved again—and for the first time into premises commensurate with its position in the city's foreign trade. The new home was at 1 Hanover Square, in a building lately vacated by the Cotton Exchange. This structure fills the short block facing the Square (a triangle, actually), between Stone and Pearl streets. Erected in 1837, it is three stories high and looks a little like something that one might see in London. It is now India House, a downtown club.

The syndicate agreement by which Grace enjoyed a favored position in the rubber trade would expire in the spring of '86. Grace's rubber business had become so large that it was decided to take it out of W. R. Grace & Co. and place it in a corporation called the New York Trading Co. By way of minimizing competition, two of Grace's rivals as rubber middlemen and a manufacturer would be taken into the corporation. They were Earle Brothers of New York, George A. Alden & Co. of Boston, and the Woonsocket Rubber Co. of Rhode Island. The arrangement was for Charley Flint to assume the presidency of the combine.[5]

The plan also contemplated that Flint should retain his partnership in W. R. Grace & Co. Late in December 1885, on the eve of the launching of the new corporation, Flint told Mr. Grace that ill health would oblige him to retire from W. R. Grace & Co. at the end of the year. Flint said that the Trading Company would be all he could attend to. Though surprised and disappointed, Grace did not attempt to dissuade Flint; he paid him $250,000 for his interest in the New York partnership. The matter was arranged with the friendliness that had always characterized the relations between Grace and his younger partner.[6]

~ The state of Mr. Flint's health did not prevent him from drawing up plans for the New York Trading Co., which dismayed Grace, who called them "Napoleonic." After this, Flint had energy enough to start his own firm, Flint & Co. These developments induced Mr. Grace to pay more attention to the establishment of the New York Trading Co. than he had expected to. He kept Flint out of the presidency and substituted George A. Alden, with Michael Grace, vice president; and Flint, treasurer. W. R. Grace took a place on the board of directors. By appealing to the "conservatism" of Alden and of Joseph Banigan of the Woonsocket Rubber Co., Grace held in abeyance the "great, speculative" moves by which Flint contemplated the domination of the rubber market overnight. In the course of this, Mr. Grace's relations with Charley Flint, whom he had been accustomed to treat as a son, were severely altered. Only after a "very heated and acrimonious discussion" did Grace's views prevail.[7]

Matters were mended none when the task of effecting a transfer to the Trading Company of 80 percent of the Grace interest in Sears & Co. of Pará was taken up. It did not appear to Grace that Flint desired to give proper recognition to Sears's important services. Flint had sent a man named Crane to Pará for the purpose of discrediting Sears, though it was clear that Flint desired to gobble up the organization Sears had created there. Grace wrote Sears that his interests would be protected. In the third month of the Trading Company's existence—March 1886—Grace began to speak of the possibility of pulling out of it and, with Sears in Pará, forming his own combine with manufacturers.[8]

The next disclosure was still more painful. Grace found that the cable codes his New York house used with rubber correspondents had been scrambled. At Flint's instigation this work had been done "surreptitiously" by Grace's cable clerk. When Grace discharged the clerk, he went to work for Flint. Burning with indignation, Grace wrote his brother John: "Flint meant to cheat us out of this business, but it has not washed." By this time—April 1—it was clear that Flint did not act alone. He had allies in Alden and Earle.[9]

Though it came at an awkward time, Grace set in motion a counter-stroke. Grace himself was head-over-heels in the multifarious duties of the mayoralty, including the fight to oust Squire. Michael was on crutches as a result of a riding accident. He was trying to reorganize Peru's foreign debt, to direct the far-ranging Grace business as a whole, and to handle in the New York house the work that Flint had abandoned. Nevertheless, the brothers set out to teach their former partner a lesson. The plan was to break up the New York Trading Co., which the Graces thought might be accomplished simply by the withdrawal of their interest. To this end, Grace offered either to sell their shares in the Trading Company or to buy those of Flint et al. In case this didn't sink the company, the Graces meant to form their own outfit and "force them [the Flint group] to wind up."[10]

Taken aback by Grace's prompt action, Flint and his people sparred for time. "They had no plan & acted like tricksters." Then they proposed that, in effect, the Grace interest remain in the Trading Company in return for "a good round sum yearly in commissions." The Graces, however, were through with Charley Flint: "We are going to be free from that crowd & we know that an association with them would end where they will end—in disaster."[11]

The first feelers in the direction of a new combine with the manufacturers were vastly encouraging. E. S. Converse of the Boston Rubber Shoe

Co., the largest manufacturer in the country, had a long discussion with Grace about it. Converse liked Grace and thought the rubber industry would do well to tie up to such a man. When he suggested a capitalization of $500,000 for a rubber-procuring firm managed by Grace, Mr. Grace said that he personally would put up that amount and get an equal amount from Sears if needed. The company would be owned half by the two Graces and Sears and half by the manufacturers.

Grace believed that nearly all the old syndicate firms would come in. Other leaders besides Converse told him they would "not under any circumstances associate themselves again with Alden, Earle, or Flint." Converse himself started missionary work among fellow manufacturers: "We will be with the only square man in the lot and free of the fellows that would stab us behind." W. R. Grace saw the project as "the biggest power ever created in this business." The company would act for the manufacturers not only in Brazil, but also in Central America and in Africa, doing a business that would amount to $5 million to $7.5 million a year.[12]

To inform themselves of Michael Grace's movements among the rubber manufacturers the Flint people put a private detective on his trail. Flint himself followed Michael to New Haven, impersonated a manufacturer on the telephone, and "burst in on" a meeting where manufacturers and Michael were discussing the proposed corporation. Michael thought these melodramatics "amusing," and an indication that Flint was in a bad way.[13]

There was still the matter of disposing of the New York Trading Co. Direct negotiations between the opposing groups having broken down, it was arranged for Kidder, Peabody & Co., the American branch of Baring Brothers, to act as arbitrator. Flint was for the continuation of the Trading Company, Grace for closing it out. The arbitration extended over a period of sixty days, and some of the sessions were lively. "Flint cut the meanest figure," Grace wrote to Sears, "having to listen to a full history of his own treachery." In the end, Grace won a clean victory. "This [New York Trading] Company goes out of existence—Sears & Co and the Manaos Trading Company [formerly Scott & Co.] in a like manner disappear.—Sears has already commenced operating for the account of the Sears Comml Co and all future business done by him will be for their account."[14]

Thus Grace summed up the result for E. S. Converse. The launching of the Sears Commercial Co. at Pará was intended as the first step in the new program.

~ In August 1886, after the successful arbitration, Michael Grace was obliged to catch a steamer for Lima on long-deferred Peruvian debt business. The day before he sailed he wrote Sears an optimistic letter. The manufacturers were sure to team up with him. "Get your business in hand; give it, as usual, close attention and we will make, after a little time, a big success with the Sears Commercial Company."

Michael's departure left William with a heavy load for a man who was at the same time mayor and conscientious about the amount of time he spared to private affairs. Some while before, City Chamberlain William M. Ivins had been made a special partner of W. R. Grace & Co. Mr. Grace tried to use Ivins in the rubber situation, but without too good results. Ivins was also a public official with a full-time job at the City Hall.

Grace's shorthanded situation was the more embarrassing because Flint, Earle, and Alden had decided to make a fight of it. They won over one manufacturer, Banigan of Woonsocket, and began to make an impression on Hotchkiss and on Christopher Meyer. At the same time they renewed efforts to undermine Sears in Brazil. Attacks were made on Sears's credit and on his business reputation. One of the young Aldens, who had served his apprenticeship in rubber under Sears in Pará, went down to further this campaign. Competitors of Sears were supported; life breathed into an old Brazilian customs suit against Sears; an attempt made to use a prince of the Brazilian royal family, whose reign over the last of New World empires was drawing to an end.[15]

Encouraged from New York but harassed in Brazil, Sears bought heavily in a rising market: in part, because activity seemed a good answer to his enemies on the ground, and, in part, because of the cheering news from the north. Tied to the mayor's desk, with Michael away and no one to replace him, in mid-August Grace realized that he was "long" on rubber in New York. He would do well to get rid of what he had at cost, plus commissions. He asked Sears to go easy on buying. He said that Flint also was stocked up on rubber and bulling the market. He expressed the opinion that prices would not hold. Two weeks later, Grace believed that Flint was operating for a drop. Either Grace was confused by Flint's tactics or he did not have the time to learn the truth of the situation. In any event he seemed rather at a loss—an unusual state of affairs for W. R. Grace.[16]

A great deal depended on the speedy lining up of the manufacturers. Even a few weeks before, this had been taken for granted. Now there was hesitation and uncertainty. For one reason the manufacturers must have noted the overbought condition of Sears in a doubtful market. Also, Flint's campaign had begun to tell. Grace found it necessary to urge his friend Converse to "pay no attention to the silly yarns [about Sears] which have been constantly circulated by my friend 'the enemy.'" Grace asked Converse to press the manufacturers, particularly Hotchkiss, for a decision: "Banigan Earle & Co are working on Mr. H daily. He should be brought into line." Grace promised to see Christopher Meyer. For that purpose the mayor made a trip to Saratoga, but missed the rubber manufacturer there.[17]

Converse could do nothing with Hotchkiss, whom Grace reported as "evidently captured by the Earle people." Grace himself had no success with Meyer, finding him "cold" to the combine proposal and "more interested in the girl he is courting than in any other business. . . . The amount of mudthrowing . . . [by] Messrs. Flint and Alden has no doubt had some effect." To counteract this, Grace wrote Converse an earnest letter: "I am absolutely not going to permit myself to be reelected as Mayor of New York, and am going . . . [to give] my undivided attention to my business." Moreover, Michael Grace soon would be through with the Peruvian bond business, and would give rubber his full attention. Grace repeated that Sears was the best man in Pará and that his house was mechanically equipped to do business economically. Contrary to the statements of Flint, rubber would be no "mere side-show" to other Grace interests. If the manufacturers would come in, Grace would guarantee the integrity of the capital for one year "and a small dividend."[18]

In the midst of this, Grace again cautioned Sears to buy lightly. Grace had more rubber in New York than he could handle comfortably. Earle was bearing the market and, "not to run any risk of weakening our connections with the manufacturers," Grace was obliged to sell at prices that came dangerously close to not covering costs.[19]

After much effort and several postponements, Grace managed to get the big rubber manufacturers, excepting Hotchkiss of L. Candee & Co. of Hartford, to meet him in Boston on September 29. Mr. Converse opened the meeting with a strong recommendation that they all stand together and join Grace. Converse's commanding position in the industry gave his remarks weight. One by one, three of the other four men present agreed to the course suggested. The last man to speak was Christopher Meyer. He said he would have to talk to his partner; and, anyway, that nothing should be done without the assent of the absent Hotchkiss. This stalled the meeting, for the rubber men, even Converse, saw the need for unanimity and peace in the industry. After the session it was arranged that Converse should try to bring Hotchkiss around and that Grace should work on Meyer.

Grace left Boston with no strong hope of success in those directions, and wrote Sears to prepare a line of retreat from the aggressive position he had taken: "If we fail to get the manufacturers into our company, we must begin to build up the company gradually." Sears was told to lay low "until we see our way clearly, or until prices decline, . . . [which] appears likely to me."[20]

When the market broke in October, hope for getting the manufacturers went glimmering. The Sears Commercial Co. held few attractions for anybody. "It is a bitter pill," Grace admitted to Sears, "to have $800,000 of rubber on hand with a falling market and nobody buying. . . . You can scarcely understand how the Flint Earle Alden people have sought to work hell here & it is unfortunate we gave them such a chance by getting so big a stock on hand."[21]

In December, Grace paid the piper. He performed that disagreeable rite in a manner that would have done credit to any man. "We have never," he wrote Sears, "made so heavy a loss in all our business experience as has been made by the Sears Coml. Co. this year; yet we don't blame any one. . . . We know you loaded us up; . . . we know, too, we could have, instead of advising you, peremptorily stopped your buying, but we . . . trusted altogether too much to the promises of the big manufacturers."

Christmas in sweltering Pará is apt to be a dismal festival, at best, for any northerner—let alone a homesick man who had seen half the accumulations of a lifetime swept away in eighty days. "I shipped you by this str. a fat lamb," Grace continued. "Your wife lately spent a few days with us; my wife enjoyed her company very much. I took them to the theatre twice & altogether I hope she had a good time. My brother will be home next month. I will be out of office Jany 1st & with our united efforts & your & our experience of the past few months, I hope you will have a happy & successful New Year."[22]

~ The new year (1887) brought no success to the Sears Commercial Co. Michael failed in a fresh attempt to line up some of the manufacturers. On the other hand, Flint, Earle, and Alden, operating under the title of the New York Commercial Co., pulled off a profitable coup. They ran up the price of rubber and unloaded two million pounds they had bought while the market was down.[23]

Eighteen eighty-eight was another year of failure. W. R. Grace was back in politics. Michael was still wrestling with the Peruvian debt in addition to supervising the business as a whole. Thus, rubber suffered from a certain amount of inattention. Flint made the most of it, outgeneraling his adversaries both in New York and Pará.

Something seems to have happened to Sears. In the early years of his Brazilian experience under the Grace aegis, everything he had touched had turned out well. Now everything turned out badly. Apart from rubber, the merchandizing business Sears carried on along the Brazilian coast lost money. This business, patterned after the trade in which Grace had been so successful on the west coast, had previously been a good money-maker.

Grace was wonderfully patient with Sears. Clearly, a desire for victory in this struggle was not altogether a matter of money with Grace. Flint had broken too many articles of the code that Grace thought should govern the conduct of businessmen. He wanted to see the transgressor get his due.

It did not end that way. In 1889, Grace sent Ivins to Brazil to see what could be done. Ivins reported Sears on the verge of collapse from insomnia. Then Ivins quit Grace and joined Flint. That finished matters for Grace. He sent Sears to Barbados for his health, and, when he was better, broke the news that the Sears Commercial Co. must be wound up. Sears was offered a position at $5,000 a year with W. R. Grace & Co. Pride seems to have kept him from taking it; and pride, at that time, was about all Sears had left.

Flint and his associates continued to operate profitably in rubber. In 1892, Flint brought about a merger of several large manufacturers into the United States Rubber Co.[24]

15 ~ The Peruvian Debt Settlement

~ Early in 1885, Michael Grace took steps toward a goal he had had in view for two or three years: the liquidation of Peru's foreign debt. The ultimate object was to make the country attractive to outside capital, for even after the war with Chile, Peru's resources were enormous.

Michael Grace did not undertake this as a work of pure altruism. Grace holdings in Peru would be enhanced by the recovery of the country. On top of that Michael hoped to be paid, and quite well, for refunding the debt. But this pay was by no means certain, and before the Graces would receive anything they would have to spend a great deal of their own money. William considered the undertaking too speculative. This is what made it so: from first to last, Michael Grace insisted on terms that would stimulate the recovery of Peru.

Nearly all parties to the long controversy voiced in public a solicitous concern for the nation's welfare. But when it came to cases, most of Peru's creditors did not care what happened as long as they got their money. Other powerful interests clearly did not wish Peru to revive; they wanted that country to remain an economic, and perhaps eventually a political, dependency of Chile. The tenacity and skill with which the Graces opposed these forces, refusing to give up when Peru's cause seemed almost hopeless, form a bright and singular chapter in the history of American commercial penetration in South America.

The bulk of the credit belongs to Michael. In the beginning, W. R. Grace opposed the effort as too much of a job. When Michael, putting the issue on lofty ground, refused to be dissuaded, the senior partner gave the project his blessing and a good deal of tangible assistance. After four years of unceasing toil, when hope for a reasonable settlement seemed extinct, a London attorney sought privately to console W. R. Grace by saying that, after all, "the business to you is purely a mercantile venture."

Grace corrected the Englishman at once:

"The business to us has not been purely a mercantile venture; for, as such, I would never have touched it. . . . My brother has had the natural and praiseworthy ambition of making for himself a great record in settling the Foreign Debt of Peru & re-establishing her in a position of prosperity, and it was the influence of this feeling in his mind and my desire to forward his wishes in that direction that induced us to spend so very large an amount of money & time, and I personally don't regret it."[1]

~ To take up matters in their order:

After obtaining operating control of the unfinished Oroya railroad, Michael had lopped deadheads off the payroll and got the line on a paying basis. Feelers were put out looking toward European financing of the completion of the road to Oroya, and then its extension to the Cerro de Pasco mines. Michael was also turning over in his mind a scheme to engage the interest of American mining magnates, including John W. Mackay of the fabulous Comstock Lode.

These stirrings, modest as they were, had an effect on prostrate Peru. They earned for Grace the gratitude of President Miguel Iglesias, whose lot was not a happy one. The Iglesias government had been formed in 1883 for the purpose of concluding the war with Chile, a piece of statecraft with which Michael Grace had had something to do. The terms had been cruelly hard, but to have let things drift would have been worse for Peru. Iglesias bore the brunt of the popular resentment of the terms. That resentment strengthened the arm of General Andres Avelino Cáceres, the sole Peruvian commander of any moment who had never yielded to the Chileans. Cáceres was still in the field with an army, his adversary, now, being Iglesias.

Michael also kept an eye on the Peruvian bondholders' committee that had been set up in London to protect the interests of the owners of Peru's defaulted foreign debt, aggregating £33 million, and with overdue interest £51 million. At the prevailing exchange this was $260,000,000. The insolvent government's most obvious assets were customs and railroads. As a railroad operator, Michael expected to hear from the committee, or to hear that the committee had approached Iglesias—which would have amounted to about the same thing. Neither happened. Instead the committee sent a lawyer named C. L. Smyles to Chile. Had Mr. Smyles gone to ask the Chileans to make a settlement with the bondholders on the ground that Chile had deprived Peru of the means to settle, Lima would have regarded it as a proper proceeding. But for Smyles to sit down with the Chileans and seek their opinion on how much could be squeezed from Peru, and in what manner, was tactless, to put it mildly.

Michael Grace set out to efface the effects of Smyles's blunder; and he did it with Castilian indirection. Having been on the west coast for some months, in April 1885, Michael called on Smyles in Santiago. They had several talks. Michael got a good idea of the Peruvian resources Smyles expected to tap in order to reimburse the bondholders. Should that program be carried out, Peru would never get on its feet. This was exactly what the government of Chile wanted—or so Michael Grace thought. Michael promised to discuss Mr. Smyles's views with the reigning powers in Lima. Moreover, he suggested that the lawyer himself visit Peru: after all, that was the country he was dealing with.

On his way north, Michael stopped in Lima between weekly steamers. He had long sessions with President Iglesias and his cabinet. When he arrived in New York, Michael had ready a letter that would run a quarter as long as this chapter. It was addressed to the chairman of the bondholders' committee in London. A copy was sent to Smyles. Ned Eyre, in Lima, was told to lay out the red carpet for the traveling attorney, and to see that he was courteously received in government circles. Eyre was also instructed to get word to Iglesias not to take Smyles too seriously, but to listen to him—and leave binding commitments to "a Peruvian commissioner in London, who would consult with me."[2]

In his letter to the head of the bondholders, Michael Grace presented the Peruvian view of the question. Though President Iglesias entertained "a real desire to do justice to the bondholders," he could not overlook the state of public opinion in his country. Peruvians were aware that the active sympathies of the bondholders had been on the side of Chile in the recent struggle; and they believed that the bondholders had given "material assistance" to Chile "in order to deprive Peru of her two great sources of income, guano and nitrate." Michael said no one could deny where the sympathy of the bondholders lay during the war, but that he thought he had been able to convince Iglesias that this had not resulted in any measurable aid to Chile.

He then took up, item by item, the Peruvian assets on which the bondholders had an eye. First were customs, amounting to £750,000 a year. Peru could give up nothing of this and exist as a nation. Next were claims Peru held against former guano consignees. Nothing there could be surrendered, as Iglesias had been obliged to pledge these assets to equip an army to fight off Cáceres.

Michael proceeded to assets that he said could be utilized for the benefit of the bondholders:

1. Guano. Though the majority of known deposits were in the hands of Chile as a measure of indemnity, it was likely that other beds would be discovered. The bondholders might work these for a period of, say, fifty years.

2. Railroads, ten in number. Nearly all were in a state of bad repair, and several needed to be completed or extended. Michael went into detail concerning the possibilities of each road, not neglecting the Oroya and the proposed Cerro de Pasco extension. It would be necessary for the bondholders to expend large sums to make these roads paying properties. He suggested that they consider this, on the basis of a fifty-year lease, paying the Peruvian government 5 percent of the gross revenues of thc roads.

3. Nitrate. It was possible that fields might be discovered in the territory remaining to Peru. The bondholders might collect a royalty on exports.

This was a much more moderate estimate of Peru's capacity to pay and still recover than anything Mr. Smyles had obtained in Chile. Yet Michael had not come to his most important point. Peru would discuss a settlement only "in exchange for an absolute quittal of all claims of its foreign creditors." That is, if the bondholders wanted any more, they would have to apply to Chile.

The object of Michael's letter was to persuade the bondholders to take a long view of the situation, and, in their own interest, work for the rehabilitation of Peru. He predicted the speedy defeat of Cáceres, and an era of tranquility and prosperity: "The great majority of the people are averse to revolutions and sincerely desirous for peace; and I consider the present troubles likely to be the last for years to come."

Michael offered his services to bring about "an equitable settlement" of the bondholders' claims on the basis outlined, "without any interest than that of having been connected in business with Peru for many years, and of having the true interests of the country at heart."[3]

~ Before Michael Grace's effort could reorient the thinking of the bondholders, Peru was beset by domestic problems that threatened to upset Michael's plan. It was the old Latin American story of armed revolt. Michael's assurance to London that there would be peace in Peru was based on negotiations then pending between Iglesias and Cáceres. A month after these assurances had been made, the negotiations fell through and Cáceres prepared to move on Lima. This embarrassed Michael more than the debt question. It created a climate unfavorable to the mining syndicate Michael meant to launch in the United States, and to the European financing of his Oroya railroad extension. It interfered with the operation of the road itself, which, in June 1885, Iglesias took over to send troops against Cáceres.[4]

Michael Grace implored Peruvians from Iglesias down to end the revolt by some means and end it soon. "In Peru they do not seem to understand the difficulties involved to persuade capitalists not only here but in Europe to invest their money in a country like Peru. The answer is always: 'But just think, Sir, the history of Peru shows that this country has never known real peace since its independence. . . . Just think of its present state.' . . . Iglesias will have to take strong measures and show no quarter to any revolutionist."[5]

In September, Iglesias put a well-equipped army of three thousand in the field. Hopeful that peace would soon be restored, Michael was preparing to go to London to press matters when his hip was broken in a fall from a horse. In bed he anxiously scanned the cables. "If Gen. Iglesias will only get rid of Cáceres and consolidate the peace by the time my leg is consolidated he will have done well, and will enable us to do something for the country." It did not turn out that way. Cáceres sidestepped the government force, seized the mountain terminus of Michael's railroad at Chilca, loaded his army on board the rolling stock, and coasted down to undefended Lima.

Both the conqueror and his late adversary behaved patriotically and wisely. Though Iglesias resigned, Cáceres refused to take the presidency except by constitutional means. That he would be elected the following year, 1886, there was never a doubt. As the man who had never bowed to Chile, Cáceres had an enormous hold on the people, whereas, ironically, Iglesias bore the onus for the treaty of '83.

The result was the promise of a truly popular government which Ned Eyre believed would tranquilize the country. Eyre managed to spread this sentiment abroad, via the Associated Press, a stroke that brought congratulations from the bedridden Michael. In Latin America, one grows accustomed to changes in government. Michael Grace decided to work with Cáceres, the victor, as ardently as he had worked against Cáceres, the aspirant to power—this in hope of winning for the cause of debt settlement the goodwill of Cáceres as he had won that of Iglesias. Ned Eyre was instructed to put five or six hundred men to work on the Oroya extension without waiting for outside financing. This earnest of faith in Peru was designed to "be a big feather in Caceres cap . . . [and] commence immediately to popularize his administration." Moreover, it was intended to infuse life into the prospects for the Cerro de Pasco syndicate, which Michael regarded as a favorable approach to the debt question.[6]

So far, so good. What Michael did not reckon on was the opposition of his older brother.

～ When Cáceres knocked out Iglesias, William hastened to the hotel in Lakewood, New Jersey, where Michael was laid up, and argued that this changed everything. With a cooperative administration the obstacles would be great enough. With the notoriously stubborn Cáceres they would be insuperable. Michael did not agree.

When Flint began to make difficulties over rubber, W. R. Grace needed Michael's help at home. Michael offered his help, but declined to give up on the debt. When the Flint trouble came to an open rupture, Mayor Grace again begged Michael to throw over the debt. Michael took his brother's hand and said:

"You had an ambition to become Mayor of New York. It was a proper one and . . . it gratified both yourself and friends. You were willing to suffer pecuniary loss. . . . I never said a word except to encourage you. . . . Now, I have an ambition to consummate one of the most daring and splendid of financial achievements. . . . I have the ambition, and I think it is an honorable one, to be known . . . as the man who negotiated with the creditors of a nation, reestablished their debt on a paying basis, and freed a Republic from a millstone that was hanging about its neck and preventing it from taking its place among the nations of the earth. Of course, if this undertaking of mine succeeds there will be great pecuniary profits both for me and for the firm of W. R. Grace & Company which has such a great interest in the development and prosperity of Peru."

William replied: "You shall never hear another word of complaint or of pleading from me. . . . I have only one suggestion to make. What is the sum of money which you will limit yourself to risk in this undertaking?"

Michael thought for a moment and named a sum "not far from a quarter of a million dollars."

William asked and received Michael's promise that when this amount had been spent without success he would give up. Thereupon William agreed to assume a share of the outlay.[7]

In the first half of 1886 matters went a little slowly because Michael remained in New York, dividing his time between rubber and the debt business. First, $100,000 was sought to send engineers to explore the Cerro de Pasco mines. This operation exhibited Michael Grace in the role of promoter on a grand scale. With John W. Mackay, W. R. Grace, and himself in for $10,000 apiece, Michael needed only seven more $10,000 subscribers. "We think this will lead to one of the largest mining enterprises in the world," he wrote. Small fry were not solicited. Michael approached Arthur Twombley, W. Seward Webb, and W. D. Sloane, all sons-in-law of the late William H. Vanderbilt; Secretary of the Treasury William C. Whitney; his brother-in-law Robert Payne of Standard Oil; Frederick Billings of Northern Pacific; Henry B. Hyde of Equitable Life; Joseph W. Drexel of Drexel, Morgan & Co.; Cornelius N. Bliss; and others. Michael enjoyed sprinkling these names through letters that would reach Peruvian bondholders in England. The money was raised in short order.[8]

The Cáceres revolt had impaired the pro-Peruvian position Michael Grace had taken on the debt. Being unable to get to London, as he had hoped, in the summer of 1885, Michael dealt with the bondholders through Henry Meiggs's son-in-law, Robertson. For Michael's purposes Robertson was an indifferent intermediary, his main concern being not Peruvian recovery but the protection of the Meiggs interest in the Oroya railroad. In this situation, Michael had agreed to concessions. He accepted the bondholders' view that the Mollendo customs house should be handed over for the period of years, and that control of the railroads be prolonged from fifty years to ninety-nine. Later he agreed that the bondholders should have the roads forever, in addition to land grants and colonization rights on the headwaters of the Amazon. Michael defended these concessions to Peruvians and urged Eyre in Lima to preach the gospel that "everything she [Peru] gives away will come back to her tenfold in future prosperity."

But on probably the most important point at issue, Michael stood his ground. He insisted that in return for whatever Peru should surrender, the country's foreign debt be marked "paid in full." As by no stretch of the imagination could Peru turn over assets worth £51 million, this would mean forgiveness of a large part—possibly half—of the debt. Michael's position was that should the bondholders care to pursue the matter further, they must look to Chile.[9]

In all, however, prospects of a settlement which Michael Grace regarded as fair to Peru looked rather dimmer in the spring of 1886 than they had a year before.

~ Within the next few months this situation changed. President Cáceres and Michael Grace were the men who did it. Though their separate labors moved events toward a common end, Cáceres and Michael were at this time by no means allies in the sense that a mutual understanding, or even a hint of one, existed between them.

To sketch things in their order:

Once old Cáceres took office and began to revive the national spirit of Peru, Michael Grace stopped giving in to the bondholders. Very soon he found himself in opposition to the bondholders on one side, and to Cáceres on the other. The bondholders demanded too much and Cáceres offered nothing at all. "Let the bondholders collect from Chile," he said, in effect, to Edward Eyre. "Chile has taken our collateral." Eyre rather admired the old man's spunk; and Michael used it as a weapon against the grasping tendencies of the creditors.[10]

In May 1886 the bondholders' committee in London proposed to make W. R. Grace & Co. its agent in dealing with the Peruvian government. It drew up terms, including provision for a contract with Grace to complete the Oroya road to Cerro de Pasco for £1.2 million. Other articles listed the items Peru should surrender. It was a longer list than Michael had suggested in 1885. In one case Peru was asked to turn over certain property that belonged to private citizens. On the other hand, Michael's insistence on Chile's responsibility bore fruit. The document contained this sentence: "The Peruvian bondholders claim that it is inequitable and unjust for the Chilean government to seize by right of conquest a large and valuable part of the security hypothecated to them without giving some adequate satisfaction to the bondholders."[11]

Michael Grace informed London that the proposals could not be accepted as a basis for negotiation without modification in favor of Peru; and that if he went to Lima as the bondholders' agent he would require wide discretionary powers. When Ned Eyre saw the proposals, he wrote Michael that it would be useless to show them to Cáceres. Michael then arranged with the bondholders to go to Lima, not as their representative but as mediator between the bondholders and the government. Designated as the bondholders' negotiator was the Earl of Donoughmore, an Irish nobleman in need of employment. Donoughmore had a great deal of personal charm, and that was about all he was supposed to have. Michael Grace was in the saddle. "His Lordship," Michael informed the bondholders, "must be given to understand that we are the men commissioned to handle the situation & that matters will be put before him for his signature."[12]

Certainly this was an improvement of Peru's position over 1884, when the confident bondholders had sent their man Smyles to Chile to arrange Peru's economic future.

Such was the state of affairs in July 1886 when Michael was trying to shake loose from the rubber battle to get to Lima. As yet the prospective mediator (with a whip hand over the bondholders) was in a difficult situation, for Cáceres simply sat back and said there was nothing to mediate. After careful preparation for the interview, Ned Eyre called at the presidential palace to try to bring the stubborn executive around.

Eyre spoke of the extensive plans Casa Grace had for Peru: the extension of the railroad to Cerro de Pasco; the opening of the famous mines. Even now a commission of distinguished engineers was en route to Peru. Michael Grace had found his efforts in these directions impeded by the bondholders who felt that they had "hypothecary rights" to the railroad properties. Though "quite independent of these people," Michael Grace had treated with them. They had "intimated a desire to come to some settlement with the Govt" whereby they could identify their interest with the interests of the Graces, whose desire was to restore the prosperity and credit of Peru. The bondholders, continued Eyre, "have manifested their desire of bringing capital & immigration & from creditors to become a source of wealth to the country." Michael Grace had promised to assist this laudable aim so long as "it was found to be in the interest of Peru."

Eyre paused to judge the effect of his carefully selected words. The old soldier-president showed "not the slightest enthusiasm." About all he said was: *"¿Como los vamos a dar nuestros ferrocarriles que nos cuestan tan caro?"* (How are we going to give them our railroads which cost us so much?)

In vain, Eyre argued that to relinquish the roads would be bread upon the waters.

Eyre went to Cáceres's minister of finance, Luis Bryce, a son of John Bryce. Bryce dismissed the question as abruptly as his superior had done. "Chile took all the guarantees Peru had given for the external debt. Peru does not owe anything."

Nevertheless, Eyre wrote his uncle that "properly put forward & with pressure" in the right places, the project "can be carried to a successful issue. Still it will be no easy task."[13]

After several cancellations of steamer reservations on account of the rubber business, Michael sailed for Lima in August 1886, making special provision for a quick crossing of Panama. He seems to have got the impression that Eyre was looking too much on the dark side. He wrote that he was not going to Peru with the idea of failing, and for Eyre to bear that in mind. Ned Eyre acted promptly. He dropped the word that the bond-holders, though disposed to be reasonable, meant business; if Cáceres would not entertain their claims, "they would be inclined to look for a government that would."[14]

~ The Lima conference was a brilliant success. Michael Grace won the confidence of Cáceres. The Peruvian Congress annulled certain existing legislation that would have prevented an understanding with the bondholders. An advocate of an understanding, José Aranibar, was named minister of the treasury and given special powers to deal with Peru's foreign creditors. In February 1887, José Aranibar and Michael Grace departed for New York on their way to London, hopeful of con-cluding their business quickly. Michael prompted Eyre to keep up Cáceres's confidence that Michael would "get for Peru a good contract."[15]

Michael did get a good contract, though he had to fight for it. He found the London group almost as suspicious and hostile as Cáceres had been a few months before. "The press [was] almost unanimously against us; . . . the large houses timid . . . the Stock Exchange very considerably opposed. . . . At times I almost despaired of success." The main stumbling block was provision for an advance of £400,000 to the destitute Peruvian government—a provision that Michael believed would go far to assure the approval of the pact by the Peruvian Congress. Pressure by Baring Brothers, heavy holders of the defaulted bonds, induced the bondholders' represen-tatives to concede this item.[16]

The other important articles provided for the cession of the railroads for sixty-six years; of Peru's share of the guano Chile was marketing for the joint account of the two countries, under the terms of the peace treaty; of certain customs revenues' in the event that railway revenues did not reach a stipulated figure; and of certain mining concessions. Also the bondholders were to receive land grants for purposes of sending immigrants to Peru and the right to establish a bank in Lima. All these affairs would be handled by a company called the Peruvian Corporation, Ltd., which the bondholders would set up.

In return for the concessions the Peruvian Corporation would under-take certain distinct obligations, in addition to the £400,000 to be advanced to the Peruvian treasury. Railroads would be repaired and extended. Above a certain sum the Peruvian government was to have

20 percent of the railway profits, and 15 percent of certain mining profits. The corporation would cancel one-half of the bonds outstanding. Michael was unable to obtain the cancellation of all the bonds because, as he said, the bondholders insisted on "the right of pursuing Chile for half the debt."

This agreement, generally known as the Grace-Aranibar contract, was signed in London in May 1887 and sent to Lima for ratification.[17]

There the contract ran into trouble. A minority of politicians opposed to Cáceres made a loud outcry, and the president himself found objections to the document. Michael advised Eyre that material modifications were possible. The clauses providing for the establishment of a bank and for land and colonization concessions could be dropped entirely; and many of the mining clauses could be dropped—though Michael believed all these articles would work for the good of Peru.

Had this been the sum of the opposition, Michael would not have been greatly disturbed. "The real power working against us in Lima is no small enemy," he wrote J. G. Meiggs. "It is nothing less than the government of Chile." A formal protest from Santiago had urged that the contract was against the interests of all Spanish America in that it represented an infringement on the sovereignty of Peru. In a grimmer tone, Chile warned that the contract was a violation of the Treaty of 1883, by which Chile had forehandedly endeavored to limit its responsibility to the creditors of Peru. "Both in London & Lima," continued Michael, "I am working to dispose of those difficulties. . . . This will be a hard rock to roll, but I have little fear that I will succeed in one way or another."[18]

The Chilean opposition had come as no great surprise. The surprise was the effect on the ordinarily stouthearted Cáceres. Eyre reported the Peruvian government "alarmed . . . to the point of considering withdrawing the contract." This brought a stream of earnest letters from Michael: to Eyre to buck up Cáceres's spirits; to Peruvians in and out of the government, extolling the merits of the contract and promising that the British government would not allow Chile to go too far.

To Cáceres himself Michael recalled his fight in Peru's behalf in London. He pointed out that the contract represented a better arrangement than any other Latin American country in financial difficulties had been able to make, and that Chile's real motives were not difficult to fathom. "Chile, who has always been so jealous to maintain its credit, now wishes to place new obstacles in Peru's way because she is convinced that Peru, once having erased the black mark of having a large debt owing in Europe, as it has more territory & resources than Chile, will surpass Chile by far in a very short time." The president was urged not to allow Congress to adjourn without approving the contract "with minor modifications"; or, if not that, authorizing the executive himself to come to satisfactory terms with the bondholders.[19]

Michael's next step was to try to enlist the aid of the world's most powerful force in the theater of international affairs—the British Foreign Office. When one spoke, in the phrase of the day, of "the long arm of England," one meant the Foreign Office, presided over, at this juncture, by the Marquess of Salisbury. Michael suggested that Her Majesty's minister in Lima, Sir Charles Mansfield, be instructed to indicate to Peru the advantages of ratifying the contract. Being on excellent personal terms with that diplomat, Michael left nothing to chance. Writing to Sir Charles directly, he put the case in plain language: "A little pressure in Lima will be an encouragement and a pretext to the [Peruvian] Government to carry out what they wish to, which is, in reality, to carry the present contract into effect, . . . and which at present they seem to be afraid to do . . . [because] of Chile."[20]

Chile beat England to it and put on the pressure first. The result was all Chile could desire. Cáceres withdrew the Grace-Aranibar contract from consideration by the Congress.

On the heels of this defeat for Michael, Cáceres instituted steps to take possession of three railroads operated by American citizens on terms similar to those by which Grace operated the Oroya. The Americans were Thorndike, DuBois, and Watson, members of the old Meiggs organization that had built the roads. To Chile's satisfaction this further muddied the water, and sent W. R. Grace to Washington to lay the case of the three Americans before President Cleveland.[21]

With matters fast getting out of his hands, Michael Grace renewed his plea for action by the British government. Thanks to the influence that members of the bondholders' committee in London were able to exert, he got it.

~ Her Majesty's government remonstrated against Chilean interference in negotiations between Peru and its creditors—but not with the result anticipated by Michael Grace. Conscious of the strength of its position in Latin America, Chile stood up to Great Britain. It argued the case, and pointed to the treaty of 1883. However, after much diplomatic maneuvering, Chile consented to negotiate for a settlement of the Chilean objections to the Grace-Aranibar contract.

While this proceeding dragged on, purposely prolonged by Chile, an ominous new development emerged. The United States had interceded so firmly in behalf of the American railroad operators that Peru hesitated to carry out its plans of expropriation. One of these roads, operated by John L. Thorndike, was the so-called Southern System. This was the first road built by Henry Meiggs. It ran from the port of Mollendo to Arequipa and on to Lake Titicaca. This road was Bolivia's outlet to the sea. Thorndike had gone into partnership with Bolivian financiers, making the road, in effect, a Bolivian line. This enterprise had the support of the Bolivian government and of the political elements in Peru who were fighting the Grace-Aranibar pact.

Behind all this Michael Grace saw the hand of Chile, whose influence in Bolivia was strong. By entrenching Bolivia in the Southern Railway System of Peru, Chile could kill two birds with one stone: prevent the agreement between Peru and the bondholders since these roads would be out of the bondholders' reach; and undermine Peru. "I am already convinced by what has happened & is happening," Michael Grace wrote to the Peruvian minister in London, "that Chile's political ambition is to dismember Peru of its southern department, giving it to Bolivia."[22]

Feeling that England, and England only, could halt the march of Chile to another diplomatic triumph, Michael strove earnestly to bestir British officialdom. Success had gone to Chile's head, he wrote. Santiago was trying "to play with and mislead your Foreign Office." "The Chilean Government is treating Her Majesty's Government without the respect due to so great a power." "I again repeat to you that Chile has got to be treated in this matter with a strong hand." At the same time he wrote anxiously to Cáceres, begging him not "to be blinded by Chile's pretended friendship," and promising that England would put that country in its place.[23]

The time had come for more strength on Peru's side in London; either that, or Peru was a goner. At this point, Michael's principal agents there were G. A. Ollard, who had succeeded Smyles as attorney for the bondholders, and John W. Grace. John had left Valparaiso ostensibly on account of his health. Actually the debt controversy was having its effect on the Grace business in Chile, and there was little John or anyone could have done about it. In March 1888, Michael decided to go to London and take charge. His primary mission would be "to find out how far the British government will go in this whole business."[24]

When at the last moment illness detained Michael, William made the journey. He boarded the steamer with enough memoranda from

Michael to occupy the voyage. This reading matter brought William up-to-date on every phase of what had become an extremely involved affair, only the main theme of which can be traced here. With dazzling prospects of power before it, Chile had played its part aggressively and well. Its adversaries were definitely on the defensive, with all disposable forces in the battle line. Any shift to reinforce one position would weaken another—and there Chile would apply the pressure. If Peru was to obtain a settlement of the debt that would permit that country to rise again, outside help was imperative. This could come only from England—in the form of a much stronger line with Chile than Her Majesty's government had yet taken. This would be difficult, not because England had compunctions against coercing lesser powers, but because imperial British finance had more at stake in Chile than in Peru.

In setting all this before his brother, candor was to be expected from Michael. The brothers concealed nothing from each other. They never dressed up unpleasant situations with smooth language. The remarkable thing about Michael's memoranda was that he told William nothing of any account that he had not already told others. In so complicated a situation, involving simultaneous dealings with various groups, each striving for an advantage, certain interim secrets were necessary. But in no case did these appear to involve deception or trickery. The ultimate object of Michael's efforts was clear to all. Steadfastly and openly he had held to that goal. He had tried to avoid a conflict with Chile, but, when it came, Michael had accepted the issue, though at heavy cost to Grace's Chilean business interests. It was a fight that W. R. Grace could go along with. He believed that the recovery of Peru would benefit all parties to the contest, including Chile. A prosperous and satisfied Peru would be a better neighbor than an impoverished, hostile one.

Michael reiterated his belief that "Chile . . . does not want Peru to be relieved from her present decrepit condition"; that the intrigue to place the Southern Railroad System "under Bolivian influence" was a long-range plan to detach the provinces of Tacna and Arica from Peru. "I have tried to impress upon the gentlemen in London that Chile cannot be handled with silk reins. . . . Her Majesty's government . . . will have . . . to bring the full pressure of her prestige to bear." Michael suggested that Britain send a commissioner to South America or invite a Peruvian envoy to London and force a settlement in the nature of the Grace-Aranibar contract. In either event, Britain must silence the opposition of Chile. Once this was done, there would be no trouble with Peru.

If England could not be induced to act along these lines, Michael was ready to admit defeat and drop the whole thing.[25]

~ In London, W. R. Grace rescued the situation from the brink of failure. His own account of how he did it cannot be given, for the letters Mr. Grace wrote during his month's sojourn in England are missing. Having already discussed smaller phases of the problem with two presidents of the United States and their secretaries of state, Mr. Grace apparently had no difficulty seeing the most eminent personages in the British Foreign Office. Shortly after his return home in May 1888, Her Majesty's government acted. Chile was notified that Britain had advised Peru to accept a modified version of the Grace-Aranibar agreement. The principal revision would embrace what Michael had long contended for: complete release of Peru from further responsibility in the matter of the bonded debt. That would leave the bondholders free to take their claims to Chile.

At the indication of the British government, Peru accepted Lord Donoughmore as the representative for the bondholders. Once more Michael Grace hastened to Lima. With Donoughmore as window dressing he negotiated a revised agreement. The English press called this the Donoughmore contract; the United States press, more realistically, the Grace contract. Embodying the most favorable terms yet offered to Peru, the pact was signed late in October 1888, and the stage cleared for speedy ratification by the Peruvian Congress.[26]

None of the friends of the contract were prepared for the cyclone that followed. Chile delivered to Peru a strong protest against the ratification of the agreement. This brought from the British government the stiffest note it had sent to Chile thus far. The attitude of Chile was called an unjustifiable interference between an independent nation and British subjects. The note did no good. On top of this, the French government solemnly protested to the British government against the consummation of the contract. The burden of the French protest was that the Grace contract discriminated against Dreyfus and other French creditors. Friends of the contract believed Chile to be behind the French protest.

This created an alarming situation in Lima, where the contract was before the Congress. There had always been a certain amount of opposition to a settlement along the line devised by Michael Grace. Part of this opposition represented an honest difference of opinion; part of it Michael Grace believed to be "traitorous" and fomented by Chilean money; part of it arose from fear. "How can we accept the Contract," a senator was quoted as saying in private, "when Chile is opposed and we have no means to resist?" Given "one or two iron-clads better than the Chileans," Federico Blume, the former railroad contractor, observed, "he [Cáceres] would not be afraid of them and would enjoy nothing better than a good fight."

With Lima in turmoil, one Sunday in December the friends of the contract called a public meeting to try to reconcile conflicting views and pour oil on the angry waters. According to one account the meeting "turned out badly," which seems an understatement. "There were cries of 'Down Cáceres,' 'death to foreigners' and one voice was heard to say 'let us attack Grace's house.' "[27]

Though these tactics had their effect on the Congress, a majority of the members stood firm for the contract. This majority had the support of most of the leading statesmen of Peru—such men as García Calderón, Marco Aurelio Denegri, Francisco Rosas, and Antero Aspígalla. The principal newspapers of Lima were on the side of the contract. Yet, by interminable oratory and parliamentary maneuvers, a vociferous minority managed to stave off a conclusive vote. This was largely due to the craft and energy of one member, the fiery liberal, José María Quimper, who, on one occasion, spoke for two days. The noisy sessions dragged through December and January. Unable longer to sustain their cause any other way, in February 1889 the minority members left their seats and withdrew from the congressional chambers. This left the legislative body without a quorum for the transaction of business. Congress adjourned without acting on the contract.[28]

The defeat "demoralized" the bondholders' committee in London— to use the word of G. A. Ollard. After four years the battle seemed definitely lost. To save expenses, Donoughmore was called home and plans considered for turning the whole problem over to the Foreign Office. That would have meant an almost certain surrender to Chile. It was at this juncture that Mr. Ollard sought to comfort W. R. Grace with the assertion that, for him, the matter was "purely a mercantile venture." To Mr. Grace's spirited rejoinder, quoted at the beginning of this chapter, was appended some advice. It would be best, Grace said, to do nothing about the contract at present: "Let it simmer in the minds of the Peruvians." Let them see "how very important the whole thing is to them." In the meantime continue to show faith by keeping up work on the Oroyo extension and the mining syndicate.[29]

Grace was really less hopeful than he seemed in his letter to Ollard. He wrote Michael that it might be a good idea to quietly bow himself out. There were opportunities in the United States where a man who worked as hard as Michael had worked for Peru would have something to show for it.[30]

Michael did not give up. Before the echo of the victorious cries of the anticontract party had died away he was in action—too busy, almost, to write letters. Old Cáceres had recovered from his fright. He stood with Michael. The two agreed upon a bold plan. A new cabinet was formed of staunch procontract men. Special elections were called to select new members of the Congress in the place of those who had quit the session. The electorate vindicated the position of the executive and returned a majority of procontract representatives. Congress, including the new members, was called to reassemble in July. These things done, Michael hastened to London to repair his lines there. Donoughmore, who had got as far as New York on his way home, was ordered back to Lima.

In an effort to soften the attitude of Chile, W. R. Grace went to work in New York. His argument was that the settlement of the debt and the consequent restoration of prosperity in Peru would be a great boon, rather than a "menace," to Chile. The Chilean minister at Washington accepted an invitation to spend a weekend at Gracefield. Though apparently this visit accomplished little, Grace had better success with Augusto Matte, then traveling in the United States. Matte was a brother of the Chilean foreign minister. Grace was able to convince Matte that "the contract is a good one for *Chile.*" Matte promised to see Michael in London and work toward its adoption.[31]

The most picturesque figure Mr. Grace saw in the course of his campaign was John Thomas North, the nitrate millionaire who twenty years before had gone to Chile as a Yorkshire mechanic. North arrived in New York with his family and a party which occupied nearly a floor in the Victoria Hotel. Newspapers called him "the Chilean Monte Cristo." The former mayor introduced North about town and entertained him at Delmonico's. Reporters described the visitor as wearing in his tie a diamond as big around as a dime, and one in his shirt bosom the size of a walnut. More impressive than either of these was the stone in a ring on his finger. In a newspaper interview, North praised the Grace contract and said he believed it would succeed.[32]

~ While the Chilean Monte Cristo was lighting his way about New York with diamonds, the new Congress in Lima took up the Grace agreement. The decorum of the scene contrasted sharply with the wild spectacle of a few months before. The contract was considered article by article. The pros and the cons had their say. Then the vote—always affirmative by a good margin. With the approval of the much-debated clause permitting the Peruvian Corporation, which was the bondholders' organization to be set up under the terms of the contract, to take £80,000 a year from the country's customs revenue, the ultimate approval of the contract seemed certain. This came about in October.

There were still some formalities. The president of Peru was required to sign the act of ratification; an enabling act was necessary to put the terms of the agreement into effect. Before anything at all could be done, Chile broke the serenity with the resounding protest that the terms of the contract violated the peace treaty of '83. Peru offered to arbitrate the question. Chile refused, though it had previously suggested arbitration. This used up the last of the patience of the British government. On November 20, 1889, the Foreign Office "advised" Peru by cable to complete the contract at once. It notified Chile of this action, adding that Chile's interference with the contract was unwarranted.[33]

Chile had successfully defied England too often to yield to this warning, peremptory as it was. W. R. Grace went to Washington to try to get the United States government to join the British protest. He reviewed the whole subject with Secretary of State Blaine. Reporters asked Mr. Grace if the talk had anything to do with Peru. That was as close to the truth as the newspapermen came, because the British action against Chile was not made public. The first Blaine knew of it was from Grace. Mr. Grace told the reporters that, of course, he had "talked about South America," and went on to throw the secretary a few bouquets. He concluded with the statement that, "as a Democrat," he hoped Mr. Blaine would not be the Republican presidential nominee in 1892.

The next day, January 3, 1890, a cable in cipher from Michael in London asked William to "request Secretary of State Washington not interfere." This was relayed to Mr. Blaine.[34]

Michael's long fight had been won. Finding that England meant business this time, Chile had given in. It consented to payments to the bondholders aggregating about £2.25 million. In exchange, Chile, like Peru, received a full quittance in the matter of the bonded debt.[35]

Formal requirements quickly out of the way, the Peruvian Corporation, Ltd., became a going concern in April 1890. Freed entirely of a foreign debt that had threatened its independence, Peru's credit in the money markets of the world was reestablished overnight. The one man but for whose perseverance and skill this would not have been achieved was Michael P. Grace. He had spent five years of his time and more than the $250,000 that had been his limit in the beginning. The money was all to come back several-fold—and not alone in the long-run benefits to the Grace business in Peru. The corporation granted W. R. Grace & Co. a contract for extending the Oroya railroad. With considerable exaggeration the London *Financial News* called this contract a "plum" worth £800,000 and marveled at the liberality of the bondholders toward Michael Grace.[36]

W. R. Grace was proud of his brother's work. He considered it on a plane with his own public services to city, state, and country, services which moved the New York *Tribune,* politically opposed to the former mayor, to say in April 1889: "Mr. Grace . . . is an honest, straightforward, sincere patriot." It would have been a simple matter for W. R. Grace, trailed as he was by newspapermen, to have gathered to himself considerable credit for the debt settlement which the press of the world applauded. He could have done this by mentioning his own contributions and omitting to speak of others. In 1888 these contributions had been vital.

Instead, W. R. Grace said that Michael had done it all. He mentioned himself only to remark that he had shortsightedly opposed his brother's going into the thing on the ground that the task was too staggering, and the expense too large, in view of the slim prospects of success. As a matter of fact, for a year or more before the successful issue, W. R. Grace had been pushing Michael into the limelight—arranging for newspapermen to interview him at critical times during the fight. So it was that, in America, Michael himself became something of a public figure, a situation few men find distasteful.[37]

When, after five years of alternating hope and despair, England had done as Michael Grace had long urged and cracked down on Chile, Michael's services came in for a measure of recognition. A measure only. Barely intimated was the story of Chile's opposition and the means by which it was resolved. Incidentally, that story has remained a diplomatic secret to the date of this writing. Naturally, the fullest accounts of Michael's contribution appeared in newspapers friendly to W. R. Grace because of his public services. The press of the world, while hailing the settlement as a statesmanlike accomplishment making possible the rebirth of a nation, buried Michael Grace's name among a long list of English dignitaries. Many of them had titles. Several had come in at the eleventh hour. In nothing this writer has seen was the name of a Peruvian mentioned. Old Cáceres and some of his colleagues deserve not to be forgotten.[38]

16 ~ Averting War with Chile

~ The Peruvian debt question out of the way, W. R. Grace turned his attention to Chile. It was time that he did so. The Grace business there was not in good shape. Virtually extinguished during the Chile-Peruvian war, it had recovered slowly. One reason for this was the stand Michael Grace had taken in the long-drawn-out debt negotiations. Competitors of Grace in Chile, mostly English, had made good use of a favorable opportunity to prejudice Chileans against the American house.

As a matter of fact the $2 million—if one includes profits on contracts for the extension of railroads—that the Grace houses stood to make directly as a result of the debt settlement was just about balanced by the business lost to them in Chile.

The huge booty acquired as a result of its military victory made Chile the richest of Latin American governments. In 1890 revenues were 58.5 million *pesos*, against 37 million in 1886 and 15 million in 1878. The money was spent as fast as it came in. New railroads were built and old ones added to. Wagon roads were repaired and greatly extended. Bridges were thrown across the rivers that tumble down from the Andes. Telegraph lines were strung, running water provided in the principal cities. Harbors and docks were improved. The educational system was modernized and hundreds of additional primary schools opened.[1]

These activities created markets for products from the world over. In supplying this market the Chilean house of Grace & Co., Valparaiso, had a disappointingly small share. This was due only in part to the setbacks Grace had received because of his role in the war and the debt settlement. The other factor was the inability of Grace to find a satisfactory head for his Valparaiso establishment. When John Grace left in 1887 the place was offered to W. R. Grace's son-in-law Holloway, but the young man asked for too much in the way of salary. Mr. Grace named

George Duval, Holloway's superior in the San Francisco house. Duval had made a good record in San Francisco which Grace expected to be duplicated in Chile.

Without much enthusiasm, Mr. Grace approved Duval's proposal to spend "four or five hundred pounds per annum in entertainment and otherwise for the cultivation of influential people." In lands where such expenditures were common, Grace had preferred to let prices and services recommend his houses to prospective customers. Duval made a rather conspicuous failure in Valparaiso, and in 1890 he and Grace parted company. Grace's nephew William S. Eyre, a brother of Ned, was sent down from the Lima house.[2]

Perhaps another impediment to the progress of the house in Chile was a series of claims Grace made against that government as a result of the war with Peru. Lynch's raiders had carried off cattle and livestock from a hacienda owned by Grace Brothers & Co. The Chilean forces of occupation had exacted indemnities in cash. But by far the largest claim had to do with the seizure of the nitrate properties, preventing the execution of the Grace contract of 1879. Grace took the position that Chile either should offer no obstacle to the performance of that agreement under Chilean control, or should indemnify W. R. Grace & Co. in the amount of $1 million. In 1882 this claim was laid before the State Department by Grace's attorney Frederic R. Coudert.[3]

Grace's was one of many claims against Chile. Toward them all Chile took a stiff attitude. Not until 1885 was the nitrate claim formally presented to the Santiago government by our minister to Chile, C. A. Logan. At home, Grover Cleveland had just assumed the presidency. The first Democrat in the White House since before the Civil War, he was beset by a clamor for the replacement of Republican officeholders. In Santiago, Mr. Logan was succeeded by W. R. Roberts, whom Grace had recommended. Logan came home burning with indignation. He wrote to Cleveland's secretary of state, Mr. Bayard, a long and bitter letter filled with misstatements, half-truths, and innuendoes about the Grace claim. This was during Grace's feud with the New York *World*. The *World* printed Logan's diatribe under sensational headlines.[4]

The publication of the Logan letter achieved what seems to have been the writer's purpose—to make the road no easier for the Grace claim. It does not appear, however, that Roberts tried to do much for the claim, perhaps because the Grace connection with the Peruvian debt controversy rendered such action inadvisable.

In 1889, Mr. Cleveland went out of office, and Roberts with him. The new Chilean minister was Patrick Egan, a man of great energy and an interesting history. As a successful Irish businessman, Egan had become an influential lieutenant of the nationalist Parnell. To escape arrest by the British he had fled to the United States. Here he succeeded in business and, unlike most Irish immigrants, joined the Republican party. His ability to turn Irish votes to Harrison in 1888 won him the post at Santiago. Though W. R. Grace had nothing to do with Egan's selection, it pleased him. Other American businessmen also counted on Egan's antipathy toward everything English to be of service to American commercial interests in Chile.

Through his connections in Chile, Mr. Grace sought to ensure Egan a pleasant reception and to enlist the minister's aid for the Grace and other American claims.[5]

The first Pan-American Congress, attended by representatives of eighteen nations, convened in Washington in 1889. This was something Grace had long favored as a means of fostering a better understanding among the nations of the two continents and of increasing Latin American trade with the United States. As the leading North American in that trade, and perhaps our best-informed citizen on the general subject of South America, W. R. Grace might reasonably have been expected to play an important role at the Pan-American gathering. As it happened he played no role because he was rather pointedly excluded from the deliberations of the congress. Naturally, Grace felt this. When the congress was drawing to a close, he made some tart criticisms of it to a newspaper reporter. Though the criticisms were valid, it was a mistake for Mr. Grace to have made them, publicly, at the time. The ex-mayor's excuse was that he thought the conversation with the newspaperman was confidential.

James G. Blaine, the father of the congress, had been recalled to the secretaryship of state by President Harrison. Grace and Blaine were friendly, and, on the whole, Grace had admired Blaine's Latin American policy; consequently the wonder that the name of W. R. Grace failed to appear on the list of ten American delegates. The delegation was headed by John B. Henderson, an ex-senator from Missouri whose qualifications for the post were indistinct. Andrew Carnegie and W. H. Trescot were the best-known members. Also on the list were W. C. Whitney and Charles R. Flint. Flint's name must have made Grace see red.

Henderson and Flint turned out to be by far the most active of the United States delegation. They made the 5,200-mile trip which took the visitors over the country. Though ignored by the American delegation, Mr.

Grace exchanged courtesies with some of the South Americans, and per-haps gave them a few unofficial hints.

When the congress was five months old, a reporter for the New York *Times* called at Mr. Grace's home. The *Times* had not been impressed by the achievements of the meeting. Mr. Grace pointed out that these were, indeed, small beside what they might have been. Delegates had been unwisely chosen. Most of the Latins were lawyers and diplomats of no commercial experience. None of the United States representatives understood the Latin people, their country, their ideas, their culture, or their language. Our tariff policies kept out South American products. No satisfactory effort had been made to bring about mutual concessions for mutual benefit.[6]

Republished throughout the country and cabled to South America, Mr. Grace's remarks were resented by friends of the congress, including the delegates. Mr. Grace explained to Secretary Blaine and to the Chilean min-ister that the *Times* article did not have his authorization. He gave another interview in which he emphasized the constructive work of the congress.[7]

Thus, owing to a combination of circumstances, large and small, in 1890 relations between the Republic of Chile and the houses of Grace fell considerably short of what Mr. Grace desired. The following year, how-ever, there began a sequence of events during which W. R. Grace was able to convince influential Chileans of his devotion to the welfare of that country. Mr. Grace played an admirable part in smoothing over an inter-national incident which for a time threatened war between the United States and Chile—incredible as that may now seem. This did a great deal more than mark a turning point in the fortunes of the Grace house in Chile. It averted a setback to Pan-American relations that would have required fifty years to repair.

∼ Trouble started with the outbreak of civil war in Chile, the background of which was this:

Progressive elements had seized the opportunity to use the country's sudden prosperity as a means of improving the lot of the common man. President José Manuel Balmaceda seemed qualified to pilot Chile through the stage of transition. Handsome, magnetic, and forty-five years old when he took office, Balmaceda was a liberal of wealthy and aristocratic heritage. But he was a strong-willed man who resented the criticisms of the Con-gress, though that body was dominated by liberals. The members of the Congress felt they had the right to share with the president the makeup of the executive cabinet. With this theory Balmaceda disagreed, and his view smacked of the old dictator principle. Congress adjourned without acting on appropriation bills, leaving the president without authority to disburse government funds in the year 1891. Ignoring the Constitution, Balmaceda announced that the budget for the preceding year would remain in force.

Early in January '91 a majority of the members of the Congress signed an act deposing Balmaceda from office. The fleet raised anchor in Valparaiso Bay and sailed to the nitrate port of Iquique, which became headquarters for the provisional government—a junta composed of three men. Quickly the Congressionalists obtained possession of all the rich nitrate territory.

The army, or at any rate the officer caste, remained loyal to Balmaceda, who took charge of populous central and southern Chile in dictatorial fashion. Balmaceda's methods were an admission of the popular strength of the Congressionalists. Balmaceda answered his adversaries' seizure of the nitrate ports with a decree closing them to foreign commerce. Britain and Germany openly disregarded this measure and dispatched warships to Chilean waters.

The situation was made to order for Patrick Egan, whose adverse opinion of the English had been lately confirmed by snubs from the British commercial set in Santiago. To him the contest was between the British parliamentary system and the American system of government. He espoused Balmaceda's cause, and saw in it a chance for American trading interests to deal their British rivals a blow in Chile. Not blind to the advantage of lining up the United States' sympathies on his side, Balmaceda instituted a campaign of official cordiality to Americans in Chile. Orders for arms were placed with Flint & Co., of New York. Flint, whose house had been doing practically no business in Chile, saw a chance to score on his rival Grace. He went to work with Prudencio Lazcaño, the Chilean minister at Washington, to popularize Balmaceda's cause in the United States. Balmaceda rejected a proffer of Anglo-German mediation, but accepted a similar proposal by France, Brazil, and the United States. Negotiations broke down when Balmaceda demanded, in substance, the surrender of the Congressionalists.[8]

The Congressionalists began to prepare for war in earnest, and they took measures to counteract the effect the Balmaceda-Egan-Flint combination was having on official and popular feeling in the United States. A considerable force of men was raised in the north, and groups of Congressionalist sympathizers were secretly organized throughout the Balmaceda territory. Lacking weapons, ammunition, clothing, and provisions, the Congressionalist force could hardly be called an army. Fortunately, some hundreds of miles of desert separated it from the Balmacedists.

The Congressionalists sent to the United States a mission headed by Pedro Montt and Ricardo Trumbull. Montt was a son of perhaps the greatest president in Chile's history. Trumbull, a Chilean born in Chile, was a graduate of Yale and kin to the distinguished Trumbulls of Connecticut. Montt's duties were largely diplomatic. Trumbull had the job of rounding up supplies.[9]

Trumbull went straight to W. R. Grace & Co. in Hanover Square. As the head of the firm was away, Trumbull dealt with John Grace, then with the New York house. John had his instructions: Grace would be pleased to supply the Congressionalists with everything they required excepting arms. Though Grace would not deal in guns and powder, the presumption is that John was able to give Ricardo Trumbull useful hints about where weapons might be had and how they might be transported quietly to Chile—matters in which the house of Grace was not without experience.

At the moment, W. R. Grace was making a leisurely transcontinental tour of the United States—half vacation and half political fence-fixing. News of the revolt in Chile had caused him to postpone his departure. W. R. Grace had been through countless Latin American revolutions. Usually he stood aloof, and, as far as the record goes, he never showed interest in a cause that was lacking in popular support. This feeling would have tended to dispose him in favor of the Congressionalists. A further incentive was the fact that Grace & Co., Valparaiso, did a large banking business for the nitrate companies that had taken the anti-Balmaceda side. The fact that Charles R. Flint was using Chile's troubles as a wedge to try to get into that business field by helping Balmaceda also may have been a factor. A little later Mr. Grace was to describe his position as neutral. As far as the Congressionalists were concerned, it was a benevolent neutrality.

John Grace made this clear enough. In no time he was on easy terms with the affable Trumbull. He related that until lately the Balmaceda government had maintained a small balance with W. R. Grace & Co. Recently, however, Minister Lazcaño had drawn it nearly all out, the legation secretary calling in person to take away the checks. "I wonder," John Grace remarked to Ricardo Trumbull, "if those rascals used our checks for any improper purpose."

Before the year was out, John would know the answer to that speculation.[10]

On April 20, 1891, W. R. Grace returned from his Western tour with a mind more on politics than on war. He found his firm busily supplying the Congressionalists with about everything short of arms. Grace's Merchants Line to the west coast of South America was all sailing vessels, but for this war business he chartered steamers. At least one had already sailed from New York on the long voyage 'round the Horn to the junta headquarters in Iquique. Three others were loading. It was a shorter journey, however, from San Francisco. The Grace house there was busy, too. Several steamers under Grace charter were loading in the bay.

Also loading in San Francisco Bay, at Oakland, was the coasting schooner *Robert & Minnie*. She was loading under the eye of Ricardo Trumbull, who had crossed the country to see the *Robert & Minnie*'s cargo safely on board. The cargo also had come by rail from New York. It consisted of fifty thousand infantry rifles packed in two hundred and fifty cases, and two million rounds of ammunition in two thousand boxes. Cases and boxes were unmarked. As a coaster, the *Robert & Minnie* was not required to make a manifest. Therefore, Trumbull saw his purchases on the schooner, believing no one to be the wiser. He had arranged with the junta at Iquique to send a vessel to meet the *Robert & Minnie* at sea off southern California and take over the schooner's cargo. Already plowing northward was the junta steamer *Itata*. Before the Congressionalists had commandeered her as a transport, the *Itata* had been a part of the fleet of the Compañía Sud Americana de Vapores, a Chilean line running to Panama. W. R. Grace & Co. were agents in the United States for that line.

Trumbull's secrecy was not attributable to the violation of any law of the United States in purchasing and shipping arms. Secretary Blaine had declared arms for either side in the Chilean war to be legitimate commerce. Charles R. Flint had dispatched from New York several consignments of weapons to Balmaceda. The reason Trumbull worked in the dark was to try to give the Congressionalists the benefit of surprise in a contemplated descent upon Valparaiso. There was no time to be lost. Already the Congressionalists' command of the sea was threatened. Two new Chilean cruisers had been hastened to completion in England and taken across the Atlantic by Balmacedists. At Montevideo they had been equipped with torpedoes sent by Flint. Continuing the voyage through Magellan, one of the new cruisers had torpedoed and sunk the historic Congressionalist ironclad *Blanco Encalada*. Much, then, depended on the cargo the *Robert & Minnie* was taking to the *Itata*.[11]

~ The stratagem of Ricardo Trumbull was not so secret as he imagined. A private detective was following Trumbull's movements. The detective knew what was in the two hundred and fifty cases and the two thousand boxes Trumbull had loaded in the *Robert & Minnie*. News of the rest of the plan—the projected meeting of the schooner and a junta vessel at sea—came from J. F. Chapman, Flint's agent in San Francisco.[12]

With these interesting facts at hand, Flint prevailed upon Lazcaño to employ as counsel the international lawyer John W. Foster, who had been, in turn, minister to Mexico, Russia, and Spain. If Foster could not prevent the *Robert & Minnie*'s arms from reaching Chile, probably no one could.

On May 3 the *Itata*, under the Chilean flag, arrived at San Diego, California. It occurred to no one to doubt the captain's story that the ship belonged to W. R. Grace & Co.; that she was en route from Iquique to San Francisco with passengers and merchandise, and had stopped at San Diego for provisions and coal. On the afternoon of May 5, however, when the reprovisioning was almost complete, a federal marshal boarded the *Itata* and took possession in the name of the United States.[13]

Large headlines in the newspapers announced the seizure of a Grace steamer for violation of the neutrality laws, and told of the search for the *Robert & Minnie*. W. R. Grace immediately denied any connection with the *Itata*, except that his house had acted as agent for the line that formerly had operated her. Mr. Grace said that although his firm had received offers or orders for arms from both sides in the Chilean struggle it had furnished none. He added that he had a pretty good idea of the identity of the "person" who had inspired the *Itata* story.

Newspaper reporters had a pretty good idea. Some of them saw the war as an extension of the enmity between the houses of Grace and of Flint. A Philadelphia editorial writer asked if the conflict "is being kept alive by the rival houses of Grace & Co. and Charles R. Flint."[14]

At the end of a little more than twenty-four hours, attention was abruptly shifted from the merchants by the audacious escape of the *Itata* from custody. This piece of work had been assisted by the laxity of our officials. The United States marshal had been hospitably received on board and treated to the best the ship had. He seemed unaware that the *Itata* was keeping up steam. On the afternoon of the second day the marshal decided to resume his pursuit of the *Robert & Minnie*. Leaving a deputy on the *Itata,* the marshal boarded a tug and put to sea. While the deputy was quenching his thirst and playing poker, the *Itata* raised anchor. The deputy was put ashore a few miles down the coast. Three days later the *Robert & Minnie* was overhauled—without a gun or a cartridge on board.[15]

The U. S. S. *Charleston* was ordered from San Francisco in quest of the fleeing *Itata*. As it was thought that the *Itata* might pick up a Chilean man-of-war off the Mexican coast, there were speculations about a sea fight. With loud unanimity our press denounced the escape as an affront to the dignity of the United States. References were made to "Chilean Pirates" and a great deal else that showed an imprecise understanding of the laws and precedents involved. Actually, when John W. Foster had prevailed on the government to put its machinery in motion, no case, or practically none, existed against the *Itata*. At most, the vessel could have been denied the use of the port of San Diego longer than twenty-four hours. But when the *Itata* broke arrest it committed an offense. More than that, it committed a blunder extremely damaging to the Congressionalist cause in the United States.[16]

Grace hurried his brother Michael to Washington, where he learned that the *Charleston* indeed had orders to take the *Itata*, even in the face of resistance. Thereupon, Michael got Pedro Montt to obtain the cabled assurance of the junta that the *Itata* would be surrendered as soon as she reached a Chilean port. Confidentially communicated to our government, this relieved the tension somewhat, though the possibility of a clash at sea remained.[17]

The situation worried Grace; and it appears to have worried Flint, whose idea it had been to detain the *Itata* at San Diego. In any event there was an intensification of the effort to connect Grace with gunrunning. Mr. Grace attributed this to Flint, as an offset to the known fact that Flint was engaged in the same activity. The New York *Herald*'s San Francisco correspondent telegraphed that the Grace-chartered steamer *Montserrat* was ready to sail for Iquique "with arms, ammunition, beef, flour, hay and other supplies."

In New York a *Herald* man put the matter to Mr. Grace. "I know nothing," replied the merchant, "about any arms or ammunition being on board." The reporter noted that Mr. Grace did not deny the presence of arms on board—merely said that he did not know of any. Mr. Grace went on to point out that "it is not a violation of the neutrality laws to ship arms to the revolutionists. Rifles and ammunition are articles of commerce." Recalling that he had shipped arms to Peru during the recent war, Mr. Grace repeated that he had decided not to furnish them to either side in this conflict.

When the reporter asked C. R. Flint if he thought the *Montserrat* carried arms, "Mr. Flint smiled significantly, swept the floor with the toe of his boot—and said nothing."[18]

Customs officers searched the *Montserrat* and found no arms.[19]

On June 4, 1891, the *Charleston* dropped anchor in the roadstead of Iquique, without having laid eyes on the *Itata*. So ended the widely heralded "chase." The day following, the *Itata* steamed in with the arms the Congressionalists needed so desperately. To learn that he could not land his precious cargo was a bitter blow to the *Itata*'s spirited captain. It was a bitter blow to the whole Congressionalist following, which believed that with those arms the war could be ended speedily. It is greatly to the credit of the integrity of the junta that it kept its word and sent the *Itata* and cargo back to San Diego. Many governments have broken promises when less was at stake.[20]

~ The surrender of the *Itata* boosted Balmaceda's stock. It raised the prestige of Charles R. Flint and lowered that of W. R. Grace. Very much the cock of the walk, Mr. Flint was appointed Balmacedist consul general in New York.

The junta, however, had another string to its bow. A shipment of German arms having reached Iquique some time after the *Itata* was turned back, in mid-August 1891, the Congressionalists landed ten thousand men just north of Valparaiso. With forty thousand, Balmaceda moved to meet them. Reports of a Balmaceda victory prompted Consul General Flint to expatiate on the boom in trade with Chile that would signalize the imminent restoration of peace. The implication was that W. R. Grace & Co. would have a small part in that boom.[21]

The report of the Balmaceda victory was premature. At the first encounter a large part of Balmaceda's army had deserted to the other side. The eventual result was a rout. Valparaiso and Santiago rose against Balmaceda. His army melted, his government fell, and the fugitive dictator shot himself. Among the first truthful reports was a cable from Valparaiso:

"COMPLETE VICTORY OPPOSITION. ALL WELL. GRACE & CO."[22]

To Congressionalist leaders far and near, Mr. Grace dispatched cables and letters of congratulations—a tactful thing to do because Americans were in such bad odor with the victors in Chile.[23]

Minister Egan's partisanship of Balmaceda had colored the views of our government. At Egan's insistence an American warship had stood guard while a cable off Iquique was cut, depriving the Congressionalist junta of direct communication with the United States. The American admiral commanding in Chilean waters was accused—mistakenly, it appears—of having given Balmaceda his first news of the Congressionalist landing. The sorest spot was the *Itata*. When the fighting was over, the vessel was released under bond. A little later a federal court held that she had been wrongfully seized in the first place.[24]

Suffering from the consequences of having backed the wrong horse, C. R. Flint tried to put Grace in the same unenviable position. To a reporter for the *Herald* the ex-consul general remarked with a great show of candor: "My interest in Balmaceda was purely of a mercantile nature. Flint & Co. sold arms to the Balmaceda government and reaped a commission, and so did William R. Grace & Co. and at the same time." Flint, however, professed to see nothing discreditable in this. Had not Baring Brothers sold to both sides in the Russo-Turkish war?[25]

Grace categorically denied the charge and called on Flint to retract. Flint declined, and a few days later the *Herald* displayed facsimiles of bills of sale from the Winchester Repeating Arms Co. to the Balmaceda government for rifles and cartridges. The transaction was trifling, involving only $6,900. But the interesting thing was a notation on the face of the bills: "Paid by Check W. R. Grace & Co."[26]

W. R. Grace & Co. at once exhibited the canceled check in question. It was a check drawn against the deposit of the Chilean legation with the Grace house, and was payable to the order of Manuel J. Vega. Vega was secretary of the Chilean legation when it was presided over by Flint's co-worker, Lazcaño. This was one of the checks that had aroused John Grace's interest earlier in the year. Endorsements showed that Vega had used the check to pay Winchester for arms the legation had ordered. Moreover, legation records exposed the untruth of Flint's accusation. Lazcaño had written his government that Grace was acting for the "insurgents" who, in this matter, had "made a wise choice," Mr. Grace being a man of "great natural talents" and far-reaching influence.[27]

Though that cooked Flint's goose, a squabble was still going on between the United States government and the victorious Congressionalists over Minister Egan, whom the administration tactlessly kept in Santiago. Egan had helped one batch of Balmacedist leaders to escape on the U. S. S. *Baltimore*. When he refused to surrender eighty others who had sought sanctuary in the legation, Chilean police surrounded the legation. Heated words flew between Santiago and Washington. President Harrison summoned to the White House the secretaries of war and navy, and the chief of the Naval Bureau of Operations. "Will Warships Go to Chile?" asked the New York *Evening World* in a headline. "WAR WITH CHILE!" screamed the *Journal*; "It Looks As Though We Were Ready To Fight."[28]

During this state of tension, on October 16, 1891, a street fight broke out in Valparaiso between Chileans and a band of seamen from the *Baltimore*. Two Americans were killed and eighteen were wounded with knives.

~ With the makings of a war in truth at hand, an undercurrent of moderation served to offset the explosions of the jingoes. The junta, ruling Chile until an election could be held to form a regular government, put forward an explanation that sensible persons knew might be true. It called the incident a sailors' brawl, and said that an investigation was under way. The domestic politics of the United States played a part in the situation. An off-year election was approaching. The result would have bearing on the national campaign a year hence, in 1892, when President Harrison intended to seek a second term. "A VERY OPPORTUNE BROIL," said a headline in the Democratic *Times*; "A Little Display of Jingoism Just Before the Election Thought to Be Beneficial to the Party." The president was said to be in favor of recalling Egan and breaking diplomatic relations with Chile. Secretary of State Blaine also nursed ambitions for the party nomination. The fact that war talk would redound to the advantage of the president was given as a reason for sharpening Mr. Blaine's zeal to settle the controversy by diplomatic means.[29]

Nevertheless, Chile maintained its inflexible attitude. To our request for indemnity and the punishment of the guilty, the government had sent a curt reply patterned after our reply to Italy, a few months before, growing out of the death of a number of Italians in New Orleans at the hands of a mob. Chile claimed sole jurisdiction in the premises and said that the investigation was proceeding.

The Valparaiso house wrote and cabled Grace that the situation grew "more difficult day by day." Wild rumors filled the streets: the Chilean legation in Washington mobbed, and so on. Responsible Chileans urgently requested Grace to go to Washington and work for peace. The main thing was to get Egan out of the country where his presence was like a red flag before a bull.[30]

Grace held long conversations with Blaine and with Pedro Montt. He had difficult personalities to work with, each of them in a difficult situation. "Montt is a cold, careful man of great caution, very slow & I think stubborn, patriotic, honest & . . . he does not understand the American character." Montt was certain that the United States had acted "in bad faith with Chile & in favor of Balmaceda; whereas I think they acted in good faith & on bad information" supplied by Egan. Blaine was a sick man: "His mind works differently under his physical troubles from day to day." He insisted that to recall Egan would mean breaking diplomatic relations, which the majority of the cabinet wanted. Grace's conclusion was that, all considered, Blaine "has . . . acted a friendly part to Chile, not that he likes Chile, which he does not, but because he wants peace & harmony with S. A." for political reasons.

Grace got Montt to promise to try to hurry up Chile's investigation and to urge the Chilean government to express regret and offer reparation. Grace carried this promise to Blaine. He drew attention to the fact that Jorge Montt, a cousin of the minister, who had just been elected president of Chile, had publicly made a friendly reference to the United States. Blaine expressed himself as satisfied—for the time being.[31]

Grace himself reported to Valparaiso: "I am actually engaged, often daily, in negotiating with & managing to influence either directly or thro' friends the members of Mr. Harrison's cabinet in favor of Chile. I am also at work off & on with the press & deem it wise to keep in with the Administration so as to be able at times to fill up any gaps not possible of being covered by Mr. [Pedro] Montt."

Grace's work with the press tended to create a climate more favorable to rational consideration of the *Baltimore* affair. The court decision in favor of Chile in the *Itata* case proved a boon to this effort. Grace was able to get editors to point out that this was not the only instance in which the present rulers of Chile had a grievance against the United States.[32]

While this was going on, Andrew Carnegie returned from London. Grace thought highly of the steelmaster: "Very liberal in his political views, a veritable Republican in the true meaning of the word." Grace learned that while abroad Carnegie had been so incensed by the London *Times'* "slanted" news of the Chilean crisis that he had cabled Harrison "to treat Chile liberally and with every consideration." Grace prevailed on Carnegie to urge this view personally on the president and the secretary of state. Grace also recommended that Pedro Montt engage John W. Foster as counsel. The idea at first shocked Montt, but Grace seems to have been able to point out that had Foster's influence and legal acumen been at the service of the Congressionalists in the *Itata* case, the issue might have been different. Probably because he had so recently represented the other side, Mr. Foster declined to take the case of the new government of Chile. All the same, Grace's work produced results. At the end of November, matters seemed on the way to an amicable adjustment.[33]

~ This did not last. On December 8, 1891, Grace wrote his brother Michael in London: "Things don't look as happy in the Chile-U. S. matter as I had hoped. The official report of Secty [of the Navy] Tracy put the thing very unfavorably & it looks to me now as if we were not entirely out of it."[34]

Tracy's report dealt with the circumstances surrounding the fight in which the two *Baltimore* crewmen were killed, and with subsequent events. Because of the state of feeling the seamen had been cautioned about their behavior, and before going ashore had been relieved of all weapons, including pocketknives. Trouble had started in a saloon. While all our seamen may not have been the models of decorum their officers claimed, a certain amount of premeditation on the part of the Chilean mob seemed very likely. When our sailors fled from the saloon, they were set upon by a swarm of armed men, probably numbering into the hundreds. The police were ineffective at best, and one of our men seems to have been killed while in police custody. Several aspects of the affair were difficult to reconcile with the Chilean claim of a spontaneous gang fight.

On December 9, President Harrison, in his annual message, treated the situation at length. He began by defending the official conduct of Egan as "impartial . . . from first to last" throughout the war. He gave an account of the *Itata* incident, in which he virtually rebuked the federal court for finding against the government and noted that the suit had been appealed. (The government subsequently lost the appeal.) Then he took up the *Baltimore* affair. Even Grace called the president's treatment of this incident "moderate"; but after Mr. Harrison's remarks about Egan and the *Itata* it would have been hard to convince a Chilean of that. The president concluded by saying that a finding in the matter was expected shortly from the Chilean government. Unless this finding came soon, and unless it was "satisfactory," the president would prepare a special message on the subject.[35]

For two days, Grace discussed the message with editors and public men in New York. One he talked to was Stephen B. Elkins, the West Virginia coal magnate. Grace ships had carried many a ton of Elkins coal to South America. Mr. Elkins told Grace of the president's offer of the secretaryship of war. This was good news, for Elkins would be another peace vote in the cabinet. Grace decided the moment had come for him personally to speak plainly to Chile—to the end that Harrison should have his "satisfactory" answer without delay. Whether he told Elkins of this does not appear, though it seems probable. In any event, on December 11, Elkins went to Washington to accept the War Office and to see Harrison and Blaine about Chile. It was also arranged for Grace to see the president privately in the residential quarters of the White House.

It now remained for Grace to obtain the cooperation of Pedro Montt. He wrote the minister a frank and firm letter. American sailors had been killed. Our government believed that the attack had been deliberate. "If tomorrow the President should send a special message to Congress demanding that Chile give satisfaction . . . I have the firm conviction that it would not only be sustained by the members of his own party, but also by the opposition." Mr. Grace advised the minister to telegraph his government to terminate its investigation and submit its report. Grace suggested that the report point out that the trouble had occurred while life in Valparaiso was still disorganized because of the war; and that it express regret and offer either to pay an indemnity or to submit the question to arbitration. Grace said the United States would accept no less than this: "You are in a position today to determine the manner in which future events will go."[36]

The day Pedro Montt received this letter he also received a long and furious cable from Manuel A. Matta, the Chilean foreign minister. This dispatch said President Harrison's message contained "errors or deliberate inaccuracies." Montt was directed to adhere to the unbending attitude laid down in Matta's earlier communications and to give certain of these communications to the American press. "Chile will maintain its dignity, notwithstanding the intrigues which proceed from so low a source [Egan] and threats which come from so high a source [the president of the United States]."

Montt had the prudence to give nothing to the press, and to say nothing to our State Department about Matta's note. That did not keep it from the American public, however. The Chilean government had given the message to the newspapers in Santiago, and had made it the basis of a circular letter to its diplomatic corps throughout the world. The New York *Herald*'s Valparaiso correspondent scored a beat by getting it to his paper in time for publication on December 13. Newspapers frequently consulted Grace about important South American news before publication. The *Herald* did so in this instance, with the result that the same issue carried an editorial headed "No Occasion for War." Grace himself may have written it.[37]

With an appearance of equanimity that cost some effort, Grace wrote to Elkins: "I will go to Washington & 'lay around' until you can give me an opportunity of having my say with the President." What passed between Grace and Mr. Harrison is not known, though it left Grace with the impression that Harrison "wanted a war," and would have it unless Chile backed down.[38]

Though Pedro Montt was wise enough to keep quiet he did seem to derive a certain satisfaction from the spectacle of little Chile pulling the tail feathers of the American eagle. He took no action on Grace's suggestion of arbitration. Considering the temper of the Chilean government, perhaps, for the moment, this was wise.

Grace's problem was to convince Pedro Montt and his government that the situation was truly serious. Grace got John W. Foster to talk to Montt. Probably through the intervention of Foster, members of the British, French, and German legations approached the Chilean minister—all with the same story: the administration meant business, but Chile could dissipate the war clouds without loss of dignity by offering to submit outstanding differences to arbitration. Like most Chileans, Pedro Montt had almost unbelievable faith in the prowess of his country. "The Americans would never dare [attack us], would they?" he was quoted as saying to a British attaché. While this was going on, Carnegie, Foster, and others begged Harrison to have patience. The president promised to await the inauguration of Chile's president-elect, Jorge Montt. Very likely, Harrison had been assured that Jorge Montt would get rid of Matta, and that this would make a difference in Chile's attitude.

At length all this began to have some effect on Pedro Montt in Washington. He was persuaded to make an accommodating gesture.[39]

It took the form of invitations to a dinner at the Chilean legation on December 26, ostensibly to celebrate the inauguration of Jorge Montt. After consultation with Harrison, Secretary Blaine accepted—and attended with his daughter in the place of Mrs. Blaine, who was ill. Among the others present were members of the Senate Committee on Foreign Relations and the House Committee on Foreign Affairs; also John W. Foster, Ricardo Trumbull, W. R. Grace, and several Latin American diplomats.

The dinner was widely talked of. Mr. Grace was given credit for arranging it, some newspaper correspondents referring to it as "Grace's dinner." The function achieved a favorable press in both countries, the New York *World* giving its account the headline: "ALL SIGNS POINT TO PEACE." Mr. Grace disclaimed any responsibility for the affair and said that he was "not in a position to know anything about diplomatic negotiations." A reporter asked if Mr. Grace thought "the Chilean government is ready to accede to our demands." "I believe," replied the New Yorker, "they are willing to do what is right and I am sure the United States will only ask what is right."[40]

The peace hopes of Grace rested on more than the fact that Mr. Blaine had enjoyed the hospitality of Señor Montt. Either shortly before or after the dinner, Pedro Montt, acting on Grace's suggestion, had asked his government to propose mediation. Private cables from Chile assured Grace that this would be done. When Grace carried the news to Blaine, the secretary of state had every reason to feel pleased with himself. He saw at hand the triumph of his policy of moderation; he saw the "war party" routed. Nor was that all. The secretary of state saw himself chalking up a thumping political advantage over his rival for the presidency, Mr. Harrison—and the nominating convention less than six months off.[41]

This prospect was strengthened by official cables from Egan. Jorge Montt had named a new cabinet. Two members Egan called "personal friends" who disapproved of the Matta note of December 11. Egan saw things on the way to a peaceful settlement.[42]

~ *N*evertheless, the hopeful aspect matters wore at the opening of 1892 rested on a slender foundation. President Harrison was determined that Chile should disavow Matta's discourteous message and make amends for the *Baltimore* attack. Grace tried to bring this home to Will Eyre, who was in touch with Chilean officialdom: "The situation here is strained & Chile should ask for arbitration as the only safe way of ending it." Delay played into the hands of the "war party." Should Harrison ask for war on the issue of "murderous assaults on our sailors because they wore the uniform of the U. S.," he would carry the country, including Blaine, with him.[43]

While trying to prod Santiago to action, Mr. Grace continued his work for Chile with the newspapers. The result was highly successful, and served in a measure to divert the public mind from Chile's vexatious delay. This was fortunate, for Chile's silence made things more uncomfortable for Blaine every day. Egan, however, remained hopeful. The police cordon had been removed from the legation and an informal arrangement made for getting the last of the Balmacedist refugees out. This was something, but not what Blaine wanted. Concerning a disavowal of Matta's note, Egan was met with evasions and quibbles. Concerning the attack on our sailors, the investigators issued a report of a hundred-odd pages that was very close to a whitewash. Even Blaine's patience was running out. Grace got Carnegie to make another trip to Washington to urge restraint upon the secretary and the president. Nevertheless, on January 16, Blaine cabled Egan to press matters—just as Grace was doing with Pedro Montt.[44]

Back came a dispatch from Santiago. Neither the Matta note nor arbitration was mentioned. What Chile asked was the removal of Patrick Egan as minister. This was the last straw. Yielding to Harrison, on January 21, Mr. Blaine sent the Chilean foreign minister a cable. Respectful language did not obscure the fact that this note constituted an ultimatum. Unless Chile made a "suitable apology" and "adequate reparations" for the assault on the sailors and withdrew "the offensive parts of the dispatch of the 11th of December," the United States would terminate diplomatic relations.[45]

When no reply to this had come after four days, the president, in a special message to Congress, made public the note of January 21. He asked Congress to support the demands of that note. Had Mr. Harrison waited a few hours longer there would have been no need for this. While his message was being read to Congress, Chile's answer to the communication of January 21 was being translated at the State Department. It acceded to everything: apology; indemnity; withdrawal of the note of December 11. The crisis was over.[46]

Though Mr. Blaine's friends could point out that the issue had been settled amicably, Mr. Harrison got most of the credit for bringing Chile to time. He deserved it, for Chile gave in only to a show of force. The president believed Chile wrong in the whole series of incidents, of which the assault of the sailors was merely the climax. In this he was mistaken. Chile had grievances against the United States that were as serious in its eyes as our grievance against Chile in the case of the seamen.

Mr. Grace's contribution to the settlement was extolled here and in Chile. His satisfaction over the ending of the crisis was modified by the manner in which it had been accomplished. He said the proud and sensitive Chileans would not soon forget our ultimatum. Other Latin countries would sympathize with Chile, thus postponing the cordial understanding between the Americas that Grace would like to see. "Blaine would have given . . . [the Chileans] time to come down gracefully & he knew that was all they wanted. Harrison & Tracy are to blame." Though his public utterances were always courteous, Mr. Grace had come to have no use for

Harrison. In these words he put the matter to his brother Michael: "He was on the war path & Tracy privately informed Dana [of the *Sun*] that a war was certain. . . . Harrison . . . fancied war would reelect him."[47]

Having worked so hard and done so much for Chile, Grace privately could not refrain from a reminder that Chile would have been better off had it taken his advice about arbitration. Replying to Will Eyre, who had conveyed the congratulations of some Chileans, Mr. Grace wrote: "We are happy to see that our friends in Chile appreciate our efforts on behalf of peace & we hope that cierto [certitude] with which we foretold the situation may fully impress them."[48]

17 ~ Climax of a Public Career

~ W. R. Grace's labors as a peacemaker in the Chilean crisis kept him out of domestic politics for four months while the lines were being drawn for the national campaign of 1892.[1]

Although he had better reasons than almost anyone for deploring the course Mr. Cleveland had taken in 1888, ending in his defeat for the presidency and the rout of the good-government forces in New York, the former mayor showed no resentment. At the same time, he did not forget Cleveland's disastrous sellout to Hill and to Tammany. Though he was for the renomination of Cleveland in '92, Grace hoped to see the candidate in better political company than he had kept four years before.

On leaving Washington in 1889, Mr. Cleveland had joined a law firm in New York City. Mr. and Mrs. Grace entertained the former White House couple at dinner. When the Clevelands moved from a hotel to a house on Madison Avenue, Grace sent some coffee "out of a special lot, imported from Central America for my own use." When Cleveland wished to join the Manhattan Club, he asked Grace to propose him.[1]

Yet the two men were not intimate personally; and between them as politicians lay the barrier arising from Mr. Cleveland's alliances of 1888.

In the heat of the rubber fight, Grace could say that he was done with politics, and mean it at the time. But he could not keep the newspapers from speculating as to what was up his sleeve; from intimating that he was secretly eager for a number of public honors; from quoting and misquoting him on free silver, the tariff, Tammany, et cetera. Mr. Grace was against the high McKinley Tariff of the Republicans. He was against the Silverites of his own party. In response to a confusing representation of his views he sent a joking personal note to Charles R. Miller of the *Times*: "I am in favor of a free flow of silver from the Peruvian mines, but that is the only silver issue . . . I take any stock in."[2]

In the spring of 1890, with a mayoralty contest in the offing, Grace gave out an interview in which he as good as said that he was a receptive candidate. Liberals of various persuasions hailed the announcement. The ring showed signs of concern, aware of the obvious truth that Grace was trying to drive a wedge between Cleveland and Tammany Hall.[3]

Though Grace said no more, the movement for him grew, aided by a typical Tammany scandal involving the incumbent Mayor Grant. A Tammany district leader who hated Grant offered to bet $10,000 that if Grace should run against Grant, Grace would not only win but would win by fifty thousand votes. Governor Hill began to get worried and to take a hand in the situation. This did not stop the onset of what one paper called a "citizens' crusade" for Grace. Through it all Mr. Grace remained silent. In mid-August he told a reporter for the ever friendly Brooklyn *Eagle* that he could not make up his mind whether to run. When another paper ran a squib about ex-Mayor Grace refusing to pay a cabby fifty cents for a twenty-five-cent ride, a writer to the letter column of the *World* said this proved Grace was no candidate: an aspirant for office would never incur the hostility of the city's hackmen.[4]

The letter writer was right about Grace not running. Instead, he tried to throw the support his name had inspired behind a ticket of the People's Municipal League, a hastily got-up group that had the backing of independents, Democratic liberals, and the Republican organization—including the state organization headed by Boss Tom Platt. An embarrassing search for a candidate took a lot of steam out of the P. M. L. After first-class men like Hewitt and former Secretary of the Treasury Fairchild had turned down the honor, it fell to Francis M. Scott, whom Grace had introduced to public life and whom Hewitt had promoted to aqueduct commissioner when that piece of public work was rescued from the clutches of Hill. Though a conscientious public servant, Scott was no rouser of the populace.[5]

Tammany renominated Hugh Grant.

Speaking two or three times a night, Grace overshadowed his candidate. To his brother Michael, Grace wrote that he was "lionized everywhere," and trying to keep from acquiring a swelled head. When Grant attempted to introduce the religious issue, Grace counseled his followers against similar tactics. A Scott worker came to Grace with a story that Grant had made a $5,000 gift to Dick Croker's infant daughter. Grace said to "avoid mud-throwing."[6]

The enthusiasm was for Grace rather than his candidate. During the campaign the patchwork P. M. L. fell apart. The unpopular McKinley

Tariff helped the Democrats throughout the country, particularly in the foreign-trade center of New York. In a light vote, Grant won by 21,000.

To Michael, Grace revealed what had been his personal political aspiration:

"If we had won I would have been next U. S. Senator from N. Y."[7]

This ambition, which escaped the newspaper writers at the time, seems to explain Grace's refusal to run for mayor. Had Grace put Scott over, Boss Platt would have been Grace's debtor. Though the Republicans in the Legislature could not have sent one of their own party to the Senate, they might have combined with the anti-Hill Democrats to elect a man like Grace. As matters turned out, however, Governor Hill was able to promote himself to the Senate seat Mr. Grace had his eye on.

~ Still, Grace did not abandon the hope of rounding out his public career in the Senate. The next chance would be in 1892, provided the Democrats won; and the 1890 sweep of the country was a good augury, regardless of how Grace felt about the result in New York City. Moreover, Mr. Grace must have been pleased to read that Grover Cleveland was said to have quietly voted the "Platt-Grace-Scott ticket." All this seemed to be working toward Grace's object of separating Cleveland from the shady elements of his party.[8]

After a delay on account of the outbreak of war in Chile, late in January 1891, Mr. Grace set out on a slow trip to the Pacific Coast, as he said, to acquaint his daughters with the beauties of their country. Along the way, party leaders flocked to see him. When he started his trip, there was almost no active opposition to the renomination of Cleveland. Anti-Cleveland Democrats had neither a man nor an issue. Mr. Grace had not traveled far, however, when this situation changed.

The old struggle between the creditor East and the debtor West centered on the silver question. With a robust disregard for Western support (but not that of the conservative, moneyed, and populous East), Cleveland, in a letter to Grace's friend Ellery Anderson, came out squarely for the gold standard. That gave the anti-Cleveland people their issue. Senator-elect Hill, embracing free silver, stepped forward as their man. Catching Mr. Grace in silver territory, these events imparted some point to his good words for Cleveland.

The San Francisco Young Men's Democratic Club gave Grace quite a reception. Introduced as the recent reform mayor of New York and "the confidential adviser of ex-President Cleveland," the visitor denied the second statement. He eulogized Mr. Cleveland. He took a mild shot at the trusts which he said the Republicans fostered. The burden of his remarks concerned the tariff. He was for "freer trade"—not free trade—and exhorted his hearers to show the courage of their convictions "as Cleveland has done . . . and the victory of 1892 is already assured." In a word of guidance he adjured his young listeners to "be ever faithful in the performance of political obligations." Possibly Grace hoped these words might reach Mr. Cleveland, too.[9]

Grace skirted the silver issue as best he could and tried to minimize the now famous "silver letter." In Denver he was expanding on the enthusiasm that praise of Cleveland had elicited in California when a reporter interrupted with: "Hill is their man."

Mr. Grace did not agree and went on to say that if Cleveland's position on silver had lost him some votes in the West, it had gained him more in the East.

On his return home, Grace repeated this thesis.

"What did you hear about Governor Hill?" asked a representative of the *Times.*

"I never heard Mr. Hill's name mentioned seriously by any prominent man," responded the ex-mayor.[10]

All the same, Grace was ready for a fight, and a fight that was to his liking because of the possibility of separating Cleveland and Hill once and for all. As Hill controlled the party machinery of the state, it would not do to underestimate him. Using the ward-heeler methods that had put him into the Senate, Hill's first move would be to try to capture the New York delegation to the nominating convention.

When the Chilean war scare was dissolved in January 1892, Grace, Ellery Anderson, and others got their heads together on ways and means of fighting Hill in the New York State convention. It was customary to hold this meeting in May, a month before the national convention, which was to be in Chicago that year. Hill struck first, however. Late in January he took his opposition unawares with a call for the state convention to assemble in Albany on Washington's birthday.

Grace at once called a meeting at his home. Only eight attended. He sent them to bring others to a subsequent meeting at the Murray Hill Hotel. This time thirty-five showed up, among them Fairchild, Anderson, Oswald Ottendorfer, Francis M. Scott, and Frederic R. Coudert. This group signed a call for a mass meeting at Cooper Union to denounce Hill's "snap" convention.[11]

At the Cooper Union meeting, four thousand filled the old hall and as many more stood outside. Hill's name was booed and the roof raised for Cleveland. Although Mr. Grace did not speak, he received a "marked ovation." A resolution was adopted calling for a protest against the Hill convention. Should that protest be unheeded, "other action" was to be taken to ensure "proper" representation of the New York Democracy at Chicago. Grace was a member of the committee that presented, in person, the protest to the Hill organization. It was, of course, denied, whereupon the good-governmenters called another Democratic state convention, to meet in Syracuse on the last day of May.[12]

The snap convention performed according to plan and selected a delegation pledged to Hill at Chicago. A Hill movement swept out into the country. Some of Cleveland's friends took alarm. Henry Watterson of the Louisville *Courier-Journal*, who lately had tried to pull Hill out of the race, wrote that Cleveland was done for.[13]

~ A great deal depended on what the anti-snappers would be able to make of their rival convention. To make anything of it would mean fast, inspired work, throwing together an organization that would penetrate every community in the State of New York. Taking the name of State Democracy, the anti-Hill forces opened headquarters on Fourteenth Street. Fairchild was in general charge, with Grace the head of the committee on enrollment, on whose success everything depended. Grace went at it like a man putting out a fire. He virtually lived at Fourteenth Street. In two days' time, four hundred and fifty signatures were obtained in one Assembly district in the city; in ten days, eight hundred in another. Grace reached into the state with equally encouraging results. The eyes of the nation were drawn to this effort. The old clean-politics faction, split and scattered by varying vicissitudes—"gone to grass," as Grace put it—was coming together again.

"You intend to contest the seating of the Hill men?" a newspaper man asked.

"Certainly," replied the former mayor. "We are going to Chicago with a fixed purpose in view, the nomination of Grover Cleveland."[14]

Grace addressed a rousing meeting in Buffalo. "That a process of awakening has been going on around us the signs of the times abundantly prove and, unless all such signs fail, we see our efforts crowned with success." Not content with his work in New York, by correspondence Grace carried his campaign against Hill into the South and West.[15]

The committee on enrollment's original goal of one hundred thousand names in New York State was passed within a month. When the lists were officially closed at the end of April, the count was over two hundred thousand. The magnitude of this outpouring was as much a source of wonder to Grace's committee as it was a source of dismay to Hill and his henchmen.[16]

Remarkably, a month before the Syracuse convention was due to assemble, the State Democracy had accomplished what it had set out to do. Hill had been stopped. The country had taken to heart the spectacle of nearly all the decent party leaders of his home state in arms against Hill, with the people rising under their banners.

The triumph of Cleveland at Chicago was so much taken for granted that it almost ceased to be news. Friendly papers, even a virtual Grace organ like St. Clair McKelway's Brooklyn *Eagle*, ceased to concern themselves especially with the doings of the State Democracy. Yet the pro-Hill *Sun* kept up its sniping. One day it said the real object of the movement was to set up Grace as a "calico candidate for Mayor." Color was lent to this by the charge of a disgruntled district worker, passed over in the selection of delegates to Syracuse, that Grace's support of Cleveland was a blind; that his true ambition was to dominate local politics.[17]

Then came the most disturbing development of all. While they had looked on with approval and satisfaction, some of the men closest to Cleveland had scarcely lifted a hand to help Fairchild and Grace to rout Hill. The fight won, two of them—William C. Whitney and Daniel Manning of Albany—came forward, publicly, with the soft plea that the Syracuse convention send only a "protesting" delegation to Chicago; that no real effort be made to unseat Hill's snappers.

Had 1888 taught Cleveland nothing? Could he still be persuaded by opportunists like Whitney to run with the hare and hunt with the hounds?[18]

The incident was not calculated to improve Grace's relations with Whitney, who had come a long way since he had left Grace's first mayoralty cabinet. At handsome profit to himself Mr. Whitney had reorganized a collection of the city's surface transit lines, and had offered Mr. Grace a participation in the enterprise. Grace refused on the ground that it would not look well for a former mayor to be engaged in a business that was so close to the city government. Next, Whitney had stepped into Mr. Cleveland's first cabinet as secretary of the navy and had made an excellent record in that office. Definitely, he was a man of success, fortune, and fashion. Grace, however, preferred the political convictions of another former cabinet officer of Mr. Cleveland—Fairchild, who was also a millionaire, incidentally.[19]

Though incensed, Grace seems to have made no effort to reach Whitney about the status of the State Democracy delegates. But he held his ground for contesting the Hill crowd's right to represent New York. He asked an Albany friend, Judge D. Cady Herrick, to intervene with Manning to stop "[this] rot about protesting delegations."[20]

Herrick failed to accomplish anything.

With its major aim achieved beforehand, the Syracuse convention was anticlimactical, though surprisingly well attended and enthusiastic. Grace was the most conspicuous and popular man there: "THE GRACE CONVENTION," the *Sun* headed its hostile account. "We had over 10,000 strangers in the city," Grace wrote to a California friend, "and a most remarkably intelligent and good-looking set of delegates." After choosing a Cleveland delegation for Chicago, the convention agreed to a sound political maneuver. On Grace's motion it named the same electors who had been chosen by Hill's snap convention. This served notice that the anti-snappers were working within the party. "With only one electoral ticket in this State," Grace explained, "there can be no fear of dangerous 'cutting' of Cleveland." Mr. Grace was asked if the delegation would contest for seats. "What do you think we came here for?" countered the anti-Hill leader.[21]

Returning home, Grace wrote buoyantly to Cleveland: "All went off with a grand hurrah." Yet the Cleveland camp seemed the reverse of pleased. Now that the danger had passed, "harmony" once more was the watchword. With the nomination in his grasp the candidate could see no reason to antagonize Hill. Even Fairchild disclaimed "any intention to create discord at Chicago." During the three weeks between the Syracuse and Chicago conventions there was constant pressure to avoid a contest.[22]

Mr. Grace rode to Chicago in the private car of Henry Villard, railroad builder and owner of the *Evening Post*, perhaps the most influential liberal newspaper of the time. Mrs. Grace and their two daughters were along—a circumstance so unusual in those days that it seemed to advertise the fact that Mr. Grace did not expect to be too seriously engrossed by the business of politics. Whitney was already on the ground. His extensive suite at the Palmer House was a focal point. There the affable New Yorker met leaders and delegates of all factions. He smoothed ruffled tempers and spread the oil of conciliation. Mr. Whitney was firm in his opposition to a contest between the rival New York delegations. Seat them both, he said—but give the Hill men the vote. Satisfied that Cleveland did not need New York's vote to win the nomination, Grace, in disgust, acceded to this arrangement. Among the disfranchised delegates were some of the most eminent men in New York. The *Post* correspondent contrasted their "quiet refined manner" to that of the Tammany-Hill aggregation.[23]

The convention met in an improvised wooden tabernacle on the lake-front. The place was as hot as an oven. During the nominating and sec-onding speeches a rainstorm cooled the air but drowned out the orators. When the roof began to leak, delegates and spectators raised umbrellas. At three o'clock in the morning of June 23 the voting roll call began, the Hill crowd having vainly moved for an adjournment. It was Cleveland on the first ballot—with 617 votes to Hill's 114, including 72 from New York.[24]

Whitney had done well at Chicago. A newspaper sketch artist caught W. R. Grace shaking the hand of Mr. Cleveland's manipulator and clapping him on the shoulder. Yet, in the opinion of the New York *Times* and a good many more, Mr. Whitney's fine work would have gone for nought except for the earlier labors of Grace, Fairchild, and the other anti-snappers who had sat voteless under their umbrellas in their dripping tabernacle on the shore of Lake Michigan.[25]

~ The campaign of 1892 was one of the quietest and cleanest in the history of the presidency. The death of Mrs. Harrison kept the Republican nominee from the platform. Mr. Cleveland at once canceled a scheduled appearance at the opening of the Chicago World's Fair, and thereafter declined to take the stump. Most of the time he spent at his summer residence, Gray Gables, on Cape Cod.

Beneath the surface, however, things were not so tranquil—particularly within the Democratic ranks in New York.

Whitney made it clear early that he favored a continuance of the policy of conciliating Tammany and Hill. He figured that the respectable elements of the party would stick to Cleveland anyway. When the Hill henchman Blue-Eyed Billy Sheehan was chosen to direct the state cam-paign, liberals were shocked. Rumors of a bolt and a third ticket, with Cleveland at its head, filled the air.[26]

Grace wrote directly to the candidate:

"I had a long talk with Messrs. Whitney & [William F.] Harrity [chairman of the National Committee] & explained to them the condition of things in this City with the Syracuse people & my obligations to them & its limitations. The organization growing out of the Syracuse enrollment is marching along, without any talk or fuss, but it is sure to be a factor next fall, & if I can keep it in control it can be made useful." Though Grace did not say what he thought would happen if he could not keep the anti-snappers in control, he dropped a hint: "The impression that the Syracuse people are being turned down is going too far for your good. You often get suggestions from me; some of them have been good ones."[27]

Whitney, too, was offering suggestions. As in '88, he was more afraid of the bosses than he was of the reformers. Recognition of the Tammany-Hill machine as the regular party organization in New York was a natural sequel to the decision to allow the Hill crowd to cast New York's vote at Chicago. Then Whitney attempted to go further. For Cleveland's signature he drafted a letter to Ed Murphy, the state chairman, inviting him to Gray Gables and promising to forget past differences among "friends." That was too much. "I'll be damned if I'll sign it!" roared Cleveland.

Whitney kept up his importunities, and Cleveland resisted. Whitney argued the "practical" politics of the case: "You do not realize that you were nominated against the united voice of your State organization." Some appeasing gesture was necessary or "you cannot carry this State." Cleveland replied that with sufficient party effort he could carry Illinois and Wisconsin, which would make up for the loss of New York.[28]

This time no knifing by the machines was feared—only that they would not get out the vote. Grace saw a possibility of remedying this by putting in the field a third ticket. The idea was that this would make Tammany stir its stumps. Grace talked over this strategy with Oswald Ottendorfer; but to Cleveland the former mayor confined himself to repeating that should the nominee embrace Tammany, Grace would have difficulty holding the honest-government people in line.[29]

After a month of refusal and hesitation, Cleveland capitulated to Whitney. He consented to see the bosses in New York.

Cleveland arrived in the city heartsick. Herrick heard him threaten to withdraw from the race. But at the Victoria Hotel he met Croker, Murphy, and Blue-Eyed Billy Sheehan. Accounts of what took place diverge. The one most creditable to Cleveland is that, though pressed, he refused to promise specific rewards for the machines' support. All the same, the parley sewed up the bosses. The Tammany *Mail and Express* exulted over the Wigwam's triumph. Hill, who had stayed away from the Victoria meeting, came into the Cleveland camp ten days later.[30]

In one of his tactful arguments for a third ticket in New York City, Grace had written: "Nothing tends to getting out the vote like a sharp local contest."[31] When Cleveland made other arrangements for getting out the vote, that argument no longer had any force. Yet, far from stilling the agitation for a third ticket, the Victoria Hotel meeting increased it. The anti-snappers were hurt and angry. They saw Mr. Cleveland mollifying the bosses, with never a friendly word for the enemies of corruption. A week after the Victoria conference Grace wrote the candidate:

"I don't know what they [the anti-snappers] may do. . . . I have pondered over this whole thing for 2 or three weeks; I want to be loyal to the men who helped me to get 77,000 names in the city . . . & I want to retain their interest in the National ticket." At the same time, perhaps not unmindful of his senatorial ambitions, he would like to please Mr. Cleveland and the national committee by coming out against a third ticket. "But I can't for the life of me decide what the effect of such an announcement will be. . . . My own idea is that it would be safer to have a 3rd ticket in the field & have me support it; but that . . . puts me in a false position with the National Committee as I am known to all as a Cleveland man above all other things." Yet, he reiterated, "there are 30 districts and what some of them may do in resentment for having been 'used and then abandoned' I don't know; that is the way they put it."[32]

To this appeal for guidance, Grover Cleveland remained silent. So Grace sent out a call for a meeting of his restive district leaders on September 22. He said he wanted to hear the popular sentiment, which, of course, he knew well enough. Actually he wanted to let the leaders blow off steam. They blew off a good deal and, overruling Grace by a vote of four to one, moved to confer with the Democratic national committee about putting a local anti-Tammany ticket in the field. National Chairman Harrity responded the next day, through the newspapers, making it clear that in his opinion there was nothing to confer about.[33]

Grace swallowed this affront to his followers. He said that while he, personally, favored a third ticket, he would do nothing about it if Cleveland and Whitney remained opposed. The situation was so tense, and so important in the eyes of the party strategists, that Harrity and Whitney decided it was up to Cleveland himself to make sure of Grace.[34]

Eighteen days after his eventful journey to New York to line up the party bosses, Grover Cleveland came from Gray Gables to line up the arch foe of those corruptionists. The only thing known about this second meeting is that it was held at the Victoria Hotel on September 30, and that Cleveland got what he wanted: Grace's pledge to oppose a third ticket.[35]

The anti-snap *Times* congratulated Grace on his decision. The anti-snap *Commercial Advertiser* accused him of bartering "for a promise of the United States senatorship." However it was, the former mayor made it clear that he had yielded against his better judgment to the candidate's and his advisers' view of party expediency. To a Virginia leader: "You may rely on the fact that I will favor nothing G. C. opposes. . . . However, . . . a 3d ticket here would have made the Cleveland ticket sure in this State." To George Apgar of Ithaca: "I bow to the wishes & convictions of many men like yourself & to the wish of the officials responsible for the management of the campaign. My judgment is the same as it was but I mean to try & prevent the Syracuse people from nominating a ticket in opposition to T. H. in this City."[36]

At some cost to his popularity, Grace turned to the distasteful work of stifling the third-ticket movement. In a practical way he succeeded, though on October 19 a few rebellious diehards did launch a local slate headed by Cleveland. It had no shadow of a chance. The city was safe for Tammany.[37]

Grace's surrender was doubtless made more palatable by the fact that it seemed to increase his chances for the Senate. In event of his election, Mr. Cleveland might be able to influence the choice of New York's next senator. No one questioned Grace's fitness; and, surely, his service to Cleveland was deserving of reward. The situation disturbed Hill and Tammany, who had their own senatorial candidate in the person of State Chairman Ed Murphy. On October 3 a reporter for the New York *Press* quoted an unnamed Tammany leader as deploring Grace's "deep" game to get the senatorship by means of Republican votes in the Legislature. This seems the first public mention of the subject. The Tammany leader was correct about Grace's strategy. Even with Cleveland's endorsement, the only way he could hope to win would be by a combination of Republicans and liberal Democrats.[38]

A week later the *Times* took delight in the Wigwam's discomfiture: "Does William R. Grace aspire to the United States Senate? He does. Keep your eyes on Grace and Cleveland, oh ye sons of Tammany." Others were not at all sure Mr. Cleveland, even as president-elect, could induce the Legislature to name Grace or any other anti-Tammany man. The *Commercial Advertiser*, which had not forgiven Grace for abandoning the third ticket, declared that Grace's chances were nil.[39]

After his clear-cut victory at the polls (which would have been won without the Tammany-Hill bargain), Mr. Cleveland showed marked attention to the anti-snap leaders, especially Grace. The president-elect attended a Reform Club victory dinner, and a smaller function given by Henry Villard. Mrs. Cleveland appeared at the coming-out reception for Lilias Grace. On the previous night the debutante's father had been closeted at the Cleveland residence with the president-elect, Whitney, Wilson S. Bissell, and former Postmaster General Don M. Dickinson discussing the makeup of the cabinet.[40]

In an effort to head off Murphy for the senatorship the *Times* proposed the name of the independent Republican Carl Schurz. Grace endorsed Schurz, and Tammany showed some signs of alarm. When not a word could be pried out of Cleveland, the Schurz boomlet expired. While this was going on, Grace privately admitted that he, too, was out of the running, writing, on November 16, to Edward Eyre: "I can't go to the U. S. Senate & I don't want to go into the Cabinet, so I will in all probability give some time to business in the future." Publicly, Grace implied that Cleveland was doing all he could to beat Murphy. When the president-elect's undercover effort failed to stem the Murphy tide, and when Murphy's victory was certain, Cleveland made public his opposition—merely as a matter of record.[41]

So it was that Senator Hill obtained a congenial and suitable colleague.

~ During the futile fight against Murphy, Grace and Cleveland seemed on the best of terms. At Cleveland's suggestion, Grace went to Washington to ask Senator John G. Carlisle of Kentucky to accept the secretaryship of the treasury, and brought back a favorable answer. In view of the fact that Grace personally would have preferred to see Fairchild again in the Treasury, the mission to Carlisle was certainly evidence of a disposition to oblige Mr. Cleveland. A roundabout offer of the post had been made to Fairchild. When Carlisle said yes, it was withdrawn. "Cleveland would be in a hole if I pressed him for anything," Grace wrote to Michael, on January 10, 1893. "I possess his confidence pretty fully, I think."[42]

Grace meant to press for anything for himself. Though he wisely refused to recommend aspirants to diplomatic posts in South America— "Mr. Cleveland was criticized last time because he appointed Roberts at my request"—the ex-mayor was in no way bashful about pushing the claims of anti-snapper friends for other jobs. Grace felt that all the patronage in New York City should go to the liberals, and he and Fairchild made up a slate. Their object was to give permanence and sinew to the reform cause by succoring a local machine in opposition to Tammany.

Very shortly, however, it developed that Mr. Cleveland was giving ear to a scheme to divide the jobs with Tammany. Grace held that in the chloroforming of the third ticket, Tammany had been treated liberally enough, and that the anti-snappers deserved all the federal patronage. He held to this view in the face of arguments by Don M. Dickinson, for whom he had a good deal of respect.

The thing flared into the open at the end of February when it was learned that Fairchild and Grace were not going to the inauguration. One published report said that sharp words had passed between the two reformers and the president-elect over patronage. Fairchild denied the sharp words and said he had never intended taking in the ceremonies. Mr. Grace declined to deny or confirm anything.[43]

Sixty days after Grover Cleveland took the oath the panic of 1893 broke. In June, on the eve of the opening of a special session of Congress called to repeal the Silver Purchase Act, doctors discovered a malignant growth in Cleveland's mouth and ordered an immediate operation. For fear that knowledge of the president's condition would intensify the panic, the surgeons worked in secret on board a yacht en route to Cape Cod.

These events gave the president little time for patronage. The plums were largely passed out by members of the cabinet. For the anti-snappers there was a shipping commissionership (Maurice Power), and the much-sought-after post of collector of the port of New York (James Kilbreath). Grace appears to have been influential in securing, over Hill's opposition, the commissionership of immigration for Joseph Senner, a naturalized Austrian who made an excellent official. The retention of Theodore Roosevelt as civil service commissioner was also a victory for the enemies of spoils. In the matter of the postmastership of New York City, Grace met defeat and took it hard. His aspirant was Henry de Forest Baldwin, a young attorney and an ardent Grace protégé who had been among the faithful eight to show up at Grace's house to start the ball rolling against the snappers. The job went to Tammany, and Mr. Baldwin had to content himself with a $3,000-a-year job—not so bad in those days—under Kilbreath.[44]

The division-of-the-spoils program so provoked Grace that by July his displeasure was common knowledge, though the newspaper headline "GRACE ON THE WARPATH!" went too far. More accurately, another journalist wrote: "The 'stubs' of Mr. Grace's check book would make a great Anti-Snapper exhibit. Has the word 'gratitude' been eliminated from the Cleveland political dictionary?" As far away as Aurora, Illinois, a newspaper expressed interest in the fact that "for some reason, which Mr. Grace professes not to understand, he is not at present *persona grata* to the administration."[45]

The last of August the country was treated to a journalistic controversy that did nothing to improve Mr. Grace's standing in the White House circle. The secret of the president's jaw operation had been well kept. Mr. Cleveland was supposed to be "resting" at his house on Buzzards Bay. During convalescence the thickness in his speech was passed off as a consequence of toothache. The president transacted government business, fished, and received a certain amount of company, with no one the wiser until the New York correspondent for the Philadelphia *Press* sent his paper a story of an operation for cancer.

The president's doctors denied there had been any operation at all. In the discussion that ensued, the St. Louis *Republic*, a paper bitterly hostile to Grace, headed, in bold type, an article from its New York man: "MR. GRACE DID IT." The body of the story was merely surmise based on Grace's disappointment over patronage and the fact that E. J. Edwards, the *Press*'s New York correspondent, was a friend of Grace who on other occasions had received tips from the former mayor. Grace vigorously denied that this had been true in the present instance. Even the consistently anti-Grace New York *Sun* called the *Republic*'s story "ridiculous and contemptible." Later Cleveland's surgeon ascribed the breach of confidence to the Philadelphia dentist who had participated in the operation to the extent of extracting two of the president's teeth.[46]

Nevertheless, while the operation-leak story was having its run in the papers, the New York *Recorder* inquired with some point:

"Has the Hon. William Grace retired from politics?—Or has Mr. Cleveland retired him?"[47]

~ After the disillusionments of 1888 and 1892, patronage was, indeed, the needle in the scale that turned W. R. Grace away from—though never against—Grover Cleveland. At least one idealist, President Benjamin Ide Wheeler of Cornell, thought this a poor reason for high-minded men to part company. Wheeler rebuked Henry de Forest Baldwin for complaining about patronage. He pointed to the Reform Club slogan: "We want no spoils." Young Baldwin came back with what was in the minds of most anti-snappers: "It was the hopes the people had of defeating Tammany . . . and not the magic of Mr. Cleveland's name which . . . [enabled us in] New York [City] to enroll more than 75,000 names."[48]

Another thing that contributed to Grace's dismay was the influence Whitney continued to exert at the White House. "Dan Lamont [secretary of war] and William C. Whitney have him [Cleveland] in their grip, and through them the Tammany tiger has its claws in his flesh," exclaimed one angry anti-snapper. Though he kept his views pretty much to himself, Grace felt about the same way.[49]

None of the anti-snap leaders took part in the off-year campaign of 1893. Yet Tammany lost in the city and Hill lost pretty generally in the state. This evidence of popular feeling gave Grace new heart. His great ambition was to break Hill. Twice, when he had had a good fighting chance, his hand had been stayed by Cleveland. Why not try it again, leaving Cleveland out of it? "I [had] made up my mind to do nothing in this State," he wrote Dickinson. "But you may rely on it that now, with or without Washington help, the Anti-Snap will be heard from."[50]

Grace and Fairchild began to gather the clan. Ottendorfer, Anderson, Coudert, and the rest were with them. The movement followed a familiar pattern. First, there was a manifesto: "It is clear that the Democratic Party in this State must be radically reorganized and purged . . . rescued from the dictation of those who have used the party organization for purely personal ends"; then a rousing meeting at Cooper Union. Neither in the manifesto nor at the meeting was Mr. Cleveland's name mentioned.[51]

The next thing on the political scene was open warfare between the president and Senator David B. Hill. By making use of other senators' grievances against the executive, Hill managed to block confirmation of Cleveland's nominee for the United States Supreme Court, Judge William B. Hornblower, of New York, an anti-Hill man. The president's next nominee, Grace's warm friend Wheeler H. Peckham, was even more offensive to Hill. He prevented Peckham's confirmation, also. Then Cleveland asked Grace's attorney, Frederic R. Coudert, to accept the nomination, but Coudert declined.

During the court fight, Grace appeared in Washington for the first time since Mr. Cleveland's second inauguration. A published report that the ex-mayor had been cordially received at the White House prompted the surmise that Cleveland's zeal to put an anti-snapper on the highest bench while Grace was reviving the State Democracy was more than a coincidence. But when it transpired that the president had not seen Mr. Grace and had taken no notice of his visit, the tails of the anti-snappers went down again.[52]

Mr. Grace returned to the work of rebuilding the State Democracy, an activity he was able to carry on without invoking the name of Grover Cleveland. What Grace really thought of Mr. Cleveland would have made interesting reading; but this was saved for a confidential letter: "I don't think our friend C is drinking; he may do that at times, but I do not think that is what has been the matter with him. I believe that he has the big head to such an extent that it would be hard to find a hatter in this country to make a hat large enough to fit his head, according to his own estimate of what it contained."[53]

Though Grace sat on the policy board, which had to do with the State Democracy's position on the tariff and other large issues, most of his work seems to have been given to the creation of disciplined, effective district units. Those are the outfits that get out the vote. Without them no political organization can amount to much. Grace was under no illusion that elections could consistently be won without the aid of a political machine. His contention was that it was possible to have a respectable machine. To one district worker, Grace dispatched a little lecture on tolerance: "The objection made by Cody and some others to Klein, on account of his being a Jew, is rather unfortunate, because most of our districts are already headed by Irishmen, and it seems to me that we are not the people to be in any sense or at any time illiberal to the Hebrews."[54]

In the spring of 1894, illness all but halted Grace's labors. On a physician's advice he planned a long European vacation with his family. Before sailing he refused a co-worker's request for a prognostication about the future. "Summer theories on politics are bad. The fall will bring things into focus."[55]

~ When Grace returned on September 28, and left the steamer in the bay by way of a tug, the situation in New York may have been in focus to the educated eye of a politician, but to anyone else it seemed a fine example of confusion.

Before Grace's departure, Hill had taken sufficient notice of the State Democracy revival to gather his lieutenants for a countermove. Then, forced by the Reverend Charles H. Parkhurst's sensational exposures, had come the Legislature's Lexow committee investigation into one phase of the city's affairs. The Lexow committee corroborated the crusading clergyman with shocking details of police protection of prostitution, gambling, and associated criminality. Heads began to roll. Croker retired as the leader of Tammany Hall. Senator Ed Murphy resigned as Democratic state chairman. Tammany's creature in the City Hall, Mayor Thomas F. Gilroy, feeling in need of a change of air, sailed for Europe. Hill stayed home and tried to make his state machine look decent.

William C. Whitney also was abroad that summer, and the newspapers speculated on a possible rendezvous with Grace. So far as is known they did not meet, but Grace and Gilroy did—in a Paris barbershop—and the newspaper correspondents and cartoonists had some fun over it.[56]

Again, Hill proved himself the tactical master of the field. The state convention assembled at Saratoga on September 25 with Hill in control, though tamed down. Passing over Lieutenant Governor William F. (Blue-Eyed Billy) Sheehan, Hill had searched long and anxiously for a respectable-looking candidate for governor. All he got were refusals. William C. Whitney arrived from abroad after the sessions had begun. As a last hope, Hill tried to land Whitney, but the traction magnate was too wary. There was nothing for Senator Hill to do but nominate himself. This was accomplished on September 26, while Grace was at sea.

From the New York pier, Grace drove straight to the Reform Club. He found the independents weakened and despondent. Having missed great opportunities, they had done little except to sit and await Grace's return.

Grace's first step was to refuse to be a candidate for mayor. This might have been expected. If Grace chose to fight Tammany for the mayoralty he, himself, would not have to run again. He did choose to fight it. The State Democracy, at Grace's bidding, backed a city ticket headed by a Republican, a sixty-eight-year-old dry-goods merchant named William L. Strong.

Grace's next move was wholly unexpected. He endorsed David B. Hill for governor. Twice Grover Cleveland had taken the hand of Hill in a political campaign. Twice in so doing Mr. Cleveland had impaired his reputation to no useful purpose and set back the cause of good government in New York as well. Could Grace do any better?

The apostle of reform had a hard time composing this announcement of the about-face on Hill. The result was painful, even to read: "This is the first time I have ever appeared upon a platform in advocacy of the election of Governor Hill. I have differed with him on lines within the party, but never out of it. Every Democrat should stand by the ticket headed by Hill."[57]

To a friend in California, Grace could be a little more candid: "I do this not for him [Hill], but because I believe the Constitutional amendments . . . passed by the Republican Legislature, would deliver this State for many years to come into the hands of the Republican ring, which is certainly but little better than the Democratic one."[58]

In that letter, Grace nearly gave himself away. If the Republican machine was a "little better," why not accept the lesser evil?

In the nature of things, Grace could tell scarcely anyone that his plan was to sell Hill a dead horse.

The Hill endorsement left Tammany in the cold. And Grace paid so much attention to Strong's candidacy that he had no time for Hill. Fortunately, there was an excuse. Strong had opposed Grace so violently on the religious issue in 1880 that now Grace had some trouble persuading certain fellow Catholics to support Strong.[59]

In the last days of the campaign, Wheeler H. Peckham, whom Hill had kept off the supreme bench, was quoted as having made the disconcerting statement that the Grace forces were going to knife Hill at the polls. Grace denied this, and Peckham denied that he had said it.[60]

It turned out, however, that the quotation attributed to Peckham was a true prophecy. Strong carried New York City by 40,000. Hill carried it by 2,795—and so lost the state.

Thus, W. R. Grace achieved one of his shining goals—the removal of David B. Hill from public life. It was an achievement deserving of the gratitude of the citizenry of New York, whatever one may think of the way it was done.

~ Grace now had an ointment for the wounds he had received at the hands of Mr. Cleveland and his political managers. He found Mayor Strong not only willing, but in some cases anxious, to listen to advice. In a month and a half Strong appointed nineteen officials, twelve of them Democrats. Of the latter the most notable was Francis M. Scott, who became corporation counsel. Another appointment—which Grace himself had once wanted to make—was that of Theodore Roosevelt as police commissioner.[61]

Exposure, internal strife, and defeat had Tammany Hall so out of it and discouraged that, momentarily, the Wigwam saw the path of virtue as the surest way to a return from Elba. Rumors began to seep about town that W. R. Grace would be asked to take over the leadership. A more abject surrender could hardly be imagined. At length, on a day in March 1895, he consented to see a delegation from the Hall. Mr. Grace had the satisfaction of telling his callers that he had no desire, then or at any time, to become head of Tammany.[62]

Shortly afterward, Grace fell quite ill of his old kidney complaint. This decided him on a step that he seems to have had in mind ever since the victory over Hill. On April 17, he submitted his resignation as chairman of the State Democracy.

"I do so," he wrote, "with the greatest possible regret. . . . The State Democracy was organized for the purpose of representing and advancing that public sentiment which had grown restless because of the dangerous tendencies of an organization which was masquerading under the name of Democracy. It is now five years since first these influences were brought or attempted to be brought into combination for the purpose of overthrowing Tammany Hall. That earlier effort was only in part successful, . . . but it sowed the seeds which brought forth the splendid harvest of election day in November last."[63]

The chairmanship was taken by Fairchild.

Grace recuperated in the country, watching the springtime turn Gracefield green. In May he passed his sixty-third birthday there. When the hay-fever season came, Mrs. Grace and he made their customary visits to the White Mountains and to Maine. In September they were back at the farm, and in October at the town house. A campaign was coming up, with a Fusion ticket in the making, headed by Strong. At Hanover Square, Grace found the big Rockefeller desk piled with political correspondence, nearly all of which he pushed aside. But he penned a note to Theodore Roosevelt:

"I congratulate you on the position you have taken with regard to the fusion ticket. . . . I think Fusion will win but I am not an expert this year. . . . With sincere wishes for your success in everything that you undertake personally."[64]

He also wrote to the president:

"F. R. Coudert talked with me some months ago about his proposed nomination for Supreme Court judge. I now *know* that if he was named for that position now, he would accept most gladly. . . . If you desire to give this graceful recognition of the most active & ablest wing of those who fought your battle for the nomination in 1892, I think . . . the public of this City & State would hear with pleasure the nomination of a man so fit in every way."[65]

Cleveland did not name Coudert to the court but, the following year, appointed him to the Venezuelan boundary commission. The letter on

Coudert seems to have been the last communication of any moment that Grace sent to Cleveland. So ended a long and troubled relationship.

Nine years later, when William R. Grace died, Theodore Roosevelt, then president, sent flowers and a letter. Nothing came from Mr. Cleveland.[66]

18 ~ New Blood
in the Business

~ *N*ext to the politicians interested in the reconstruction of corrupt party machines, the person who most welcomed Mr. Grace's retirement from public life in 1895 was his wife. Though, as an official hostess, Mrs. Grace had discharged her responsibilities in a manner that had brought published compliments flattering enough to have turned the heads of some women, she had never cared for the role. Yet Lillius Grace was anything but a recluse. She liked to have people at Gracefield and at the town house; and she liked to visit. Her criticism of official functions was that there was too much ostentation about them, and too little friendliness.

The manner of Mrs. Grace's introduction to official social etiquette became a family joke. After Mr. Grace's first election as mayor in 1880, a carriage stopped in front of the Grace residence on Seventeenth Street. On the box was not only a coachman but also a footman. The Graces had always had a coachman, though never a footman. Moreover, they knew no one who had a footman. The presence of a footman on a box was usually a mark of Mrs. Astor's Four Hundred, or of aspirants to membership in that circle. The Graces were neither.

The footman mounted the Grace steps, rang the bell, and departed. It was discovered that he had left the card of Mrs. Cooper, whose husband Mr. Grace would succeed as mayor on the first of January.

Being new to the business, Mrs. Grace determined to return the "call" in the exact manner in which it had been made. She borrowed Michael Grace's coachman, turned him into a footman, and so left her card at the Cooper house. That was the only time, however, that Mrs. Grace felt the need to pretend that she had a footman.[1]

Lillius Grace was grateful for her husband's retirement from politics for other reasons. For some time she had been anxious about his health, and rightly so, because the threefold responsibility of public figure, head of a great international business, and father of a large family was too much for W. R. Grace. Though Mr. Grace had neglected business for politics, and vice versa, he had never neglected his duties as a parent. Grace was more than a father to his children. He was their companion and friend; but no flatterer. In 1895 four children were at home: Joe, 23, who had been graduated from Columbia and was studying law at New York University while breaking in as a minor clerk at Hanover Square; Lilias, 21; Louise (called Lulu), 19; Russ (William Russell junior), 17 and in school.

In a letter to an Irish niece, Grace gave a candid picture of this brood:

"Lill is much taller than her Mother, is a fair french scholar and has great taste for painting and a very manageable girl and not much of a kicker. Joe is short, not very manly looking, but is considerable of an athlete, moderate in his views, a good steady worker, likes his study and keeps at it; he is a moderate-tempered fellow, good natured, but with an opinion of his own and firm. Lu is younger and less settled; she is tall, strong, well-built and rough, very nervous, much inclined to catch cold, very affectionate but sensitive and hates to be demonstrative; very proud but I think entirely conscientious and truthful. Russ is a long boy for his age, quick-witted, very good tempered, very affectionate, mischievous, very cautious, a poor student and a poor scholar, finds it very disagreeable work to have to study. All go regularly to their monthly Communion, Russ being the only one who needs a reminder. Lulu has a fine high voice. Russ has a good voice too, but he is not cultivating it."[2]

Frequently the eldest of the Grace children, Alice Holloway, born at sea off the Chincha Islands, was at home with the first, and as yet the only, Grace grandchild, "Billee" (William Grace Holloway), aged nine. Alice's husband had died in 1892 as a result of a riding accident. Mr. and Mrs. Grace received the news while attending the Democratic national convention in Chicago. Alice's inheritance of her husband's interest in the San Francisco house, plus a gift from her father, made the young widow independent financially. In the early years of her widowhood, Alice traveled a good deal, often abroad. During these absences, Billee sometimes stayed with his Grace grandparents.

Grace had seen to his daughter's financial security only after the death of her husband. When a woman had a husband, it was Grace's belief that she should look solely to him. After the birth of her boy, Alice had a term of poor health. The expense was too much for Holloway's earnings, so Grace made his son-in-law (not his daughter) an allowance. "It has occurred to me," he wrote, "that a woman is always better subject to her husband in all things and dependent on him alone for all financial help. . . . I am a little old fashioned in my ideas, and I want my daughter to feel towards her husband as I like to have my wife feel toward me, dependent on me and me alone."[3]

Though Mr. Grace gave away a good deal of money, most of it to charities under the control of his church, he did not have a high opinion of the efficacy of gifts of money. He preferred to give opportunities, particularly to young people. What was made of the opportunities would be up to the recipients.

When the celebrated Parker House in Boston changed hands, the headwaiter did not care to remain under the new management. Mr. Grace went to considerable trouble to reestablish the man in New York. A servant girl who wished to marry was disturbed about the long hours her fiancé was obliged to work. As a feeder in the stables of the American Express Co., he had to be on the job before dawn and was not through until late at night. After investigating the case, Grace asked an officer of the company to give the young man "reasonable hours of labor." The following from a letter to an executive of the Lincoln Bank was typical: "I will be happy to try to do something for your brother, but remember one thing, if he takes a position in any enterprise in which I am engaged he will be expected to be active. . . . Otherwise he won't last very long. . . . The wages you may be sure will not be very high."[4]

The esteem in which Grace held his father-in-law never diminished. Yet when Captain Gilchrest failed in business owing to the rascality of a partner, Grace does not appear to have advanced a dollar to help the old man. The only thing I can make of this is that the captain, still as independent as when he walked the deck of his own ship, refused assistance. From the wreck, Gilchrest saved a few acres of land adjoining Gracefield. There, with his own hands, he built a little house in which he spent his last days. Time had mellowed the old mariner. He was a great favorite of the Grace boys, Joe and Russ. In the dead of winter Joe would leave the town house when school was out on Friday to spend the weekend with his grandparents in the little house at Great Neck. After the captain's death, Mary Jane Gilchrest stayed on there until she died in 1886.[5]

In the city, Grace had moved far uptown—to Seventy-ninth Street and Madison Avenue, where in 1893 he had purchased a mansion. In front burned, all night, the two ornate gas lamps that marked the residences of mayors of New York, past and present. The custom of providing this illumination went back to Dutch times when the mayor was also the captain of the guards and commander of all other troops stationed in the city. In those days it might be necessary to find the mayor in the middle of the night and find him quickly. Though the most pretentious house that Grace ever owned, the Seventy-ninth Street place was the least used of his abodes. Particularly after he quit politics, the family spent more and more time at the Great Neck farm.

All the Grace youngsters had their gangs of friends whom they were encouraged to bring to the house; and Gracefield was a young people's paradise. There were swimming and sailing, tennis courts, a golf course ("links" they called them in those days), a polo field, and a stable of polo and all kinds of other horses. When a friend asked Mr. Grace if he didn't think he was extravagant in indulging the whims of his children, the squire of Gracefield replied: "Not a bit. It keeps 'em home." This from a man who regularly had his hotel bills gone over by a secretary with instructions to question doubtful items; who could write his Fifth Avenue tailor: "Be sure and make your bill moderate, for if you do not you won't hear from me again"; who could reprimand the superintendent of Gracefield for an unauthorized expenditure of $12.50, then give him a bonus and use his influence to get the man's son into West Point.[6]

Mr. Grace had a horror of the gambling habit. This did not apply to an occasional sporting wager, such as Grace himself might make. But he believed that a bettor should bear the consequences of his losses and not pass them on to others. One time Joe, as a lad, tramping the estate with his father, offered to bet a dollar he could throw a stone and hit an indicated tree. Joe threw and missed until he owed his father several weeks' allowance. Mr. Grace never refused permission for his children to bet at horse races or in the casino at Monte Carlo or other European resorts. He would make advances on their allowances. But when the money was gone, the children would be in for a lean spell.

Mr. Grace enjoyed the game of poker, which he had learned from Americans as a young man in Peru. He taught it to his children, girls and boys alike. In the family they played for pennies and each loser paid up from his own funds. When Joe was in college, there was a poker game nearly every Saturday night at the Grace home, attended mostly by young bloods from Columbia. At these sessions, quantities of beer were consumed. Before retiring, Mr. Grace usually strolled in to meet the boys and see how the luck was running.[7]

The golf links and the polo field at Gracefield were among the first privately owned places of their kind in the United States, both games being new here in the nineties. The Grace polo string was a good one. Joe and Russ became fine players. Among other frequenters of the field were Pat Collier, of the *Collier's Weekly* family; Bob Bacon, later ambassador to France; Jim Appleton, a five-goal man; Morgan Grace, junior, formerly of New Zealand; and Stewart Iglehart, Joe's classmate and crony at Columbia.

A spectacular rider in his young days, Mr. Grace had given up the saddle during his last years in public life. Shortly after his retirement he mounted Lilias's horse. The animal was spirited and Mr. Grace had put on weight. He imagined he cut so poor a figure that on dismounting he said: "This is not for me any more." He never got on a horse again. This seems singular, for one does not forget how to ride any more than one forgets how to swim. With a little patience, Mr. Grace could have attained an excellent form for a man his age. The incident suggests the survival of the vanity that characterized Grace as a boy when he had no use for anything he couldn't do well.[8]

It is difficult to separate the Grace clan from the Grace business. Both continued to grow. The stream of letters between the heads of the scattered houses began "Dear Uncle," "Dear Mich'l," "Dear Jack," "Dear Will." As always, they often contained family as well as business news. In the early nineties, all Grace houses, excepting San Francisco, were in charge of members of the family; and in San Francisco, Frank Grace, a son of John, was on the staff. In New York was "the chief," assisted by Edward Eyre and John Grace. Michael had removed with his family to London, where he directed M. P. Grace & Co., which had been formed during the last stages of the Peruvian debt negotiation. Lima remained the most important house in South America. Will Eyre was shifted from Valparaiso to take charge. With the adjustment of the differences between the United States and Chile in 1892, Grace's Chile business picked up. Jack Eyre was sent there from Lima to replace his brother Will. In 1894 the long-debated Grace claims against Chile arising from the Chile-Peruvian war were settled by an international commission. By a divided vote the commission ruled against Grace on the ground of Grace's activity in support of Peru during the conflict.

Every head of a large business has the problem of finding competent subordinates. For Mr. Grace the problem was complicated by a desire to find them within the family. "I wish my boys were grown up and could be of some use," he wrote in 1892, "but probably they are better as they are." One thing Mr. Grace made plain to his sons: they could select their own careers. Much as he wanted them in the family business, he insisted that their choice in that regard should be wholly their own. When Joe decided to top off his B. A. with a law degree, he would have been perfectly free to follow that profession. As it fell out, Joe decided to stick with W. R. Grace & Co., where his legal training was by no means lost.[9]

~ Michael Grace's long work of relieving Peru of the burden of its foreign debt proved the key to the economic restoration of that country in the nineties. When the Peruvian Corporation, Ltd., took over the debt in exchange for railroad and other concessions, it will be recalled that Grace interests held the operating lease on the Oroya railroad. Grace further benefited by obtaining the principal contracts for the rehabilitation and extension of that road.

Though most of the engineering problems had been solved under the stimulus of the driving enthusiasm of Meiggs, there was much to be done. The supervision of this undertaking was Ned Eyre's last work in Peru, and that which won his promotion to second-in-command of the New York house. William H. Cilley being dead, the principal engineers were H. D. B. Norris, who had served Grace in Costa Rica, and J. L. Thorndike of the old Meiggs organization. The first task was to replace the Verrugus bridge which had collapsed in 1889—one of the few engineering failures on a work of Henry Meiggs. This cantilever span was 575 feet long, and 300 feet above the gorge of the Rímac.

Chilca, where Meiggs had abandoned the road, was eighty-seven miles from Callao and 12,215 feet above it. Under Grace's direction the line was extended fifty miles, to Oroya. The continental divide was crossed at 15,660 feet by way of a tunnel 3,855 feet long. Thus was completed perhaps the most daring, imaginative, and costly piece of railroad engineering ever undertaken. The wonder to me is that more tourists in Peru do not make the trip over the line simply to view the magnificence of the scenery.

The headquarters of the Peruvian Corporation were in London. Its chairman was Sir Alfred Dent, a financier who had never been to Peru. The Peruvian representative of the company was Lord Donoughmore, whose son and heir presently married a daughter of Michael Grace. Though extremely fond of him, Michael had no great confidence in the ability of Donoughmore. Before building operations on the Oroya line were finished, Michael came to the conclusion that the Peruvian Corporation would never realize all that might reasonably be expected of it under more competent management. Accordingly, he decided to take the Graces out of the railroad business in Peru. This was accomplished in 1893 by selling the Oroya lease to the corporation for £382,911, payable in 6 percent bonds of the corporation. Time was to prove this a wise move. Though by no means a failure, the Peruvian Corporation did not achieve the success that many had hoped for.[10]

When the panic of 1893 struck, few large American business houses came through that calamity and the three trying years that followed more handsomely than the Grace interests. This was a result of foresight, sharpened by the experience of the brief "Baring panic" of 1890. For many years the great London banking house of Baring Brothers had acted as bankers for Grace in the international field, and had financed numerous Grace undertakings. In November 1890 it became apparent to some that, due to overextension in Argentine railways, the Barings were in a critical situation. Michael Grace accumulated £100,000 in cash in London and advised his brother by cable to make similar provisions in New York. William quickly raised $400,000, partly by borrowing on his personal credit. Three days later Baring Brothers suspended.

"The failure of Barings," Grace wrote, "has brought ruin to thousands; where it will end, God knows." W. S. Bissell, Cleveland's former law partner, was with Grace and several others when the news came over the ticker that the Bank of England had assumed the Baring obligations. Some of the men who were scanning the tape thought this would be the end of the trouble. Grace took Bissell's arm and said in a low voice: "The panic is stopped, no doubt; but the consequences of this failure will be a shriveling of credit all over the world which will be felt for several years."

In immediate need of another international banking connection, Grace turned to J. P. Morgan, with whom he had only a slight acquaintance. "Morgan showed a very friendly disposition," he wrote Michael, "but he is shrewd and a grabber." Grace thought the banker's terms pretty stiff. "Yet it may be that this is the best we can do for the present."

In any event, Morgan succeeded Baring as the Grace bankers.[11]

~ 𝒥n 1892, W. R. Grace made a momentous decision concerning the Grace shipping interests. Urged by Michael and by Edward Eyre he consented to go into steam—not as the charterer of an occasional vessel but as the owner and operator of a regular line that one day would replace the sailing ships of the Merchants Line, which had proved so successful that the regular run of its vessels out of New York had been extended from the west coast of South America to San Francisco.

The decision was made reluctantly. Grace had shipped before the mast as a boy. He had an affection for sailing ships, and no one in the world had a better knowledge of the problems of their management. In the face of the virtual collapse of the American merchant marine (in 1892 our tonnage in foreign trade was less than it had been in 1810) and of the eclipse of sail generally, he continued to increase his prosperous fleet of windjammers on the tough Cape Horn route. "I hate to embark on so thoroughly new a business," he wrote Eyre, "but it seems almost a necessity and I have concurred and hope and think they can be made to pay and add to our com'l strength."[12]

Grace feared that unless he took up steam some foreign line of steamers would go into competition with his Merchants Line. The ability of steam to drive out sail had been abundantly shown. More than that, foreign steam could drive out American steam because foreigners built and operated their vessels more economically. Grace noted that the American-owned Brazil Mail Steamship Co. (in which C. R. Flint had an interest) was "going to pieces" in the face of competition from British-owned Lamport & Holt.[13]

The British built better steamers than we built. Inasmuch as our laws prohibited Americans from purchasing vessels abroad and operating them under the American flag, Grace decided, against his personal inclinations, to begin his steam operations under the Union Jack. In explaining this to the bureau of navigation of the Treasury Department, he recommended a change in our laws. So it was that, late in 1892, the New York & Pacific Steamship Co., Ltd., was incorporated in London. The Grace brothers and the Eyre nephews were by this time all American citizens; thus, the unusual spectacle of an American shipping business under the British flag. The Merchants Line of sailing ships continued to fly the Stars and Stripes. Grace was proud of that and looked forward to the time when his steamers would do the same.[14]

In 1893 an English-built steamer was purchased and three others were ordered. The vessels were about three thousand tons each. They were given Incan names: *Coya, Condor, Capac,* and *Cacique.* When all were in service, there were regular sailings from New York, forty-five days apart. After coaling in the West Indies or at Montevideo, the first cargo stop was at Coronel, in southern Chile, eighty-five hundred miles from New York. The vessels proceeded up the coast as far as Guayaquil, Ecuador. Knowing he had much to learn, Grace followed in great detail the construction and operation of the steamers. He urged his younger associates to do the same, writing: "El ojo del amo engorda el Caballo (The eye of the master fattens the horse)."[15]

The New York & Pacific Steamship Co. was the first arm of the Grace business to be incorporated. For years, Mr. Grace had spoken with pride of the fact that the Grace business was no corporation but a series of partnerships. Perhaps there was only one larger unincorporated business in the United States—E. I. du Pont de Nemours & Co. of Delaware. This also was a family firm, which did not become a corporate entity until 1899.

In 1894, however, W. R. Grace & Co. was incorporated in West Virginia, and modestly capitalized at $3 million. The precise reasons for this step do not appear. Presumably they had to do with the fact that the general tendency of the time was toward incorporation of partnership businesses. The action may well have been part of a plan to consolidate the several Grace partnerships and to provide for continuity of ownership and management of the whole in a way that would have been impossible, or very difficult, under the partnership form. One moving reason for the existence of corporations—limitation of personal liability—seems to have been scarcely a factor. Upon incorporation the individual partners in the several houses did not withdraw the personal accounts due them from those houses. More unusual still, they left in the corporation certain surplus funds for the various houses "to guarantee unliquidated accounts, said funds to be undivided as long as the Directors of the Company may require and thereafter to be payable in whole or part to each of the partners in the said firms." Some months after the incorporation the surplus funds were liquidated by the issuance of additional common stock.

"It's just a family affair," said Mr. Grace, explaining the incorporation to newspapermen. "We're all just the same, only turned around a bit." A family affair, indeed! There were thirteen stockholders, no more—all members of the Grace clan. W. R. Grace was president; M. P. Grace, first vice president; John W. Grace, second vice president; and Edward Eyre, secretary. They and Lillius G. Grace comprised the board of directors. The only officer not a member of the family was J. Louis Schaefer, the treasurer.

Though they were allotted no stock, generous treatment was accorded men outside the Grace family who had risen in the company's service, some of them to junior partnerships in the various houses. Twelve such men, all young and only two of them members of the Grace family, were given shares in the profits in addition to their salaries. The combined participations amounted to 41.25 percent of the common stock dividends.[16]

~ $\mathcal{S}$ome years back, Mr. Grace had realized that his business was outgrowing the capacities of the Grace clan to handle in all its far-spread details. He brought young men into his organization with the idea of advancing them as far and as fast as their talents would justify. Thus, he began to build an organization calculated to survive him, and to survive the whole Grace family, for that matter, should the second generation produce no one capable of directing the operations of W. R. Grace & Co.

Mr. Grace, who liked people and particularly young people, made a pleasure of this farsighted work. His door was open at any time to anyone in his employ. He would listen as patiently to a subordinate's personal problem as he would to a matter affecting the firm. Yet he expected his youngsters to work, and to work hard. All started in lowly positions. At least two of the Eyre boys had made their first passages to South America as seamen.

All the nonfamily men who participated in the profits of the corporation in 1894 had started with Grace when they were young, and most of them when they were boys. When he became treasurer of the corporation, Louis Schaefer had been with Grace for thirteen of his twenty-eight years. An example of the advice Mr. Grace gave these juniors appears in a letter to John Fowler (ex-office boy) who in 1893 went to Chile as a junior partner in the Valparaiso house (and in 1894 became a sharer of the profits of the corporation): "Be prudent, modest and careful, and you are sure of success. But if you should become inflated with a notion of your own abilities you can be pretty certain that disaster will follow any such idea. The men who are really successful are those who do not over estimate their own abilities. . . . I think if you confer with that good, sensible wife of yours from time to time . . . you will probably find that in her you have a pretty safe adviser."[17]

Among his young men, Mr. Grace encouraged frankness and got it to an unusual degree. This was a good thing for the characters of the young people, and for W. R. Grace & Co. An instance:

The supply of young Eyres was apparently inexhaustible. In 1899 one was working under his brother Will in Lima. Wishing a line on the young man from an outside source, Mr. Grace asked Lawrence Shearman, who had grown up in the New York office and was in Lima on a special mission, five very direct questions. Shearman replied:

"1st. 'Is he a man of good judgment?' I don't think he is possessed of either remarkably good or bad judgment. At times he has a tendency to let his prejudices get away with his judgment but this is usually in little things and I don't think he does so to such an extent as to amount to a serious matter.

"2nd. 'Is he growing and likely to grow?' Yes.

"3rd. 'Is he devoted to his business and unswerving in pursuit of its success?' Unquestionably—His best point is the interest he takes in the business and his readiness to serve it day and night when occasion requires and to the best of his ability.

"4th. 'Is he adapted to his present work and duties?' Fairly—He has a good deal to do and all things considered does his work well.

"5th. 'Is he a man of shrewdness?' No. In my opinion he is a man of ordinary ability who has the interests of the house at heart, is willing to work hard and will with time get on. I don't think he will ever be possessed of anything like the ability of Don Eduardo [Edward Eyre] or the hard common sense shrewdness and energy of Jack [Eyre]. His worst point, that is, the one most dangerous to himself, is a tendency to a 'big head.' "[18]

Shearman made such a good impression on that trip that he was directed to stay in Lima, where eventually he succeeded Will Eyre as head of the Peru house. (For years after the incorporation the old custom persisted of calling the main branches "houses.")

With the business expanding and the directing heads getting old, it was more than a satisfaction to the founder to note the enthusiasm and energy with which his son Joseph P. had buckled down to work. Joe showed more than zeal. He showed ability and imagination. In 1896, when Joe had been on the job full time for a year, the head of the San Francisco house died. With a new man to be installed, Mr. Grace decided to give that branch an overhauling. Joe was sent out to assist, and to transmit the home-office point of view. It was his first large independent assignment. Joe did the job so competently that in 1897 he was promoted to be secretary and a director of the company.

John Grace's health was failing. He disliked New York and asked Michael for a transfer to London. Michael demurred, thinking it would throw too great a burden on William. By 1898, however, Joseph P. Grace had come along so well that Michael believed John could be spared. He suggested that John go "to London to work with me . . . three days a week and play the balance. . . . [Edward] Eyre and JPG [can] practically run the N Y House under the Chief."[19]

The change was made. J. P. Grace was twenty-six when he undertook his new responsibilities. In 1899 the company was reincorporated in

Connecticut. The new charter contained broader powers. The capitalization was, more realistically, $6 million. The shares were owned by nineteen stockholders, all Graces or Eyres.[20]

By this time, twenty managers and submanagers of outlying branches were participating in the profits of the corporation, exactly as if they were the holders of common stock. This participation aggregated 34.75 percent of the common stock dividends. Of the twenty young men enjoying this liberal treatment, fourteen were not members of the Grace family. Of those fourteen, seven were, during the coming generation, to distinguish themselves in the service of the company. D. Stewart Iglehart was to become president; Louis Schaefer, Maurice Bouvier, Lawrence Shearman, John Fowler, Alberto Falcon, Frederick Wrightman, and John H. Rosseter, vice presidents. Three other juniors who had not, in 1899, reached the profit-participation stage were also, eventually, to become vice presidents. They were Luis Valverde, Gale H. Carter, and E. T. Ford.

One can imagine the pride the founder took in the fact that his son, Joseph P. Grace, had shown himself qualified for the leadership of the corps of hustling, able young men in the company's service. In 1899, Joe was made second vice president.

Thus, W. R. Grace achieved his goal of an organization to carry on after him. While bringing in talent from the outside and treating it liberally, it was obvious that Mr. Grace wished control of the firm to remain in the family. Each share of preferred stock had three votes to one for a common share. By a provision in his will, Mr. Grace formed a trust of preferred shares carrying control, this trust to endure for the lives of his two youngest grandchildren, the maximum permitted by the law. The trust is governed by five self-perpetuating trustees. A majority of these trustees have at all times been members of the Grace family.

An example of how the young men worked together may be had from a look at the business relationship between Joseph P. Grace and his Columbia chum and polo-playing friend, Stewart Iglehart. Iglehart was a son of a Methodist clergyman. Starting as a junior clerk, Iglehart had risen rapidly. In 1900, he was ranging the west coast of South America examining the varied Grace activities with a sharp eye and a keen mind. Long letters passed between "Dear Joe" and "Dear Igle"—letters in which Igle commented every bit as freely on personnel as Shearman had done. Though some of Iglehart's recommendations were fairly sweeping, he did not lose sight of the minutiae of the trade which had formed the solid foundation of Grace's success in South America and had gone a long way toward preserving the business there after the Meiggs collapse.

"I spent," wrote Iglehart, "three days last week in Santiago visiting our clients there and was surprised to see the amount of American goods in the market in this specific line; and also the German goods which I think can be replaced from the New York market.

"I mention the following as a few lines which although some of them are not new to us, we have hitherto made only spasmodic efforts to push:

Sewing machine oil	Wall paper
Shoe-pegs	Cutlery, especially
Grindstones	the cheaper grades
Glassware, especially	Lamps
the better quality	Tools
Shoenails	Files
Tacks	Plated ware
Stoves	Machinery
Scales	Novelties."[21]

Though J. P. Grace had been in South America enough to know what Iglehart was talking about, he was definitely destined for the home office in New York. Just as definitely, Iglehart was destined for South America, where he remained for fifteen years. From the start they made a great team.

~ The matter of finding investments for his large fortune naturally brought W. R. Grace in touch with businesses other than his own. He preferred the role of investor to that of manager, though in a few instances he became involved in the problems of management. One was the case of the New York Bank Note Co., which Grace and the penny-pinching millionaire Russell Sage came to control. However, Grace's principal venture in management outside the family business was the Ingersoll-Sergeant Drill Co.

This company manufactured rock drills and other mining machinery. Grace had done business with it from the time he was buying for the Costa Rica railroad. In 1890 the company was in the hands of a young man named Robert W. Chapin, who had inherited the business. Though carelessly operated, the company made money. The Baring crash caught Chapin on the wrong side of the stock market, with most of his equity in the Ingersoll-Sergeant Co. pledged for loans he could not meet. The loans amounted to $120,000. Grace offered to take over the pledged stock for

$182,000. He agreed to retain Chapin as an officer of the company. Though this represented a bargain for Grace, apparently it was the best offer Chapin received. At any rate, he took it.[22]

Mr. Grace reorganized the business in all its departments—manufacturing, engineering, and sales. He moved the plant from an old horsecar barn on Ninth Avenue to Easton, Pennsylvania. Through the Grace connections with international trade, within a few years Ingersoll-Sergeant products were being sold all over the world. When things were going on the new basis, Mr. Grace virtually turned the conduct of the company over to George Doubleday, who had assisted in the reorganization. Yearly profits amounted to more than Grace had paid for his interest. The business was so sound and so profitable that he recommended its shares to old friends such as Judge Pratt and Don M. Dickinson. Other blocks of stock were set aside for his children. In addition to his duties with W. R. Grace & Co., Joe Grace helped his father with Ingersoll-Sergeant. When the younger son, the "poor scholar" Russell, had all the schooling he would take, he went to work on the foundry floor of the plant and, in time, rose to the first vice presidency of the company.

The Easton plant was the scene of the only strike with which W. R. Grace had to deal in an enterprise of his. Though a small, a very small, affair as strikes went, it affected Mr. Grace as profoundly as anything affected him in the last years of his life.

Grace bore the name of a good employer. Certainly his interest in the general welfare of his workers went beyond that of the average employer of his time. During his public life, Grace had received a large share of the labor vote. He addressed labor unions—which the average public man did not do. He had come to admire Henry George, and when George died (before the Ingersoll-Sergeant strike was settled), Grace paid a tribute to the late leader: "He was honest, fearless, and sincere." Yet when a molders' union called a strike in the Easton plant, and certain workers walked out in sympathy, Grace thought the men had been badly advised. He set out to teach them a lesson. The issue, as he saw it, was whether unions or management should run the plant. As the strike went on, Mr. Grace's temper cooled considerably, but he stuck to his main point.[23]

Grace thought the strike an "injustice"—the word was his—both to him and to the men. It came about over the introduction of piecework as an incentive to the molders to produce more, and incidentally to earn more, than the then-prevailing union scale of $2.65 a day. Grace believed that by the piecework method, molders would earn from $3.00 to $3.50 a day. He said the strike was called "precipitately," before the new system had been given a fair trial. Altogether about eighty-five of the plant's two hundred-odd workmen quit.[24]

The common way of ending a strike in those days was to hire strikebreakers. Strikebreakers were of two kinds: professionals who went from place to place specifically to break strikes; and ordinary nonunion workmen who were willing to take strikers' places. Professional strikebreakers were paid above the going wage, often double it. When a strike was broken, they would be let out and the old men would be taken back for what the employer was ready to pay.

Grace hired no professionals, but he did bring unemployed molders and machinists from New York and New England. Permanent jobs were promised to those who made good. Many were released after a few days. This disturbed Grace. He cautioned his superintendent to give the men "a fair trial of at least a week's duration." Grace was also disturbed about the plight of the strikers and their families. He urged that efforts be made to induce as many as possible to come back, married men especially. They did not have to give up their union affiliation. But Grace would deal only with the men individually, and not with the union officials. And the men would have to come back on the old terms. Thus, union membership, while tolerated, was of no particular benefit to a workman in the case at hand. Mr. Grace, however, sent a man to New England to study the piecework question further.[25]

Near the end of March, when the strike had been under way for two months, Mr. Grace was returning by train from Easton to New York when a strike leader named Dougherty asked for a subscription to an entertainment for the benefit of the strikers' families. Dougherty must have been surprised when Mr. Grace wrote a check for $5,000. That was nearly equal to a month's pay for all eighty-five strikers. "Dougherty," said Grace, "you get work for every man who is idle, and make up your mind to one thing—under no circumstances will it be possible for the men who struck ever to go back to the Ingersoll works except as individuals, applying personally to the superintendent." Dougherty said the men would not do it, and that they would win their strike because the plant could not get along without them. Grace said they would never win, and that the strike was "the most ridiculous baby play I had ever seen a sensible man take part in." Mr. Grace told his plant superintendent that this conversation was entirely friendly. "Dougherty . . . talked well, sustaining his side of the argument like a gentleman."[26]

Mr. Grace sent an unsolicited donation to the building fund of the Catholic church in Easton. That gave him an excuse to ask the priest "to call on me for a subscription at any time necessary for the poor of Easton under your charge or the poor strikers who are so foolishly wasting their energies." Rarely, if ever, had strikers been so well taken care of by an employer. It seems a safe assumption that there was little suffering at Easton—this in a day when hunger was the prime strikebreaker.[27]

Though Grace did not yield on the piecework issue, strikers began to drift back. How many of the eighty-five eventually returned cannot be ascertained, though in six months' time the plant was running normally. The union did not formally call off the strike until more than a year later, however. No figures are available to indicate whether Mr. Grace or the union was correct about the ultimate effect of the piecework system on the men's wages.

Some months before the formal ending of the strike, Mr. Grace asked union representatives what, in their opinion, was the best thing he could do to improve the living conditions of working people. One of the men replied: "Teach our girls to sew and to cook."

"That settled it with me," Mr. Grace said in a later reference to the conversation. "I took up the scheme in earnest and the more I studied it the better I liked it. Our industrial schools offered splendid advantages to boys but no help is offered to needy girls and women."[28]

Such was the beginning of the Grace Institute.

Mr. Grace got in touch with Grace Dodge, who, as a member of the Board of Education during Grace's second term as mayor, had introduced manual training in the city's public schools. He consulted trade-school specialists. The thing nearest to what he wanted he found in Jersey City, where the Catholic Sisters of Charity conducted night classes in cooking and dressmaking which girls walked miles to attend. Mrs. Grace, who for many years had helped working girls on her own, took part in the survey.

In the spring of 1897 the Grace Institute was incorporated. The Legislature granted it tax exemption up to $2 million. Mr. Grace and his brother Michael set aside $200,000 to begin work. Grace was still undecided about details. The Sisters of Charity had the experience and were willing to organize a school. They offered their services for $300 a year each, which was much less than Mr. Grace could have employed other teachers and administrators. Miss Dodge, a Protestant, spoke enthusiastically in favor of the sisters. Yet Mr. Grace feared the engagement of the sisters might lead to a misconception of the project, which was to be nonsectarian. Girls of any creed, or those professing no creed, were to be eligible.

An understanding was reached with church authorities whereby there should be no religious instruction in the school. An old mansion on West Sixtieth Street was purchased and remodeled. Under the management of the Sisters of Charity the first classes were opened in January 1898, with three hundred girls in attendance. Instruction was given in cooking, sewing, and laundry work. Soon classes in millinery, stenography, and bookkeeping were added. In its second year, Grace Institute had five hundred pupils.

Mr. Grace would have preferred that the school not bear his name. In this he said he had yielded to the wishes of his family. He expressed the hope that others would contribute to the school's endowment; in that event he would change the name if desired. But if no one else contributed, he said that his will would provide for the school's future.[29]

19 ~ The Nicaragua Canal Project

~ W. R. Grace's last great undertaking was to try to dig an interoceanic canal across Nicaragua. He probably would have succeeded had not the United States government decided to do the job on its own, subsequently taking over the old French concession in Panama where work had been abandoned in 1889. Whether the government acted wisely in accepting the Panama route was questioned by impartial experts at the time. Though a canal in Nicaragua would have been longer, they said engineering problems would have been simpler. Moreover, according to Mr. Grace's engineers, the cost would have been much lower. These theories may yet be put to the test, for at this writing (1948) there is talk of easing the load on the Panama waterway by running a canal across Nicaragua.

The bankruptcy of de Lesseps's project brought to life a number of schemes to finish that work or to construct a canal elsewhere. William L. Scott, a Pennsylvania railroad and coal mine owner, asked Grace about the feasibility of a canal. Notwithstanding the support he had given the French project, Grace was not sure that a canal would pay its way; he advised Scott to assemble statistics on shipping movements. The death of Scott in 1891 ended the matter.[1]

By that time another scheme, with Nicaragua as its seat of operations, had made considerable headway. This was the Maritime Canal Co., which had obtained a concession from the Nicaraguan government and had begun construction of workshops and a breakwater at Greytown, the proposed Atlantic terminal. In the manner of railroad promoters of the day (and long after), the canal promoters had taken small risk on the profitable operation of the canal. They intended to make their money digging it. Should the waterway prove a financial disappointment, others would hold the bag.

In addition to the Maritime Canal Co., which was the operating corporation, the promoters had created for their particular benefit the Nicaragua Construction Co. The plan was to sell Maritime Company stock and bonds to the public, and, if possible, get the United States government to guarantee the bonds. The Maritime Company would give the Construction Company $275,000,000 worth of these securities to do work estimated to cost from $65,000,000 to $100,000,000. The Construction Company was to receive $12,000,000 for right-of-way that had cost at most $500,000.[2]

Though Grace had no part in the formation of this enterprise, he knew some of the guiding spirits, among whom were Smith M. Weed and Warner Miller. Weed was a corporation lawyer who usually had been on Grace's side in politics. Warner Miller was a manufacturer who had amassed a fortune from a new process for making paper of wood pulp. Miller had served as a Republican in both houses of Congress. In 1888 he had narrowly missed beating Grace's foe, David B. Hill, for the governorship. A trustee of the Construction Company whom Grace knew only slightly was James Roosevelt of Hyde Park, whose son, Franklin Delano Roosevelt, was, at this juncture, nine years old.

The project was launched with fanfare. It was the subject of speeches on the floor of the United States Senate. John Tyler Morgan of Alabama said the canal would be the means of raising the South from the ashes of the Civil War by opening Pacific trade with the Gulf ports. Money came slowly, however. When the Construction Company had spent $6 million, there was no more in the till and work stopped. A refinancing campaign ran into the 1893 panic.

In this situation the promoters, through Weed, approached W. R. Grace. They made a handsome offer—the presidency, at a large salary, of the Construction Company. Though admitting to his brother Michael that "the program looks very pretty," Grace declined the proposal on the ground that his health would not stand the additional burden. Without Grace, the promoters failed to get anywhere, though Morgan made one appeal after another for Congress to rescue the Maritime Company, possibly even buy it out and build the canal as a government venture. This, of course, would have been in violation of the Clayton-Bulwer Treaty with Britain, which all our efforts had not succeeded in amending. In 1896 the canal people made another effort to interest the Graces, writing this time to Michael. W. R. advised his brother "against having anything to do with that project."[3]

Grace had not so much lost interest in the canal as he had lost faith in the Maritime outfit. Having read in the original Spanish its Nicaraguan franchise, he pronounced the agreement "a very poor one."[4]

~ Though efforts to draw W. R. Grace back into politics during the dramatic national campaign of 1896 failed, he was something more than a spectator. The party in power is always blamed for hard times. On top of that, the Democrats in '96 were so divided on the silver issue that long before the nominating convention it seemed doubtful whether the party would support President Cleveland's "sound money" stand. Grace contributed to the "sound money" factions in various states, but refused to go to the Chicago convention as a delegate-at-large from New York. Thus, he avoided a futile fight, for the silver people carried the day easily and nominated Bryan.

Before sailing for Europe three weeks later, Mr. Grace declared for the Republican nominee, McKinley. A few days before the election, Grace wrote Mr. McKinley that a story was abroad to the effect that, if elected, McKinley would remove a lot of officeholders because they were Catholics. Grace said he believed and hoped the story untrue. It was untrue; and, in office, President McKinley showed Mr. Grace a few small courtesies but, as we shall see, nothing more.[5]

The declaration of war against Spain in 1898, and especially the *Oregon*'s dash around the Horn, reawakened interest in the canal question. Before the brief fighting was over—it began in May and ended in July— Grace was in the field with a canal scheme of his own.

Prior to that, however, he had dealt with a war question that lay closer to home. William Russell Grace, junior, twenty years old, wanted to join up. As there was no holding the boy, Grace carried the matter to the secretary of war and landed a berth for Russ on the staff of a general who was bound for Puerto Rico. Before the young man could report for duty, a barn at Gracefield caught fire. In an effort to extinguish the blaze, Russ fell and broke a leg. By the time he was well, Spain had sued for peace, and Grace, with the rest of New York, was welcoming home New York's particular hero, Theodore Roosevelt.[6]

Concerning the canal, Grace's active interest seems to have dated from a meeting with Edward F. Cragin, a promoter who had broken with the Maritime group. After talking with Cragin, Grace's idea was to take over what was worth salvaging in the Maritime organization; and then, with a new and better agreement with Nicaragua, fresh capital, engineering brains, and general management, get things started in earnest.

Grace sent Cragin with letters to a number of wealthy and influential friends: "I now think the time is ripe for securing control of this enterprise. . . . Mr. Cragin will explain to you the facts in connection with the project for the formation of an association for securing control. . . . With the right men a great success can be made."[7]

Thus, early in August the Nicaragua Canal Syndicate came into being. Fifteen subscribers put up $1,000 apiece for immediate expenses and each pledged an additional $10,000. Grace was still sending out letters—to such men as Andrew Carnegie, August Belmont, and F. W. Vanderbilt. "The sentiment of this country is unquestionably for the construction of the canal. . . . [Because of the Clayton-Bulwer Treaty] the United States Government cannot undertake the work for its own account, and it therefore remains for private enterprise to do it." An executive committee of the syndicate had been formed consisting of Grace; John A. McCall, president of the New York Life Insurance Co. (of which Grace was a trustee); Clement A. Griscom, president of the International Navigation Co.; William Barbour of the Hanover National Bank; and— oddly—Charles R. Flint.[8]

Grace instituted inquiries into the character and abilities of Frank S. Washburn, the contracting engineer who had been tentatively settled upon. From Washburn himself he got detailed memoranda on the methods of organizing a large-scale construction job, with particular attention to the problems entailed by importing a large body of laborers "into a new country remote from their homes and in a tropical climate." He was apparently well satisfied both with what he heard of Washburn, and what he got from him, for the engineer remained with the syndicate.[9]

Grace sought an interview with his old friend Stephen B. Elkins, former secretary of war and now representing West Virginia in the United States Senate. "The matter in question is one which I would much rather discuss with you personally [than put in writing]." It related to the political aspects of the venture. The Maritime Company, which Grace hoped to replace, drew considerable water in official Washington. Blocks of its stock had been distributed among senators and representatives.[10]

There was also the matter of obtaining a concession from Nicaragua. The Maritime concession had only a little more than a year to run, that is, until October 1899. Though Grace did not want to operate under this contract, which he considered badly drawn, he would have taken it over for reasons of policy and then tried to amend it. Definitely he did not wish Nicaragua to extend the old concession. For his own project he desired a much broader franchise. To this end he arranged to send Cragin and the experienced Edward Eyre to Nicaragua.

These things provided for, Mr. Grace sailed for Europe early in August 1898. He intended to enlist the help of his brother Michael and to take a short vacation.

~ *J*n Europe, Mr. Grace had a slight stroke, from which he was never fully to recover. This prolonged his sojourn. While "the chief" was recuperating at a French watering resort, Michael Grace hurried to New York early in October, full of zeal for the canal enterprise and anxious to lighten his brother's labors. William was supposed to stay and rest for another month or so.

In Nicaragua, Eyre and Cragin were doing well, though they had their problems. Both were excellent negotiators, and Cragin knew the ins and outs of the Maritime arrangement. Behind them was the prestige of the Grace name. Washburn was on hand to give engineering advice. President Zelaya of Nicaragua had received the visitors cordially and had talked frankly and confidentially. Nicaragua was anxious for a canal—one built by private capital. Grace's connection with the enterprise seemed a guarantee of success. On the other hand, the only hope for the Maritime project was that the United States government come to its rescue. Nicaragua feared this would mean the "absorption" of the country. Zelaya would have liked to cancel the old concession forthwith, and give Grace an immediate and clear field.[11]

At the same time, Zelaya feared to offend the United States. He cabled his minister to ascertain whether Washington would object to the forfeiture of the Maritime franchise. From London, Michael Grace cabled his nephew Joseph P., temporarily looking out for matters in New York, to call on President McKinley and also to get John A. McCall to see what he could do to get a favorable reply to Zelaya's inquiry. Eyre suggested that former Senator Warner Miller be approached with a proposal to come over to the Grace side. Failing in that, Eyre suggested that Senator Elkins be asked to help.

Whatever happened, it accomplished nothing. The Maritime crowd was too well dug in at Washington. The Nicaraguan minister in Washington was informed that the United States opposed cancellation. The

American minister at Managua was instructed to work to that end. This diplomat was a forceful old retired sea captain named Merry. He made the most of his instructions, and the idea of eliminating Maritime then and there was dropped. Eyre and Cragin did the only thing left to do. They went ahead with negotiations for a concession effective on the expiration of the Maritime contract.[12]

A few days before the arrival of Michael Grace to take charge of his brother's canal syndicate, John Hay became secretary of state. Hay also plunged into canal matters, exerting his considerable acumen and charm toward obtaining a revision of the troublesome Clayton-Bulwer Treaty. Hay had always got along well with the British Foreign Office. In the treaty matter, too, he made progress—which was more than any predecessor of his had done in thirty years. Though privately incensed by the free talk of congressmen about building a canal whether England liked it or not, Hay went along with the administration policy and assured Senator Morgan that his bill would be no embarrassment to the treaty negotiations. The secretary went further. He impressed upon Ambassador White, in London, the advisability of speed, pointing out that when the Maritime Company concession expired in October '99, "we shall be confronted with new difficulties." Though Mr. Hay did not say so, unless life was infused into the Maritime enterprise one of these difficulties would be Grace.[13]

There were also other canal schemes, each with advocates in Washington. Most notable was a plan for reviving, under American aegis, the defunct Panama enterprise. To this end a new Panama company had been formed. In theory it had resumed the work of construction. Practically, however, it was devoting its energies to the creation of a Washington lobby with the object of selling the concession to the United States government at an outrageous price. More than that, since 1897, there had been in Central America an official Washington commission headed by Admiral Walker. Its mission was to settle once and for all the controversy over routes.

Not only did the administration hamper Grace by continuing its blessing of the Maritime Company's moribund stock-jobbing scheme; on the Democratic side, too—where Grace had the most political influence—the old company had fortified its lines. Senator Morgan of Alabama continued to urge the government to bail out Maritime and build the canal with public funds. He was preparing to introduce a bill to that end in the forthcoming Congress, which would convene in December 1898.

Michael Grace went to Washington to see what could be done about the opposition to the Grace syndicate. After talking to Vice President

Hobart, Senator Mark Hanna, and others, he decided very little could be done by direct means. By indirect means much might be done. Michael proposed that the Grace crowd capture the Maritime Company, and by that side door come into the administration's favor. The scheme frightened some of the syndicate members. John Claflin withdrew. McCall and others would have done so but for the personal influence of W. R. Grace, who, unable to sit on the sidelines any longer, had unexpectedly returned from Europe.

"The chief" acted vigorously. He reorganized the syndicate, dropping the discontented members, including Flint. He directed Eyre to go ahead with his concession negotiations, then in the final stage; and he kept close watch on those negotiations. He moved to acquire control of the Maritime Company stock. First, Warner Miller was induced to join the new Grace syndicate. Then it was planned to offer $100,000 for depreciated stock of the Nicaragua Construction Co., which had a par value of $1,500,000. With Miller's holding, this would give Grace control of the Construction Company, which in turn controlled the Maritime Company.[14]

On October 31, 1898, four days after the reorganization of the Grace syndicate, Eyre cabled in code from Nicaragua that the Congress of that country "has approved our concession with unimportant modification which we accepted."[15]

~ The Eyre-Cragin contract was a masterly document, reflecting by far a firmer grasp of the realities of canal construction and eventual operation than any similar concession negotiated up to that time.

Grace was to form a corporation, to be known as the Interoceanic Canal Co., within six months after the Nicaraguan government's contract with the Maritime Company "ceases to have legal existence," which in no case should be later than October 9, 1899. In other words, the old contract would not be renewed, as Senator Morgan, for one, contended it must be. The Interoceanic Company's franchise to build and operate the canal was exclusive. It pledged itself to complete a railroad across the isthmus within three years; to begin work on the canal within two years, and to complete it within ten. If these terms were not fulfilled, Nicaragua could cancel the contract or impose heavy financial penalties.

Nicaragua was to give the company certain public lands, and the use of public waters along the canal route, plus an additional grant of a million acres. The company was to purchase whatever private lands it might need.

Provision was made for the regulation of tolls, the exemption of the canal property from taxation, and the neutrality of the canal ports. The company was to receive police power, and absolute jurisdiction over a belt of land three miles wide on either side of the canal. The concession was in perpetuity—one of several conditions never before granted in a Latin American canal franchise.

The company was to receive all the profits from the canal during the first one hundred and ninety-nine years of its operation. After that, Nicaragua would have a share which, in the course of a hundred years, would be increased to 50 percent. Nicaragua was to have free use of the canal's railways and telegraph lines "for purposes of state." The syndicate agreed to pay $100,000 within three days after the ratification of the contract and $400,000 more within four months after the organization of the Interoceanic Canal Co.[16]

W. R. Grace advanced the initial $100,000, and was later reimbursed by the syndicate.

With this franchise in his hands and Warner Miller in his syndicate, Grace seemed to feel that capturing control of the Maritime stock would be easy. If so, he was mistaken. The Grace offer for the Maritime securities was refused by Miller's late colleagues in Maritime, and a New York bank. Apparently the Maritime crowd still believed their political pull was worth more than Grace's contract. Specifically, they hoped for the passage of the Morgan bill which would bring the United States government to the aid of their scheme. Thereupon, Grace undertook the second reorganization of his syndicate within a month. This was completed in January 1899, when twenty-six men had chipped in $10,500 apiece. Formidable names had been added: George Westinghouse, John Jacob Astor, Levi P. Morton, George T. Bliss, James Stillman, and Robert Goelet.[17]

In the meantime, Mr. Grace had begun to woo the administration, certain that, of the two Nicaragua concessions, his would be of greater benefit to the United States. After former Senator Miller—who had been largely responsible for Maritime's politically favored position—had paved the way, Michael Grace visited the capital with a letter of introduction from his brother to President McKinley. Both the executive and Secretary Hay received Michael pleasantly. The president spoke of sending "the strongest kind of a message to Congress" on the canal question; but he did not say which project he would favor. With a jest the genial Hay simply passed Michael on to Senator Morgan.

Michael spent nearly four hours with that statesman, who had done more than anyone else in public life to keep the Maritime enterprise alive. Without having seen the Grace contract the senator had attacked it in a speech. Michael Grace asked Mr. Morgan to read the contract. The senator did so and without hesitation pronounced it much better than the Maritime Company's. Yet he added that it was "a great pity that the Maritime Company had been interfered with." Why couldn't the two groups get together before Congress convened? Michael replied that representatives of the Grace group had "gone with their hats in their hands to the old company for the special purpose of avoiding a conflict."

Morgan said that personally he favored the building of the canal by private enterprise, but that the majority of Congress wanted the government to have a hand in it. Michael said the Grace syndicate was willing to give the government a third interest. That did not satisfy Morgan. He said the Grace people should have a national charter, granted by Congress, such as Maritime had, and that the only way they could get one would be to make a deal with Maritime. Michael said he thought a charter of incorporation issued by one of the states would do just as well. The senator did not agree. He kept saying that Maritime had been unfairly treated, presumably by Grace, and repeated that the two groups should get together. The senator admitted that his bill to rescue Maritime probably would not pass, and remarked again that the best way for the Grace group to advance its interests was to come to terms with its rival.

It was a curious interview. The senator gave no reason of any consequence for his stubborn championship of Maritime in face of his confession that Grace had the better franchise.

Returning to New York, Michael recommended that another effort be made to acquire the Maritime stock. The executive committee of the syndicate voted unanimously against this, and decided to carry the issue, on its merits, straight to Mr. McKinley.[18]

The corporate setup planned by the Grace group did not differ essentially from that of Maritime. There was to be an owning corporation and a construction corporation. The public would be invited to invest in the owning corporation. Insiders would control the construction corporation, which would receive from the owning corporation securities with a face value of $225,000,000 with which to build a canal estimated to cost $100,000,000. Should the canal prove successful, the construction company securities, originally sold at a discount, probably would go to par.

Thus the promoters would reap large profits on a relatively small investment. Should the canal prove unprofitable the loss to the construction company (insiders) would be small by comparison with the loss to the owning company (outsiders).

Mr. Grace made a better proposal of government participation in his project than Senator Morgan was urging on behalf of Maritime. He suggested to the president that the United States help finance and control the owning company. This company would be incorporated for $100,000,000, with the privilege of issuing mortgage bonds not exceeding $150,000,000. In exchange for the right to regulate tolls on the canal the United States government was asked to guarantee interest of at least 3 percent on $50,000,000 worth of the company's bonds. This guarantee was not to be effective until the company had spent $20,000,000 of its own money. As security the government would be given a second mortgage on the company. In addition, the government would receive one-fourth ($25,000,000 worth) of the stock of the company and have the right to name five of the fifteen directors.[19]

Mr. McKinley was not impressed by the syndicate's offer. Two days after it was received at the White House the executive's annual message was made public. Concerning the canal this document said only two things positively: a canal would be built; the United States would control it. The matter of a route must wait upon the report of the Walker commission. The claims of the rival concessionaires were in a vague way referred to Congress. The president, however, mentioned the Maritime Company by title. The Grace syndicate was called "another association," which "appears" to have obtained "an optional concession . . . to become effective on the expiration of the present grant." The implication, faint but there, was that the unnamed "association" was a sort of interloper.[20]

Nothing was left for Grace but to get together a lobby and fight the Morgan bill. This was done at a confusing session. Washington swarmed with lobbies interested in the canal issue. The Maritime lobby was making its last stand. The railroad lobby was against any canal. The Panama lobby was against any other canal. Those were merely the principal lobbies. Hitherto, the Grace people had been content to dwell upon the excellence of their own concession, without reflecting specifically upon their rival. Grace now provided material for riddling the Morgan bill and its proposed beneficiary. Controlled by stockholders, Maritime securities had been worked up and down to the profit of insiders. Officers drew large salaries for doing very little. "The board of directors of the old Company is known as the Pick Wick Club, nice gentlemen to talk to but could not build canal." In the middle of February, Grace was able to write Michael, who had returned to London, that the bill would be beaten. "The old concession must lapse, and then we will have our innings."[21]

～ Always moderate in appraising his achievements, Mr. Grace did not claim to have defeated the Morgan bill. He was merely part of a coalition that downed it. Later, William Nelson Cromwell, attorney for the Panama Company, took credit for killing the bill. Possibly he deserved it. Not only was Cromwell the cleverest lobbyist on the scene in Washington that winter; he was also one of the least troubled by scruples. Cromwell played a waiting game. With the Walker commission (though it had not made its report) known to favor the Nicaragua route, Cromwell aimed at eliminating not only the Maritime Company but also Admiral Walker.

After voting down the Morgan bill, Congress had adopted a resolution providing for a restudy of routes. Cromwell tried to exclude from the new commission all members of the Walker body. He failed. Though several new men were added, Walker and his principal assistants were retained. Among those retained was Louis Haupt, a real champion of Nicaragua, originally appointed at the suggestion of W. R. Grace. This was before Mr. Grace had any idea of entering the canal picture. Grace would have liked to have seen George S. Greene of the New York City Department of Docks added to the new Walker commission, but he did not urge it. He cautioned his associates not to "exhaust" their credit with the administration over the selection of an engineer.[22]

The Panama crowd went to work on the new members of the enlarged Walker commission. Mr. Grace was less disturbed by this than by the growing sentiment for a government-built canal. He sketched out some opposing arguments: "Bulwer-Clayton treaty obligations. Slowness, lack of steadfastness. Political interests paramount, absence of a single purpose. A physical problem, not primarily a political or governmental one. Uncertainty of government enterprises. Absorption of Nicaraguan sovereignty. Example of Albany capitol. Time 30 years, cost 20 millions, worth 3 millions."[23]

At the same time, Mr. Grace wrote: "If it is the will of the American people, as expressed by the representatives in Washington, that the Government should build the Canal . . . the gentlemen with whom I am associated are entirely ready to act the part of good citizens."[24]

Matters drifted until October 10, 1899, when the Maritime concession lapsed and the Grace contract became effective. Still matters drifted, and not until the last day permitted by the terms of the contract—April 10, 1900—did the Interoceanic Canal Co. come into existence. Four months thereafter a payment of $400,000 would be due Nicaragua. This sluggishness, so uncharacteristic of W. R. Grace, seems attributable in part to the decline of his physical energy. Moreover, late in March 1900, Mr. Grace had slipped and fallen, in front of his office in Hanover Square, dislocating a shoulder. He did not leave his town house again until May, when he went to Gracefield for his sixty-eighth birthday. After that he came to the city only once or twice a week.

Belatedly addressing himself to the task of raising money to pay Nicaragua, Mr. Grace offered to double his original contribution of $10,500 to the syndicate. Other members were asked to do likewise. The response was so disappointing that Grace had to seek fresh sources of funds. One of his letters, dated May 29, was to James D. Phelan, banker and mayor of San Francisco. Grace had known Phelan's father, a native of Ireland who had gone to California with the gold rush.

"I shall be pleased to have you join us," the letter read, "and if you care to put the matter before one or two other equally prominent Californians whom you know to have an interest in the accomplishment of the work, I could no doubt arrange to have them come in too. . . . If our Syndicate builds the Canal, the investment should be highly remunerative."

Grace went on to say what was really on his mind: "It was not expected when this matter was taken up by the Syndicate that the intention of having the canal built by our own Government would have manifested itself so strongly, and I confess it is with grave fears that I see our Congress launched on such a course.

"We hope that after the election, more prudent counsel may prevail. . . . If, on the other hand, Government ownership is insisted upon, our concession, which is absolute and exclusive, can be surrendered for a consideration which can be decided on later; personally I should have no objection to step aside on payment only of the money expended.

"I want the Canal built by private enterprise, so that it can be availed of for the commerce of the world in six or eight years, and we all have the desire of connecting our names with this great enterprise. I am satisfied that if the work is confided in the executive, the completion of the canal must be deferred for many years, to say nothing of what it may finally cost the country."[25]

Mr. Grace did not exaggerate the rising tide of sentiment for a government canal. Shortly before he wrote Phelan the House of Representatives had overwhelmingly passed the Hepburn bill, calling for the United States to build, fortify, and operate a canal across Nicaragua. This measure ignored both the Grace concession and the Clayton-Bulwer Treaty. Though the Senate declined to act on the Hepburn bill before summer adjournment, it made the measure a preferred order of business on the reconvening of Congress in December. Meantime, Secretary Hay was progressing with his negotiations for an amendment or abrogation of the treaty. This would clear the way for the Hepburn bill, or for any plan for a government-owned canal, without offense to Britain. Another development that boded no good to Grace was the activity of Cromwell for Panama. Though most of the Walker commission still favored Nicaragua, Senator Mark Hanna showed increasing interest in the Panama route. Mark Hanna was the most powerful man in the United States. He had made William McKinley president and was currently setting the stage for his protégé's reelection.

Phelan declined Grace's invitation to contribute. In fact, Grace had no luck at all, and in August the Interoceanic Canal Co. defaulted on its payment to Nicaragua. This had a chilling effect on the Latin American republic, where Grace's prestige had lately been so high. Our minister there, Captain Merry, who had been sniping at Grace all along, was in a position to say "I told you so." Secretary Hay lost no time opening talks with Nicaragua looking toward a government concession, if and when Congress should authorize the president to acquire a route there.

In November 1900, Mr. McKinley was reelected. Edward Eyre later told a story of how Mr. Grace visited the White House to make a last plea for the government to support the Grace concession. According to Eyre, the president treated the old merchant with great consideration but was firm in his refusal. He said any canal would have to be a government undertaking solely. This interview may have taken place, though neither Mr. Grace's correspondence nor the surviving records of the syndicate contain any allusion to it.[26]

December saw the end, for practical purposes, of Mr. Grace's effort to build a canal. On the first day of the month, Secretary Hay signed a protocol with Nicaragua giving the United States prior rights. Forthwith that republic declined Grace's request for an extension in the matter of the overdue $400,000, and declared the Interoceanic Canal Co.'s concession forfeited. One small hope remained. The government of Nicaragua intimated that should the United States not act promptly, Nicaragua might be willing to renew the Grace franchise.

On the last day of 1900, Mr. Grace relayed tidings of these developments to the members of his syndicate. In the same letter he returned to each subscriber $4,000. That left a small balance which Mr. Grace said would maintain the legal existence of the Interoceanic Canal Co. for a while, on the long chance that something might turn up.[27]

～ *N*othing turned up that was of any benefit to the Interoceanic Canal Co. W. R. Grace remained an interested, if aging and sometimes weary, spectator of the procession of events. Hay managed the abrogation of the Clayton-Bulwer Treaty; sentiment in favor of a government operation became insurmountable. When McKinley died of an assassin's bullet in September 1901, the succession of Theodore Roosevelt to the presidency assured a vigorous canal policy. Roosevelt had long been for a government project, and had done much to shape public opinion in that regard. Shortly after Roosevelt was sworn in, the Walker commission reported unanimously in favor of Nicaragua. A factor in the finding was the avarice of the Panama promoters who asked $109,000,000 for their concession.

Then came the upset few would have predicted a year before: the swift triumph of the Panama over the Nicaragua route, due to a masterpiece of lobbying and an act of God. In May 1902, while the Senate was considering rival routes, Mount Pelée in Martinique erupted and killed thirty thousand people. Then Mount Momotombo in Nicaragua went into action. When the Nicaraguan government denied the existence of an active volcano there, Panama lobbyists placed on each senator's desk a Nicaraguan postage stamp showing one in eruption. That represented one of the lobby's modest expenditures. On June 28 the Senate authorized the president to acquire the old French concession for $40,000,000, the promoters having came down to that figure.[28]

Mr. Grace wrote to his friend in the White House:

"I think Congress exercised rare wisdom in consigning to your care the Isthmian Canal in toto. . . . I feel as a citizen and merchant that great advantage must accrue to the commerce of the world, and to that of the United States in particular, through the Isthmian link between the oceans. . . .

"All interest I and my associates formerly had in the Nicaragua route ceased upon our reaching the conclusion that the policy of the Government was for Governmental construction and control."[29]

Mr. Grace refrained from saying that he remained unconvinced that the canal should not be built by private enterprise or that Panama provided the better route.

With $40,000,000 going into the pockets of the Panama speculators, the Republic of Colombia felt entitled to something. Though eighteen years later we paid Colombia $25,000,000, in the autumn of 1902 less creditable means were taken to ensure the canal. The Panama Company clique plotted a revolution on the isthmus which came off in November. Panama declared its independence and achieved it without blood, thanks to the liberal use of money from the canal company's treasury and to the guns of the United States navy. The people of the United States approved this Big Stick procedure, and the Republicans carried the November elections. Mr. Grace was moved to write the president again:

"From my position on the political side lines, I can see but one indication from yesterday's results that interests me, and that is the accentuation of the view I have held for some time now—that your services to the country must entitle you to be the next Republican Presidential candidate, and that the prospects of your success then are much brighter than they were a few days ago.

"I need hardly say that this is a matter of personal pleasure to me, and my only hope is that my judgment in this respect may not be warped by the strong feeling I have always had for you."[30]

Fourteen days after the Republic of Panama was proclaimed, Secretary Hay concluded a treaty with it giving the United States a strip ten miles wide on which to build, fortify, and operate in perpetuity a ship canal. It must have afforded Mr. Grace satisfaction to note that several features of this agreement had been taken bodily from his contract with Nicaragua, which otherwise our government had snubbed so thoroughly.

~ Perhaps it was fortunate for him that W. R. Grace did not get the task of directing the construction of a canal, for after the shoulder accident in 1900 he was never again a well man. Yet had he been in charge, the mistakes Theodore Roosevelt made during the first year of active operations at Panama would have been avoided. Nearly all these errors proceeded from the lack of business experience of the president's subordinates.

Before the work started, Grace had recommended William L. Saunders as a member of Mr. Roosevelt's canal commission. The recommendation was inspired by patriotism, for Saunders was a man Grace could have spared only with difficulty. An engineer with excellent talents for business, Saunders was in virtual charge of the Ingersoll-Sergeant Drill Co. He had been a consultant on the Chicago Draining Canal and on the improvement of navigation in the Danube through the Iron Gate. Though the president failed to appoint Saunders, it was not until he eventually got men of that stripe that the work, so badly begun, really moved forward.[31]

In various ways it was evident that the sands were running out for Mr. Grace. Though he still exercised carriage horses at the farm, he no longer drove them in town where for a generation his handling of spirited teams had been a familiar sight. Yet on occasions there was a flash of the old fire. Sometimes Mr. Grace rode on the Third Avenue Elevated from his home at Seventy-ninth Street to Hanover Square. One day in his seventieth year he arose to give his seat to a lady. A young man dropped into the seat. Mr. Grace took the young man by the collar and lifted him to his feet.[32]

The family tried to persuade Mr. Grace to have a man accompany him on his rounds about the city. He would not have it, but he consented to engage an electric hansom. In this way the family succeeded in having him escorted, as the driver helped his passenger in and out, passed him through doors, and so on. Toward the end of 1902, Mr. Grace was painfully injured by flying glass when the hansom skidded against a Sixth Avenue "L" pillar.[33]

In the year 1903, Mr. Grace was quite active. At W. R. Grace & Co. he still held the reins, though his son Joseph P., then second vice president, assumed more and more responsibility. The senior Grace directed a policy of expansion at Ingersoll-Sergeant, which had become a large concern. The management of his personal fortune of $10,000,000 took a good deal of time. Charities, and in particular Grace Institute, received an increasing share of his attention. In honor of the founder's seventy-first birthday on May 10, the Institute got up a celebration which Mr. Grace attended. He had lately enlarged the building, bringing the outlay for the school to $500,000.

On December 7, Mr. Grace left his office in Hanover Square and went straight to bed at the town house. For several days he had been suffering from a cold. Pneumonia developed in both lungs. The children all came home. Michael hurried over from London. Doctor Morgan Grace had died earlier in the year in New Zealand—the first of the four brothers to go. John, in London, was too ill to come.

The patient survived the crisis, rallied, and seemed on the way to recovery. He sent for his secretary and began to transact business in bed.

Early in March the kidney complaint from which Mr. Grace had suffered periodically for forty years reasserted itself. This brought on a general physical collapse. On the morning of March 20, 1904, Mr. Grace asked concerning the arrival of one of his steamers. Shortly after that he slipped into a coma. The following forenoon he died without regaining consciousness.[34]

So passed the genius of his century in the Latin American trade, and the man who did as much as any other in his time to foster understanding between the peoples of the two continents of this hemisphere. So passed one of the great chief magistrates of New York's whole history, whose influence for integrity in politics and courage in public places went far beyond the confines of the city he governed so well. So passed the last great master of sailing ships under the American flag—or perhaps any flag. As proof that time does not stand still, his last inquiry was about a steamer, a kind of ship this old foremast jack had hoped never to be obliged to own.

20 ~ Casa Grace

~ Any man worth writing a book about leaves something that lasts longer than he does. The achievements of thinkers (like Confucius) survive longer than the achievements of doers (like Caesar). W. R. Grace was a doer, and his field was that of commerce, where changes have been more profound within the past half century than in many other fields. Let any veteran reflect how differently any business is conducted today [1948] from what it was when he started out. W. R. Grace & Co. has changed. Its airplanes cover the distance between the United States and Peru in twelve hours whereas in 1904 its sailing ships, a good many of which were still in service, took a hundred days. Yet basically the business has altered very little. This is not because Mr. Grace's successors have fallen behind the times. It is because the founder was ahead of his time; and because his house had been built upon principles that are enduring.

Without going into the intricacies of multiple corporate structure, W. R. Grace & Co. is, in effect, the parent corporation of about sixty corporations engaged in a wide variety of undertakings. Some of its activities are carried on by the parent company and others by the associated companies. But W. R. Grace & Co. is neither a holding company nor an investment trust. It is essentially an operating company, and its managerial activity extends to all of the enterprises in which it is interested. In the United States the older officers and employees still speak of the parent corporation as "the house." In South America it is "Casa Grace," perhaps the best-known commercial name on the west coast, from Panama to Cape Horn.

As far back as the days of Bryce, Grace & Co., the standing of that house was such that its drafts, called "*damas verdes*," circulated as currency. The name came from the fact that those early Grace drafts were ornamented with the figure of a woman printed in green ink. This became

317

an identifying symbol of good "money." Particularly in the recurrent times of monetary uncertainty was there a demand for "*las letras de la dama verde*" (the drafts of the green lady).

Later, Peru witnessed an even more striking example of the confidence of its people in the financial stability of the house of Grace. The outbreak of war in Europe in 1914 so upset money markets that the New York Stock Exchange was closed to avoid what was feared might degenerate into a panic. The effect was even more serious in South America. In Peru, gold and silver money disappeared. People were afraid to accept paper. The country was without a circulating medium. A supply of United States currency was hastily imported in the hope that the prestige of the American government would make it acceptable. Certain mill and mine workers, however, refused even this. A Peruvian lawyer had what proved to be a stroke of inspiration. At his suggestion the United States currency was "*Garantizado por la Casa Grace.*" With this endorsement, the workers took it.

What kind of business is Grace in nowadays? Just about all kinds. For diversity of activity there is today no other concern like it. The remarkable thing is that, transportation excepted, most of these businesses are small by United States standards. Only in the aggregate do they bulk large. Now, as sixty years ago, the prestige of Grace on the west coast is something that cannot be measured by assets. For two generations it has been perhaps the principal factor in the development of trade relations between South America's west coast and the United States.

Cultural and political relations follow trade, or usually do. But it is only by this indirect means that W. R. Grace & Co. has exercised any influence within the past fifty years and more on political factors in Latin America.

As a matter of fact, during the lifetime of W. R. Grace the Grace interests kept singularly aloof from Latin American politics, the standards and practices of the time considered. That was one of the reasons Grace bore a good name in those countries, and one reason for the sustained commercial success of the Grace house over the years. The period of Grace's growth to a position of importance on the west coast—say, from 1855 to 1900—was one of almost unrestrained intervention in political matters by foreign business and financial interests. Whole countries in Latin America were practically dependent, economically, on foreign interests, largely English, French, and German. Grace made his way by other means: by the punctual fulfillment of contracts; by delivering goods that were as represented to be; by superior service and fair prices; in other words, by competence and honesty. When young Grace started in business in Peru, honesty was enough of a novelty on the part of the foreign trader to be made note of and remembered. His climb to the top was slower than those who were out for quick turnovers and high profits. But Grace has lasted.

One thing that strikes the student of the fifty thousand-odd letters that comprise Mr. Grace's preserved correspondence over fifty years is the degree of his abstention from Latin American politics in a day when nearly every foreign trader was in it up to his neck.

So strict is the no-politics rule in W. R. Grace & Co. today that it applies to officers and employees not only acting for the company but also acting in their capacities as citizens. In South America, many of the Grace executives and all but a few of the thousands of other Grace employees are citizens of the countries where Grace does business. If they wish to take an active part in politics, they must sever their connections with Grace. The head of W. R. Grace & Co. in Lima is Doctor Carlos García Gastañeta. Some years ago Doctor García was mentioned as a possible candidate for the presidency of Peru. I do not know how seriously Doctor García took this boomlet. I know only that he stayed with Grace. Raúl Simón, a Chilean, runs the affairs of Grace in Chile, as did Jorge E. Zalles, a Bolivian, in Bolivia. The no-politics rule applies to them as it does to anyone identified with Casa Grace.

Control of stock ownership in W. R. Grace & Co. by the Grace family was assured for a long time to come by the will of the founder. Control of the management has been preserved to the clan by the competence of Mr. Grace's descendants. But not for many years have there been enough Graces or Eyres to man all the top management posts. First, the founder's young men mentioned in an earlier chapter came to the front in administration and responsibility, and, with J. P. Grace, formed a "partnership" group to which younger men coming along have been added. But the family spirit has always been maintained and so, after nearly a hundred years (centennial in 1951), it remains a family business.

When W. R. Grace died in 1904, the presidency of the corporation went to the founder's nephew, Irish-born Edward Eyre, who had joined the firm in Callao in 1867, having made the passage as a seaman in the old and unlucky Grace clipper *Nereus*. The notable achievement of the Eyre administration was the assumption of the Transandine Railroad contract by Grace, which resulted in the completion of the first transcontinental railway in South America uniting the Pacific and the Atlantic coasts. After long planning, two Chilean brothers, Juan and Mateo Clark, had begun construction toward the Argentine border in 1886. Owing to financial difficulties they were obliged to stop work three years later. The project languished until 1899, when an English company obtained control of both the Chilean and Argentine ends. Work progressed slowly, however, until 1904, when W. R. Grace & Co. was awarded the contract for finishing the western end. The work, completed in 1910, marked a new era in the commercial development of Argentina and Chile.

By that time, J. P. Grace had succeeded his cousin as president of W. R. Grace & Co. The change took place in 1907. J. P. Grace and his father had points in common. They were about the same height and build. Both were splendid horsemen. Both had a delightful sense of humor. Both were modest men. J. P. Grace had previously declined the presidency on the grounds of age and limited experience. Under his leadership and with the cooperation of the young men his father had brought up in the business, the firm experienced far-reaching growth and development on all fronts. Under his administration the management base was broadened and the founder's principle of compensation based on a participation in profits was expanded to include department heads and many others. Opportunity for ownership of common stock was also given to the staff through sale at attractive prices on easy payment terms.

In 1929, J. P. Grace assumed the chairmanship of the board of W. R. Grace & Co. His Columbia classmate and best friend, Stewart Iglehart, the Methodist minister's son, became president. These friends worked as well together in business as they had on the polo field. They were the authors of modern Grace, a thumbnail sketch of which will follow in a moment. Together these friends and workmates, and a remarkable corps of associates they had gathered about them, saw the Grace empire through the dark days of the great depression.

In 1945, Messrs. Grace and Iglehart retired. In 1946, Mr. Iglehart died. Mr. Grace's successor as chairman was William Grace Holloway, whom the reader last glimpsed as the founder's first grandchild, Billee—Alice's son. Mr. Holloway had worked his way through the ranks of the company, in New York, San Francisco, London, and South America. Adolf Garni and Harold J. Roig, who had also risen to senior positions in the "partnership" group, were elected vice chairmen. While not members of the family they became, with three members of the family, trustees of the stock control trust under the will of the founder. Mr. Iglehart's successor as president was Joseph Peter Grace, junior—called Peter to distinguish him from his father, who is called Joe. As a young man coming up the ladder he was Peter to his associates, including the clerks and secretaries. When Peter became president, they began calling him Mr. Grace. Peter corrected that. These four men, with Vice Presidents John T. Kirby and Andrew B. Shea, both of whom had risen from the ranks by way of the home office and South America, compose the operating "executive committee." With them, many men and women with many talents in many lands in all ranks today carry on the varied activities of the firm.

The company is still at Hanover Square, where it has been since 1885. One building houses the headquarters activities of W. R. Grace & Co. and the Grace National Bank, formed in 1915, originally to take over banking activities entrusted to Grace by South Americans and other friends of the house. The bank, of which Chester R. Dewey is president, does a general business, with the accent on the foreign field. It does not finance the Grace business. Any such business done with Grace, even ordinary commercial letters of credit, is secured by United States government bonds. Across the square another building houses the offices of the Grace Line, successor to the old Merchants Line of sailing ships.

The Grace business falls into three general categories: export and import trade, transportation, and industry.

Of these, trade is the oldest. When William Grace joined the firm in 1851, John Bryce & Co. were ship chandlers with a slight interest in foreign trade. It was young Grace who took the company into export and import trading on a large and profitable scale. It was Grace who took the firm into shipping and integrated that business with trading, making it a commercial power on the west coast.

Although its form has undergone a radical change from buying and selling, largely on commission, to dealing as merchant principals, the trading feature of the Grace business differs little, in essence, from what it was when the founder started it. In simplest terms it means the marketing of the products of Ecuador, Peru, Bolivia, Colombia, Chile, Venezuela, and Central America in the United States, and taking products of the United States there in return. To itemize all the articles involved in this trade would fill several pages of this book. The principal ones moving north in which the firm deals as merchants are coffee, cocoa beans, metals, sundry produce, long-staple cotton, and wool. The principal ones moving south are machinery, manufactured goods, lumber from the Pacific Northwest, and foodstuffs. Due largely to the enterprise of Grace, the United States now stands first in trade relations with the west coast of South America, where thirty years ago it stood third or fourth among the commercial nations.

Ocean transportation, with all its related port facilities, is and always has been the circulatory system of the Grace business. From the time that the founder in 1893 began to replace his sailing ships with steamers the Grace transportation interests moved forward rapidly. The opening of the Panama Canal in 1914 halved the distance between the South American west coast and the Atlantic seaboard of the United States. Grace was ready for this. The founder's successors were proving as astute operators of steam as the founder had been of sail. The name Merchants Line was dropped in favor of Grace Line. Gradually the American flag replaced the British flag on the Grace steamers, the last ships being converted to American registry in 1915.

At the present time, Grace Line operates three main routes and some feeder services. The main routes are from New York to Valparaiso, with intervening stops for passengers and cargo; New York to Colombia and Venezuela; and Puget Sound and West Coast United States ports to Valparaiso. The modern Grace fleet is largely the creation of the late Daulton Mann, whose immediate successor, R. R. Adams, is the present head of the Grace Line.

Though they represent less than half of the Grace commercial empire, the Grace businesses best known, in fact about the only Grace businesses that are known at all to the average American, are the Grace Line, the Grace National Bank, and PANAGRA. PANAGRA (Pan American-Grace Airways, Inc.) is the Grace interest in air transportation. The company is owned half by Grace and half by Pan American Airways, a union engineered in 1928 by Robert V. Patchin, vice president of Grace. The first flights comprised a purely local service in Peru. This was swiftly expanded to link the principal cities of the west coast and Buenos Aires on the east coast. Then came the link with the United States, so that within a matter of hours one may be in almost any large city in South America. PANAGRA is operated under the direction of Harold J. Roig, its first president.

The third arm of the Grace business is industry. Though in the days of the founder Grace owned the Cartavio sugar plantation and mill, the industrial development is the world of the founder's son, J. P. Grace, and of Stewart Iglehart and colleagues. This development has meant taking initial capital and technical and commercial skills to South America; building factories and industrial establishments there; developing organizations (operatives, foremen, and managers) of nationals to carry on these enterprises; leaving in the countries where the plants are located not only taxes, wages, and salaries, but plowing back earnings year after year to build up the business and associating with local interests through stock ownership by nationals of the countries where the business is carried on.

The sugar estates in Peru now comprise 20,000 acres of cane and employ 15,000 persons, with mills producing refined as well as brown sugar. Related to this, and using in large part the cane pulp as the basis for its product, is a plant making paper and paperboard products and a bag and box factory turning out paper bags and cardboard boxes and containers for a wide variety of uses. This paper plant, the only one of its kind in existence, was developed by Vice President Gaston J. Lipscomb.

For many years Chilean nitrate of soda, production in Chile and shipment and distribution in the United States, was the basis of a very important Grace activity. In 1930 the Grace *oficinas* with the other producing properties were purchased and merged with a Chilean government monopoly.

From importing textiles, manufacturing them was a natural step. Grace operates several cotton mills in Peru and Chile and has an important interest in a cotton mill in Colombia. Most of these mills combine in one unit all of the textile-making processes—carding and spinning, weaving, bleaching, dyeing, and printing.

Other Grace industries in South America include an edible-oil mill and solvent plant, a soap factory, sugar refinery, flour mills, paint factories, coffee and cocoa cleaning plants, candy and biscuit manufacture, a highway asphalt and a cement plant, manganese and tin mines, and a commercial radio station, which was the first in Chile. In the United States the firm has for many years carried on a business in commercial fertilizer (begun as an outlet for Chilean nitrate of soda) and has recently made a beginning in some other industrial lines.

These industries are incorporated in the countries in which they do business. Though the Grace management operates most of them, a substantial part of the stock ownership of many of them is in the hands of South Americans. In some instances this interest is more than 50 percent. These industries have been a boon to the economy, not only of the countries in which they are situated, but to the whole west coast of South America. Integrated with the Grace transportation and trading interests, the Grace industries have immensely stimulated commerce and general understanding between the west coast and the United States. That was a big part of the founder's dream.

~ Notes

~ CHAPTER 1

1. Morgan S. Grace, *A Sketch of the New Zealand War* (1899), 10; Joseph Wilhelm, *The Family of Grace* (1911), 21.

2. Mrs. Grace addressed her son as "Billy." See her letter to him, undated but probably written in October 1868, Grace Papers, W. R. Grace & Co., Hanover Square, New York City. James Grace apparently called his son "William." See Morgan S. Grace to W. R. Grace, October 27, 1894, collection of J. P. Grace, New York. Ellen Grace's comment on the possible relation between her son's love of the sea and his birthplace is taken from an unpublished biography of W. R. Grace written prior to 1941 by Katherine Burton. Mrs. Burton talked to older members of the Grace family and to associates of Mr. Grace who are now dead. Some of the material thus obtained can be proved wrong by the records. Though the item here referred to cannot be proved one way or the other, surely it is probable. Hereafter this source will be cited as Burton.

3. Samuel Leigh, *New Pocket Road-Book of Ireland* (1833), 100, 109; Samuel Lewis, *A Topographical Dictionary of Ireland* (1837), I, 141.

4. Sir Charles Coote, *General View of the Agriculture and Manufactures of Queen's County* (1801), 37; Richard R. Griffith, *General valuation of Ireland, Ballyadams barony* (1850), 14, 15, 17.

5. Valuation Office, Ely Place, Dublin, Surveyors' Field Books, Ballyadams Barony (1849); Coote, 107; Genealogical Office, Dublin Castle, Betham Red Books, Second Series, III, 105; Wilhelm, 124, for the canal reference. On p. 142 the same author mentions an incident that has become traditional with later generations of the Grace family. It is that James Grace went to law with Lord Annsley to recover old Grace lands held by that peer and, after long and costly litigation, lost his suit. R. J. Hayes, director of the National Library of Ireland, and T. P. O'Neill of the Irish Historical Society, who conducted the writer's research in Ireland, could find nothing in existing records to confirm any such litigation. The story possibly

arises from other land disputes involving members of the numerous Grace family. In the course of the family's long history in Ireland, there were many such cases.

6. M. S. Grace to W. R. Grace, October 17, 1894, collection of J. P. Grace; Joseph P. Grace, a son of W. R. Grace, to the writer.

7. J. P. Grace and his sister, Lilias Grace Kent, to Bessie Rowland James.

8. Indenture, October 3, 1727, between Walter Weldon and Michael Grace, Registry of Deeds, Henrietta Street, Dublin, Book 55, p. 122, No. 36181; Lewis, I, 141.

9. Wilhelm, 20–21; James Fraser, *Hand Book for Travellers in Ireland* (1844), 158.

10. Wilhelm, 43–44, 58–80; Sheffield Grace, *Memoirs of the Family of Grace* (1823), 10–26.

11. J. P. Grace to B. R. James.

12. Manuscript of a speech by Mr. Grace, about September 1882, when Mr. Grace was mayor of New York, Grace Papers; Henry de Forest Baldwin to Jonathan Grossman, research assistant; J. P. Grace to B. R. James.

13. Manuscript of speech, *op. cit.*; Seumas MacManus, *The Story of the Irish Race* (1944), 594–95.

14. W. R. Grace to the Reverend J. K. Fitzgerald, September 26, 1884, Grace Papers.

15. William O'Connor Morris, *Ireland, 1494–1905* (1909), 198–248; Edmund Curtis, *History of Ireland* (1936), 284–87.

16. MacManus, 603.

17. *Ibid.*, 607.

18. Wilhelm, 143; *Compressed Air*, a New York trade publication, April 1904; Registry of Deeds, Dublin, 1851, Book 12, No. 167, Deed, Michael Grace to Anthony Weldon; W. R. Grace in an undated autobiographical memorandum, probably written in May 1882, Grace Papers. Doctor Cahill died in Boston while on a lecture tour and in 1885, W. R. Grace participated in the effort that resulted in transporting his remains to Dublin.

19. MacManus, 610.

20. Thomas Johnson to Brother Vernon, November 3, 1887, Grace Papers; manuscript of biographical sketch, probably written in 1896, *ibid.*; Burton; Utica (N. Y.) *Observer*, April 6, 1901; New York *Daily News*, March 21, 1904; Cincinnati *Enquirer*, March 22, 1904. The Utica *Observer* and Cincinnati *Enquirer* items are pieces of reminiscence about Mr. Grace by men who knew him well. The former, signed "Observer," was written by W. S. Bissell, postmaster general during Cleveland's second term; the latter, signed "Holland," by E. Jay Edwards of Philadelphia.

21. M. S. Grace to W. R. Grace, October 27, 1894, collection of J. P. Grace.

22. Scholastic honors list, Belvedere College, *Freeman's Journal* (Dublin), July 9, 1839.

23. Cincinnati *Enquirer,* March 22, 1904; New York *Daily News,* March 21, 1904.

24. Advertisements of William Russell Grace & Co., *The Nation* (Dublin), various dates from July to November 1850; note on mode of operation of passage brokers, T. P. O'Neill of the Irish Historical Society to the writer.

25. Advertisements of William Russell Grace & Co., *The Nation,* various dates from July to November 1850.

26. *Ibid.,* July 20, 1850.

27. *Ibid.,* October 5, 1850.

28. *Ibid.*

29. From a memorandum, dated February 18, 1946, from Doctor Manuel C. Gallagher of Lima, a grandson of Doctor John Gallagher. Doctor Gallagher is a distinguished attorney who has held high posts in the Peruvian government.

30. London *Times,* April 10 and October 28, 1851; Edward Eyre, "Early Reminiscences of the Grace Organization," an unpublished account by a nephew of W. R. Grace who went to Peru under Grace auspices in 1873. Hereafter cited as Eyre manuscript.

31. Quoted from the London *Times,* October 18, 1851.

32. M. P. Grace to J. W. Grace, August 21, 1873, Grace Papers.

~ CHAPTER 2

1. Eyre manuscript; Manuel Gallagher memorandum; Wilhelm, 144; James Grace to John Bryce, November 11, 1851, Grace Papers. In this communication, written when the colony was less than four months old, Grace mentioned the effects of illness on the colonists and added that he was getting rid of others because of an "indisposition to work."

2. Percy F. Martin, *Peru of the Twentieth Century* (1911), 67.

3. William R. Manning, editor, *Diplomatic Correspondence of the United States* (1938), X, 540. Hereafter cited as *Diplomatic Correspondence.*

4. Carl C. Cutler, *Greyhounds of the Sea* (1930), 152, 362, 373.

5. Eyre manuscript; "Reminiscences of Mrs. W. R. Grace, May 24, 1921," an unpublished memoir, written from her dictation. Hereafter cited as Mrs. Grace, "Reminiscences." Eyre refers to the original firm as that of Pablo Vivero, but Romero is correct. Judging from advertisements in *Gazeta Mercantil* of Lima, the firm did a large business in the 1830s when Bryce went to work there. Records preserved in the Callao office of W. R. Grace & Co. show that Marguerita Romero, Pablo's widow, took an active part in the firm's affairs as late as 1850.

6. George W. Peck, *Melbourne and the Chincha Islands* (1854), 143–46.

7. Years later, when W. R. Grace had located in New York, a friend of his early days in Callao wrote about the racing situation there in a vein that suggests that Grace had been *au courant* with turf affairs in Peru. (G. T. Mayne to W. R. Grace, August 20, 1870, Grace Papers.)

8. Frederick Walpole, *Four Years in the Pacific* (1849), II, chapters 1 and 2; Charles Darwin, *Journal of . . . the Voyage of H. M. S. Beagle* (1846), II, 131; A. J. Duffield, *Peru in the Guano Age* (1877), 13–14, 45–47; New York *Times,* December 6, 15, 1868. For certain details of the description of Lima the writer also is indebted to conversations with Limenians who know the city as of the period under review.

9. E. R. Cummins to W. R. Grace, May 10, 1869, Grace Papers.

10. J. P. Grace to the writer. In 1899, J. P. Grace visited Guayaquil for the first time and found several importing houses who had been Grace customers since his father's visit forty-five years before.

11. Boston *Pilot,* February 26, 1887, a reprint from the *American Exporter.*

12. Martin, 67–68; Duffield, 16; Dana Gardner Munro, *The Latin American Republics* (1942), 330–32.

13. *Diplomatic Correspondence* X, 659, 756, 765–66, 778, 793–98.

14. *Ibid.,* X, 686, 750, 759, 767, 770.

15. Roy F. Nichols, "Latin American Guano Diplomacy," in A. Curtis Wilgus, editor, *Studies in Hispanic American Affairs* (1933), 517–22.

16. *Diplomatic Correspondence* X, 248–49.

17. *Ibid.,* X, 249, 592, 595, 598–600, 602–8, 616–17, 636–41, 644–51.

18. *Ibid.,* X, 636, 663.

19. New York *Times,* April 12, 1868; Mrs. Grace, "Reminiscences"; *State Department Documents, U. S. Foreign Affairs, 1857–59,* XLVIII, pt. 3, p. 63; Peck, 206–13.

20. *Diplomatic Correspondence* I, 647; Duffield, 89; *State Department Documents, op. cit.,* XLVIII, pt. 3, p. 21; New York *Times,* April 12, 1868. When the writer passed the Chincha Islands in 1947, twenty miles at sea, they appeared "perfectly white." Having been scraped bare in 1869, the islands are producing guano again—under Peruvian government supervision which affords protection to the indispensable sea birds.

21. Mrs. Grace, "Reminiscences"; Eyre manuscript.

22. New York *Times,* April 12, 1869; Mrs. Grace, "Reminiscences"; a manuscript by Lilias Grace Kent of recollections of her mother's stories of her early years. Hereafter cited as Mrs. Kent, "Recollections." The writer also has drawn on the substance of letters in the Grace Papers to W. R. Grace from sea-captain friends.

23. Winthrop L. Marvin, *The American Merchant Marine* (1903), 267–68, quoting Lindsay, British merchant-marine historian.

~ CHAPTER 3

1. Mrs. Grace, "Reminiscences"; Lilias Grace Kent, "Recollections"; *The Grace Log* (house organ of W. R. Grace & Co.), November–December 1922; Burton. Characterizations of Mary Jane and Lillius Gilchrest are drawn from a wealth of correspondence in the Grace Papers.
2. Mrs. Grace, "Reminiscences"; Basil Lubbock, *The Down Easters* (1929), 27.
3. George W. Gilchrist (*sic*) pledge, dated October 8, 1828, collection of J. P. Grace.
4. Gilchrest family records, *ibid.*; Lilias Grace Kent to B. R. James.
5. Burton; Lilias Grace Kent to B. R. James; Lilias Grace Kent, "Recollections"; Eyre manuscript.
6. J. P. Grace to the writer; J. C. Smith to W. R. Grace, September 20, 1858, Grace Papers.
7. Consular records, Callao, volume 3, National Archives, Washington.
8. Mrs. Grace, "Reminiscences"; New York *Times*, April 12, 1868; John Brown to Michael P. Grace, dated Chincha Islands, May 24, 1865, Grace Papers. Captain Brown, an American shipmaster, wrote: "Mrs B. is quite well. No increase in the Brown family yet but in daily expectations."
9. Lilias Grace Kent, "Recollections."
10. *Diplomatic Correspondence* X, 810, 850–51; New York *Times*, December 3, 4, 1860.
11. Lilias Grace Kent, "Recollections."
12. Mrs. Grace, "Reminiscences."
13. Eyre manuscript.
14. J. P. Grace to the writer.
15. Various correspondence of W. R. Grace, Grace Papers; Registry of Deeds, Henrietta Street, Dublin, 1863, Book 26, No. 31; Wilhelm, 176–77.
16. Eyre manuscript; Wilhelm, 178.
17. W. R. Grace to B. Burney, February 26, 1864; to Alfred Stevens, March 28, 1864; to R. A. Davis, October 3, 1864: Grace Papers.
18. W. R. Grace to James Ross, March 10, 1864; to Charles Evans, March 17, April 11, 1864; to Alfred Stevens, March 28, 1864; to M. I. Hamilton, April 12, 1864: *ibid.*; Lilias Grace Kent, "Recollections."
19. Mrs. Grace, "Reminiscences"; Lilias Grace Kent, "Recollections."
20. W. R. Grace to R. A. Davis, December 3, 1864, Grace Papers.
21. Various letters of W. R. Grace, 1864, *ibid.*
22. W. R. Grace to Page Richardson & Co., February 28, 1864; to Washington Ryan, May 24, 1864: *ibid.*
23. William H. Prescott, *The Conquest of Peru* (1847), book I, *passim*; C. Reginald Enoch, *Peru* (1912), 14–30.
24. Watt Stewart, *Henry Meiggs, Yankee Pizarro* (1946), 71; A. P. Hovey to W. H. Seward, January 14, 1867, State Department Papers, Foreign Relations, volume 21, National Archives, Washington.

25. Stewart, 32, 39.
26. Manuel Pardo, *Estudio sobre la Provincia de Juaja* (1862), *passim*; Jorge Basadre, *Historia de la Republica del Perú* (third edition, 1946), II, 62–63; Stewart, 68–74.
27. *Ibid.*, 41–43.
28. Francis Bryce to Seymour, Peacock & Co., December 28, 1864; W. R. Grace to Snow & Burgess, January 13, March 13, March 28, 1865; to George Seymour, February 27, 1865; to Francis Bryce, September 1, November 1, 1865; Francis Bryce to W. R. Grace, July 13, September 25, October 12, November 27, 1865: Grace Papers.

~ CHAPTER 4

1. Burton; J. P. Grace to B. R. James; Charles R. Flint, *Memories of an Active Life* (1923), 5–6, 20.
2. Richard C. McKay, *South Street* (1934), 417–24; W. W. Bates, *Our Early Shipping Policy* (1897), *passim*.
3. Marvin, 319–53; United States Works Progress Administration, *A Maritime History of New York* (1941), 180–84.
4. A. N. Miller to W. R. Grace, March 12, 1869, Grace Papers; Cincinnati *Enquirer,* March 28, 1904. An article about Mr. Grace by his friend Doctor E. J. Edwards, who signed himself "Holland."
5. J. P. Grace to B. R. James; *The Grace Log,* May–June 1923; G. C. Smalley to W. R. Grace, August 18, 1869, Grace Papers.
6. "William R. Grace in a/c. current with M. P. Grace 1867–68," Grace Papers. The writer is indebted to G. Spottiswoode, of W. R. Grace & Co., for an interpretation of this record.
7. Eyre manuscript; articles of agreement, dated Lima, March 13, 1868, Grace Papers. In the body of the document, July 1, 1867, is given as the date of the inception of the partnership.
8. W. R. Grace to M. P. Grace, August 30, 1869; M. P. Grace to W. R. Grace (two letters), October 13, 1869; J. H. Brown to W. R. Grace, April 30, 1869: Grace Papers.
9. John Bryce to W. R. Grace, December 29, 1868, *ibid.*
10. A. P. Hovey to Hamilton Fish, August 22, 1870, United States State Department, *Papers Relating to Foreign Relations,* 1870, part II, 505–6; Basadre, 421–26; T. J. Hutchinson, *Two Years in Peru* (1873), I, 234. Hovey waited six years, or until the eve of his retirement from office, to confess to his superior his violation of neutrality in support of Peru in 1866.
11. A. P. Hovey to W. H. Seward, January 27, 1867, *Papers Relating to Foreign Relations,* 1867, part II, 736–38.

12. A. P. Hovey to Hamilton Fish, August 22, 1870, *ibid.,* 1870, part II, 506.

13. J. A. García to W. R. Grace, May 26, 1869, Grace Papers.

14. New York *Times,* March 14, 1869; Paulding, Kimble & Co. to W. B. Hilton, March 5, 1869; J. A. García to W. R. Grace, March 20 and April 29, 1869; Bureau of Ordnance, United States Navy Department, to W. R. Grace, April 24, 1869: Grace Papers.

15. W. B. Hilton to W. R. Grace, December 15, December 30, 1868, January 3, 24, 1869; J. A. García to W. R. Grace, December 17, 1868, January 7, September 13, 1869: *ibid.*; New York *Times,* March 8, March 27, 1869.

16. A. P. Hovey to Hamilton Fish, August 22, 1870, United States State Department, *Papers Relating to Foreign Relations,* 1870, part II, 509.

17. Aurelio García to W. R. Grace, May 27, 1870, Grace Papers.

18. J. G. Meiggs to Henry Meiggs, August 1, November 1, 1867, Meiggs Papers, archives of Peruvian Corporation, Lima.

19. The original contract expressed monetary figures in *soles.* In 1868 a Peruvian *sole* was worth ninety-five cents.

20. Stewart, 43–52; A. P. Hovey to W. H. Seward, January 14, 1868, United States State Department, *Papers Relating to Foreign Relations,* 1868, part II, 841; Hovey to Hamilton Fish, August 22, 1870, *ibid.,* 1870, part II, 507.

21. New York *Times,* March 10, 1878.

22. A. P. Hovey to Hamilton Fish, August 22, 1870, United States State Department, *Papers Relating to Foreign Relations,* 1870, part II, 507; Stewart, 96.

~ CHAPTER 5

1. Stewart, 5–21, 26–28, 30–31, 34–37.

2. New York *Sun,* October 11, 1877.

3. M. P. Grace to W. R. Grace, April 14, 1869; G. T. Mayne to W. R. Grace, February 10, 1870: Grace Papers; A. P. Hovey to Hamilton Fish, August 22, 1870, United States State Department, *Papers Relating to Foreign Relations,* 1870, part II, 507.

4. W. R. Grace to Bryce, Grace & Co., February 27, 1869, Grace Papers. The holder of the notes was James Phelan, a fellow immigrant from Queens County, Ireland. A son of his, of the same name, was later a United States senator from California.

5. John Bryce to W. R. Grace, December 28, 1868, Grace Papers.

6. M. P. Grace to W. R. Grace, April 14 and October 13, 1869, *ibid.*

7. M. P. Grace to W. R. Grace, April 14, 1869, *ibid.*

8. Bryce, Grace & Co. to W. R. Grace, July 28, 1869; W. R. Grace to G. W. Gilchrest, July 2, 1869; J. R. Cushier to W. R. Grace, July 7, July 31, 1869,

January 11, 1871; Lydia Cushier to W. R. Grace, April 20, 1869; W. R. Grace to C. R. Flint, March 5, October 5, 1870: *ibid.*

9. J. W. Sheridan to W. R. Grace, December 18, 1868; W. R. Grace to C. R. Flint, March 7, 1870; C. R. Flint to W. R. Grace, June 14, 1871: *ibid.*; Flint, 8; New York *City Directory,* 1870–71, 1871–72.

10. John Bryce to W. R. Grace, October 5, November 22, 1870, July 30, November 9, 1871: Grace Papers; Stewart, 270.

11. Bryce, Grace & Co. to W. R. Grace, December 27, 1869, Grace Papers.

12. Stewart, 153; S. L. Crosby to W. R. Grace, January 23, 1871, Grace Papers.

13. Lydia Cushier to W. R. Grace, various letters, 1869–71, *ibid.*

14. S. L. Crosby to W. R. Grace, December 22, 1870, *ibid.*

15. S. L. Crosby to W. R. Grace, January 23, 1871, *ibid.*

16. Bryce, Grace & Co. to W. R. Grace, February 2, 1871, *ibid.*

17. Various letters, 1868–71, between W. R. Grace and M. P. Grace, *ibid.*; Eyre manuscript.

18. Bryce, Grace & Co. (Michael's handwriting) to W. R. Grace, October 13, 1869; C. R. Flint to W. R. Grace, June 14, 1871; W. R. Grace to C. R. Flint, May 12, 20, 1871; E. P. Fabbri to W. R. Grace, June 14, 1871; John Bryce to W. R. Grace, July 30, 1871: Grace Papers. No articles of agreement continuing the partnership can be found. Grace's letter to Flint of May 20 mentions the increase in capitalization to "280,000 soles." Later correspondence (notably to M. P. Grace, February 14, 1873) reveals that this was a slip of the pen for $280,000.

19. Stewart, 115, 121, 125, 129–51; New York *Sun,* October 11, 1877.

20. *Scribner's Monthly,* July 1877; New York *World,* October 12, 1877.

21. Stewart, 173–85.

22. New York *Sun,* October 11, 1877; Stewart, 47, 247–49.

23. M. P. Grace to W. R. Grace, September 22, 1871; J. G. Meiggs to W. R. Grace, November 21, 1870; Bryce, Grace & Co. (Michael's handwriting), October 21, 1871: Grace Papers.

24. M. P. Grace to W. R. Grace, September 22, 1871; Bryce, Grace & Co. (Michael's handwriting) to W. R. Grace, October 21, 1871: *ibid.*

25. J. G. Meiggs to W. R. Grace, January 21, 1872; Dreyfus Brothers & Co. to W. R. Grace, September 1, 1871: *ibid.*; Stewart, 266–72.

26. C. L. Aldana to W. R. Grace, January 21, 1872; Bryce, Grace & Co. (Michael's handwriting) to W. R. Grace, November 21, 1871; M. P. Grace to W. R. Grace, November 22, 1871: Grace Papers.

27. J. G. Meiggs to W. R. Grace, January 21, 1872, *ibid.* As only incoming letters in Grace's New York office have been preserved for this period, it has been necessary to reconstruct Grace's attitude toward Meiggs, his directions to the Callao office, etc., from the replies to his communications concerning such matters. This has been fairly easy to do.

28. W. R. Grace to Pope & Talbot (Grace's San Francisco agents), August 31, 1871; Bryce, Grace & Co. to W. R. Grace, November 21, 1871; M. P. Grace to W. R. Grace, November 22, 1871, April 23, 1872; John Bryce to W. R. Grace, March 25, 1872; Federico Blume to W. R. Grace, June 9, 1872: Grace Papers.

29. John Bryce to W. R. Grace, November 24, 1871, February 29, 1872: *ibid.*

30. Stewart, 273, 280; John Bryce to W. R. Grace, February 20, 1872, Grace Papers.

31. J. G. Meiggs to W. R. Grace, January 21, May 21, 1872; Antonio A. dela Plaza to W. R. Grace, May 3, 1872; William & Roberts (Grace's Liverpool agents) to W. R. Grace, January 16, May 7, 1872; S. D. Hazen to W. R. Grace, June 14, 1872: *ibid.*; Stewart, 273.

32. M. P. Grace to W. R. Grace, May 23, June 23, 1872: Grace Papers.

33. Stewart, 283; Federico Blume to W. R. Grace, June 21, July 13, 1872, Grace Papers.

34. M. P. Grace to W. R. Grace, May 23, 1872; S. D. Hazen to W. R. Grace, July 8, 1872; Federico Blume to W. R. Grace, July 12, 1872: *ibid.* The statement about Michael's frequent visits to the presidential palace rests on the assertion of Blume. Michael's letters do not mention them, though they make clear his leanings in the electoral campaign.

~ CHAPTER 6

1. H. M. Keith to W. R. Grace, July 21, September 20, 1871; M. P. Grace to W. R. Grace, July 22, 1871; J. G. Meiggs to W. R. Grace, September 12, 1871; M. Baird & Co. to W. W. Evans, October 3, 1871: Grace Papers. Evans, an engineer, was an adviser to Meiggs, Spinney, and Grace on technical purchases.

2. J. G. Meiggs to W. R. Grace, September 21, 1871; H. M. Keith to W. R. Grace, September 25, 1871: *ibid.*; J. B. Blair to Hamilton Fish, September 13, 1871, United States State Department, *Papers Relating to Foreign Relations, 1871*, part II, 252.

3. Samuel Crowther, *The Romance and Rise of the American Tropics* (1929), 143–44; N. Hoatling to W. R. Grace, December 4, 1871, Grace Papers.

4. J. G. Meiggs to W. R. Grace, November 21, 1871; H. M. Keith to W. R. Grace, undated; W. H. Russell to W. R. Grace, February 7, 1872: *ibid.*

5. H. M. Keith to W. R. Grace, November 30, December 8, 23, 30, 1871: ibid.

6. Guillermo Nanne to W. R. Grace, December 11, 1871; E. E. Verebely to W. R. Grace, December 30, 1871: *ibid.*

7. Jackson & Sharp Co. to W. R. Grace, December 20, 1872; Guillermo Nanne to W. R. Grace, October 22, November 1, 1872; H. M. Keith to W. R. Grace, April 10, 1872; Mc. W. Gray to W. R. Grace, September 15, 1872: *ibid.*; New

York *World*, February 22, March 10, 1873. Grace had nothing to do with the labor or opium contracts, though he was informed of them. Keith told Grace the Chinese were for work on the coffee plantations, and this was doubtless his original intention. They were used on the railroads, however.

8. Williams & Roberts to W. R. Grace, January 2, 20, 1872; S. W. D. Jackson to W. R. Grace, November 13, 1871; H. M. Keith to W. R. Grace, May 12, September 9, 1872; M. C. Keith to W. R. Grace, December 4, 10, 1872; M. C. Keith & Co. to W. R. Grace, February 4, 1873; W. R. Grace to J. G. Meiggs, March 10, 1873; Guillermo Nanne to W. R. Grace, October 5, 1873: Grace Papers.

9. H. M. Keith to W. R. Grace, May 12, June 16, 1872: *ibid.*

10. W. R. Grace to C. R. Flint, July 19, 25, 26, 1872; C. A. Arthur to A. O. Vanderpool, July 12, 1872: *ibid.*; New York *Herald,* July 18, 1872; *Harper's Weekly,* August 10, 1872.

11. R. M. Douglas to W. R. Grace, July 17, August 20, 1872; J. H. Blackfan (superintendent of foreign mails) to W. R. Grace, October 18, 1872: Grace Papers.

12. W. R. Grace to S. D. Hazen, October 24, 1872, *ibid.*

13. Guillermo Nanne to W. R. Grace, May 13, July 16, 1872; Ezekiel Gutiérrez (secretary to H. M. Keith) to W. R. Grace, October 12, 1872: *ibid.*; *Money Market Review* (London), February 7, 1874.

14. W. R. Grace to Guillermo Nanne, October 24, 1872; W. R. Grace to M. P. Grace, November 25, December 10, 1872; Guillermo Nanne to W. R. Grace, December 5, 1872; H. D. B. Norris to W. R. Grace, December 26, 1872; W. R. Grace to J. G. Meiggs, November 20, 1872; Tomás Guardia to W. R. Grace, January 28, 1873: Grace Papers.

15. Bryce, Grace & Co. to W. R. Grace, July 20, 1872, *ibid.*; Stewart, 284.

16. D. J. Williamson to W. R. Grace, July 25, 1872; Bryce, Grace & Co. to W. R. Grace, July 22, 27, 1872; S. D. Hazen to W. R. Grace, July 27, 1872: Grace Papers; Faustino Silva, *Revolución de Julio* (1924), *passim*; New York *Times*, August 19, 1872; Stewart, 285–86.

17. Bryce, Grace & Co. to W. R. Grace, August 7, 1872; W. R. Grace to M. P. Grace, October 11, 1872: Grace Papers

18. S. D. Hazen to W. R. Grace, August 26, 1872, *ibid.*

19. Stewart, 289–93; New York *Times*, December 2, 1872; John Bryce to W. R. Grace, July 18, 1872; clipping from an unnamed Peruvian newspaper, February 21, 1873: Grace Papers.

20. W. R. Grace to M. P. Grace, January 31, 1873, December 31, 1872, February 19, 1873, *ibid.*

21. Bryce, Grace & Co. to W. R. Grace, February 5, 14, 28, 1873; J. G. Meiggs to W. R. Grace, February 13, 1873; M. P. Grace to W. R. Grace, February 28, 1873: *ibid.*

22. W. R. Grace to M. P. Grace, February 14, 19, 1873, *ibid.* In the first letter William's emotion is shown by a jumbling of topics that was rare for Grace. No matter how complex or varied the subject, he usually wrote well-ordered and clear letters. To render his thought more readily intelligible the writer has rearranged the sequence of some of the sentences quoted.

23. W. R. Grace to C. E. Pratt, June 11, 1872; to S. D. Hazen, January 31, 1873; to H. J. Moody, October 15, 1872; to G. W. Gilchrest, September 24, 1874: *ibid.*; J. P. Grace to B. R. James.

24. Various letters, Grace Papers; Lilias Grace Kent to B. R. James.

25. Louise Grace, a daughter of W. R. Grace, to B. R. James; J. P. Grace to the writer.

26. Louise Grace to B. R. James; concerning the purchase and first putting to rights of the new place, a numerous collection of letters between W. R. Grace and T. J. Northall, L. Kane, G. W. Gilchrest, J. W. Grace, Pat Delaney, 1871–74: Grace Papers.

27. J. P. Grace to B. R. James.

28. W. R. Grace to S. D. Hazen, January 31, 1873; Mother Superior Francis Xavier Warde to W. R. Grace, January 9, 24, 1871; J. S. McLellan to W. R. Grace, February 2, 1871; Father Farley to W. R. Grace, August 31, 1871; Sister M. Camilus to W. R. Grace, August 25, October 11, 1871: Grace Papers.

29. Various letters Edna Norris, Lillie T. Keith, Emily Jarvis, F. J. Kurtze, Elena L. A. de Gonzales, and Eduardo Gonzales to W. R. Grace, 1871–74, *ibid.*

30. J. W. Grace to M. S. Grace, undated; various letters J. W. Grace to W. R. Grace, 1872–73; M. P. Grace to W. R. Grace, June 23, 1872; W. R. Grace to M. P. Grace, February 14, March 22, 1873: *ibid.*

~ *CHAPTER 7*

1. Quoted from Samuel Eliot Morison, *A Maritime History of Massachusetts* (1921), 373. Mr. Morison points out that chanteys, the productions of unlettered and unknown seamen, comprise the best poetry of America's golden age of sail.

2. *Ibid.*, 352–57.

3. *Ibid.*, 257, 354. In 1947 the writer had the accidental good fortune to travel to and from the west coast of South America in Grace ships commanded by veteran masters of the vanishing school of sea captains who began their careers as foremast hands in sail. Captain Vladimir Cernescu of the *Santa Isabel*, a native of Rumania, ran off to sea when he was fourteen. Captain Duncan Cook of the *Santa Barbara,* born in Scotland, was introduced to the forecastle when he was sixteen. They were kind enough to read the manuscript of this chapter and, after some urging, to offer helpful suggestions.

4. L. H. Stevens to W. R. Grace, December 27, 1873; A. J. Brown to W. R. Grace, November 3, 1869: Grace Papers.

5. Mary Watkins to James E. Watkins, undated but written in England in January 1876, *ibid.*

6. Grace Papers.

7. Elizabeth Hall to W. R. Grace, January 13, 1877; Eliza Kelly to W. R. Grace, October 28, 1870: *ibid.*

8. M. E. Weymouth to Bryce, Grace & Co., June 6, 1869; to W. R. Grace, June 10, 1869: *ibid.* The latter letter contains a notation of Grace's reply.

9. D. Baker to W. R. Grace, March 19, 1871, *ibid.*

10. Mrs. C. G. Godfrey to W. R. Grace, May 26, 1870; W. R. Grace to H. D. B. Norris, December, 1872; Norris to Grace, March 16, 1873; M. J. Hamilton to W. R. Grace, January 24, 1874; Mrs. C. G. Hamilton to W. R. Grace, January 26, 1874: *ibid.*

11. Morison, 351; W. A. Lord to W. R. Grace, July 18, 1870, Grace Papers.

12. Burgess Wingate to W. R. Grace, March 3, 1872, *ibid.*

13. F. A. Soule to C. R. Flint, January 20, June 26, 1870, *ibid.*

14. N. P. Caner to W. R. Grace, November 28 and December 8, 1870, *ibid.*

15. C. K. Limstrong to W. R. Grace, May 13, 1873, *ibid.*

16. Lubbock, *The Down Easters,* 89. The reputation of the *M. P. Grace* seems to have had contemporaneous repercussions on Michael Grace himself. The author just cited does not appear to have known that Michael was a brother of W. R. Grace. He refers to him as "Mike Grace, the Irish-American millionaire who became notorious at one time for sundry escapades in Europe." Though, as we shall see, Michael eventually went to live in England, nothing in his behavior there that this writer has discovered is deserving of such characterization.

17. "William R. Grace in a/c current with M. P. Grace, 1867–68," Grace Papers.

18. H. M. Nickels to W. R. Grace, October 13, 1868, *ibid.*

19. A. N. Miller to W. R. Grace, February 13, March 12, July 2, 1869, *ibid.*

20. A. N. Miller to W. R. Grace, November 14, 1869, *ibid.*

21. R. J. Hancock to W. R. Grace, October 20, 1869; W. R. Grace to Mrs. H. M. Nickels, November 11, 1869; A. N. Miller to W. R. Grace, November 23, 1869, January 9, 1870; Gillchrest & Patton to W. R. Grace, November 15, 1869; R. Gillchrest to W. R. Grace, November 15, 16, 1869: *ibid.* The Gillchrests of Gillchrest & Patton, ship brokers of Liverpool, were not related to W. R. Grace's father-in-law.

22. W. R. Grace to C. R. Flint, February 28, March 1, 3, 1870; A. N. Miller, May 20, 1870: Grace Papers.

23. Bryce, Grace & Co. to W. R. Grace, February 20, 1871, *ibid.*

24. S. C. Jordan to W. R. Grace, June 9, 25, August 6, 1870; W. Gillchrest to W. R. Grace, June 16, 1870; T. R. Herbert (with enclosures) to W. R. Grace, June 25, 1870: *ibid.*

25. S. C. Jordan to W. R. Grace, July 16, 1870; Bryce, Grace & Co. to W. R. Grace, February 20, 1871; T. R. Herbert to W. R. Grace, March 20, 1871: *ibid.*

26. M. P. Grace to W. R. Grace, July 27, 1871; W. R. Grace to C. R. Flint, April 18, 1871; W. R. Grace to M. P. Grace, August 16, 1871: *ibid.*

27. Bryce, Grace & Co. to W. R. Grace, February 20, 1871, *ibid.*

28. Basil Lubbock, *Nitrate Clippers* (1935), 4, 35–36.

29. J. R. Law to M. P. Grace, July 10, 1870, Grace Papers.

30. R. C. Mears to W. R. Grace & Co., May 25, 1872, *ibid.*

31. R. C. Mears to W. R. Grace & Co., August 5, 1872, *ibid.*

32. R. C. Mears to W. R. Grace & Co., February 19–20, 1873, *ibid.*; Lewis Mumford, *Herman Melville* (1931), 36.

33. R. C. Mears to W. R. Grace & Co., February 19–20, 1873, Grace Papers. Excepting deletions as indicated and some changes in punctuation, the only liberties the writer has taken with Captain Mears's letter has been to alter the sequence of a few of his sentences.

34. Report of the United States Shipping Commissioner for the Port of New York, Charles C. Duncan, January 1, 1876, *ibid.*

~ CHAPTER 8

1. W. R. Grace to M. P. Grace, February 14, 1873, Grace Papers.

2. *Ibid.*

3. Bryce, Grace & Co. to W. R. Grace & Co., April 12, 1873; W. R. Grace to J. G. Meiggs, March 10, 1873; J. G. Meiggs to W. R. Grace, November 10, 1873; M. P. Grace to W. R. Grace, August 14, 1873: Grace Papers.

4. Emiliano Llona to W. R. Grace & Co., January 11, 1873; W. R. Grace to John Bryce, August 26, 1874; M. P. Grace to W. R. Grace, August 14, 1873: *ibid.*; Richard Gibbs to W. M. Evarts, April 26, 1878, Diplomatic Despatches, XXX, National Archives.

5. M. P. Grace to W. R. Grace, November 14, 1873; W. R. Grace to M. P. Grace, December 19, 1873: Grace Papers.

6. C. R. Flint to W. R. Grace & Co., April 20, May 27, 1874, *ibid.*

7. Stewart, 224, 229, 295–98; C. R. Flint to W. R. Grace & Co., June 12, 16, 1874, Grace Papers.

8. C. R. Flint to W. R. Grace & Co., June 5, 13, 20, 1874, *ibid.*

9. W. R. Grace to Bryce, Grace & Co., September 4, 1874; to John Bryce, August 26, 1874: *ibid.*

10. W. R. Grace to John Bryce, August 26, 1874; to M. P. Grace, September 3, 1874: *ibid.*

11. John Bryce to W. R. Grace, August 24, 1874; W. R. Grace to John Bryce, September 16, 1874; to M. P. Grace, September 24, 1874: *ibid.*

12. W. R. Grace to M. P. Grace, October 5, 1874, *ibid.*
13. W. R. Grace to W. R. Grace & Co., October 19, 1874, *ibid.*
14. W. R. Grace to W. R. Grace & Co., October 19, November 5, 1874; to H. J. Moody, November 12, 1874: *ibid.*
15. W. R. Grace to W. R. Grace & Co., October 19, November 23, 1874: *ibid.*
16. W. R. Grace to W. R. Grace & Co., October 21, 31, November 4, 5, 23, 1874: *ibid.*
17. W. R. Grace to H. J. Moody, November 12, 1874, *ibid.*
18. M. P. Grace to W. R. Grace, December 6, 1874; W. R. Grace & Co. to W. R. Grace, December 11, 1874: *ibid.*
19. W. R. Grace to W. R. Grace & Co., March 6, March 13, 1875: *ibid.*
20. M. P. Grace to W. R. Grace, May 13, 1875, *ibid.*
21. W. R. Grace & Co. to S. G. and C. G. Ward, December 21, 1875; W. R. Grace to M. P. Grace, January 13, 1876: *ibid.*
22. Stewart, 314–17; M. P. Grace to W. R. Grace, January 28, 1877; W. R. Grace to M. P. Grace, January 29, 1876: Grace Papers.
23. C. H. Watson to J. S. Spinney, July 20, August 20, 1877, Meiggs Papers, Lima.
24. C. H. Watson to J. G. Meiggs, August 12, 1877, *ibid.*; M. P. Grace to W. R. Grace, September 13, 1877, Grace Papers.
25. M. P. Grace to W. R. Grace, August 28, September 13, 21, 1877: *ibid.*; Basadre, II, 50.
26. W. R. Grace to M. P. Grace, June 10, 1873, July 13, 1875; J. G. Meiggs to W. R. Grace, July 13, 1873; Guillermo Nanne to W. R. Grace, July 15, 1873; W. R. Grace to W. R. Grace & Co., July 14, 1873: Grace Papers.
27. Guillermo Nanne to W. R. Grace, October 10, 1875; Grace's reply, October 29: *ibid.*
28. Various letters between M. C. Keith and W. R. Grace & Co., 1872–75; W. R. Grace to W. R. Grace & Co., January 27, 1875: *ibid.*
29. A. K. Brown to W. R. Grace & Co., February 10, 16, 22, April 16, 1876: *ibid.*
30. M. C. Keith to W. R. Grace & Co., February 16, 1876, *ibid.*
31. H. D. B. Norris to W. R. Grace, September 9, 1876, *ibid.*

~ CHAPTER 9

1. W. R. Grace to M. P. Grace, November 2, 1873, Grace Papers.
2. C. R. Flint to W. R. Grace & Co., July 9, 1874; S. D. Hazen to C. R. Flint, December 13, 1873, March 20, 1874: *ibid.*
3. C. R. Flint to W. R. Grace & Co., July 9, 1874, *ibid.*
4. C. R. Flint to W. R. Grace & Co., June 26, July 3, July 18, 1874, *ibid.*
5. Various correspondence 1877–78, W. R. Grace & Co., Grace Brothers & Co., Baring Brothers & Co.: *ibid.*

6. Luis Galdames, *A History of Chile,* translated by Isaac Joslin Cox (1941), 169, 224, 323–24; S. D. Hazen to W. R. Grace, October 25, 1874, Grace Papers.

7. Various letters and cables exchanged among W. R. Grace & Co., Grace Brothers & Co., and Baring Brothers & Co., November 1878 to February 1879; see especially, W. R. Grace & Co. to Grace Brothers & Co., December 26, January 8 and 9; to Baring Brothers & Co., January 8; see also, W. R. Grace to C. R. Flint, December 24, 1878: *ibid.* See also, Michael P. Grace, "The Evolution of W. R. Grace & Co.," *The Grace Log,* June 1918.

8. W. R. Grace to F. R. Coudert, February 14, 1882; to M. P. Grace, April 14, 1879: Grace Papers.

9. W. R. Grace to M. I. Prado, June 9, 1879, *ibid.*

10. W. R. Grace to M. P. Grace, April 14, 1879, *ibid.*

11. W. R. Grace & Co. to Grace Brothers & Co., April 10, 1879, *ibid.*

12. W. R. Grace to Grace Brothers & Co., March 31, May 29, 1879; to M. P. Grace, May 31, July 19, 1879: *ibid.*

13. W. R. Grace & Co. to S. F. Chester and William Lee, April 10, 1879; to Grace Brothers & Co., April 10, 21, 1879; H. D. Winston to S. F. Chester, May 1, 1879; W. R. Grace to M. P. Grace, June 9, 1879: *ibid.*

14. Flint, 85–86.

15. C. R. Flint to Enrique Lara, June 1, 1879; W. R. Grace & Co. to Grace Brothers & Co., June 20, 1879; W. R. Grace to Enrique Lara, July 1, 1879; to P. G. de Paredes, July 10, 1879; de Paredes's reply, August 6: Grace Papers.

16. Enoch, 79–81; New York *Times,* July 3, 1879.

17. W. R. Grace to M. P. Grace, May 31, 1879; W. R. Grace & Co. to Grace Brothers & Co., June 19, 1879; W. R. Grace to Enrique Lara, June 25, 1879; C. R. Flint to M. P. Grace, June 30, 1879: Grace Papers.

18. W. R. Grace to M. P. Grace, August 7, 13, 1879; to J. F. Canevaro, August 25, 1879: *ibid.*; Flint, 87. For accounts of Read, who deserves more attention from historians, see *South Atlantic Quarterly,* October 1929, and *Munsey's* magazine, July 1916.

19. W. R. Grace & Co. to Grace Brothers & Co., August 20, 1879; W. R. Grace to Carlos Pividal, August 25, 1879: Grace Papers.

20. W. R. Grace to M. P. Grace, September 4, 1879; New York *World,* April 25, 1886.

21. F. H. Snyder to "Dear Brother," October 1, 1879; F. H. Snyder to "Dear Friend," November 15, 1879: *ibid.*

22. New York *World,* April 25, 1886; F. H. Snyder to "Dear Friend," November 15, 1879, Grace Papers.

23. W. R. Grace & Co. to Grace Brothers & Co., January 26, 1880; W. R. Grace to L. G. Astete, February 28, 1880: *ibid.*

24. W. R. Grace to J. W. Grace, November 29, 1879; to M. P. Grace, December 26, 1879; to Ellen Grace, December 17, 1879: *ibid.*

25. Many letters between W. R. Grace & Co., C. R. Flint, and various correspondents, including John Ericsson, 1879–1880, *ibid.*

26. Various letters exchanged among the New York, Callao, and San Francisco houses, and among the Grace brothers, W. R., M. P., and J. W., 1873–1880; the letter quoted is dated December 20, 1879: *ibid.*

27. Various letters between W. R. Grace & Co. and Baring Brothers & Co., 1879; the letter quoted is dated December 22, 1879: *ibid.*

28. W. R. Grace to M. S. Grace, November 15, 1879, *ibid.*

29. M. S. Grace to W. R. Grace, February 4, 1876, *ibid.*

30. W. R. Grace to M. S. Grace, November 15, 1879, March 3, 1880: *ibid.*

31. New York *Herald,* February 4, 1880.

32. W. R. Grace to M. P. Grace, February 12, 1880; to Edward O'Brien, February 27, 1880; to Editor, New York *Herald,* March 16, 1880; to L. P. Morton, March 18, 1880; to T. B. Connery, March 16, 17, 1880: Grace Papers; New York *Herald,* various dates, February–March 1880.

~ *CHAPTER 10*

1. Gustavus Myers, *Tammany Hall* (1917), 258–66; Matthew Josephson, *The Politicos* (1938), 216–24; Stephen Fiske, *Offhand Portraits of Prominent New Yorkers* (1884), 217–21, 324–28; New York *Tribune,* June 2, 1886; J. P. Grace to the writer.

2. New York *Herald,* August 21, 1878; C. R. Flint to M. P. Grace, August 21, 1878, Grace Papers; Myers, 259.

3. W. R. Grace to Eugene Kelly, December 1, 1879, Grace Papers.

4. W. R. Grace to G. A. Crosby, May 5, 1880, *ibid.*

5. Brooklyn *Eagle,* June 21, 1880; W. R. Grace to G. A. Crosby, May 5, 1880; to J. H. Rossiter, May 19, 1880; to John Kelly, October 2, 1879, May 25, 1880; to A. D. Payne, May 25, 1880: Grace Papers.

6. W. R. Grace to Samuel Watts, April 8, 1880; to J. H. Rossiter, May 19, 1880: *ibid.*

7. W. R. Grace to J. M. Forbes, April 30, May 13, 1880, *ibid.*

8. W. R. Grace to G. A. Crosby, May 5, 1880; to A. D. Payne, May 25, 1880: *ibid.*

9. W. R. Grace to Thomas Ruffin, April 30, May 13, 1880, *ibid.*

10. W. R. Grace to L. V. Baughman, May 3, 13, 1880, *ibid.*

11. W. R. Grace to G. A. Crosby, May 5, 1880, *ibid.*

12. Ellis Paxson Oberholtzer, *A History of the United States Since the Civil War* (1931), IV, 72–81, 92–95.

13. W. R. Grace to Henry Amy, June 15, 1880; to the proprietors of the Emery House, Cincinnati, June 15, 1880; to E. F. Winslow, June 16, 1880: Grace Papers.

14. Cincinnati *Enquirer,* June 20, 21, 1880; Cincinnati *Commercial,* same dates; Cincinnati *Daily Gazette,* June 19, 1880; W. R. Grace to M. P. Grace, July 12, 1880, Grace Papers.
15. Cincinnati *Daily Gazette,* June 19, 1880; Cincinnati *Commercial,* June 20, 21, 1880; Cincinnati *Enquirer,* same dates; New York *World,* June 19, 22, 1880; New York *Herald,* June 22, 1880.
16. New York *Times,* June 20, 21, 1880; New York *Herald,* June 22, 1880; New York *World,* June 21, 22, 1880.
17. New York *Herald,* June 21, 1880.
18. Cincinnati *Enquirer,* June 22, 1880; New York *Times,* same date; W. R. Grace to M. P. Grace, July 12, 1880, Grace Papers.
19. Brooklyn *Eagle,* June 21, 22, 1880; New York *Evening Post,* June 22, 1880; New York *World* and *Times,* same date; New York *Herald,* June 21, 1880; Cincinnati *Times,* same date; W. R. Grace to M. P. Grace, July 12, 1880, Grace Papers.
20. W. R. Grace to M. P. Grace, July 12, 1880, *ibid.*
21. New York *Times,* June 23, 1880; Brooklyn *Eagle,* same date; Cincinnati *Enquirer,* same date; W. R. Grace to J. H. Rossiter, July 8, 1880, Grace Papers.
22. W. R. Grace to M. P. Grace, June 28, July 12, 1880, *ibid.*
23. W. R. Grace to M. P. Grace, June 28, 29, 1880, Grace Papers; Lilias Grace Kent, "Recollections"; H. D. Baldwin to Jonathan Grossman; Brooklyn *Eagle,* July 29, 1880; New York *Evening Mail,* June 29, 30, 1880; New York *Herald,* June 30, 1880; New York *Times,* June 29, 30, 1880.
24. W. R. Grace to J. M. Forbes, July 8, 1880; to J. A. Donahue, Mrs. C. F. Batchelder and others, same date, Grace Papers; Burton.
25. W. R. Grace to M. P. Grace, August 21, September 25, 1880; to D. J. Williamson, December 20, 1880: Grace Papers.
26. Myers, 259; J. P. Grace to the writer.
27. New York *Times,* October 19, 20, 1880.
28. New York *Times,* October 20, 1880; New York *Tribune* and *Evening Post,* same date.
29. New York *Times,* October 19, 1880.
30. New York *Herald,* October 19, 1880; New York *World* and *Evening Post,* same date.
31. New York *World,* October 24, 1880.
32. *The Nation,* October 21, 28, 1880.
33. New York *Herald,* October 30, 1880.
34. New York *Times,* October 30, 1880.
35. *Ibid.,* October 26, 1880; New York *Tribune,* October 26, 27, 1880.
36. *Ibid.,* October 27, 1880.
37. New York *Times,* October 28, 1880.

38. New York *Tribune,* November 1, 1880.
39. W. R. Grace to M. P. Grace, September 25, 1880; to W. D. English and J. H. Rossiter, November 6, 1880: Grace Papers.
40. New York *Times,* November 3, 4, 6, 1880; New York *Evening Post,* November 3, 4, 1880; Fiske, 97; Burton; *Harper's Weekly,* November 15, 1884, p. 748; W. R. Grace to W. D. English and J. H. Rossiter, November 6, 1880, Grace Papers.
41. New York *Tribune,* January 6, 1881.
42. "W. R. Grace as Underwriters' Agent," a report by M. P. Grace, undated, Grace Papers.
43. New York *Tribune,* January 6, 1881.

~ CHAPTER 11

1. William L. Riordan, *Plunkitt of Tammany Hall* (1905), 182 ff.
2. New York *Herald,* November 10, 11, December 12, 1880; New York *Tribune,* November 22, 1880; *Truth* (New York), October 22, 1884.
3. New York *Tribune,* December 11, 12, 1880; New York *Herald,* same dates.
4. New York *Tribune,* December 13, 14, 15, 25, 1880; New York *Herald,* December 13, 14, 1880.
5. Burton; J. P. Grace to the writer.
6. New York *Tribune,* March 2, 1881.
7. W. R. Grace to F. A. Prince, March 19, 1881, Grace Papers.
8. New York *Times,* August 24, 1881.
9. New York *Herald,* March 19, April 7, 9, 13, 15, 1881; New York *World,* April 7, May 4, 1881.
10. New York *Times,* May 25, June 5, 1881; New York *World* and *Herald,* same dates.
11. New York *World,* May 7, 14, 1881; New York *Herald,* April 15, 1881.
12. New York *Times,* August 24, 1881; New York *Herald,* August 24, September 15, 1881.
13. New York *Times,* January–February, 1881; New York *Tribune,* same dates; New York *Herald,* September 14, 1881; Philadelphia *Press,* March 27, 1904; Syracuse *Post Standard,* same date.
14. New York *Times,* December 27–31, 1881.
15. New York *Herald,* New York *World,* April 29, 1881.
16. New York *World,* May 11, 1881.
17. New York *Times,* December 27–31, 1881; New York *Herald,* May 11, 14, 1882.
18. New York *Herald,* June 1, 1882.
19. *Truth,* October 22, 1884.

20. New York *Herald,* April 1, April 4, 1882; W. R. Grace, "Confined Naturalized Citizens in Ireland," Grace Papers; New York *Herald,* April 4, 1882.
21. New York *Herald,* March 9, 1882; New York *Commercial Advertiser,* April 12, 1882; W. R. Grace to J. W. Covert, April 13, 1882, Grace Papers.
22. New York *Times,* July 3, September 21, 1881, January 22, March 19, 1882; New York *Herald,* same dates.
23. W. R. Grace to E. A. Hart and others, October 26, 1881, Grace Papers.
24. New York *Times,* December 13, 1881; Philadelphia *Press,* March 27, 1904.
25. W. R. Grace to R. J. Morrison, October 8, 1881; to W. C. Kingsley, October 11, 1881; to D. E. Sickles, October 12, 1881; to J. H. L'Hommedieu, October 18, 1881: Grace Papers.
26. New York *Herald,* October 10, 1881.
27. New York *Sun,* September 20, 1882; W. R. Grace to C. A. Dana, same date, Grace Papers.
28. W. R. Grace to Henry Purroy, September 19, 1882, *ibid.*
29. Allan Nevins, *Grover Cleveland, A Study in Courage* (1933), 99–106; Myers, 261; New York *Herald,* September 23, 1882; New York *Times,* same date.
30. New York *Herald,* October 15, 24, 1882.
31. New York *Times,* October 16, 18, 20, 21, 24, 1882; New York *World* and *Herald,* same dates.
32. W. R. Grace, "Speech before Citizens' meeting at Cooper Institute," Grace Papers.
33. New York *Herald,* October 24, November 9, 1882; Myers, 262; W. R. Grace to J. P. Morgan (and others), October 31, 1882, Grace Papers.
34. New York *Mail and Express,* December 13, 14, 1882; W. R. Grace to J. S. Coleman, December 31, 1882, Grace Papers.
35. New York *Evening Post,* December 30, 1882.
36. New York *Staats-Zeitung,* December 3, 1882.
37. New York *Tribune,* January 2, 1883.
38. New York *Evening Post,* December 30, 1882; New York *Herald,* December 31, 1882.

~ CHAPTER 12

1. W. R. Grace to H. D. B. Norris, January 29, 1883, Grace Papers; Burton.
2. W. R. Grace to Manuel Llaguno, August 21, 1880; to J. W. Grace, August 31, 1881; M. P. Grace to J. W. Grace, December 30, 1880; to Ellen Grace, January 5, 1881: Grace Papers.
3. I. P. Christiancy to J. G. Blaine, May 4, 1881, United States State Department, *Papers Relating to Foreign Relations, 1881,* 899–904; M. P. Grace to

W. K. Rogers, January 29, 1881; various letters from Grace Brothers & Co., 1881: Grace Papers.

4. W. R. Grace & Co. to Baring Brothers & Co., March 18, June 22, 1881; M. P. Grace to Noel West, January 31, 1882: *ibid.*; Basadre, II, 185–86.

5. M. P. Grace to Mr. Petrie, July 12, 1881; to Grace Brothers & Co., December 1, 1881; to J. W. Grace, January 21, 1882; W. R. Grace & Co. to Grace Brothers & Co., November 22, 1881: Grace Papers; New York *Herald,* January 27–29, 1882; United States State Department *Documents,* Vol. 89, Report No. 1790 of the 47th Congress.

6. M. P. Grace to Noel West, January 31, 1882; to Edward Eyre, same date: Grace Papers.

7. M. P. Grace to J. W. Grace, February 10, 1882; J. W. Grace to M. P. Grace, April 8, 1882: *ibid.*; Basadre, II, 191.

8. J. W. Grace to M. P. Grace, March 2, 8, 1882, Grace Papers.

9. New York *Times,* March 1, 1883; M. P. Grace to Edward Eyre, same date, Grace Papers.

10. J. W. Grace to M. P. Grace, April 6, 1882; M. P. Grace to Edward Eyre, August 9, 17, 1883; to Nicolás de Piérola, May 28, 1883, *ibid.*; W. J. Dennis, *Documentary History of the Tacna-Arica Dispute* (1927), 220–24.

11. M. P. Grace to Edward Eyre, August 29, 1884; to J. F. Elmore, March 9, 1886; "Prospects of the Central Grinding Company to be Established on the Estate of Cartavio," manuscript copy dated July, 1886: *ibid.*

12. M. P. Grace to Edward Eyre, February 19, 20, 1883, January 30, August 29, September 19, 1884; to W. H. Cilley, March 5, September 4, October 30, 1883; to W. R. Grace, September 4, 1883: *ibid.*; New York *World,* October 12, 1877.

13. W. R. Grace to R. F. Sears, April 28, 1882, January 19, 1883, March 3, April 11, 1884: Grace Papers.

14. C. R. Flint to W. R. Grace & Co., June 26, 1874; W. R. Grace & Co. to Grace Brothers & Co., August 21, 1882; M. P. Grace to E. S. Moyna, February 21, 1883; to J. W. Grace, October 30, 1883; W. R. Grace to J. W. Grace, January 16, 1884: *ibid.*

15. Dwight C. Miner, *The Fight for the Panama Route* (1940), 3–23; Oberholtzer, IV, 706–12; New York *Times,* April 11, 1883. Grace did not overlook the advertising value of his dinner to the Grace business, particularly in Latin America. See his letter to J. W. Grace, April 10, 1883, Grace Papers.

~ CHAPTER 13

1. W. R. Grace to Grover Cleveland, February 5, 1883, Grace Papers.

2. W. R. Grace to J. R. McPherson, February 6, 1883; to Titus Sheard, February 20, 1884: *ibid.*

3. W. R. Grace to Theodore Roosevelt, April 10, 1884; to Oswald Ottendorfer, February 29, 1884; to C. A. Dana, July 7, 1884: *ibid.*

4. W. R. Grace to an unidentified friend, June 17, 1884, *ibid.*

5. W. R. Grace to Grover Cleveland, July 14, 1884; to C. R. Flint, September 22, 1884: *ibid.*

6. W. R. Grace to J. W. Grace, February 29, August 1, 1884, *ibid.*

7. W. R. Grace to T. L. James, May 14, 1884; to J. W. Grace, May 22, 1884: *ibid.*

8. Oberholtzer, IV, 166–67; Benson J. Lossing, *Our Country* (undated revised edition), 1811–12.

9. W. R. Grace to H. O. Thompson, September 15, 1884, Grace Papers.

10. W. R. Grace to Grover Cleveland, September 26, 1884, *ibid.*

11. W. R. Grace to W. R. Roberts, September 29, 1884; to A. P. Gorman, October 7, September 30, 1884; to J. P. Townsend, October 14, September 29, 1884; to S. L. M. Barlow, October 10, 1884; to W. D. English, September 29, 1884; to A. P. Gorman, October 10, 1884; to Grover Cleveland, September 29, October 9 (two letters), 1884: *ibid.*

12. W. R. Grace to Mrs. W. M. Ivins, November 7, 1884; to J. W. Grace, November 20, 1884; to W. L. Brown, November 8, 1884; to Daniel Manning, October 12, 1884; to Harold Frederic, November 18, 1884: *ibid.*; New York *Star,* October 21, 26, 1884; New York *Commercial Advertiser,* October 22, 1884; New York *Truth,* October 29, 1884; New York *Journal,* October 21, 24, 31, 1884.

13. New York *Evening Post,* December 30, 1884; New York *Journal,* October 21, 1884; New York *Sun,* October 22, 1884.

14. New York *Star,* October 29, 1884; New York *Tribune,* same date; New York *Times,* October 31, 1884; New York *Evening Post,* same date.

15. W. R. Grace to Daniel Manning, November 12, 1884, Grace Papers.

16. W. R. Grace to Dennis O'Brien, November 6, 1884; to W. L. Brown, November 8, 1884; to W. D. English, November 8, 1884: *ibid.*

17. New York *Evening Post,* December 30, 1884.

18. W. R. Grace to M. P. Grace, December 1 and 9, 1884, Grace Papers.

19. In any New York City newspaper from December 15 to 31, 1884, the course of the fight over the nominations can be traced. See especially editorial comment in *Times* and *Tribune,* December 16; *Evening Post,* December 17; *Commercial Advertiser, Times, World* and Brooklyn *Eagle,* December 31.

20. Various New York newspapers, January 2, 1885; New York *World,* August 2, 1886.

21. New York *Tribune,* January 13, 1886, June 21, 1885; New York *World,* September 1, 1886, June 18, 1885; New York *Guide,* July 4, 1885; New York *Sun,* May 20, 1888; W. R. Grace to G. F. Canfield, February 23, 1887, Grace Papers.

22. New York *Times,* June 30, 1885.

23. John Quinn to W. R. Grace, March 14, 1885, Municipal Library of New York; W. R. Grace to James Daly, February 24, 1885; to the *Times*, February 13, 1885; R. J. Morrison to Hugh McLaughlin, March 11, 1885: Grace Papers.

24. Burton; W. R. Grace to W. R. Roberts, March 19, 1886; to Harold Frederic, November 18, 1884: Grace Papers.

25. Allan Nevins, *Abram S. Hewitt* (1935), 496; New York *Herald*, June 17, 1885; New York *Tribune*, June 18, 1885.

26. Lossing, 1812; New York *Sun*, July 24, 1885; Brooklyn *Eagle*, April 27, 1887.

27. New York *News*, August 11, 1885; Brooklyn *Eagle*, April 27, 1897; New York *Sun*, April 18, 1897.

28. New York *Times*, January 2, 1886; New York *Commercial Advertiser*, August 7, 1885.

29. New York *Times*, April 24, 1888; New York *Graphic*, August 30, 1885; New York *Telegram*, April 21, 1888; New York *Commercial Advertiser*, April 27, 1888.

30. New York *Herald*, January 1, 1886; New York *Times*, January 2, 1886, April 24, 1884.

31. New York *Sun*, August 10, 1886; New York *Telegram*, July 20, 1886.

32. New York *Sun*, August 10, 1886; New York *Tribune*, August 3, 1886.

33. New York *Star*, December 5, 1885, September 25, 1886; New York *Sun*, December 1, 1885; New York *Times*, September 19, 1886; W. R. Grace to Oswald Ottendorfer, October 24, 1889; to Elliott Roosevelt, June 14 and June 28, 1886: Grace Papers.

34. New York *Tribune*, November 22, November 25, 1885; New York *World*, November 27, 1885; New York *Sun*, November 25, 1885; W. R. Grace to Oswald Ottendorfer, October 24, 1889, Grace Papers.

35. James W. Barrett, *The World, the Flesh and Messrs. Pulitzer* (1931), 13 ff; Nevins, *Cleveland*, 234–52.

36. New York *Herald*, November 29, 1885; New York *World*, November 30, 1885.

37. W. R. Grace to Ferdinand Ward, September 16, 1880; to Grant & Ward, June 6, 1882: Grace Papers.

38. New York *World*, November 30, 1885.

39. New York *Evening Post*, December 4, 1885.

40. New York *Tribune*, December 5, 1885; New York *World*, December 9, 1885.

41. New York *Tribune*, March 26, 1886.

42. The library of the state supreme court in the courthouse of New York County contains no record of the Grace *vs*. Pulitzer suit.

43. Document dated April 13, 1889, by which Grace released the Grant & Ward "estate" from a claim in the amount of $70,000, Grace Papers.

44. "Occasional" (W. S. Bissell) to Utica (New York) *Observer,* April 2, 1904.
45. W. R. Grace to W. R. Roberts, June 29, December 7, 1886: Grace Papers; New York *Journal,* September 13, 1886; New York *Herald,* September 19, 1886.
46. Nevins, *Hewitt,* 460–69; W. R. Grace to Grover Cleveland, November 3, 1886; to A. S. Hewitt, October 12, November 3, 1886; to W. R. Roberts, January 10, April 1, 1887: Grace Papers.
47. W. R. Grace to D. S. Lamont, March 10, 1887; to Grover Cleveland, July 13, 1888: *ibid.*
48. W. R. Grace to D. S. Lamont, February 4, 1888; to Grover Cleveland, August 4, 1888: *ibid.*
49. New York *Evening Telegram,* June 17, 18, 20, 1885; New York *Journal,* June 22, 1885; New York *Herald,* June 21, 1885.
50. W. R. Grace to W. R. Roberts, April 1, 1887, Grace Papers.
51. W. R. Grace to St. Clair McKelway, May 18, 1888; to Oswald Ottendorfer, December 15, 1887: *ibid.* The McKelway letter shows that Grace and the editor had had earlier discussions on the same subject.
52. Galveston (Texas) *News,* February 4, 1888.
53. New York *Herald,* February 13, 1888; W. R. Grace to D. S. Lamont, March 2, 1888; to Grover Cleveland, March 5, 1888: Grover Cleveland Papers, Library of Congress, Washington.
54. P. McHugh to D. S. Lamont, March 20, 1880, *ibid.*; New York *World,* March 20, 21, 25, 1880.
55. W. R. Grace to D. C. Herrick, March 21, 1888; to Hugh McLaughlin, March 22, 1888: *ibid.*
56. New York *Evening Graphic,* May 14, 1888; Brooklyn *Eagle,* May 15, 1888; Brooklyn *Standard-Union,* same date; New York *Tribune,* May 16, 1888; New York *Herald,* May 17, 1888; Peter Hevner, *A One-Sided History of William R. Grace, the Pirate of Peru* (1888).

In Peru the writer has searched court archives, newspapers, and other sources that might throw light on the charges Hevner made against W. R. Grace or, more accurately, his brother Michael. Not the slightest corroboration could be found, aside from the fact that seamen unquestionably were shanghaied to fill out crews on Grace ships, as they were on virtually all ships touching Callao at the time. I have already said as much elsewhere in this book. The more serious charges, alleging the swindling of heirs of Henry Meiggs, have no basis at all. The account of the night escape from Peru of Michael Grace, in flight from a cloud of legal actions brought by Hevner, seems wholly fictitious. No trace of the suits can be found. M. P. Grace was not in Peru within almost a year of the time of the supposed flight. Though the pamphlet seemed untrustworthy on its face, I investigated it because it is listed, with no indication as to its character, in the bibliography appended to the sketch of W. R. Grace in the *Dictionary of American Biography,* ordinarily a dependable source.

57. W. R. Grace to D. S. Lamont, May 28, 1888, Cleveland Papers; W. R. Grace to D. S. Lamont, May 23, 1888, Grace Papers.

58. Nevins, *Hewitt*, 517–19.

59. New York *Telegram*, July 21, 1888; New York *World*, same date; New York *Times*, August 24, 1888.

60. W. R. Grace to Grover Cleveland, July 13, 1888, Cleveland Papers.

61. Grover Cleveland to W. R. Grace, July 14, 1888, *ibid.*

62. W. R. Grace to Grover Cleveland, September 20, 1888. Grace Papers; J. L. Britton to Grover Cleveland, September 21, 1888, Cleveland Papers.

63. W. R. Grace to G. A. Ollard, December 28, 1888, Grace Papers.

~ CHAPTER 14

1. W. R. Grace to R. F. Sears, April 17, 1882, Grace Papers.

2. W. R. Grace to J. W. Grace, August 1, 1884, *ibid.*

3. W. R. Grace to R. F. Sears, August 3, 1886; to C. R. Flint, September 22, 1884: *ibid.* Flint's original report on Sears cannot be found, but Grace's letter to Sears cited above mentions the nature of it.

4. W. R. Grace to A. O. Bourne, March 31, 1883; W. R. Grace & Co. to George A. Alden & Co., May 28, 1886: *ibid.*

5. W. R. Grace to R. F. Sears, December 18, 1885, *ibid.*

6. W. R. Grace to J. W. Grace, January 9, 1886; W. R. Grace & Co. to Baring Brothers & Co., March 19, 1885: *ibid.*

7. W. R. Grace to R. F. Sears, February 27, March 12 (two letters), 1886: *ibid.*

8. W. R. Grace to R. F. Sears, February 27, 1886, March 12, 1886 (two letters), March 26, 1886: *ibid.*

9. W. R. Grace to R. F. Sears, April 5, 1886; W. R. Grace & Co. to S. V. Storm, April 21, 1886; M. P. Grace to George Chambers, same date; to Furth & Campbell, same date; W. R. Grace to J. W. Grace, April 7, 1886: *ibid.*

10. W. R. Grace to R. F. Sears, May 8, 1886, *ibid.*

11. W. R. Grace to R. F. Sears, April 17, 22, 1886; M. P. Grace to H. L. Hotchkiss, May 13, 1886: *ibid.*

12. W. R. Grace to R. F. Sears, April 5, 8, 22, 1886, *ibid.*

13. M. P. Grace to E. T. Sawyer, May 3, 1886, *ibid.*

14. W. R. Grace to Kidder, Peabody & Co., June 11, July 9, 1886; to R. F. Sears, July 23, August 3, 1886; to E. S. Converse, August 12, 1886; M. P. Grace to E. S. Converse, June 12, 15, 1886: *ibid.*

15. M. P. Grace to R. F. Sears, June 18, August 13, 1886; R. F. Sears to W. R. Grace & Co., June 23, 1886; W. R. Grace to R. F. Sears, June 30, 1886: *ibid.*

16. W. R. Grace to R. F. Sears, August 16, 28, 1886; to M. P. Grace, August 28, 1886: *ibid.*

17. W. R. Grace to E. T. Sawyer, August 27, 1886; to M. P. Grace, August 28, 1886; to E. S. Converse, August 28, September 2, 1886 (two letters): *ibid.*

18. W. R. Grace to R. F. Sears, September 17, 1886; to E. S. Converse, September 15, 1886: *ibid.*

19. W. R. Grace to R. F. Sears, September 17, 1886, *ibid.*

20. W. R. Grace to R. F. Sears, September 30, 1886, *ibid.*

21. W. R. Grace to R. F. Sears, October 19, 28, 1886, *ibid.*

22. W. R. Grace to R. F. Sears, December 16, 1886, *ibid.*

23. W. R. Grace to R. F. Sears, March 10, May 11, 1887; R. F. Sears to G. A. Lewis, November 4, 1887: *ibid.*

24. The final stages of the rubber fight, 1888–1890, are told so briefly that reference to particular letters would be of no use. The correspondence from which the synopsis in the text was written is extensive. Most of it was between Grace and Sears. The letters appear in Books 13 to 18, Grace Papers.

~ CHAPTER 15

1. G. A. Ollard to W. R. Grace, February 19, 1889; Grace's reply, March 5: Grace Papers.

2. M. P. Grace to C. L. Smyles, May 20, 1885; to Edward Eyre, May 21, 1885; to A. R. Robertson, July 22, 1885: *ibid.*

3. M. P. Grace to Chairman, Peruvian Bondholders' Committee, May 18, 1885, *ibid.*

4. M. P. Grace to A. R. Robertson, June 5, 1885; to Manuel Galup, July 18, 1885: *ibid.*

5. M. P. Grace to E. A. del Solar, November 30, 1885; to A. R. Robertson, June 16, 1885; to Miguel Iglesias, October 31, 1885: *ibid.*

6. M. P. Grace to Edward Eyre, October 19, December 9, 10, 19, 1885, January 6, 1886: *ibid.*

7. Philadelphia *Press*, January 14, 1890. This article was written by the New York correspondent of the *Press*, E. J. Edwards, a personal friend of W. R. Grace. Without doubt Edwards's informant was Grace himself.

8. M. P. Grace to A. R. Robertson, April 28, May 14, June 17, 1886, Grace Papers.

9. M. P. Grace to Manuel Galup, July 18, 1885; to A. R. Robertson, July 22, August 18, 1885; to Grace Brothers & Co., August 19, 1885; to Edward Eyre, August 25, 1885; to Aurelio García, September 15, 1885; to J. A. Ribeyro, March 26, 1886: *ibid.*

10. Edward Eyre to M. P. Grace, July 10, 1886, *ibid.*

11. Bondholders' proposal, dated May 1886, *ibid.*

12. M. P. Grace to A. R. Robertson, June 16, 17, 21, July 2, 9, 1886; to Edward Eyre, July 13, 1886; Edward Eyre to M. P. Grace, June 12, 1886: *ibid.*

13. Edward Eyre to M. P. Grace, July 10, 1886, *ibid.*
14. Edward Eyre to M. P. Grace, August 3, 1886, *ibid.*
15. M. P. Grace to Edward Eyre, March 18, 19, 1887, *ibid.*
16. M. P. Grace to Edward Eyre, August 31, 1887, *ibid.*
17. New York *Times,* June 28, 1887; M. P. Grace to Edward Eyre, August 31, 1887, Grace Papers.
18. M. P. Grace to J. G. Meiggs, September 2, 1887, *ibid.*
19. M. P. Grace to J. A. Miro Quesada, August 31, 1887; to Alejandro Garland, September 9, 1887; to A. A. Cáceres, August 31, 1887: *ibid.*
20. M. P. Grace to G. A. Ollard, September 2, 1887; to Charles Mansfield, same date: *ibid.*
21. M. P. Grace to G. A. Ollard, February 14, 1888; to Edward Eyre, February 20, 1888: *ibid.*
22. M. P. Grace to J. A. Miro Quesada, February 25, 1888; to Smyles, Binyon & Ollard, March 7, 1888; to Edward Eyre, March 9, 1888; W. R. Grace to T. F. Bayard, March 9, 1888; to J. G. Blaine, December 26, 1889, with enclosure: *ibid.* The enclosure in W. R. Grace's letter to Secretary of State Blaine is a long synopsis of the debt-settlement negotiations. This document, which had been prepared by Michael Grace, makes the positive assertion that Chile was behind a move to deprive Peru of the province of Tacna.
23. M. P. Grace to Smyles, Binyon & Ollard, February 25, 1888; to G. A. Ollard, same date; to A. A. Cáceres, March 1, 1888: Grace Papers.
24. M. P. Grace to Edward Eyre, April 20, 1888, *ibid.*
25. M. P. Grace to W. R. Grace, several memoranda dated March 21, 1888, *ibid.*
26. W. R. Grace to J. G. Blaine, December 26, 1889, with enclosure, *ibid.*
27. W. R. Grace to J. G. Blaine, December 26, 1888, with enclosure; G. A. Ollard to J. Domis, January 8, 1889; Federico Blume to G. A. Ollard, January 5, 6, 8, 1889: *ibid.*
28. G. A. Ollard to W. R. Grace, February 8, 15, 1889, *ibid.*; Basadre, II, 228–30.
29. G. A. Ollard to W. R. Grace, February 19, 1889; Grace's reply, March 5: Grace Papers.
30. W. R. Grace to M. P. Grace, March 14, 20, 1889, *ibid.*
31. W. R. Grace to M. P. Grace, June 17, 21, 25, July 13, 1889, *ibid.*
32. W. R. Grace to J. T. North, May 28, 1889, *ibid.*; New York *Times,* July 3, 1889; New York *Journal,* July 4, 1889; New York *Star,* July 12, 1889.
33. *Export and Finance* (New York), October 26, 1889; W. R. Grace to J. G. Blaine, December 26, 1889, with enclosure, Grace Papers.
34. W. R. Grace to J. G. Blaine, December 26, 1889, with enclosure, and January 3, 1890, *ibid.*; New York *Sun,* January 4, 1890.
35. New York *Journal of Commerce,* January 14, 1890.
36. London *Financial News,* March 11, 1890.
37. New York *Tribune,* April 8, 1890; Philadelphia *Press,* January 14, 1890.

38. Philadelphia *Press,* December 30, 1889, April 20, 1890; Brooklyn *Eagle,* January 15, 1890; Brooklyn *Times,* January 16, 1890; London *Times,* February 14, 1890; New York *Tribune,* April 13, 1890. The contemporary literature in Peru on the subject of the contract is voluminous and highly controversial. The instrument is spiritedly attacked and defended. I asked Doctor Jorge Basadre, director of the National Library of Peru, his opinion of the merits of the argument. Doctor Basadre is one of the most distinguished living Latin American historians. His record is sufficient, and more than sufficient, to protect him from an assumption of partiality to foreign interests in Peru. He told me that, all considered, he thought the contract a good one and doubtless the most favorable arrangement that could have been made for Peru at the time.

～ CHAPTER 16

1. Galdames, 338–43.
2. W. R. Grace to J. W. Grace, October 24, 1887; to G. L. Duval, August 16, September 19, 1889; to Edward Eyre, July 21, 1890: Grace Papers.
3. W. R. Grace & Co. to F. T. Frelinghuysen, February 2, 1882, *ibid.*
4. New York *World,* December 21, 1885.
5. W. R. Grace to J. T. North, May 28, 1889; to Patrick Egan, March 21, April 24, 26, 1890; to Edward Eyre, June 6, 1890: Grace Papers.
6. New York *Times,* March 11, 1890.
7. New York *World,* March 16, 1890; *Export & Finance,* March 15, 1890; W. R. Grace to C. R. Miller, March 12, 1890; to J. G. Blaine, March 12, 1890; to E. C. Varas, March 13, 1890: Grace Papers.
8. Galdames, 342–46; Munro, 310–11; Henry Clay Evans, Jr., *Chile and Its Relations with the United States* (1927), 136–39.
9. Evans, 138; Washington *Post,* May 6, 1891.
10. New York *Herald,* September 29, 1891; Philadelphia *Press,* October 4, 1891. The *Press* article, by its New York correspondent E. J. Edwards ("Holland"), a friend of W. R. Grace, is a review of certain aspects of the Chilean civil war. In all probability Edwards's informant was Mr. Grace.
11. New York *Times,* April 21, 1891; Osgood Hardy, "The Itata Incident," *Hispanic American Historical Review,* May 1922, pp. 202–4; New York *Herald,* May 6, 1891.
12. Hardy, 205–6. An odd minor detail of the situation was the fact that the Balmacedist vice consul at San Francisco, Walter D. Catton, was an employee of the Grace San Francisco house. What was a member of Grace's official family doing in the service of Balmaceda? It seems to me there were three possibilities: (1) Grace let Catton keep the position as evidence of the proclaimed neutrality of the Grace house; (2) Grace used Catton as a listening post to find out secrets

of the Balmacedists; (3) Grace had a foot in both camps, dealing with the Balmacedists as well as the Congressionalists.

As we shall see, Flint later made the charge last-named. Flint cited Catton's presence at San Francisco and the fact that Catton transmitted to Lazcaño in Washington certain intelligence about the *Robert & Minnie*. Flint's accusation was wholly false, a fact Flint must have known when he made it. Lazcaño reported to his government that Catton "seriously compromised" his Balmacedist efforts to thwart the delivery of the *Robert & Minnie* arms to the junta. (New York *Herald,* September 28, 1891; New York *Evening Post,* November 21, 1891.)

Therefore, it seems to me that Catton's presence as a Balmacedist vice consul was for a combination of purposes (1) and (2), above.

13. Washington *Post,* May 6, 1891; Hardy, 204–5.
14. New York *Herald,* May 6, 1891; New York *Tribune,* same date; Philadelphia *Bulletin,* May 7, 1891; Boston *Transcript,* same date.
15. Hardy, 209–13.
16. New York *Commercial Advertiser,* May 7, 1891; New York *Times,* May 8, 1891; New York *Herald,* same date; New York *Evening Post,* May 9, 1891; New York *Tribune,* May 10, 1891.
17. Philadelphia *Press,* October 4, 1891.
18. New York *Herald,* May 9, 1891.
19. San Francisco *Call,* May 15, 1891.
20. Hardy, 217, 220–22.
21. New York *Herald,* August 27, 28, 1891; New York *Journal,* August 28, 1891.
22. New York *Press,* August 30, 1891.
23. W. R. Grace to Augusto Matte, September 8, 1891, Grace Papers. This communication, written in Spanish, rather apologized for Grace's guarded support of the Congressionalists during the war: "We have not allowed the belief that we were partisans to gain ground, because of the business that we might have transacted in the shipment of arms & ammunition." When I first saw this passage I thought it a hint or tacit admission that Grace *had* supplied arms to the Congressionalists. All direct evidence, however, is against this interpretation. On February 20, 1892, when Trumbull was leaving the country, Grace wrote a letter of farewell (Grace Papers) in which some allusions were made to the *Itata* case, then closed. It does not appear to be the sort of letter Grace would have written if he had had anything to do with loading that steamer; and no other shipment of arms to the Congressionalists was made from the United States.
24. Hardy, 141–42, 224; New York *Times,* November 4, 1891.
25. New York *Herald,* September 22, 1891.
26. *Ibid.,* September 28, 1891.
27. *Ibid.,* September 29, 1891; New York *Evening Post,* November 21, 1891.

28. New York *Evening World,* September 29, 1891; New York *Journal,* same date.
29. New York *Times,* October 27, 30, 1891.
30. Grace & Co. to W. R. Grace & Co., November 4, 1891, Grace Papers.
31. W. R. Grace to M. P. Grace, November 16, 1891, *ibid.*
32. W. R. Grace to W. S. Eyre, December 8, 1891; to Ballard Smith, November 4, 1891; to J. A. Scrymser, same date; to C. R. Miller, same date; to W. S. Eyre, same date: *ibid.*; New York *World,* November 3, 1891.
33. W. R. Grace to M. P. Grace, November 16, 1891; to Pedro Montt, December 4, 1891: Grace Papers.
34. W. R. Grace to M. P. Grace, December 8, 1891, *ibid.*
35. New York *Times,* January 10, 1891; W. R. Grace to Pedro Montt, December 9, 1891, Grace Papers.
36. W. R. Grace to Pedro Montt, December 11, 1891, *ibid.*
37. M. A. Matta, *Cuestiones Recientes con La Legación l el Governo de los Estados Unidos de Norte-America* (1892), 126; United States State Department, *Papers Relating to Foreign Relations, 1891* (1892), 267–69; New York *Herald,* December 13, 1891; W. R. Grace to Pedro Montt, December 14, 1891, Grace Papers.
38. W. R. Grace to S. B. Elkins, December 17, 1891; to W. S. Eyre, December 30, 1891: Grace Papers.
39. New York *World,* December 28, 1891; Chicago *Times,* December 29, 1891; January 1, 1892.
40. New York *World,* December 27, 1891; New York *Herald,* same date; New York *Recorder,* same date; Boston *Journal,* January 1, 1892; Chicago *Inter Ocean,* January 2, 1892; Chicago *Times,* January 3, 1892.
41. Chicago *Times,* December 29, 1891; W. R. Grace to M. P. Grace, February 12, 1892, Grace Papers.

    In Santiago the writer asked permission to consult, in the Ministry of Foreign Affairs, the original files on the *Baltimore* incident. They probably would throw light on the case that cannot be obtained elsewhere. In the present instance the date and form of Pedro Montt's recommendation of mediation would have been of interest. I was informed that it would be impossible to inspect the files; and also unnecessary, because the principal documents had been published. I was provided with M. A. Matta's *Cuestiones Recientes con La Legación l el Governo de los Estados Unidos de Norte-America.* This highly nationalistic condensation was not of great help.
42. United States State Department, *Papers Relating to Foreign Relations, 1891,* 284.
43. W. R. Grace to W. S. Eyre, December 30, 1891, Grace Papers.
44. United States State Department, *Papers Relating to Foreign Relations, 1891,* 284–87; W. R. Grace to Pedro Montt, January 12, 14, 19, 20, 21, 22, 1892, Grace Papers.

45. United States State Department, *Papers Relating to Foreign Relations, 1891,* 307–8.
46. James D. Richardson (compiler), *Messages and Papers of the Presidents* (1898), IX, 215–27; United States State Department, *Papers Relating to Foreign Relations, 1891,* 309–12.
47. W. R. Grace to E. P. Bailey, January 28, 1892; to M. P. Grace, February 12, 1892: Grace Papers.
48. W. R. Grace to W. S. Eyre, February 10, 1892, *ibid.*

~ CHAPTER 17

1. Philadelphia *Ledger,* May 4, 1889; W. R. Grace to Grover Cleveland, July 9, 1889, Grace Papers; Grover Cleveland to W. R. Grace, July 15, 1889, Collection of J. P. Grace.
2. W. R. Grace to C. R. Miller, February 19, 1890, Grace Papers.
3. New York *Tribune,* April 8, 1890; New York *Sun,* same date.
4. New York *Mail and Express,* May 10, 1890; New York *Journal,* June 17, September 14, 1890; New York *World,* August 1, September 16, 1890; Brooklyn *Eagle,* August 17, 1890.
5. W. R. Grace to E. L. Godkin, October 1, 1890; to Wheeler Peckham, October 2, 1890; to T. F. Neville, October 20, 1890: Grace Papers; D. F. Alexander, *Four Famous New Yorkers* (1923), 140; New York *World,* October 11, 1890.
6. New York *Sun,* October 29, 1890; Rochester *Post-Express,* October 23, 1890; W. R. Grace to M. P. Grace, October 30, 1890; to Wheeler Peckham, October 2, 13, 1890; to F. M. Scott, October 20, 1890; to P. A. Collins, October 21, 1890; to C. R. Miller, October 23, 1890; to G. H. Schwab, October 27, 1890: Grace Papers.
7. W. R. Grace to M. P. Grace, November 20, 1890, *ibid.*
8. Brooklyn *Eagle,* December 14, 1890.
9. Charleston (S. C.) *News and Courier,* February 23, 1891; St. Paul *News,* same date; San Francisco *Examiner,* April 5, 1891; New York *Daily News,* April 12, 1891.
10. *Rocky Mountain News,* April 12, 1891; New York *Times,* April 21, 1891.
11. New York *Tribune,* January 30, 1892; Henry de Forest Baldwin to Jonathan Grossman, research assistant. Mr. Baldwin, at the time a young lawyer and one of the rising generation of independent Democrats Grace was drawing about him, attended both meetings.
12. New York *Herald,* February 12, 1892; New York *Daily News,* same date; New York *World,* February 23, 1892; Baltimore *Sun,* same date.
13. Nevins, *Cleveland,* 485.
14. New York *Telegram,* March 22, 1892; W. R. Grace to Albert Shaw, March 11, 1892, Grace Papers; New York *World,* March 25, 1892; New

York *Tribune,* March 15, 20, 1892; New York *Times,* March 20, 1892.

15. New York *Times,* March 27, April 6, 1892.

16. New York *Recorder,* May 1, 1892.

17. New York *Sun,* April 6, 1892; New York *World,* May 18, 1892.

18. New York *Times,* May 27, 1892.

19. J. P. Grace to the writer—on Whitney's offer to W. R. Grace of participation in the street-railway venture.

20. W. R. Grace to A. H. Prescott, March 25, 1892; to D. Cady Herrick, May 26, 1892: Grace Papers.

21. W. R. Grace to A. A. Taylor, June 2, 1892; to C. W. Buck, June 3, 1892; to J. J. Valentine, April 14, 1892: *ibid.*; New York *Sun,* May 31, 1892; New York *Recorder,* same date.

22. W. R. Grace to Grover Cleveland, June 2, 1893, Grace Papers; New York *World,* June 1, 1892; Chicago *Herald,* June 2, 1892.

23. New York *Herald,* June 22, 1892; New York *Evening Post,* same date; Chicago *Tribune,* June 20, 23, 1892.

24. W. R. Grace to Carter Harrison, June 29, 1892, Grace Papers; Henry de Forest Baldwin, "Before the Democratic National Convention at Chicago," a manuscript account in the Baldwin Papers; Oberholtzer, V, 201.

25. New York *Times,* June 23, 1892; Philadelphia *Press,* June 22, 1892; New York *Evening Post,* December 31, 1892.

26. Hartford *Post,* August 12, 1892.

27. W. R. Grace to Grover Cleveland, August 2, 1892, Grace Papers.

28. Nevins, *Cleveland,* 494–96.

29. W. R. Grace to Oswald Ottendorfer, July 6, 1892; to Grover Cleveland, August 16, 1892: Grace Papers.

30. Nevins, *Cleveland,* 496–98; New York *Mail and Express,* September 8, 1892; New York *Morning Advertiser,* September 10, 1892.

31. W. R. Grace to Oswald Ottendorfer, July 6, 1892, Grace Papers.

32. W. R. Grace to Grover Cleveland, September 16, 1892, *ibid.*

33. New York *Times,* September 22, 1892; New York *Tribune,* September 23, 24, 1892.

34. New York *Sun,* September 28, 29, 30, 1892; New York *Telegram,* September 29, 1892.

35. New York *Mail and Express,* September 30, 1892; Chicago *Tribune,* October 11, 1892.

36. New York *Times,* September 30, 1892; New York *Commercial Advertiser,* October 10, 1892; W. R. Grace to G. W. Apgar, October 4, 1892; to Thomas Smith, October 4, 1892: Grace Papers.

37. New York *Sun,* September 23, 1892; New York *Times* and New York *Tribune,* October 8, 9, 19, 20, 21, 1892.

38. New York *Press,* October 3, 1892.

39. New York *Times,* October 9, 1892; New York *Commercial Advertiser,* October 11, 1892.

40. New York *Times,* December 18, 1892; New York *World,* December 19, 1892.

41. W. R. Grace to Edward Eyre, November 16, 1892, Grace Papers; Boston *Globe,* November 22, 1892; New York *World,* December 28, 29, 1892; Baltimore *Sun,* December 30, 1892.

42. New York *World,* December 31, 1892; C. R. Breckinridge to C. S. Fairchild, January 17, 1893, Fairchild Papers, New-York Historical Society; J. P. Grace to the writer; W. R. Grace to M. P. Grace, January 10, 1893, Grace Papers.

43. W. R. Grace to W. J. English, March 29, 1893, *ibid.*; New York *Recorder,* February 27, 1893; New York *World,* February 28, 1893; New York *Times,* March 3, 1893; New York *Tribune,* March 17, 1893.

44. New York *Recorder,* June 25, 1893; New York *Tribune,* July 29, 1893; Baldwin Diary, 1893, Baldwin Papers. The patronage question even caused minor rifts among the anti-snappers. The selection of Kilbreath, Fairchild's choice for collector of the port, over Robert Grier Monroe, a Grace lieutenant, was said to have caused a temporary estrangement between Grace and Fairchild.

45. New York *Commercial Advertiser,* July 23, 1893; New York *Recorder,* July 25, 1893; Aurora (Illinois) *News-Times,* December 28, 1893.

46. Nevins, *Cleveland,* 532–33; St. Louis *Republic,* September 3, 1893; New York *Sun,* September 7, 1893.

47. New York *Recorder,* September 4, 1893.

48. B. I. Wheeler to H. D. Baldwin, July 27, 1893, and an undated draft of Baldwin's reply, Baldwin Papers.

49. J. P. Grace to B. R. James; New York *Commercial Advertiser,* July 23, 1893.

50. W. R. Grace to D. M. Dickinson, November 13, 1893, Grace Papers.

51. New York *Sun,* November 29, 30, December 2, 1893; New York *Tribune,* November 29, 1893; New York *Evening Post,* December 22, 1893.

52. New York *Mercury and America,* February 25, 26, 1894.

53. W. R. Grace to A. A. Taylor, October 3, 1894, Grace Papers.

54. W. R. Grace to John Kelly, April 19, May 14, 1894, *ibid.*

55. W. R. Grace to J. A. Girdner, June 20, 1894, *ibid.*

56. New York *Telegram,* September 11, 1894.

57. New York *Sun,* October 19, 1894.

58. W. R. Grace to A. A. Taylor, October 3, 1894, Grace Papers.

59. W. R. Grace to F. D. Hoyt, October 12, 1894; to G. S. Falvey, October 13, 1894; to W. S. Logan, October 20, 1894; to Archbishop M. A. Corrigan, October 25, 1894: *ibid.*

60. New York *Tribune,* October 30, 1894; New York *World,* November 1, 1894; W. R. Grace to W. H. Peckham, October 31, 1894, Grace Papers.

61. W. R. Grace to W. L. Strong, January 5, 1895, *ibid.*; New York *Press,* February 18, 1895; *Tammany Times,* February 16, 1895.

62. New York *Press,* March 17, 1895; New York *Evening Telegram,* March 20, 1895; New York *Commercial Advertiser,* March 21, 1895; New York *World,* March 21, 1895; New York *Press,* March 22, 23, 1895.

63. New York *Morning Advertiser,* April 18, 1895.

64. W. R. Grace to Theodore Roosevelt, October 17, 1895, Grace Papers.

65. W. R. Grace to Grover Cleveland, October 7, 1895, *ibid.*

66. J. P. Grace to the writer.

~ CHAPTER 18

1. J. P. Grace to B. R. James.

2. W. R. Grace to "Dear Kathleen," January 15, 1891, Grace Papers.

3. W. R. Grace to W. E. Holloway, December 4, 1888, *ibid.*

4. W. R. Grace to Mrs. Ashman, September 10, 1889; to John Hoey, March 5, 1888; to W. R. Murphy, April 22, 1896: *ibid.*

5. Various letters, 1883, *ibid.*; J. P. Grace to the writer.

6. J. P. Grace to the writer; various letters, 1890–98, Grace Papers.

7. Lilias Grace Kent to B. R. James; J. P. Grace to the writer.

8. J. P. Grace to B. R. James and to the writer.

9. W. R. Grace to Edward Eyre, August 8, 1892, Grace Papers; J. P. Grace to the writer.

10. The rebuilding and extension of the Oroya railroad can be traced through the correspondence exchanged among the New York, London, and Lima houses, 1890–93. The sale of the lease by M. P. Grace in 1893 appears in the records of the Peruvian Corporation at Lima.

11. W. R. Grace to M. P. Grace, November 19, 21, 1890; to Edward Eyre, November 19, 1890 (two letters): Grace Papers; Philadelphia *Press,* December 10, 1890; Utica (New York) *Observer,* April 2, 1904.

12. W. R. Grace to Edward Eyre, November 16, 1892, Grace Papers.

13. W. R. Grace to M. P. Grace, October 31, 1892; March 17, 1893: *ibid.*

14. New York *Times,* December 28, 1892; W. R. Grace to M. P. Grace, July 20, 1893; to E. T. Chamberlain, April 6, 1894: Grace Papers.

15. W. R. Grace to M. P. Grace, July 20, 1893; January 25, 1895; March 11, 1895: *ibid.*

16. Minute Book of W. R. Grace & Co. of West Virginia, *passim.* The first corporate name was American Export Co., and the incorporators were dummies. This probably was done to avoid publicity until the reorganization should be consummated. Once the corporation was formed, the dummies resigned, Grace took their places, and the name was changed to W. R. Grace & Co.

17. W. R. Grace to J. F. Fowler, August 2, 1893, Grace Papers.

18. L. H. Shearman to W. R. Grace, August 13, 1899, *ibid.*

19. M. P. Grace to J. P. Grace, January 30, 1898, *ibid.*

20. The Connecticut charter of 1899, under which W. R. Grace & Co. still operates, is unusual in that while it fixes the total amount of the authorized capital and the original number of shares and par value, it leaves to the corporation, without requiring amendment of its certificate but by mere by-law provision, the privilege of classifying the capital into preferred and common shares, fixing the rights of the different classes of stock, and restricting "the right to vote on either class of said stock, in such manner as it deems proper."
21. J. S. Iglehart to "New York House," July 23, 1900, Grace Papers.
22. Various correspondence, 1890–91, Letter Book 19, *ibid.* See especially W. R. Grace to M. P. Grace, December 16, 1890; to J. Q. A. Holloway, January 3, 1891.
23. W. R. Grace to Henry George, Jr., October 29, 1897; to J. C. Manion, January 27, 1896; to John Eyre, January 29, 1896: *ibid.*
24. New York *Times,* January 28, 1896.
25. W. R. Grace to G. R. Elder, February 7, April 24, 28, 1896, Grace Papers.
26. W. R. Grace to G. R. Elder, March 21, 1896, *ibid.*
27. W. R. Grace to the Rev. Father J. McGivirn, April 4, 1896, *ibid.*
28. New York *World,* May 22, 1898.
29. New York *Daily News,* March 25, 1897; *Catholic News,* March 28, 1897; W. R. Grace to Eda M. Chapman, April 13, 1897; to Sister Mary Rose, May 21, 1897: Grace Papers.

~ CHAPTER 19

1. W. R. Grace to W. L. Scott, April 1, 12, 1890, Grace Papers.
2. 51st Congress, 2nd Session, *Senate Document No. 1944.*
3. W. R. Grace to M. P. Grace, July 21, 1893, March 14, 1896, Grace Papers.
4. W. R. Grace to John Claflin, July 13, 1898, *ibid.*
5. W. R. Grace to Henry Hentz, March 28, 1896; to C. J. Faulkner, April 27, 1896; to M. P. Grace, June 16, 1896; to William McKinley, October 26, 1896, June 21, 1896; William McKinley to W. R. Grace, March 7, 1897: *ibid.*; New York *Tribune,* August 1, 1896.
6. W. R. Grace to Major General J. J. Coppinger, June 1, 15, July 29, 1898; to R. A. Alger, June 15, 1898: Grace Papers.
7. W. R. Grace to J. A. McCall, July 6, 1898, *ibid.*
8. W. R. Grace to H. W. Webb, July 28, 1898; to F. W. Vanderbilt, July 29, 1898: *ibid.*
9. F. S. Washburn to A. S. Bacon, July 23, 1898; "Replies to Possible Objections," an undated memorandum; W. R. Grace to F. M. Scott and to W. L. Saunders, November 28, 1898, *ibid.*
10. W. R. Grace to S. B. Elkins, July 19, 22, 1898; J. P. Grace to W. R. Grace, October 5, 1898: *ibid.*

11. Edward Eyre to W. R. Grace & Co., London, September 20, 1898, (code cable); to W. R. Grace & Co., New York, October 11, 1898, (code cable): *ibid.*

12. Edward Eyre to W. R. Grace & Co., September 26, 1898, (two code cables); September 30, (code cable); October 2, October 5, (code cables): *ibid.*

13. William Roscoe Thayer, *Life and Letters of John Hay* (1915), 216–18.

14. M. P. Grace to W. D. Sloane, October 12, 1898; to Edward Eyre, October 27, 1898: Grace Papers.

15. Edward Eyre to W. R. Grace & Co., New York, October 31, 1898, *ibid.*

16. Copy of contract, dated October 31, 1898, *ibid.*

17. Minutes, executive committee, Nicaragua Canal Syndicate, November 21, 1898; syndicate agreement, November 23, 1898; M. P. Grace to G. G. Williams, H. W. Webb, W. D. Sloane, October 31, 1898; W. R. Grace to J. A. McCall, November 29, 1898; unsigned letter to J. A. Zelaya, January 25, 1899: *ibid.*

18. Minutes, executive committee, Nicaragua Canal Syndicate, November 11, 1898; "M. P. Grace's trip to Washington," an account dictated by Michael Grace, November 21, 1898; minutes, executive committee, December 1, 1898: *ibid.*

19. W. R. Grace to William McKinley, December 2, 1898, *ibid.*

20. New York *Evening Post,* December 5, 1898.

21. "Memorandum regarding Morgan bill," undated; "Replies to Possible Objections," undated; various correspondence, December 1898–February 1899; W. R. Grace to M. P. Grace, February 17, 1899: Grace Papers.

22. W. R. Grace to R. A. Alger, June 29, 1897; to J. A. McCall, March 9, 1899: *ibid.*

23. "Replies to Possible Objections," typed notes, undated, with additions in W. R. Grace's handwriting, *ibid.*

24. W. R. Grace to R. J. Lowry, January 3, 1899, *ibid.*

25. W. R. Grace to J. D. Phelan, May 29, 1900, *ibid.*

26. Typewritten memorandum by Edward Eyre, undated but apparently written long after the event described, Grace Papers. J. P. Grace is also under the impression that the meeting took place.

27. W. R. Grace to members of the Nicaragua Canal Syndicate, 25 identical letters, December 31, 1900, *ibid.*

28. Samuel Eliot Morison and Henry Steele Commager, *The Growth of the American Republic* (1937), II, 402–4.

29. W. R. Grace to Theodore Roosevelt, July 3, 1902, Grace Papers.

30. W. R. Grace to Theodore Roosevelt, November 5, 1902, *ibid.*

31. W. R. Grace to Theodore Roosevelt, July 3, 1902, *ibid.*

32. Lilias Grace Kent to B. R. James.

33. J. P. Grace to B. R. James.

34. New York *Times,* March 22, 1904; New York *World,* same date; Cincinnati *Enquirer,* March 28, 1904; various letters, February–March, 1904, Grace Papers.

~ Bibliography

~ MANUSCRIPT SOURCES

Henry de Forest Baldwin Papers, New York. A scattering of letters and papers bearing on Grace's public career. Consulted by courtesy of Mr. Baldwin, who has since died.

Grover Cleveland Papers, Library of Congress, Washington. Bearing on Grace's public career.

Edward Eyre, "Early Reminiscences of the Grace Organization." Recollections of a nephew who, on the death of the founder, became president of the company. In the possession of W. R. Grace & Co., New York.

Charles H. Fairchild Papers, New-York Historical Society. Bearing on Grace's public career.

Grace Papers, Lima. A relatively small collection of business letters, numbering about five hundred items, apparently overlooked when the early Grace foreign correspondence was consolidated in New York.

Grace Papers, New York. This large collection forms the principal source of this book. Comprising some 55,000 items bound in 140 volumes, it is the most valuable private manuscript collection concerning our business relations with Latin America between 1868 and 1904 that has come to light. Some of the letters go back to the year of Grace's arrival in Peru, 1851. Moreover, the papers touch, at times intimately, upon contingent matters of Latin American politics and diplomacy. They also relate to W. R. Grace's public career in the United States. As the Grace business was a family business, business and domestic concerns were often mingled in the same communication, imparting a flavor not to be found in any other collection of business papers with which this writer is acquainted. In the possession of W. R. Grace & Co., New York.

Joseph P. Grace Collection, New York. A few of his father's personal letters.

Lillius Gilchrest Grace, "Reminiscences of Mrs. W. R. Grace, May 24, 1921." A memoir written at her dictation. In the possession of W. R. Grace & Co.

Lilias Grace Kent, a memoir written by a daughter of W. R. Grace. In the possession of W. R. Grace & Co.

Meiggs Papers, Lima. A considerable collection of the letters of Henry and John D. Meiggs. Owned by the Peruvian Corporation, Ltd.
Municipal Library of New York. Various letters and papers dealing with Grace's terms as mayor.

~ PUBLIC RECORDS

Court and property records were consulted in Ireland in connection with Grace's ancestral background.
Court records were consulted in Peru and in New York in connection with various phases of his career.
The archives of the Ministry of Foreign Affairs, Lima, were extensively consulted in connection with the settlement of the Peruvian foreign debt, as related in Chapter 15. Diplomatic papers of the United States were consulted at the National Archives, Washington.

~ PRINTED SOURCES

~ Books

Alexander, D. F. Four Famous New Yorkers (1923).
Barrett, James W. The World, the Flesh and Messrs. Pulitzer (1931).
Basadre, Jorge. Historia de la Republica del Perú (3rd ed., 1946).
Bates, W. W. Our Early Shipping Policy (1897).
Commager, Henry Steele. See Morison, Samuel Eliot.
Coote, Sir Charles. General View of the Agriculture and Manufactures of Queen's County (1801).
Crowther, Samuel. The Romance and Rise of the American Tropics (1929).
Curtis, Edmund. History of Ireland (1936).
Cutler, Carl C. Greyhounds of the Sea (1930).
Darwin, Charles. Journal of . . . the Voyage of H.M.S. Beagle (1846).
Dennis, W. J. Documentary History of the Tacna-Arica Dispute (1927).
Duffield, A. J. Peru in the Guano Age (1877).
Enoch, C. Reginald. Peru (1912).
Evans, Henry Clay, Jr. Chile and Its Relations with the United States (1927).
Fiske, Stephen. Offhand Portraits of Prominent New Yorkers (1884).
Flint, Charles R. Memories of an Active Life (1923).
Fraser, James. Hand Book for Travellers in Ireland (1844).
Galdames, Luis. A History of Chile, translated by Isaac Joslin Cox (1941).
Grace, Morgan S. A Sketch of the New Zealand War (1899).
Grace, Sheffield. Memoirs of the Family of Grace (1823).
Griffith, Richard R. General valuation of Ireland, Ballyadams barony (1850).

Hevner, Peter. *A One-Sided History of William R. Grace, the Pirate of Peru* (1888).

Hutchinson, T. J. *Two Years in Peru* (1873).

Josephson, Matthew. *The Politicos* (1938).

Leigh, Samuel. *New Pocket Road-Book of Ireland* (1833).

Lewis, Samuel. *A Topographical Dictionary of Ireland* (1837).

Lossing, Benson J. *Our Country,* undated revised edition.

Lubbock, Basil. *The Down Easters* (1929).

———. *Nitrate Clippers* (1935).

Martin, Percy F. *Peru of the Twentieth Century* (1911).

Marvin, Winthrop L. *The American Merchant Marine* (1903).

McKay, Richard C. *South Street* (1934).

MacManus, Seumas. *The Story of the Irish Race* (1944).

Manning, William R., editor. *Diplomatic Correspondence of the United States* (1938).

Matta, M. A. *Cuestiones Recientes con La Legación I el Governo de los Estados Unidos de Norte-America* (1892).

Miner, Dwight C. *The Fight for the Panama Route* (1940).

Morison, Samuel Eliot. *A Maritime History of Massachusetts* (1921).

Morison, Samuel Eliot, and Commager, Henry Steele. *The Growth of the American Republic* (1937).

Morris, William O'Connor. *Ireland, 1494–1905* (1909).

Mumford, Lewis. *Herman Melville* (1931).

Munro, Dana Gardner. *The Latin American Republics* (1942).

Myers, Gustavus. *Tammany Hall* (1917).

Nevins, Allan. *Abram S. Hewitt* (1935).

———. *Grover Cleveland, A Study in Courage* (1933).

Nichols, Roy F. "Latin American Guano Diplomacy," in A. Curtis Wilgus, editor, *Studies in Hispanic American Affairs* (1933).

Oberholtzer, Ellis Paxson. *A History of the United States Since the Civil War* (1931).

Pardo, Manuel. *Estudio sobre la Provincia de Juaja* (1862).

Peck, George W. *Melbourne and the Chincha Islands* (1854).

Prescott, William H. *The Conquest of Peru* (1847).

Richardson, James D., compiler. *Messages and Papers of the Presidents* (1898).

Riordan, William L. *Plunkitt of Tammany Hall* (1905).

Silva, Faustino. *Revolución de Julio* (1924).

Stewart, Watt. *Henry Meiggs, Yankee Pizarro* (1946).

Thayer, William Roscoe. *Life and Letters of John Hay* (1915).

United States Works Progress Administration. *A Maritime History of New York* (1941).

Walpole, Frederick. *Four Years in the Pacific* (1849).

Wilhelm, Joseph. *The Family of Grace* (1911).

~ Newspapers

Bulletin, Philadelphia
Call, San Francisco
Catholic News, New York
Commercial, Cincinnati
Commercial Advertiser, New York
Daily Gazette, Cincinnati
Daily News, New York
Eagle, Brooklyn
Enquirer, Cincinnati
Evening Graphic, New York
Evening Mail, New York
Evening Post, New York
Evening Telegram, New York
Evening World, New York
Examiner, San Francisco
Export and Finance, New York
Financial News, London
Freeman's Journal, Dublin
Gazeta Mercantil, Lima, Peru
Globe, Boston
Guide, New York
Herald, New York
Inter Ocean, Chicago
Journal, Boston
Journal, New York
Journal of Commerce, New York
Ledger, Philadelphia
Mail and Express, New York
Mercury and America, New York
Morning Advertiser, New York
News, New York
News, St. Paul
News and Courier, Charleston, S.C.
News-Times, Aurora, Ill.
Observer, Utica, N.Y.
Pilot, Boston
Post, Hartford
Post, Washington
Post-Express, Rochester
Post Standard, Syracuse
Press, New York

Press, Philadelphia
Recorder, New York
Republic, St. Louis
Rocky Mountain News, Denver
Staats-Zeitung, New York
Standard-Union, Brooklyn
Star, New York
Sun, Baltimore
Sun, New York
Tammany Times, New York
Telegram, New York
Times, Chicago
Times, London
Times, New York
Transcript, Boston
Tribune, Chicago
Tribune, New York
Truth, New York
World, New York

~ *Miscellaneous*

City Directory, New York, 1870–71, 1871–72
Compressed Air, a trade publication, New York
Directory of American Biography
Grace Log, The, house organ of W. R. Grace & Co.
Harper's Weekly
Hispanic American Historical Review, May 1922—article by Osgood Hardy, "The
    Itata Incident"
Money Market Review (London)
Munsey's magazine
Nation, The (Dublin)
Nation, The (New York)
Scribner's Monthly
South Atlantic Quarterly
United States State Department, *Papers Relating to Foreign Relations,* 1867; 1868;
    1870; 1871; 1881; 1891.
State Department Documents, U. S. Foreign Affairs, 1857–59
United States State Department *Documents,* Vol. 89, Report No. 1790 of the 47th
    Congress
51st Congress, 2nd Session, *Senate Document No. 1944*

~ Acknowledgments

~ The greatest single debt Mrs. James and I owe in connection with the work of research and writing that went into this book is to Joseph Peter Grace, son of the subject of this biography. Mr. Grace turned over to us—or rather to my wife—the whole collection of his father's papers. No restriction was placed upon their use; and neither Mr. Grace nor anyone else had much of an idea as to what the letters contained. I am sure Mrs. James is the only one who has read them all. Mr. Grace also gave us certain private letters of his father which were apart from the general collection. He helped us whenever we asked him with his recollections, which served to clarify several points in the latter days of the life of W. R. Grace.

The bulk of the research was done at the offices of W. R. Grace & Co. in Hanover Square, New York City. C. W. Hopkins, head of the cable department, through which the Grace headquarters keeps track of its affairs in foreign lands, got the job of answering any question Mrs. James or I might ask, and of doing anything we wanted done to facilitate this work. If all researchers and writers were as well served as we were by Mr. Hopkins, they would be lucky.

To name all the officers and employees at Hanover Square who helped us would be to recite a long list. We cannot forbear, however, mentioning a few upon whom our impositions were especially heavy. They are Harold J. Roig, vice chairman of W. R. Grace & Co., and his secretary Blanche E. Boucher; and Vice Presidents Raúl Simón, Andrew B. Shea, and J. T. Kirby.

We are also indebted to R. J. Hays, of the National Library of Ireland, and to T. P. O'Neill of Dublin for assistance in research in connection with Grace's ancestral background and boyhood. Mr. Hays kindly read that portion of the manuscript. Our thanks are due Dr. Jonathan Grossman of the College of the City of New York for research in connection with W. R. Grace's public career.

In the Lima office of W. R. Grace & Co. we are indebted to Carlos Velarde C., Manuel Ulloa, Moisés Woll, John D. J. Moore, and C. J. Billwiller. Mr. Billwiller is an old-timer who, as a young man, remembered Michael Grace. Mr. Ulloa undertook work in the archives of the Foreign Office in connection with the negotiations to refinance the Peruvian debt, as related in Chapter 15.

I am deeply indebted to Doctor Jorge Basadre, the distinguished South American historian and head of the National Library of Peru. Doctor Basadre is an objective and impartial scholar. He oriented me on a good many points and read in manuscript all the chapters dealing with Peru. His suggestions were very helpful.

In the Santiago office, we are indebted to Walter F. Koch, executive vice president, and to Guy de Morás.

Both in Peru and in Chile the United States embassy people lightened our burdens. I cannot refrain from mentioning Thomas Dozier, then press attaché in Lima, and Heath Bowman, cultural attaché in Santiago. My thanks are also due and hereby conveyed to Carol Henderson, my secretary during this undertaking.

M.J.
1948

~ Index

Latin American Silhouettes
Studies in History and Culture

William H. Beezley and
Judith Ewell
Editors

Volumes Published

William H. Beezley and Judith Ewell, eds., *The Human Tradition in Latin America: The Twentieth Century* (1987). Cloth ISBN 0-8420-2283-X Paper ISBN 0-8420-2284-8

Judith Ewell and William H. Beezley, eds., *The Human Tradition in Latin America: The Nineteenth Century* (1989). Cloth ISBN 0-8420-2331-3 Paper ISBN 0-8420-2332-1

David G. LaFrance, *The Mexican Revolution in Puebla, 1908–1913: The Maderista Movement and the Failure of Liberal Reform* (1989). ISBN 0-8420-2293-7

Mark A. Burkholder, *Politics of a Colonial Career: José Baquíjano and the Audiencia of Lima,* 2d ed. (1990). Cloth ISBN 0-8420-2353-4 Paper ISBN 0-8420-2352-6

Kenneth M. Coleman and George C. Herring, eds. (with Foreword by Daniel Oduber), *Understanding the Central American Crisis: Sources of Conflict, U.S. Policy, and Options for Peace* (1991). Cloth ISBN 0-8420-2382-8   Paper ISBN 0-8420-2383-6

Carlos B. Gil, ed., *Hope and Frustration: Interviews with Leaders of Mexico's Political Opposition* (1992). Cloth ISBN 0-8420-2395-X Paper ISBN 0-8420-2396-8

Charles Bergquist, Ricardo Peñaranda, and Gonzalo Sánchez, eds.,
Violence in Colombia: The Contemporary Crisis in Historical Perspective (1992). Cloth ISBN 0-8420-2369-0   Paper ISBN 0-8420-2376-3

Heidi Zogbaum, *B. Traven: A Vision of Mexico* (1992). ISBN 0-8420-2392-5

Jaime E. Rodríguez O., ed., *Patterns of Contention in Mexican History* (1992). ISBN 0-8420-2399-2

Louis A. Pérez, Jr., ed., *Slaves, Sugar, and Colonial Society: Travel Accounts of Cuba, 1801–1899* (1992). Cloth ISBN 0-8420-2354-2   Paper ISBN 0-8420-2415-8

Peter Blanchard, *Slavery and Abolition in Early Republican Peru* (1992). Cloth ISBN 0-8420-2400-X   Paper ISBN 0-8420-2429-8

Paul J. Vanderwood, *Disorder and Progress: Bandits, Police, and Mexican Development*. Revised and Enlarged Edition (1992). Cloth ISBN 0-8420-2438-7   Paper ISBN 0-8420-2439-5

Sandra McGee Deutsch and Ronald H. Dolkart, eds., *The Argentine Right: Its History and Intellectual Origins, 1910 to the Present* (1993). Cloth ISBN 0-8420-2418-2   Paper ISBN 0-8420-2419-0

Jaime E. Rodríguez O., ed., *The Evolution of the Mexican Political System* (1993). ISBN 0-8420-2448-4

Steve Ellner, *Organized Labor in Venezuela, 1958–1991: Behavior and Concerns in a Democratic Setting* (1993). ISBN 0-8420-2443-3

Paul J. Dosal, *Doing Business with the Dictators: A Political History of United Fruit in Guatemala, 1899–1944* (1993). ISBN 0-8420-2475-1

Marquis James, *Merchant Adventurer: The Story of W. R. Grace* (1993). ISBN 0-8420-2444-1

John C. Chasteen and Joseph S. Tulchin, eds., *Problems in Modern Latin American History: A Reader* (1993). Cloth ISBN 0-8420-2327-5   Paper ISBN 0-8420-2328-3